W9-CPC-068

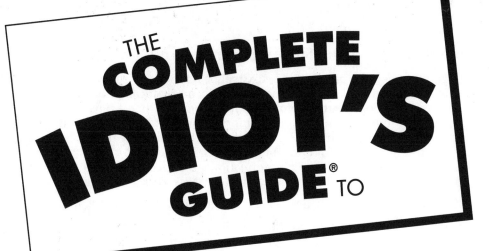

THE COMPLETE IDIOT'S GUIDE® TO

Impeachment of the President

by Steven D. Strauss &
Spencer Strauss

alpha books

A Division of Macmillan General Reference
A Simon & Schuster Macmillan Company
1633 Broadway, New York, NY 10019-6785

Steven D. Strauss lovingly dedicates this book to his wife Maria, who makes all things possible.

Spencer Strauss dedicates this book, with love, to his mother.

Copyright © 1998 by Steven D. Strauss and Spencer Strauss

All rights reserved. No part of this book shall be reproduced, stored in a retrieval system, or transmitted by any means, electronic, mechanical, photocopying, recording, or otherwise, without written permission from the publisher. No patent liability is assumed with respect to the use of the information contained herein. Although every precaution has been taken in the preparation of this book, the publisher and author assume no responsibility for errors or omissions. Neither is any liability assumed for damages resulting from the use of information contained herein. For information, address Alpha Books, 1633 Broadway, 7th Floor, New York, NY 10019-6785.

THE COMPLETE IDIOT'S GUIDE TO and design are trademarks of Prentice-Hall, Inc.

Macmillan Publishing books may be purchased for business or sales promotional use. For information please write: Special Markets Department, Macmillan Publishing USA, 1633 Broadway, New York, NY 10019.

International Standard Book Number: 0-02863156-0

Library of Congress Catalog Card Number: 98-88701

00 99 98   8 7 6 5 4 3 2 1

Interpretation of the printing code: the rightmost number of the first series of numbers is the year of the book's printing; the rightmost number of the second series of numbers is the number of the book's printing. For example, a printing code of 98-1 shows that the first printing occurred in 1998.

Printed in the United States of America

13.954
572

Alpha Development Team

Publisher
Kathy Nebenhaus

Editorial Director
Gary M. Krebs

Managing Editor
Bob Shuman

Marketing Brand Manager
Felice Primeau

Senior Editor
Nancy Mikhail

Editor
Jessica Faust

Development Editors
Maureen Horn
Phil Kitchel
Amy Zavatto

Assistant Editor
Maureen Horn

Production Team

Development Editor
Phil Kitchel

Cover Designer
Mike Freeland

Photo Editor
Sue Moseson,
Go Fish Images, Inc.

Illustrator
Jody P. Schaeffer

Designer
Nathan Clement

Indexers
Ginny Bess
Cheryl Jackson

Layout/Proofreading
Angela Calvert
Mary Hunt

51,280

Contents at a Glance

Part 1: A Quick Civics Lesson   **1**

  1 How Did We Get Here?   3
*The Clinton/Lewinsky scandal and the ensuing Starr report
have already radically altered politics in America.*

  2 American Government 101   13
*The Founding Fathers were pretty clever with that "three
branches of government" stuff. How will it work here?*

  3 The Impeachment Process   23
*"High crimes and misdemeanors" is a standard intended
to remove Presidents who commit serious crimes against
the state.*

  4 Impeachment in History   31
*Impeachments are nothing new: Presidents, supreme court
justices, and many others have endured the process.*

Part 2: The Making of a President   **39**

  5 No Wonder They Call It Hope   41
*Bill Clinton grew up brilliant, gifted, and knowing he
would be President.*

  6 Family Matters   51
*Hillary Clinton tied her own promising career to the man
she loved and believed in.*

  7 On the National Stage   61
*The 1992 election was Clinton's chance to fulfill his
destiny—and the nation's first chance to see his strengths
and his flaws.*

  8 Liar, Liar, Pants on Fire   71
*Clinton's history of lying and infidelity foreshadowed the
current crisis.*

  9 Jones v. Clinton   85
*Paula Jones' lawsuit, although dismissed as without merit,
would still prove to be Clinton's undoing.*

Part 3: The Road to Impeachment?   **97**

  10 Scandals of the Past   99
*If we were to dismiss the legacy of every President tainted
by scandal, our history would be the weaker for it.*

11 Watergate and Its Aftermath 107
This was a lot more than a "third-rate burglary," and it led to the means by which we investigate the Executive branch today.

12 The Independent Counsel 117
The statute that gave Kenneth Starr such power was intended to prevent abuse of power, not enable it.

13 A "Vast Right-Wing Conspiracy"? 129
While Clinton's enemies may not literally be conspirators, they know each other well, and help each other when they can.

14 The Report on Starr 137
Some background on the independent prosecutor: his personal and professional past, and the current legal and political affiliations that may tarnish his investigation.

15 Whitewatergate 145
Whitewater, Travelgate, Filegate: Learn the facts.

Part 4: A Scandalous Affair **159**

16 Sex in the White House 161
Clinton isn't the first or the worst President to play around, and his predecessors were a lot more randy.

17 Enter the Intern 173
Clinton knew his dalliance with Monica Lewinsky was wrong, but he proceeded anyway.

18 "It's Illegal to Threaten the President" 187
Once Clinton ended the affair, Lewinsky began to play hardball.

19 Sex, Lies, and Audiotape 197
Linda Tripp and her tapes intrigued Ken Starr, and he pounced.

20 The Role of the New Media 211
The Internet, cable television, and around-the-clock news affected the story as much as it reported it.

21 Stand by Your Man 221
Hillary remains strong, despite her anger and hurt.

Part 5: The President on Trial **229**

22 Starr Chambers 231
Once news of the affair became public, all bets were off, and there are legal stains on more people than just the President.

23 Is Sex an Impeachable Offense?   241
    An analysis of Starr's case. Is that all there is?

24 The Impeachment Scenario   255
    How this entire matter will likely be decided in Congress.

25 What Does the Future Hold?   271
    *It will take years to know the impact on our political
    system of the scandal, the investigation, and an impeach-
    ment, but a few projections are possible.*

Appendices

A Excerpts from the Starr Report   285
   *An exhaustive compendium of the report's most salient
   features.*

B Timeline   331
   A roadmap in time to better understand the order of events.

C The Cast of Characters   337
   The major players and the roles they've played.

D Further Reading   345
   An annotated bibliography to help you keep learning more.

E Glossary   349
   *A listing of some of the terms you may not have been
   familiar with before we had to become constitutional
   scholars.*

   Index   353

Contents

Part 1: A Quick Civics Lesson   **1**

1 How Did We Get Here?   **3**

It Was Wrong 4
A Legacy in Doubt 6
"I did not have sexual relations with that woman,
 Miss Lewinsky." 6
Where Does He Come Up with This Stuff? 8
The Starr Report 9
Unanswered Question 11

2 American Government 101   **13**

Founding Fathers 14
Separation of Powers (Is This Any Way to Run
 a Country?) 15
The Real Supremes 16
The Congress of the People 16
The Chief Executive 18
No Angels Here 20

3 The Impeachment Process   **23**

The History of Impeachment 23
What Are High Crimes and Misdemeanors? 24
How the Process Works in Theory 26
How It Would Work in Practice 27
What Is the Role of the Courts? 28

4 Impeachment in History   **31**

The Impeachment of Senator William Blount 31
The Impeachment of Supreme Court Justice
 Samuel Chase 32
The Impeachment of President Andrew Johnson 34
Other Notable Impeachments 37

Part 2: The Making of a President — 39

5 No Wonder They Call It Hope — 41

Birth of a President 41
Boy Wonder 43
The Draft Dodge 44
A Yale Man 45
Professor Who? 46
The Political Prodigy 47
Birth of the Comeback Kid 48
State-Wide to Nation-Wide 48

6 Family Matters — 51

Hillary's History 52
Into the Fray 53
Hillary Rodham, Esq. 55
Hippie Hillary 55
'Till Death Do Us Part 57
Thoroughly Modern Hillary 58
  A Bull Market 58
  Brighter Skies Ahead 59

7 On the National Stage — 61

The Not Ready For Prime-Time Player 61
The Seven Dwarves 62
The Perot Factor 63
"It's The Economy, Stupid" 63
Clinton Upsets the Right Wing 65
President William Jefferson Clinton 66
  The Price of Inexperience 67
  Cracks in the Dike 67
  A Showdown and a Shutdown 68

8 Liar, Liar, Pants on Fire — 71

Clinton's Alleged History of Infidelity 72
  Dolly Browning 72
  *What Did the Troopers Know and When Did They
    Know It?* 73
Gennifer Flowers 74

Kathleen Willey 76
Paula Jones 79
"I did not inhale." 79
Promises, Promises 80
Are All Lies Alike? 83

9 Jones v. Clinton   85

The Background on the Jones Case 85
Her Legal Claims *88*
The Supreme Court Sets the Stage 89
The Case Goes Forward 90
How Monica Lewinsky Fits In 91
Judge Wright Tosses the Case Out 92
Why Paula Jones Lost 94
The Damage Done 94

Part 3: The Road to Impeachment?   97

10 Scandals of the Past   99

Money and Manifest Destiny 99
The Whiskey-Ring Scandal 100
The Teapot-Dome Scandal 101
Abscam 102
Iran-Contra 102

11 Watergate and Its Aftermath   107

Deep Background 108
The Waters Rise 110
All the President's Men 112
Who Was Deep Throat? 112
Aftermath 113
How Does the Watergate Scandal Compare to Today's? 115

12 The Independent Counsel   117

The History of the Independent Counsel Statute 118
Watergate Sets the Stage *118*
A Law Is Born 119
What the Statute Says *119*
Powers of the Prosecutor *120*

How the Statute Works in Reality 121
The Ghosts of Prosecutors Past 122
Upon Further Review… 123
Building a Better Bill-Trap 124
Tactics of an Independent Counsel 126
What Choice Do We Have? 127

13 A "Vast Right-Wing Conspiracy"?   129

What Is a Conspiracy? 130
The "Ringleader": Ken Starr 130
Who's Richard Mellon Scafie?! 132
Lucianne Goldberg, Linda Tripp, Paula Jones … 133
The Clinton Chronicles 135
Untangle This Mess, Please 135

14 The Report on Starr   137

The Son of a Preacherman 138
Right-Wing Conspirator or Tough Prosecutor? 139
An Unhealthy Obsession 141
Surf's Up! 143
In Conclusion… 143

15 Whitewatergate   145

Whitewater 146
Fraudulent Transactions 146
Web Hubbell and Hillary Clinton, Attorneys at Law 148
Travelgate 150
The Death of Vince Foster 153
Filegate 154
How Ken Starr Entered the Picture 155
  Farewell to Fiske 155
  Starr Wars 156
Criminal Incompetence? 157

Part 4: A Scandalous Affair   159

16 Sex in the White House   161

Jefferson's "Black Venus" 162
James Buchanan and His "Better Half" 163

Grover Cleveland: Ma, Ma, Where's My Pa? 164
Warren G. Harding: Sex in the White House Coatroom .. 165
Franklin and Eleanor: They Had a "New Deal" 166
JFK: Some Like It Hot 168
Lyndon Baines Johnson: No Cows Please 169
The Gentlemen's Agreement 171

17 Enter the Intern   **173**

Initial Contacts with the President 173
Sex with the Commander in Chief 174
"We need to talk about our relationship ..." 177
Breaking Up Is Hard to Do 178
Secret Service Suspicions 179
Lewinsky's Transfer to the Pentagon 180
Playful Monica 181
Betty Currie's Role 182
The Blue Dress 184
Can We Still Be Friends? 186

18 "It's Illegal to Threaten the President"   **187**

Her New Friend, Linda 187
Monica's Job Search 188
Fatal Attraction 189
Fireworks 190
Vernon Jordan: Super Lawyer! 191
"I Am Not a Moron" 194
Advice from Uncle Vernon 195

19 Sex, Lies, and Audiotape   **197**

Secret Tapes: A Washington Cliché 197
   Monica's Motives *198*
   Tripp's Trepidation *199*
The Talking Points 200
Monica's Affidavit in the Jones Case 202
The Big Payoff 203
Starr's Circuitous Path from Whitewater to Sex 204
The President's Deposition in the Jones Case 205
Extra, Extra, Read All About It! 208

20 The Role of the New Media   **211**

The Good Old Days 212
Dawn of a New Age 213
Stand By for News! 214
Birth of a New Medium 216
An Unhappy Populace 218
A Return to Civility 218

21 Stand by Your Man   **221**

Hillary Puts On a Good Face 222
A Private Woman in a Public World 224
A Woman Scorned 225
A Woman in Love 226

Part 5: The President on Trial   **229**

22 Starr Chambers   **231**

The Risks of Angering a Prosecutor 231
Legal Ramifications of the Investigation 232
Definition of Terms 233
Kenneth Starr: Yep, Him Too 234
Monica Is Almost Out of the Woods 236
Vernon Jordan Had Better Be a Superlawyer 237
Linda Tripp May Reap What She's Sown 238
Hillary Clinton: What, She Didn't Kill Vince Foster? 239

23 Is Sex an Impeachable Offense?   **241**

The Charges 242
Perjury (Counts 1, 2, 3, 4, and 8) 243
Obstruction of Justice (Counts 5, 6, 7, and 10) 247
Witness Tampering (Count 9) 250
Abuse of Power (Count 11) 250
The New House Charges 252
So, What Does It All Mean? 253

24 The Impeachment Scenario   255

Our Course Is Clear? 255
Clinton's in the House 257
Resignation Situation *258*
Playing the Impeachment Odds *259*
What's Impeachable? 260
Let the Courts Decide 260
Will the Witness Please Rise? 261
The Role of the House 264
"The chair recognizes the Senator from…" 265
Then What? 267

25 What Does the Future Hold?   271

Prosecutor or Persecutor? 271
No More Independent Counsels, Ever! 273
A Disturbing Legal Legacy 274
Democrats, Republicans, Citizens and Voters 276
The Comeback Kid 277
Afterglow 280
And Now, the End Is Near 280

Appendices

A Excerpts from the Starr Report   283

B Timeline   331

C The Cast of Characters   337

D Further Reading   345

E Glossary   349

Index   353

Foreword

One of the strongest memories of my college years is a lecture on Greek drama given by a professor who was something of a joke on the campus of the University of Chicago because of his obsession with Plato as the beginning and end of all knowledge. The basic point of this particular lecture was the distinction between tragedy (which he defined as men acting above their normal standards) and comedy (which he said was based upon men acting below their normal standards).

The professor had a vivid style, which made the things he said seem to be not only real but contemporary. He could croak "coax" with the same vigor depicted by Aristophanes in his play *The Frogs*, and his students would later walk across the campus imitating him. But it was not his style that kept him alive in my later years of life. What really did it was my period as a journalist covering the U.S. government in Washington, D.C., and the period I spent as a government official in the U.S. Senate and the White House. In both capacities I encountered dramatic tragedy and comedy on a scale far beyond anything imagined by the Greeks.

At the present time the whole nation is confronted with the spectacle of a fantastic farce, which is obviously heading towards a major historic tragedy. The principle characters are two men who would have inspired Aristophanes to a major effort. One is a political leader and one is a legal prosecutor, but even though they are battling each other they seem to share one common characteristic—an obsession with kinky sex.

The battle between the two protagonists involves the issue of one allegedly lying about an affair with a woman who had what can be charitably described as "accommodating" moral and ethical standards. To back this charge, the accuser is invoking untested sources of fantastic power—especially one known as "impeachment." The result of this charge is the involvement of the entire structure of government, which otherwise might be engaged in such matters as public health, financial support of the elderly, and the education of the nation's children.

Beyond this point, however, the resemblance to the classic Greek comedy comes to an end. The audiences in Athens came to see the plays because they enjoyed them; the audience for this farce (the public) is sick and tired of the spectacle and wants it to go away. In Greek comedy no truly decent people got hurt; in our current version a whole system of government that has worked well for two centuries can go down the drain. Finally, what should be little more than pornographic amusement is becoming a classic story.

The public needs to understand the nitpicking characteristics of this incredible happening. I hope that in pursuing the details our sense of humor will predominate. More truth will be found in wit than in mourning. This book is dedicated to presenting the facts accurately but in perspective. About the only saving grace that can help us now is to keep this event basking in the light of the farce that it is. If we do, we might survive.

—George E. Reedy, retired professor of communications at Marquette University, is a former White House press secretary under President Lyndon B. Johnson; former staff director of the U.S. Senate Democratic Policy Committee; and a former journalist who covered Congress for a number of years.

Introduction

"I did not have sexual relations with that woman, Miss Lewinsky." With those words, President William Jefferson Clinton set the stage for a colossal struggle. Of course, now we all know more than we want to about what he did with that woman, even if he is not sure what to call it. And our government is speeding towards a possible impeachment of a President for only the third time in history.

This entire episode raises a host of troubling questions. How did it ever become proper to ask the leader of the free world about his sex life, let alone conclude that we deserve an honest answer? Should a sitting President have even been asked those questions? Should Independent Counsel Kenneth Starr have been allowed to go from investigating a failed land deal in Arkansas to allegations of sexual misconduct in the White House? In this book, we answer these questions, and a whole lot more, sorting the wheat from the chaff.

The Lewinsky scandal and the tale of pathos in the Starr report is remarkable, but it's only part of the story. To understand why we are now in the midst of very real Presidential crisis, you also need to know how Clinton's history, and his enemies' tenacity, made this crisis practically inevitable; how the Paula Jones lawsuit played into that and created a legal precedent that will endanger Presidents for years to come; and how a well-meaning independent counsel law created a monster.

What's in It for Me?

In *The Complete Idiot's Guide to Impeachment of the President*, we attempt to give you a comprehensive overview and thorough analysis of the situation. You will learn how impeachment works in theory and what will happen in reality. The history of sex in the White House, Watergate, the impeachment of President Andrew Johnson, Iran-Contra, Whitewater, the Starr report—it's all here.

Some say this is "just about sex." Others disagree. Is Ken Starr a "right-wing conspirator" or a tough-as-nails prosecutor? Whatever you think, you will find in this book the tools to defend your point of view.

Part 1, "A Quick Civics Lesson," lays out the players and the process. The intentionally vague constitutional term "high crimes and misdemeanors" will be made simple. This section overviews the current situation, explains the basic set-up of our government, describes how the impeachment process is outlined in the Constitution, and how past impeachments have been conducted.

Part 2, "The Making of a President," tells how Clinton rose from a family dealing with an alcoholic step-father to become regarded by those around him as a young man who would someday become President. It recounts his early days, his rise from governor to candidate to President, and details the many "bimbo eruptions" that has beset his career, including the monster of them all, *Jones v. Clinton*.

Part 3, "The Road to Impeachment?," sets the stage for the Starr report. You get a quick look at past scandals, including a chapter on the Watergate scandal, which brought the modern independent counsel law into being; an exploration of the alleged "vast right-wing conspiracy;" a look at its supposed henchman, Ken Starr; and finally an examination of Whitewater and its many cousins.

Part 4, "A Scandalous Affair," is the juicy stuff. A lascivious intern named Monica, a wily President named Clinton, a treacherous friend named Tripp, a zealous prosecutor named Starr, a committed wife named Hillary—it's all here, as is the role of the media in feeding the firestorm.

Part 5, "The President on Trial," analyzes the impact of the Starr report on the President, Congress, and the country. It explains just how strong (or weak) Starr's case against the President actually is, and gives you an insider's view of what we will be witnessing in the months, or years, to come.

Throughout the book you will also encounter many more tidbits of information that have been highlighted by friendly icons. Here is what to expect:

Mumbo Jumbo

Much of politics and law is laced with arcane words and phrases. This section will translate them into English.

Media Alert

The media has played a very large part in this story. This snippet will relay the role of the media, both past and present, in American politics.

Become a Pundit

Insider information, facts, knowledge, and gossip is the currency of politics. Find it all here.

Sound Bites

The incessant stream of talk about Clinton and Lewinsky has resulted in some very good quotes. Read them here.

White House Confidential

The men and women who have occupied the White House were all too human. Stories of their sometimes surprising peccadilloes should prove to be entertaining.

Acknowledgments

The authors would like to thank Eric Jones for all his work. Chapter 2, "American Government 101," was written because of him. They would also like to thank Amy Czechorosky for quickly jumping into this project. Without her, Chapter 6, "Family Matters," couldn't have been written.

Steven D. Strauss would also like to thank his fantastic literary agent, Sheree Bykofsky, for making this book possible. He is also grateful to Rick Tuttle for fostering his love of politics. Mark Sobel, Jeff Eichen, Sydney and Mara, and Jillian Lewis were also very helpful.

Spencer Strauss would like to especially thank Marty Stone for his patience and support. He would also like to thank Seymour Fagan, Glenn Bozarth, Susan Garber-Yonts, Kevin Hoban, and Larry Strauss. He is grateful to his brother Steve for this great opportunity and for teaching him "what one man can do, another can do."

Finally, both authors would like thank Jessica Faust, Phil Kitchel, and everyone else at Macmillan who assisted in this intense experience.

The authors are also grateful to Jennifer Basye Sander for her inspiration.

Part 1
A Quick Civics Lesson

While it's unlikely they could have predicted a scandal of this nature, our Founding Fathers did a pretty good job setting up the Constitution and the government to cope with one. In the next few chapters, you'll take a look at how the Clinton/Lewinsky saga developed, then explore how our three branches of government are set up to check up on each other.

You'll also look at how an impeachment takes place, constitutionally, and at the few cases of impeachment that will serve as the example in the case of President Bill Clinton.

Chapter 1

How Did We Get Here?

In This Chapter

➤ The President admitted his affair after a series of strenuous denials

➤ The lawsuit brought by Paula Jones, although dismissed, has still harmed Clinton greatly

➤ The Starr report tells us more than we may want to know

➤ Many questions remain to be answered

It was a shocking sight, really. The 42nd President of the United States, William Jefferson Clinton, went before the American people on national television and admitted to being an adulterer. While explaining that he had misled people, including his wife, he insisted that he had not actually been lying either.

It was a sad, disheartening, embarrassing day for many Americans. We want to be able to say to our children, "Look at the President. Some day, if you study and work hard, that could be you." All of a sudden, we weren't so sure we wanted our children to be like him.

Clinton's speech of August 17, 1998, was a far cry from where he had been only six months earlier. With a booming economy and stock market, his approval rating was at an all-time high. How he went from king of the world to walking wounded is a story that will be told for generations. It is a story that results from equal parts stupidity, duplicity, arrogance, and inquisition. Rest assured that none of the major players will escape from this with their reputation or dignity untarnished.

The White House.
Adam Woolfitt/Corbis

It Was Wrong

Clinton had every reason to look awful the night he admitted his adultery on TV. He
had just concluded four grueling hours of embarrassingly graphic questioning by
Independent Counsel Ken Starr's lawyers. Moreover, little did the nation know, but
Clinton had been meeting with his national security advisors for a week in preparation
of an air-raid on suspected terrorist sites in the Sudan and Afghanistan.

White House Confidential

Although we all know that George Washington was married to Martha, the love of his life was not his wife but his mistress, a woman by the name of Sarah "Sally" Fairfax. While married to Martha, he once wrote to Sally, "The world has no business to know the object of my Love, 'tis obvious; doubt it not, nor expose it." Especially don't expose it.

While his poor delivery that night can be justified, the content of the speech left many people bewildered. In that missed opportunity, Clinton was able to turn the tide of public opinion … against himself. What could have effectively ended months of crisis instead ensured months of crisis. It was one of the defining moments, if not the defining moment, of the Clinton presidency. For the most gifted politician of his generation, it was a rare, and potentially fatal, blunder.

This afternoon in this room, from this chair, I testified before the Office of Independent Counsel and the grand jury.

I answered their questions truthfully, including questions about my private life, questions no American citizen would ever want to answer.

As you know, in a deposition in January, I was asked questions about my relationship with Monica Lewinsky. While my answers were legally accurate, I did not volunteer information. Indeed, I did have a relationship with Miss Lewinsky that was not appropriate. In fact, it was wrong.

I know that my public comments and my silence about this matter gave a false impression. I misled people, including even my wife. I deeply regret that.

Media Alert

In 1952, as Eisenhower's vice-President running mate, Richard Nixon was accused of financial impropriety. Nixon gave an unprecedented televised speech to plead his case. He denied misuse of a campaign fund, speaking of his humble means and his wife's "respectable Republican cloth coat." The only gift he had kept, he said, was the cocker spaniel, Checkers. The "Checkers speech" saved Nixon's career and became the standard for all subsequent political confessions.

Clinton then went on to lay much of the blame for his current problems on his nemesis, Ken Starr. At this point, Clinton lost many people. Until that point, the nation had been generally willing to forgive the President his indiscretion. But his lack of contrition, coupled with his obvious anger and finger-pointing, convinced many that he was not deserving of exoneration.

A Legacy in Doubt

Without question, the President has much to be angry about. He has been investigated, examined, and reviewed more than almost anyone in history. Yet despite it all, he was largely untouched by Starr's investigation. Before the turn of 1998, Clinton was widely considered to be on the verge of, if not greatness, at least very-goodness.

Become a Pundit

In 1997, 719 historians and former politicians were asked to rank the Presidents in terms of character and integrity. Abraham Lincoln came in first, followed by George Washington. Richard Nixon came in last.

Prior to the Lewinsky mess, such were Bill Clinton's fortunes that much of his time was spent contemplating his place in history. The press openly worried that he was spending too much time golfing, thinking about the future, resting on his laurels, and generally becoming a lame duck before his time. Clinton assured everyone that he would be as involved as ever. All was well in the kingdom.

His advisors liked to play a game: They would list Clinton's best and worst deeds and then assess how history would rank each one. There were many things on the positive side: a tamed deficit, a booming economy, welfare reform, reduced crime, peace at home and abroad. In comparison, the negatives—the scandals and misdeeds both real and alleged—while plentiful, seemed to pale in the rosy glow of a second term.

Then along came Linda Tripp and her tapes, and Ken Starr and his grand jury, and Monica Lewinsky and her stained dress, and nothing was the same. Camelot would not be revisited. Clinton had been hoisted by his own petard.

"I did not have sexual relations with that woman, Miss Lewinsky."

No one would want to admit to marital infidelity, let alone do so on national television. That Bill Clinton put himself in that position is inexcusable. Clinton has a well-chronicled history of adultery, but many people thought he had put that behind him when he became President. He hadn't. His odd relationship with Monica Lewinsky (it can hardly be called an affair in the conventional sense) meant that he had again cheated on his wife, Hillary Rodham Clinton. Especially given that he was being sued by Paula Jones for sexual harassment, and had to know how closely he was being watched, why would Bill Clinton be so stupid as to cheat on his wife and give his enemies more ammunition?

As much as he wanted to blame Ken Starr, Bill Clinton had no one to blame for this debacle but himself. He had been mincing words and parsing meaning for months. His explanations had become increasingly unbelievable, his use of language ever more tortured.

Sound Bites

Everyone lies about sex. Without lying there'd be no sex.

—Jerry Seinfeld

Since the news of his relationship with the 22-year old intern had first broken, Clinton tried to avoid telling the truth without actually lying. He reverted to his pattern of truth-shading (like admitting that he smoked pot as a young man but "did not inhale") and his legal training in an attempt to avoid an admission of adultery—and, by extension, an admission of perjury in his deposition for Paula Jones's lawyers.

White House Confidential

In 1897, senator and one-time Presidential hopeful Arthur Brown began an affair with Anna Bradley. When she got pregnant, Brown abandoned the Senate and his wife and ran off with Bradley to Idaho. In 1906, Bradley learned that Brown had taken a new mistress. She shot him and was later acquitted.

On Day One of the scandal, January 21, 1998, the President was interviewed by Jim Lehrer. In retrospect, Clinton's answers would be funny if they were not so pathetic.

> *Q: The news of this day is that Kenneth Starr, independent counsel, is investigating allegations that you suborned perjury by encouraging a 24-year-old woman, a former White House intern, to lie under oath in a civil deposition about her having had an affair with you. Mr. President, is that true?*

> *A: That is not true. That is not true. I did not ask anyone to tell anything other than the truth. There is no improper relationship.*

> *Q: "No improper relationship"—define what you mean by that.*

> *A: Well, I think you know what it means. It means that there is not a sexual relationship, an improper sexual relationship, or any other kind of improper relationship.*

Q: You had no sexual relationship with this young woman?

A: There is not a sexual relationship—that is accurate.

We can see now that Clinton was trying very hard not to lie, but struggling to not tell the truth either. That is why he used present-tense phrases like "there is not a sexual relationship" (the relationship was over) and the term "no improper relationship" (apparently he considered it proper as long as it did not include intercourse).

That same day, Clinton was interviewed by the Capitol Hill newspaper *Rollcall*. In this interview, he was again asked about his relationship with the intern.

Q: Was it in any way sexual?

A: The relationship was not sexual. And I know what you mean, and the answer is no.

Despite his attempts to avoid lying without admitting he was a careless adulterer, Clinton looked worse and worse. The next day, in reference to requests for more information about the scandal, he promised "more rather than less, sooner rather than later." Of course, the reality was that he offered less rather than more, later rather than sooner.

Media Alert

Many people find it no coincidence that Clinton finally and forcefully denied the affair only after his friend, television producer Harry Thomason, had spent a week with Clinton at the White House. Thomason is known to be media savvy and many people think he penned Clinton's remarks that day.

The coup-de-grace was his statement during a White House ceremony on January 26, 1998. Wagging his finger and speaking more forcefully than he had since the story broke, the President looked the American people in the eye and said:

I want to say one thing to the American people. I want you to listen to me. I'm going to say this again. I did not have sexual relations with that woman, Miss Lewinsky. I never told anybody to lie, not a single time—never. These allegations are false. And I need to go back to work for the American people.

Clinton then spent the next several months stonewalling, avoiding answers, giving convoluted explanations, and attacking the Starr office. All the while, details of the affair (allegedly leaked illegally from the Office of the Independent Counsel) made Clinton look more and more dishonest.

Where Does He Come Up with This Stuff?

Clinton's insistence that he had not had "sexual relations" with Lewinsky stemmed from the deposition he gave in the Paula Jones sexual-harassment case. In that deposition, Jones's lawyers presented Clinton with a definition of "sexual relations" that seemed to include intercourse and fondling only, if one were to construe the definition very narrowly. This allowed Clinton a way out. Using their own definition, Clinton was able to deny that he had had "sexual relations" with Lewinsky (since they had never had intercourse). This was not a term he invented, it was given to him by his adversaries.

Was this a lie, or was it just a sharp lawyer outfoxing his sworn enemies? Understand this: It was not Clinton's job to make it easy for Jones's attorneys. It was not his job to admit every infidelity, if he could truthfully avoid doing so. It was his job not to give them any damaging evidence, while remaining truthful. That is the duty of any deponent.

Lawsuits are a civilized form of war. The other attorneys are out to get you. This was even more true in the Jones case. Hillary Clinton's assertion that a "vast right-wing conspiracy" is out to get her husband may or may not be true, but it is indisputable that by the time Jones was permitted to take Clinton's deposition, right-wing enemies of Clinton's were financing and directing the case. Jones's attorney were out to get Clinton.

It would be asinine for Clinton, or any defendant in any case, for that matter, to give opposing lawyers damaging evidence if he could avoid it. Any good lawyer would tell any client being deposed the same thing. The Jones lawyers gave Clinton a strange definition of sexual relations. He certainly wasn't going to admit to adultery if their definition permitted him to avoid it without perjuring himself.

Mumbo Jumbo

In a civil lawsuit, the **deponent** is the person who is having his deposition taken, under oath.

The problem today is that Clinton thinks he was able to do so, and Ken Starr disagrees.

The Starr Report

After Clinton's deposition, Starr began his investigation of the Clinton-Lewinsky matter in earnest. White House aides were subpoenaed and the White House tried unsuccessfully to block their testimony by invoking "executive privilege." Starr took the heretofore unprecedented step of subpoenaing Secret Service agents, and the White House was again unsuccessful in its attempt to block that testimony by invoking the never-before-heard-of "protective function privilege."

Mumbo Jumbo

A **subpoena** is a command to appear at a certain time and place and give testimony regarding a certain matter.

Then things got bad. Lewinsky, the President's one-time lover copped a plea with the independent prosecutor and spilled whatever beans were left to spill. Evidence that went beyond the unreliable and unimpeachable "he said/she said" variety surfaced in the form of a stained blue dress. Clinton was forced to testify before Starr's grand jury.

Starr, after years of seemingly fruitless efforts to get Clinton, finally had something. All other investigations—Whitewater, Travelgate, Filegate, Gategate—were set aside while the prosecutor went about proving that the President lied about sex. Impeachment was finally at hand!

On Friday, September 11, 1998, Starr delivered to Congress and the country his verdict on Clinton. Starr's 455-page report maintained that he had "substantial and credible" evidence that the President had committed 11 impeachable offenses. Some seemed trivial. Starr asserts that Clinton's effort to mount a vigorous defense by invoking executive privilege warrants impeachment. Others are more serious. Starr alleges that Clinton obstructed justice when he and Lewinsky colluded to have her lie under oath.

As you read and think about this situation, a critical moment for the nation, the political system, and the traditions that anchor our society, keep in mind the following:

Impeachment was intended to remove public officials from office, for the good of the country, if their behavior seriously undermines the law, the legitimacy of the government, or the Constitution. It must be decided on the basis of what is good for the country and its future, not on our emotional whims of the moment. Impeachment is not intended as punishment or retribution: It is intended to safeguard the legitimacy of the system, and the rule of law.

Impeachment is considered quite apart from whether or not illegal acts occurred. If they undermine our system, illegal acts could be part of impeachable offenses. Many illegal acts might not be considered impeachable offenses—even if a person is tried and found to have committed illegal acts, that person could still, in some circumstances, continue to hold office. Conversely, a public official could be impeached even if no illegal acts were committed. Impeachment is political in the high sense of the word; it is a judgment about what is good for the country and what supports our faith in our system. It is political, not legal.

Finally, this case is not about sex. None of the charges relate specifically to the fact that Clinton had some form of sex with a young intern. He is not charged with rape, assault, sexual harassment or anything else. His "inappropriate conduct" is not the issue. The charges have to do with whether he lied under oath, obstructed justice, or abused his position of power and authority. The charges would be the same regardless of what he might have tried to cover up.

It is unfortunate, but perhaps no accident, that Ken Starr saw fit to include inflammatory details that were certain to preoccupy the public and the media, so that the charges themselves would be underplayed. For many, the sexual behavior Starr took pains to describe is

Sound Bites

The President is mentally and emotionally unstable.

—Ross Perot, September 26, 1998

worthy of punishment by itself, even though it is not, in fact, illegal. The sexual details are a polarizing influence, a wedge almost certain to eliminate sensible debate on the issue of the President's committing or not committing perjury in a civil suit that was later dismissed.

Unanswered Question

The entire affair raises serious constitutional and public policy concerns. The most basic is: What now?

Starr's report is just the opening salvo in a drama that is sure to grip the nation for some time. The House of Representatives is empowered with investigating the matter and bringing charges of impeachment, should such charges be deemed justified. During Watergate, the House Judiciary Committee spent many months just learning the facts and deciding whether President Nixon's misdeeds were impeachable. Given Clinton's misdeeds and the political capital a Republican Congress could reap by dragging this matter out, there is every likelihood that this affair won't go away anytime soon.

Starr himself is not done until he concludes all investigations and brings indictments or clears targets of alleged wrongdoing, at which point he reports to the attorney general. As the statute that gives him his power does not require him to make his ongoing investigations public, we don't know what he is looking into at this point. It is safe to assume that his original charge—Whitewater—is probably at the top of the list. Long ago, it seems, he ceased to be an independent prosecutor and became a personally obsessed inquisitor. His seeming lack of objectivity has unfortunately tainted his investigation, his results, and the office he holds.

Finally, whither William Jefferson Clinton? He has disappointed so many people and squandered such enormous promise, that if he could be impeached for that, he might be. Beyond that, his utter lack of judgment (some have called it character) has tainted *his* office and his allies.

But consider this: People lie. Politicians lie. Presidents lie. Lyndon Johnson lied about Vietnam. Ronald Reagan lied about selling arms to terrorists in trade for hostages, then using the profits to aid Central-American guerrillas against a specific congressional resolution. The Iran-Contra affair was perhaps the most serious constitutional crisis of this century, and George Bush continued to lie about it even after his involvement was clear. No impeachment was discussed. We must seriously consider whether these lies of Clinton's are so

Become a Pundit

Probably the most famous line to come out of Watergate was uttered by Senator Howard Baker (R) of Tennessee. Inquiring about Nixon's knowledge of the break-in and its aftermath, Baker asked, "What did the President know and when did he know it?"

much worse than those of his predecessors that we should be discussing the impeachment of a President for only the third time in our nation's history.

Other than war, impeachment is about as serious a business as a country can face. We surely don't want to impeach a President—any President—because his definition of a word differed from that of a prosecutor's. Yet that is exactly where we stand. Operators in Washington have discovered that a civil deposition can now be used as a political tool; even the most intimate details must be answered honestly or a perjury charge is imminent. At which point the sensible instincts of the public (evident in the polls) are ignored and the President's enemies and friends alike can only watch and shrug as the machinery of government turns out the executive office on the most trivial of pretexts.

Perjury is a crime, if indeed perjury was committed. We don't want to be shy of impeachment, however unpleasant, if a President did in fact obstruct justice or commit perjury before a grand jury. But impeachment does not automatically follow upon the commission of crime, just as there need not be a crime present for impeachment to be considered. So we're in a real national quandary: Did he commit perjury? (And can it be proven or disproven without the unpleasant sight of congressmen and senators arguing whether his or her intent was to gratify when he or she handled this or that?)

Some people may count Bill Clinton out. Don't be too sure. If ever there was a politician whose political instincts and skills are enough to reverse an apparently doomed presidency, it is the self-styled Comeback Kid.

The Least You Need to Know

➤ Clinton's speech of August 17, wherein he admitted being an adulterer, failed to turn the tide in his favor, mainly because of its tone.

➤ Prior to admitting the truth, Clinton spent many months feebly denying the affair.

➤ Clinton had hoped to achieve greatness, but the Paula Jones suit and his own philandering got in the way.

➤ The Starr report alleges 11 impeachable offenses against Clinton, ranging from the trivial to the considerable.

➤ This national crisis will take a long time to play itself out, and its long-term effects will take years to understand.

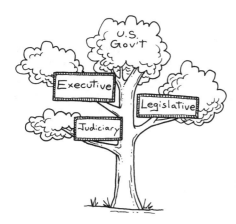

Chapter 2

American Government 101

In This Chapter

➤ Our Founding Fathers invented a brand-new form of government

➤ We have three branches of government, and each acts as a watchdog upon the others

➤ Congress can pretty much do whatever it wants

➤ The President's ultimate power stems from his power to persuade

---

To outside observers, and sometimes to many of us, our government looks like a three-ring circus run amok. The Clinton-Lewinsky saga seems but the latest example of a government at odds with itself—the independent counsel is after the President, the President is mad at Congress, the House rails against the Senate, and on it goes.

Yet the United States government is one of the oldest continuous forms of governments in the world. For the most part, our democracy works. Of course it is ugly sometimes, and yes it can be bloated and unresponsive, but for the most part, it works remarkably well. Strange as it may seem, the political circus that we see today is going (almost) exactly according to plan.

The framers of the Constitution (the document that sets forth exactly how the government is to run and what powers are designated to whom) intended for there to be friction between the different "branches" of government. Their plan worked remarkably well.

Founding Fathers

The men (there's no getting around it, very few women were involved in this process) who created this country were, for the most part, born in England. They came here in search of adventure and looking for more freedom than they had back home. But they weren't revolutionaries; at least they never set out to be.

White House Confidential

Bill Clinton is not the first President to have his sex life paraded in front of the media. Thomas Jefferson had several inflammatory poems about his sexual proclivities published in the major newspapers of his day.

As years past and the American colonies grew and prospered, a rift with Great Britain inevitably began. Although the fledgling colonies were part of the British Empire and subject to English rule and law, they had little say in how their land was run. King George III would make an edict and colonists far away were expected to carry it out. The colonists were given no formal representation in England. Worst of all, they were forced to pay taxes to a crown they were growing to resent. "No taxation without representation!" was the cry.

The Great Seal of the President of the United States.
Archive Photos

Had King George simply allowed the colonists some say in the running of their own affairs, it's unlikely the United States would have ever been born; there would have been no need to revolt. But the colonists felt they had no choice, and they did revolt. The Declaration of Independence, when viewed anew, is a remarkably beautiful and revolutionary document.

> *We hold these truths to be self-evident, that all men are created equal, that they are endowed by their Creator with certain unalienable Rights, that among these are Life, Liberty, and the pursuit of Happiness. That to secure these rights, Governments are instituted among Men, deriving their just powers from the consent of the governed. That whenever any Form of Government becomes destructive of these ends, it is the Right of the People to alter or to abolish it, and to institute new Government, laying its foundation on such principles and organizing its powers in such form, as to them shall seem most likely to effect their Safety and Happiness.*

Never before in the history of mankind had such sentiments been expressed—that those who govern do so at the consent of the governed. However noble the sentiments, the question remained: How to create such a government?

Separation of Powers (Is This Any Way to Run a Country?)

Above all, the people who created the United States of America wanted to avoid the kind of autocracy they had been subject to under King George. No one person or branch of government would be above the others. Accordingly, the government would be divided into three branches and each would serve to "check and balance" the other. This is called "separation of powers." The idea was to create some inherent tension between these three branches of government so that no one branch would be supreme. In this way, the tyranny of a minority would hopefully be avoided.

Supreme Court Justice Louis Brandeis once observed,

> *The doctrine of the separation of powers was adopted by the Convention of 1787, not to promote efficiency but to preclude the exercise of arbitrary power. The purpose was, not to avoid friction, but by means of the inevitable friction incident to the distribution of the governmental powers among the departments, to save the people from autocracy.*

Mumbo Jumbo

An **autocracy** is a government in which one person possesses unlimited power.

Become a Pundit

The term "Congress" actually has two meanings. While it describes both the House and the Senate combined, more often it is used to refer to the House alone. That is why members of that institution are called "congressmen."

The first branch of our government is the executive branch. It is the only branch of our government headed by a single person—the President. The judicial branch is made up of the federal judiciary. The legislative branch is made up of Congress.

Each branch has a different function, and no branch can operate independently of the others. For example, judges on the Supreme Court are nominated by the President and confirmed by the Senate. As Justice Antonin Scalia pointed out in his confirmation hearings, the purpose of these checks and balances among the three branches is to assure that "no one of them can run roughshod over the liberties of the people."

The Real Supremes

The easiest branch of government to understand is also the most autonomous (by intention)—the judiciary. Made up of district court judges, appeals court judges, various other special judges, and the Supreme Court, the job of the judicial branch is to interpret the laws of the country.

The Supreme Court has the final say on the constitutionality of any law, and the interpretation of what the Constitution says. That may sound simple—it says what it says, right? Not necessarily. Some judges are called "strict constructionists." Tending to be more conservative, these judges look at the exact words of the Constitution to interpret its meaning. A "well-armed militia" (2nd Amendment) means a well-armed militia.

Other judges are not so narrow in their interpretation. They think that their job is to look at the document as a whole and interpret its meaning in a bit broader, possibly more contemporary, context. For example, while many of us think that we have a constitutional right to privacy, nowhere in the Constitution is that right explicitly granted. We have that right because one of these judges, the legendary William O. Douglas, read the Constitution and found an overriding respect for privacy to be a guiding principle. The "right to privacy" then became part of an important Supreme Court decision.

Become a Pundit

William O. Douglas was appointed to the Supreme Court by Franklin Roosevelt. He served there longer than any other justice in the history of the country—36 years. Former Secretary of War Edwin Stanton, appointed by U.S. Grant, served the shortest time. He died four days after being confirmed by the Senate.

The Congress of the People

Efficiency was not a top priority in designing our government. For example, in Article I, the Constitution allocates legislative power to Congress, but it then divides Congress into two houses. Why? By having two houses in Congress, no single group could make the laws.

The House of Representatives is made up of members who represent relatively small geographic areas. It all depends upon the population of an area. A dense area such as

Los Angeles would have more congressmen than the same area in North Dakota. In addition, members of the House must run for reelection every two years. In this way it was hoped that members of the House would be more responsive to their constituents than their brethren in the Senate.

While some states have far more congressmen than others (California for example), every state has two senators. This was intended to create equality among the states. While a less populated state like Nevada is overshadowed by New York in the House, in the Senate they are equal. Senators are elected every six years. This was done in order to hopefully make it a more deliberative, thoughtful arena (which it is).

These two bodies are forced by the Constitution to work together, and with the President. In order to become law, a bill that imposes new taxes, for instance, must originate in the House, then be approved in the Senate, before being sent to the President for his signature or his veto. If he signs it, the bill becomes law.

If the President disapproves of the bill, he vetoes it. But even that is not the last say. Congress can override a Presidential veto if it can garner a two-thirds majority in both houses. If so, then the bill can become law. In this way, neither Congress nor the President can create a law without working with the other.

Become a Pundit

In his final term as speaker of the House, John White gave a speech that was actually an old speech of Aaron Burr's. When the truth of his plagiarism came out, White killed himself.

One of the main functions of Congress is called "oversight." Oversight takes many forms. The first is annual congressional hearings on agency budget requests. Agencies have to justify their funding to the satisfaction of the Congress.

Another method of oversight includes investigation. Any congressional committee can instigate matters under its jurisdiction. Most of these investigations relate to small matters in which members inquire about specific concerns of their own or their constituents. Larger investigations, such as the Senate Whitewater investigation, are also appropriate.

Become a Pundit

The only reason McCarthy went after communists in the first place is because he was facing a tough reelection fight and his campaign manager thought it might make a good campaign issue.

Now, some members may take their oversight investigations too seriously and use them as a political vendetta. This is what happened in the 1950s when Senator Joseph McCarthy began the infamous "Army-McCarthy" hearings. McCarthy alleged that communists had infiltrated the highest reaches of our government. Using intimidation and blackballing, McCarthy turned the country and the government upside down on a witchhunt to find commies. McCarthy was finally shut down when one of his colleagues said to him on national television, "Have you no sense of decency, sir, at long last? Have you left no sense of decency?" This sentiment galvanized the country against Senator Joe, and he was later reprimanded by the Senate.

Other congressmen use their oversight responsibilities as an excuse to travel all over the world (at government expense) to see how federal programs and policies are operating. These visits are derisively called junkets, but they are an important part of the oversight process. Some members of the Congress simply cannot understand why it is necessary to vote for money for American forces in NATO unless they first visit Europe and make a thorough investigation of the situation. "Jones, I need to know more about that new European monetary union—better book a trip to Paris!"

In addition to government-funded inquiries, members of Congress often find it necessary to consult lobbyists. Lobbyists are experts in their field and can often help a legislator understand a particular issue better. Just as often, however, these lobbyists are trying to use their significant financial resources to "buy" a vote, although it is usually far more nuanced.

In exchange for access to the halls of power, lobbyists give members of Congress money, trips and other "freebies." For instance, their generosity may include free plane trips. These are perfectly legal as long as congressional business is discussed. If there is a plausible legislative purpose to the trip, special interests can fly members of Congress to the most elegant resorts in the world, put them up in the costliest hotels, and buy all their food and drink.

White House Confidential

The man who has accused President Clinton of unethical behavior, Ken Starr, has continued to lobby for the tobacco industry during the entire four years of his Whitewater investigation.

The Chief Executive

Under the Constitution, the President is expressly granted the following powers:

➤ To act as commander in chief of the armed forces.

➤ To require written opinions of executive officers.

- ➤ To grant reprieves and pardons for federal offenses, except in cases that arise from impeachment.

- ➤ To make treaties, subject to approval by two-thirds of the Senate.

- ➤ To appoint ambassadors, public ministers (including Cabinet members), and justices of the Supreme Court, with the consent of the Senate.

- ➤ To fill vacancies that occur during recesses of the Senate.

- ➤ In order to carry out these responsibilities, the President has the right and means at his disposal to enforce and execute the nation's laws.

In addition to these express powers, the President has other implied authority, especially the ability to commit military forces in the absence of a declaration of war (which must come from Congress).

The Oval Office.
Wally McNamee/Corbis

Become a Pundit

Besides being President, Theodore Roosevelt ("TR") was a war hero, an avid outdoorsman, an adventurer and an author. He wrote 15 books, mostly about nature.

In reality, the President's greatest power comes from his ability to use the authority of his office to persuade others to adopt his ideas. Teddy Roosevelt called this the "bully pulpit." As the sole voice of the executive branch, the President is in a unique position to introduce new ideas, shape compromises, and direct the ebb and flow of news.

Presidential power has greatly increased in this century. Some have come to call this the "imperial presidency," meaning that the office of the presidency has become more powerful than the other two branches of government: an imperial office.

The cause of this increase in Presidential power can be traced to the emergence of the United States as a world power at the beginning of this century. The end of World War I saw President Woodrow Wilson introduce his "14 points" and the forerunner to the current United Nations, the League of Nations. With these developments, the U.S. became a world leader and nascent "superpower."

This made the President a more powerful figure on the world stage, and consequently at home too. In the 1930s, FDR's New Deal greatly expanded the federal government, and as a result, the presidency. America's post-World War II emergence as a superpower has only accelerated this trend.

Another development that has increased Presidential power has been the growth of the Executive Office of the President (EOP). The EOP is made up of, among others, the White House staff, the Office of Management and Budget, the National Security Council, the Council of Economic Advisors, and several other advisory boards. These departments have largely taken over the task of advising the President and originating policy priorities within the executive branch. Cabinet officials have gradually focused their efforts more on department management. The result is to centralize the general formation of policy goals around the office of the President.

No Angels Here

How should we view this conflict between the executive and legislative branches? In an effort to have the Constitution adopted, James Madison, Thomas Jefferson, Alexander Hamilton, and John Jay wrote essays on how the new government was supposed to work. Entitled "The Federalist Papers" the essays are eerily relevant even today.

In Federalist No. 51, Madison wrote:

> *"But what is government itself, but the greatest of all reflections on human nature? If men were angels, no government would be necessary. If angels were to govern men, neither external nor internal controls on government would be necessary.*

But controls are needed. Bill Clinton, Ken Starr, Al Gore, Orrin Hatch—no angels in that group. One of those controls, a new invention, is the independent counsel. Yet Kenneth Starr's investigation has operated largely outside the system of checks and balances that governs normal investigations. Starr is operating under the provisions of a statute specially created to investigate the executive branch. Criticism of the independent-counsel statute has come from both the left and the right. Having a prosecutor shadowing the executive branch was never part of the original plan. No matter what the ultimate result of the current scandal turns out to be, many predict that the total lack of control over Starr's investigation will yield a wide-ranging re-evaluation of the independent counsel's role in the government.

In the end, it seems that, for all the conflict that our checks and balances create, for all the inherent tension (some might call it "gridlock"), they also ultimately force all the branches of government to work closely together.

The Least You Need to Know

➤ Our Founding Fathers tried to create a system of government that would avoid autocracy.

➤ Our government has three branches—the legislative, executive and judicial—that were designed with a degree of conflict between them.

➤ The Supreme Court has the final say on all matters legal.

➤ Congress can investigate almost anything, including agencies of the government, even itself, at any time.

➤ The President is far more powerful today than the framers of the Constitution ever anticipated.

Chapter 3

The Impeachment Process

In This Chapter

➤ The history of the impeachment clause

➤ The meaning of "high crimes and misdemeanors"

➤ How the process is designed to work

➤ How it will likely work

It's been almost 25 years since the word "impeachment" has been tossed around as much as it has in 1998. Not since Watergate (which you'll learn about in Chapter 11) has the country actually considered the removal of its chief executive. It's a serious business, so it is therefore important to understand what impeachment is and how it's supposed to work.

Impeachment is an often misused and misunderstood term. Many people think that when a President is impeached, he is removed from office. Not so. Impeachment is the beginning of the process by which the President, Vice President, federal judges, and all civil officials of the United States may be removed from office. It takes a trial in the Senate to remove a President from office.

To better understand how the process was designed to work, it may be helpful to go back to and see where the idea of impeachment came from.

The History of Impeachment

Impeachment existed in ancient Greece, as a process known as the *eisangelia*. "Modern" impeachments did not originate until the latter part of the 14th century in

England. The English system began as a means of enforcing responsibility of the king's ministers to Parliament. It was used heavily after the accession of James I in 1603.

However, since the unsuccessful impeachment trial of Lord Melville in 1806, it has fallen into disuse.

At the time the Constitution was being written (1787) the practice of using impeachment for political gain was still common in England. The framers of our Constitution wanted to avoid this. On September 8, 1787, the working draft of the Constitution permitted removal of the President for bribery and treason only. George Mason proposed that "maladministration" be added to the list. James Madison objected, noting that such a term was far too vague. In any case, many delegates concurred, an election every four years would prevent "maladministration." Mason then offered a term that had been used in British law since at least 1386—"high Crimes and Misdemeanors."

In the end, the delegates chose the phrase "Treason, Bribery or other high Crimes and Misdemeanors" to be the standard for impeachment.

Become a Pundit

Historians routinely trace the genealogy of Presidents after they are elected. Many of our Presidents descend from royal blood. George Washington had three kings in his family tree. George Bush has four. The President with the most kings in his family's history? Franklin Roosevelt with five.

What Are High Crimes and Misdemeanors?

The first thing to notice is the entire phrase. When lawyers read a statute, which this is, the words are analyzed very carefully. A criminal statute that has the word "and" is very different than one that has the word "or." The results of these two words are completely different.

Here, the entire phrase is "treason, bribery or other high crimes and misdemeanors." The key phrase is "or other." In this sentence, high crimes and misdemeanors are being compared to treason and bribery. As such, the first thing to realize is that impeachment was intended to be reserved for very serious offenses against the state, such as treason and bribery. There is no other way to read the law.

This is borne out when you look at the history of the English word "misdemeanor." Today we think of a misdemeanor as a petty offense, as opposed to a felony, which is a major crime. Accordingly, when people usually think of "high crimes and misdemeanors" they believe that the phrase was intended to apply to any offense a President might commit, large and small alike. But the framers had a far different meaning in mind when they chose the word.

Mumbo Jumbo

As defined in the U.S. Constitution, **treason** is a crime committed by a U.S. citizen who helps a foreign government to overthrow, make war against, or seriously injure the U.S.

In 18th-century England, the phrase "high misdemeanor" referred to crimes against the state, as opposed to crimes against people or property. Historically, the phrase was analogous to "great offences" considered impeachable in common-law England. In addition to treason and bribery, these "high misdemeanors" normally included misapplication of funds, abuse of official power, neglect of duty, interference with the legislative process, or corruption. Charles Pinckney, one of the Constitutional Convention delegates, explained it this way: Impeachment was for "those who behave amiss, or betray the public trust."

This analysis is borne out in modern times as well. In 1973, the House Judiciary Committee was considering impeachment proceedings against President Nixon. The special counsel to that committee was John Doar. Doar wanted to have a study done on the history of impeachment and the meaning of the obtuse phrase "high crimes and misdemeanors." Doar hired Yale historian C. Vann Woodward to lead the study. Doar then told Woodward that he would be working with a bright young woman on Doar's staff by the name of Hillary Rodham.

That study later became part of a report published in February 1974. That report defined impeachment broadly. Not all crimes were impeachable offenses, and not all impeachable offenses were crimes, it maintained. For example, if a President simply stopped performing his duties, while not criminal, it certainly is impeachable.

The head of that report, Joseph Woods, stated "We thought that the most important thing was the 'take Care' clause of the Constitution—the provision of Article II that defines the President's duty as being to 'take Care that the Laws be faithfully executed.'"

Woods believed that this clause is the crux of the President's job. Violation of that clause "is the basis of considering whether his conduct ought to be rewarded with impeachment." Woods and his staff concluded that "it was a perversion of the office" that demanded impeachment.

The report concludes that impeachment is a "remedy addressed to serious offense against the system of government," and impeachable offenses are "constitutional wrongs that subvert the structure of government, or undermine the integrity of office and even the Constitution itself." Thus, it seems clear that a high crime or misdemeanor is, as Alexander Hamilton stated in the Federalist No. 65, an offense that relates "chiefly to injuries done to the society itself."

Mumbo Jumbo

Common Law has its origins in England and grows from ever-changing custom and tradition.

Become a Pundit

In 1974, the House Judiciary Committee received a 60-page report from Watergate prosecutor Leon Jaworski, but did not make it public.

In the case of President Clinton, it's highly debatable whether the conduct as alleged by Starr constitutes a crime against the state. Certainly what the President did was wrong, but would the Congress impeach him over it?

How the Process Works in Theory

Article II, Section 4, of the U.S. Constitution specifies the procedures to be used to remove the President, Vice President or other officials from office. The procedure is complex, reflecting its 18th-century roots.

The process opens in the House. Although there are several options, the impeachment process traditionally begins with a House vote on an inquiry of impeachment. The Judiciary Committee is then authorized to investigate the charges against the President.

Already the process will be different, as Starr has already investigated the matter. The Starr report will surely make Congress' investigation quicker. If Congress decides to investigate matters beyond Lewinsky (Whitewater et al), the investigatory stage could take quite awhile. After the investigation, a member of Congress can take the more serious step of introducing a resolution of impeachment. All other work must stop until a decision is reached.

At this point, either the President is cleared of the charges through the investigation, or the Judiciary Committee votes to send articles of impeachment to the full House.

White House Confidential

In the Watergate case, the Judiciary Committee voted to send three articles of impeachment against Richard Nixon to the full House.

The House then votes on the articles of impeachment. If the House approves articles, the matter is sent to the Senate. The Senate has the sole authority to conduct impeachment trials. In cases of trials impeaching the President, the Constitution specifies that the chief justice of the Supreme Court shall preside over the trial. Conviction on the impeachment charges requires a two-thirds majority vote of the Senate.

The reason that Nixon was pardoned by Gerald Ford is that, once removed from office, the Constitution states that the President remains "liable and subject to indictment, trial, judgment, and punishment."

Once removed from office, the President would be replaced by the Vice President. The new President would then nominate a new Vice President, to be approved by a majority vote of both Houses of Congress.

How It Would Work in Practice

Because the Constitution does not specify how the House is to conduct an impeachment investigation, the House must decide upon its own rules. It is likely to follow the Watergate precedent.

Articles of impeachment have been compared to a grand-jury indictment. That is, the articles can be seen as prosecutorial in nature. But the 1974 House Judiciary Committee regarded itself as having a role that was more adjudicatory than prosecutorial—they thought of themselves more as judges than prosecutors. For example, the committee permitted the President's counsel to offer arguments and examine witnesses.

It is important to realize that the Starr report is based entirely upon evidence that has not been challenged. Unlike Nixon, Clinton and his attorneys have been given no opportunity to cross-examine the witnesses who have testified against the President, or otherwise challenge the credibility of the evidence presented.

Think about that for a moment. What if your greatest enemy was in charge of a prosecution against you, and he called against you several witnesses who hated you? Imagine that you had no opportunity to challenge what those people said. Finally, consider the possibility that a report was written about you based upon this testimony. As such, the evidence Starr presented against Clinton in the report must be taken with a grain of salt.

In 1974, the Judiciary Committee set for itself the standard of "clear and convincing evidence" as the appropriate standard of proof required before approving an article of impeachment. That means that the committee had to be given evidence of a crime that was "clear and convincing." If the evidence did not meet this high standard, an article of impeachment would not be approved.

Become a Pundit

At the height of Watergate, in 1974, Samuel Byck planned to assassinate Richard Nixon. Byck intended to hijack a plane, shoot the pilot, and fly the plane into the White House, thereby killing Nixon. Byck got as far as the airport, where he killed a Delta security guard and a copilot. He was shot by security guards and then killed himself.

Mumbo Jumbo

For a jury to be convinced **beyond a reasonable doubt**, it must be fully satisfied that the person is guilty. This is the highest level of proof required and is used only in criminal trials. It does not mean "convinced 100 percent," but it comes close.

Although five articles were originally brought against Nixon, only three met this standard and were forwarded to the whole House.

Legally, this a very high standard of proof. In a normal lawsuit, the standard of proof is "by a preponderance of the evidence" which is normally thought to be about 51 percent—a fairly easy threshold to meet. To prove someone was negligent in a civil suit, you need to prove it was more likely than not that they made a mistake. A "clear and convincing" standard is higher. It means that you have to be damn sure you can prove the allegations.

The Senate has never adopted a uniform standard of proof for impeachment trials. In the case of then-Judge Alcee Hastings, who was impeached and convicted in 1989, the Senate expressly refused to adopt a "beyond a reasonable doubt" standard, as the judge urged. Without such a rule, each senator, at the conclusion of a Presidential trial, would have to decide for themselves whether enough evidence was presented to warrant removal from office.

What Is the Role of the Courts?

Impeachment is inherently more a political process than a legal one. Then-Representative Gerald R. Ford, who would become President after Nixon resigned, once said,

> *An impeachable offense is whatever a majority of the House of Representatives considers [it] to be at a given moment in history; conviction results from whatever offense or offenses the other body considers to be sufficiently serious to require removal of the accused from office.*

Ford's position is not legally accurate. The House cannot simply decide what is and is not impeachable. The Constitution sets forth the standard as a "high crimes and misdemeanors." If the House were to impeach a President for smoking cigars, their constituents would rightly conclude that their representatives had violated their oath to uphold the Constitution.

Become a Pundit

Gerald Ford was one of only 12 Presidents to lose a bid for another term. (Technically, when he ran in 1976, Ford was seeking election and not reelection.)

Yet there is an important truth to Ford's observation. Even the Supreme Court thinks that the impeachment process is more political than legal. In a 1993 case, *Nixon v. United States* (no, not Richard), the Supreme Court dismissed a challenge to the Senate's impeachment procedures brought by a judge, Walter Nixon. The Court concluded that impeachment is a matter best left to the political branches of government, not the judiciary. (You can read more on this in Chapter 20.)

Judge Nixon had been impeached and convicted on charges of lying to a federal grand jury. In that case, the Senate delegated the initial evidence-gathering phase of the trial to a Senate subcommittee. Judge Nixon alleged that this practice violated the Constitution. He believed that the Constitution required that the entire Senate should have sole power to try all impeachments. Using a sub-committee was unconstitutional, he alleged. The Supreme Court disagreed. Actually, the Court concluded that impeachment was none of its business.

The Supreme Court concluded that Nixon's allegation presented what the court historically has called a "political question." The Court normally refuses to resolve such matters. Political questions, the Court has historically concluded, are simply not proper issues for Supreme Court adjudication. The Court believes that the Constitution intends for the elected branches of the national government to resolve overly political issues, such as impeachment. Judicial interference is improper. In the Nixon case, the Court held that the Senate had the right to make its own impeachment rules and they are not subject to judicial oversight.

This means that in the future, even if the Court thinks that Congress could go awry in implementing its impeachment powers, the Court nonetheless lacks the power to correct the error. For this reason, impeachment is best considered a political process in legal clothing. Given that the stakes are so high, it is therefore imperative that Congress implement the constitutional design faithfully, and exercise true, *nonpartisan* statesmanship. Congress is in the unenviable position of needing to avoid all appearances of politics in this highly political environment.

And so the question remains: Are Clinton's offenses impeachable? You will, in fact, be the judge. One of many.

The Least You Need to Know

➤ The phrase "Treason, Bribery, or other high Crimes or Misdemeanors" means that the founders of our country intended impeachment to be reserved for a crime against the state.

➤ Impeachment is a highly political process.

➤ It is highly likely that the Supreme Court would stay out of any impeachment fight.

Johnson

Chapter 4

Impeachment in History

In This Chapter

➤ The first impeachment

➤ The impeachment of a Supreme Court justice

➤ The first impeachment of a President

➤ Other impeachments

➤ The censure option

When we consider whether to impeach President Clinton, we should understand what kind of behavior has historically constituted an impeachable offense. Not every wrong a President or other elected official may commit is necessarily worthy of impeachment.

While many people are aware that only two Presidents have even come close to being impeached (Richard Nixon and Andrew Johnson) fewer know that many lesser officers have also faced impeachment, and several have been tried and convicted in the Senate. (Watergate was such a big scandal, it gets its own chapter—Chapter 11.)

It might be helpful to keep the following thought in mind when reading about these scoundrels and miscreants: How does what Clinton has been accused of compare?

The Impeachment of Senator William Blount

On July 5, 1797, a motion was made on the House floor by Representative Samuel Sitgreaves of Massachusetts. The congressman announced, "Resolved, that William Blount, from the State of Tennessee, be impeached for high crimes and misdemeanors." There it was: The first impeachment in the history of the United States had begun.

What were Senator Blount's high crimes and misdemeanors? Conspiracy, my good man, conspiracy! He was secretly plotting with the British to wrest Florida and Louisiana away from the Spanish. Had his plan been successful, he could have dragged the United States into war with Spain.

In a letter he sent to James Carey, a U.S. interpreter to the Cherokee nation, Blount explained he and the British would be able to get Indians and frontiersmen to attack the Spanish armada. Carey was instructed to read the letter three times and then burn it, but before he did, President Adams got a copy of the letter and sent it on to Congress.

Recall that impeachment is a two-step process. The House first has to vote on articles of impeachment and then the Senate conducts a trial on the articles as forwarded by the House. The problem with regard to Blount was that there had never been an impeachment proceeding before—the Constitution was only 10 years old! Instead of following the process outlined in the Constitution, Congress got it backwards.

Become a Pundit

Unlike Presidents, who can only be elected to two terms, Senators can run for reelection as many times as they choose.

On July 5, the House voted to bring articles of impeachment. But just three days later, the Senate unanimously agreed that William Blount, "having been guilty of a high misdemeanor entirely inconsistent with his public trust and duty as a Senator, be, and he hereby is expelled from the Senate of the United States." The Senate was so anxious to get rid of Blount that they forgot to hold the impeachment trial!

By expelling Blount, the Senators created a new set of questions that they were ill-equipped to answer. Could a private citizen face impeachment? No one knew. Did expulsion from the Senate eliminate the opportunity to try him? Probably so. Can a private citizen even be tried by the Senate? Probably not. There were no easy answers for the young country and inexperienced lawmakers.

Mumbo Jumbo

Jurisdiction is the right and power of a court to adjudicate a matter pending before it.

In the end, our first attempt at following the intent of the framers fizzled. The House brought former Senator Blount up on five articles of impeachment, but the Senate dismissed the charges. After much debate, the Senate decided that, since Blount was no longer a member of the Senate, they no longer had jurisdiction over him.

The Impeachment of Supreme Court Justice Samuel Chase

Associate Justice Samuel Chase was a bad judge—smart, but bad. His conduct on the bench was described as "unfair," "biased," "partial," and "oppressive." Consequently, in December 1804, Congress sent eight articles of impeachment bearing Chase's name over to the Senate.

In his 1992 book, *Grand Inquest*, Supreme Court Chief Justice William Rehnquist cited as reasons for Chase's impeachment his improper conduct in the trials of John Fries and James Callender. The House had little respect for Justice Chase generally, and the Fries case permitted them to dislike him specifically.

Fries was a small-time farmer and a veteran of the Revolutionary War. In 1798 he organized neighboring farmers in his county in what amounted to a minuscule armed resistance to war taxes. He was arrested and hauled into federal court. Justice Chase accused Fries of treason. Chase was outraged by Fries' actions but a charge of treason was overreaching. Charging the small-time farmer, who had merely banded together his neighbors to decry war taxes, with treason was preposterous.

Become a Pundit

Ronald Reagan nominated Associate Justice William Rehnquist to be Chief Justice of the Supreme Court on June 17, 1986.

Nevertheless, Fries was tried, found guilty, and Justice Chase sentenced him to hang. This upset more than a few members of Congress.

White House Confidential

Before John Fries could be put to death for treason, President John Adams pardoned the farmer, against the advice of his Cabinet, and averted national disgrace.

In the James Callender case, Judge Chase's behavior on the bench was even worse. During the election of 1800, Callender wrote a book that criticized President Adams. He wrote, "take your choice, then, between Adams, war, and beggary, and Jefferson, peace, and competency." He also called Adams a "toady to the British Monarchy." Penny-ante stuff, really, in a land of free speech.

But for Justice Chase, Callender's vilification of President Adams was unacceptable. True to form, Chase found Callender guilty of violating the Sedition Act. The Sedition Act protected the country from people advocating the overthrow of the government. To allege that Callender was advocating the overthrow of the federal government by calling President Adams a "toady" was unbelievable, even by the standards of Samuel Chase.

At the impeachment proceeding, Justice Chase's lawyers argued that Chase had neither committed any crime nor violated any law. Instead, they said, his impeachment was political in nature and based on the fact that he was widely hated. Chase's lawyers argued that this failed to meet the impeachment criteria as set forth in the Constitution. To compare Chase's bad legal judgment and harsh personality with "treason, bribery, or other high crimes and misdemeanors," they said, was also ludicrous.

The prosecution vehemently disagreed. They argued that Judge Chase had displayed a "corrupt partiality and predetermination unjustly to oppress those who differed from him in political sentiments." In other words, Chase had a reputation as a biased judge who consistently ruled against those whose politics he disagreed with.

But, as one pundit puts it "the Constitution does not make honest error impeachable." The Senate agreed. On March 1, 1805, they acquitted Justice Chase on every count.

Lessons can be learned from the Chase case. Impeachment is not meant to be a political tool. Differences in ideology and temperament are not reason to impeach a federal officer. The process is designed and intended to be non-partisan.

The Impeachment of President Andrew Johnson

The lesson that impeachment is supposed to be a non-partisan endeavor hopefully devoid of most political calculations was not an easy one for this country to learn. The politically inspired impeachment of President Andrew Johnson proved that.

In 1864, Andrew Johnson shared the Republican party ticket with Abraham Lincoln. The election made Johnson the Vice President to the man who would be considered the greatest President of all time. Johnson's days as Lincoln's Vice President were short-lived. Lincoln was assassinated at Ford's Theater on April 14, 1865, and Andrew Johnson had become America's 17th President.

Ascending to the Presidency is not the same as being elected. Lincoln was the nation's hero, had fought to abolish slavery, and had finally won the Civil War. His death was a tragedy unprecedented in the country's history. Even though Johnson said he would be true to Lincoln's policies, Lincoln, as they say, was a tough act to follow. Johnson entered the Presidency with two strikes against him.

Become a Pundit

Johnson himself might have been assassinated the same night as Lincoln, except the assassin assigned to kill the Vice President decided to get drunk instead.

Johnson was unable to get along with Congress, especially the so-called "radical Republicans." Few Congressmen respected the new President's authority. Johnson decided to assert his power and shake things up by firing someone. He ousted a long-time nemesis, Secretary of War Edwin M. Stanton. Stanton, however, was a radical Republican, so firing him just angered Congress all the more.

Andrew Johnson.
Corbis-Bettmann

They retaliated by passing the Tenure of Office Act, which ended up being the basis for Johnson's impeachment. This law prohibited the President from dismissing any official who had been appointed with Senate consent without first obtaining Senate approval. This meant that the President could not fire his own Cabinet members without asking the Senate's permission. The law was eventually proven unconstitutional, but, at the time, it resulted in Stanton getting his job back.

White House Confidential

Before giving his Vice Presidential inaugural address, Andrew Johnson, it was said, "took a wee drop to illuminate his thoughts." His drunken address was both rambling and incoherent.

Johnson knew that the Tenure of Office Act was enacted for one purpose—to weaken his powers as President. He bucked the absurd law and fired Stanton a second time. Congress didn't blink. On February 24, 1868, they brought 11 articles of impeachment against the President. They hoped that with three strikes Andrew Johnson would be out.

At the time of trial in the Senate, nine Democrats and three Republicans sided with Johnson. Of the remaining 42 senators, the radical Republicans could count on 35 votes to impeach. This left seven senators who were undecided. One by one, six of the seven jumped ship and voted to acquit the President.

A ticket to President Andrew Johnson's impeachment trial in the Senate.
AP/Wide World Photos

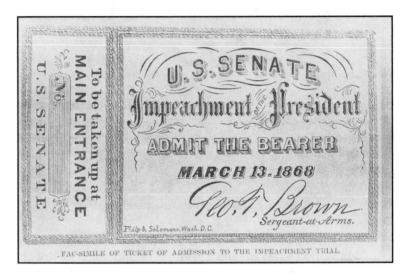

Johnson's fate rested in the hands of Republican Senator Edmund G. Ross of Kansas, the last undecided voter. On May 16, 1868, after receiving countless threats and bribes from his fellow Republicans, Ross made up his mind and cast the deciding vote to acquit. Andrew Johnson stayed in office by that one vote.

Although Andrew Johnson stayed in office, his name lives on in infamy as the only President (to date) to have ever been impeached.

The Johnson case illustrates the necessity of avoiding impeachment for partisan political purposes. The process would carry no weight if it was used for reasons other than investigation into legitimate "high crimes and misdemeanors."

Media Alert

The story of Senator Ross and his political bravery in saving President Johnson, while facing heavy political pressure to do otherwise, was made famous by Senator John F. Kennedy in his Pulitzer Prize-winning book, *Profiles in Courage.*

White House Confidential

Besides being the only President to have been impeached, Andrew Johnson also held the distinction of being the first ex-President to be elected to the U.S. Senate. Six years after his impeachment, voters sent him back to Washington.

Other Notable Impeachments

John Pickering (U.S. District Court judge, NH), was a federal judge and a mentally unbalanced alcoholic. On March 12, 1804, Pickering was impeached for "wickedly, meaning and intending to injure the revenues of the United States." During his trial he challenged President Jefferson to a duel. After a deliberation over whether the mentally insane could be tried, the Senate voted 20-6 to remove Judge Pickering from office.

West Hughes Humphreys (U.S. District Court judge, TN) Humphreys accepted an appointment in the Confederate judiciary, without giving up his U.S. judgeship. Seven articles of impeachment were adopted against Humphreys, but he could not be personally served because he had fled Union territory. The House charged Humphreys with rebellion and provoking revolt. He was convicted on June 26, 1862, in a one-day trial. Humphreys was disqualified from holding further office on a 36-0 vote.

William Belknap (Secretary of War in the Grant Administration) confessed to taking a kickback for granting Indian trading-post concession rights. He was impeached and forced to resign as secretary of war pending trial in the Senate. Despite resigning, the Judiciary Committee continued to work on impeachment articles, and ended up charging him on five counts. He went to trial but, in the end, the Senate decided that they no longer had jurisdiction over him. On August 1, 1876, he was acquitted.

Charles Swayne (U.S. District Court judge, FL) faced impeachment charges including wrongly jailing lawyers for contempt of court, padding expense accounts, using railroad property for his personal benefit, misusing contempt power, and living beyond the boundaries of his district. He admitted to some of his crimes and on February 27, 1905 the Senate acquitted him of all charges. They felt his wrongs did not live up to the standard of "bribery, treason, or other high crimes and misdemeanors."

Halsted L. Ritter (U.S. District Court Judge, FL) was impeached for a plethora of misdeeds including practicing law while on the bench, extortion, misconduct, and income-tax fraud. Taken individually, none of the judge's misdeeds were considered

Mumbo Jumbo

Extortion: Obtaining property from another by the wrongful use of actual or threatened force, violence, or fear.

Become a Pundit

In 1992 Hastings was elected to the House of Representatives—the same body that impeached him. He remains a Democratic Representative from Florida today.

impeachable offenses. However, one article of impeachment said that his wrongs, if taken altogether, merited removal from the bench. The Senate convicted Ritter on April 17, 1936, but an order to disqualify him from holding further office was defeated by a count of 0-76.

Alcee L. Hastings (U.S. District Court judge, FL) was impeached and convicted on October 20, 1989, for leaking wiretaps, allegations of bribery, and lying under oath. He had already been acquitted by a jury but the Senate convicted him on 8 of 11 articles of impeachment.

Walter L. Nixon, Jr. (U.S. District Court judge, MS) was impeached and convicted by the Senate on November 3, 1989, on perjury charges. At the time of his conviction in the Senate, Walter Nixon was already in prison, serving a five-year sentence for that very crime.

Besides these official impeachments, the only other time a President has ever been reprimanded by Congress occured in 1834. The Whig-controlled Senate censured Democratic President Andrew Jackson because Jackson had vetoed a bill favored by the Whigs in the Senate. It was a patently ridiculous move, clearly unconstitutional, and the censure was expunged from the Senate's official record the next year.

It is surprising how few individuals alleged to have committed high crimes and misdemeanors have actually been impeached, tried, and convicted of the charges. Sometimes they have been acquitted because the charges were blatantly political. Other times, the charges failed to clear the high bar set by the Constitution. Before we go impeaching somebody, we better be certain his crimes are high crimes.

The Least You Need to Know

➤ The first impeachment showed that the Senate was not quite ready to execute its Constitutional duties properly.

➤ The impeachment of Supreme Court Justice Chase failed for lack of proof of an actual crime having been committed.

➤ The first impeachment of a President failed as it was more a political vendetta than a trial on the merits.

➤ Other officers have been impeached with varied levels of success.

Part 2
The Making of a President

Some think the flaws in Bill Clinton's "character" that may bring him down have been apparent since his earliest days in politics. Others look at President Clinton and still see the brilliant, gifted young man who overcame a difficult upbringing to overachieve in high school and go on to Georgetown, Yale, and a Rhodes Scholarship to Oxford University in England.

Whether he did or didn't inhale, dodge the draft, or pick up more women than an Arkansas ferris wheel, there's no arguing with the fact that, again and again, Bill Clinton has proven himself a talented politician, a committed public servant, and a compassionate leader. His personal paradoxes are almost Shakespearean, and his story begins here ….

Chapter 5

No Wonder They Call It Hope

In This Chapter

➤ Roots

➤ Boy wonder

➤ The Draft Dodge

➤ Professor Who?

➤ The Political Prodigy

➤ The Comeback Kid

Jefferson might seem like an unusual middle name—after all, not many 20th-century mothers name their sons after 18th-century Presidents. But Virginia Kelly was no ordinary mother, and, it turns out, her first born was no ordinary son.

It seems like Bill Clinton was destined to become President; the signs were all there. The name, the early recognition by others, meeting Kennedy. Yet, when you look at his history, it's amazing that he got where he did. Certainly many gifted children born into poverty and alcoholism never achieve their potential. What made Bill Clinton different?

Birth of a President

Bill Clinton was born William Jefferson Blythe III on August 19, 1946, in Hope, Arkansas. His mother, Virginia Dell Blythe, lost her new husband, Bill Blythe, in a car accident on May 17, 1946, three months before the future President was born. Not long after, she met Roger Clinton, a car salesman from Hot Springs, whom she would eventually marry four years after Bill was born.

By first grade, Billy Blythe had come to be known as Billy Clinton. Already, Bill showed both a bright mind and a desire to impress. His second-grade teacher predicted that he would someday become President of the United States. He was president of his junior class in high school.

Become a Pundit

Thomas Jefferson penned the Declaration of Independence. He was also Governor of Virginia, third President of the United states, an architect who designed his own home (Monticello), and the founder of the University of Virginia.

Virginia Kelly's marriage to Roger Clinton was not a happy one. They had a child together, Bill Clinton's half-brother Roger Jr., but Roger Senior had a problem—he was an alcoholic. And he was violent. Much later, Bill Clinton would recall that he was present during one of his stepfather's violent eruptions. "I was present March 27, 1959, and it was I who called my mother's attorney, who in turn had to get the police to come to the house to arrest [my stepfather]."

The family was in turmoil. Virginia divorced Roger in 1962, took him back two months later, and remarried him that same year. His drinking continued, and young Bill tried to avoid it. It isn't easy being the child of an alcoholic, let alone an abusive, alcoholic step-parent, and it affected the future President. As one noted psychologist explains, Adult Children of an Alcoholic (ACOA) often share certain traits. They tend to:

➤ Lie automatically

➤ Thrive upon chaos

➤ Be filled with self-doubt

➤ Struggle with a feeling of loss

➤ Avoid confrontation

Sound Bites

He cannot help but lie.

—Paul Fick, Ph.D, *The Dysfunctional President*

A child in an alcoholic home often learns that truth has little value. First, he may be continually lied to by the alcoholic parent—promises to attend school plays and ball games are often not kept. Further, the child learns that there are no negative consequences to telling a fib, and that appearances seem to count more than honesty. Finally, it is often just easier for the child to learn to get along by lying, like the rest of the family does, than to go against the grain. It becomes part of the family code.

But he sure could achieve. Clinton was quickly gaining a reputation as a bright, articulate, exceptional young man.

Boy Wonder

Boys Nation is an educational organization that rewards children who have achieved academically. Of course, Bill Clinton was asked to join. Shining there, as he had everywhere, Clinton was selected to go to Washington as a national delegate in 1963.

On July 21, 1963, Clinton and the other young men went to the White House to meet President Kennedy. Meeting in the Rose Garden, Kennedy complimented the young men on a statement they had put out. "Racism is a cancerous disease," the statement had declared. Kennedy told them, "[W]e were impressed by it." Kennedy came from behind the podium with the intention of meeting only a few of the boys. Sixteen-year-old Bill Clinton was the first to shake his hand.

Media Alert

JFK's book, *Profiles in Courage*, won the Pulitzer Prize.

Bill Clinton at 16, meeting President John F. Kennedy. Archive Photos/Arnie Sachs

Clinton graduated in 1964, and was one of three speakers at his graduation ceremony. As part of his benediction, Clinton said: "We pray to keep a high sense of values while wandering through the complex maze which is our society."

Become a Pundit

John F. Kennedy is the President with the most public schools named after him: 103. The next most is 75, held by Thomas Jefferson.

He entered Georgetown the next year and was promptly elected president of the freshman class (although he lost his bid to become student body president in 1967.) In 1966 he clerked for the Senate Foreign Relations Committee, one of only three students to be so honored. While working at the Capitol, Clinton got to know the committee chairman, Arkansas Senator William J. Fulbright.

As he neared graduation, Clinton was encouraged by Fulbright to apply for a Rhodes Scholarship, which accepted only 32 people every year to study in Oxford, England. Clinton did, and was accepted. He sailed to England in October 1968.

The Draft Dodge

In 1969, while in England, Clinton received an induction notice. On January 13, 1969, Clinton took his preinduction physical exam at a U.S. airbase near London.

Clinton, like most young people of the time, opposed the war. On May 1, 1969, he received a draft notice. Many years later, while running for President, he would fail to mention that he ever received this draft notice. In 1969, Clinton's problem was that, given the career he hoped to have, he couldn't just dodge the draft; even then he knew it would be political suicide. So Clinton wrote to his local draft board and asked them to postpone his draft notice until the end of his term at Oxford.

Once he concluded his first year of studies in England and returned home, there was little he could do to avoid the draft. He knew that joining the ROTC would delay induction, but all the spots were full. Clinton contacted his old pals in Senator Fulbright's office, and suddenly, Colonel Holmes, the local head of the Arkansas ROTC, began to get calls from the draft board, who had been contacted by Fulbright's office, asking whether he could "help young Bill Clinton." A spot in the heretofore full ROTC opened up, Clinton joined, and his induction notice was nullified. (This is more or less the same way Dan Quayle avoided military service in the Vietnam era.)

Become a Pundit

Before Bill Clinton, the last President to not serve in the military was Franklin Delano Roosevelt.

The draft board granted Clinton a 1-D deferment as a reservist, and Clinton went back to Oxford for another year, even though he should have been at the ROTC (he was also given special permission to conclude his studies). Clinton then had serious misgivings about this decision. Oxford was ending, he did not want to serve in the ROTC, did not want to go to Vietnam, and did not know what to do. He decided to give up his deferment. Col. Holmes, who got him in the ROTC, now helped him get out.

Clinton knew that troops were starting to be sent home, and that if he got himself reclassified as eligible, he might not get drafted. He did so, knowing the risk, and submitted himself to the largest draft in history, 850,000 young men. He drew a high number, and never went to Vietnam.

In December 1969, he wrote to Colonel Holmes and stated, "First, I want to thank you ... for saving me from the draft." In that same letter, Clinton confesses to the Colonel, "I decided to accept the draft in spite of my beliefs for one reason: To maintain my political viability within the system."

Early in the 1992 campaign, when asked why he did not serve in Vietnam, Clinton said, "It was simply a fluke that I wasn't called up ... I was just lucky, I guess," and denied having received any unusual or favorable treatment. It's another example of Clinton, in his desire to seem to never have done anything morally questionable, trying to cover something up and looking like he's done something worse. The cover-up is worse than the "crime."

A Yale Man

In the fall of 1970, Clinton began his law studies at Yale. Although he was anxious to begin a political career, he was reluctant to return to Arkansas without an advanced degree from a prestigious institution. Yale fulfilled that need.

White House Confidential

During the 1992 campaign, when talk of Clinton's infidelity was in high gear, Yale graduate President George Bush was rumored to have had an affair with one of his aides. Denials were issued and the stories were never proven true.

Clinton rarely attended class, and spent as much time as he could working on various political campaigns. At one point, a pal of Clinton's by the name of Cliff Jackson wrote to Clinton, asking him how to get a White House Fellowship (not unlike

Monica Lewinsky's White House internship). Clinton wrote Jackson back, relaying this story:

> *About the White House Fellowships: The best story I know on them is that virtually the only non-conservative who ever got one was a quasi radical woman who wound up in the White House sleeping with LBJ. [He] made her wear a peace symbol around her waist whenever they made love. You may go far, Cliff; I doubt you will ever go that far!*

One day, an editor at the Yale Law Journal was trying to convince Clinton to join the staff, telling Clinton that he could get a great job in Manhattan as a result. Clinton was not interested. He was staring across the room at Hillary Rodham, and absent-mindedly telling the editor that he planned to go back to Arkansas after graduation and run for office.

Hillary noticed his stare, got up and walked across the room and said, "Look, if you're going to keep staring at me and I'm going to keep staring back, we should at least introduce ourselves. I'm Hillary Rodham."

Clinton loved her bold move. They shared a mutual sense of social commitment and pragmatism. Yet, while he was easygoing and relaxed, she was precise and demanding. They found in each other a perfect complement. And she was his match: smart, ambitious, independent, tolerant. (You'll read about Hillary's background in Chapter 6.)

Mumbo Jumbo

A **law journal** is a periodical that publishes scholarly legal articles, run by the top students of any law school.

Professor Who?

Clinton returned to Arkansas nine years after he left. The boy wonder was now a man wonder. He now had degrees from Georgetown and Yale and was a Rhodes Scholar. Although clearly in a hurry, he couldn't run for President quite yet.

Become a Pundit

Nixon was only the second President to have articles of impeachment brought against him in the House.

His first job out of law school was as a professor at the University of Arkansas Law School. Clinton soon developed a reputation for giving out high grades. Because of his clear lack of prejudice and desire to treat everyone equally, the black law students dubbed Clinton "Wonder Boy." One of them said, "He did not let race treat you any differently, that's why we called him 'Wonder Boy.' It was a miracle, the way he was."

In 1974, at the height of Watergate, not content to be a small fish, Bill Clinton announced that he was running for Congress. At the same time, Hillary Rodham was working in Washington as a staffer to the

House Judiciary Committee's impeachment inquiry staff. Her friends at the time note that she was uncharacteristically crazy about Bill Clinton. According to her friend Tom Bell, she said more than once, "You know, Tom Bell, Bill Clinton is going to be President of the United States someday!"

Nixon resigned on August 9, and Hillary moved to Arkansas soon after, having accepted a teaching position at the law school in Fayetteville, where Clinton taught.

The Political Prodigy

Clinton was now teaching law and driving the backroads of Arkansas, hustling for votes. Clinton was constantly on the go from one town to the next, staying in the homes of old friends or new allies. He also had no shortage of women vying for his attention. It was during this first campaign that his reputation as a womanizer began.

Starting with 12-percent name recognition and little money, Clinton's brains, energy, and work ethic easily won him the Democratic nomination to Congress. But the general election in November had a different ending. Clinton lost by a mere 6,000 votes—two percentage points. He wasn't discouraged. He had become well-known and well-liked in Arkansas politics. That in itself was a victory. It is said that the morning after the election, Clinton was already shaking people's hands in downtown Fayetteville. The next race, for Governor, had already begun.

Bill Clinton and Hillary Rodham were married on October 11, 1975, in a traditional Methodist ceremony. A few months later, they honeymooned in Acapulco. It was not lost on Clinton that his idol, Jack Kennedy, honeymooned there with his new bride, Jacqueline Bouvier.

In 1976, Clinton ran for attorney general of Arkansas. In the May primary, Clinton received 55 percent of the vote and avoided a runoff. He was 29 years old.

The job suited him perfectly. He did not have to sit behind a desk; he could give speeches, travel, and meet new people. But it was not enough. In the fall of 1977, Clinton's chief of staff called a young political consultant he knew in New York. His name was Dick Morris. Morris came down to meet the up-and-coming politician.

Clinton was torn, unsure whether to run for senator or Governor. Morris' polls showed that Clinton could be elected to the governership with no problem. The Senate was possible, too. In the end, even though he would have to run for reelection every two years in Arkansas, Clinton opted to run for Governor. When he won in 1978 with 63 percent of the vote, he was the youngest Governor in the United States in 40 years. He was 32.

Media Alert

The rest of America did not know that Clinton was the "Comeback Kid" until 1992 when he came in (only) second in the New Hampshire primary after the accusations of Gennifer Flowers almost derailed his campaign.

Clinton was bursting with ideas: preschool, secondary education, the environment, solar energy, forestry, and on. One thing Clinton did immediately was to raise the tax on car registration to pay for an ambitious highway program. By 1980, the 'car tag' issue had come back to haunt him. For the first time, too, his wife became an issue in a campaign: She had continued to use her maiden name after her marriage.

Clinton's lofty agenda, combined with an unpopular Southern President (Carter), an unpopular car-tag increase, and a poor economy, doomed Clinton's reelection bid in 1980. He lost, and lost bad. The legend of the Comeback Kid was now to be born.

Birth of the Comeback Kid

Clinton hated private life. Now a practicing attorney, he began to travel the state, trying to learn from his defeat. Once a month, he met with Dick Morris to plan his comeback. Clinton wanted to run for Governor again. Morris' poll's revealed that the voters of Arkansas thought that Clinton had patronized them. But they still liked him. He could come back. But first he needed to apologize.

Morris told Clinton that they needed a television ad to begin his redemption. He told Clinton, "You have to recognize your sins, confess to them, and promise to sin no more. And in the act of contrition, you have to be humble. You have to say, 'I am very sorry, ashamed, I know I did wrong and I'll never do it again.'"

The two had what can only be described as a prophetic conversation. While discussing the contents of the ad, they had a long, heated debate as to whether the word

Mumbo Jumbo

A **poll** is a random survey of people designed to elicit general opinions. Almost all politicians now use polls before they announce any policy action.

"apology" needed to be in it. Clinton didn't want it in and Morris did. In the end, Morris played with the words and, according to one biographer, "Clinton managed to say that he was sorry without saying he was sorry."

The ploy worked, and by 1982, Clinton was a private citizen no longer. This time around, he was more cautious. Morris tested ideas before they were announced. Clinton had an air of earnestness now, instead of arrogance.

He did in fact learn his lesson, and he became a very popular Governor. Running for reelection every two years, by 1986, he had a 72 percent approval rating.

State-Wide to Nation-Wide

Clinton decided that education reform would be the cornerstone of his new Governership—he wanted to be known as the "education Governor." Meetings were chaired by Hillary Clinton (on leave from the Rose Law Firm) all over the state, to gather ideas and infuse people with Clinton's plan. The package included teacher-competence testing, and was opposed by many teachers. In the end, the bill passed, Clinton had a major victory, and the people of Arkansas came to like their improved schools. They liked what Clinton could do.

Clinton also used his power as Governor during the 1980s to forward many of his integrationist goals. Blacks were appointed to state boards in record numbers, and the first black ever to serve on the Arkansas Supreme Court was nominated by Clinton.

His new successes were not going unnoticed. He became active in the national Democratic Party, and helped facilitate a group of rising Democratic stars who were committed to moving the party to the center. Clinton was a key figure in this group of so-called "New Democrats," which included others like senators Bill Bradley and Al Gore. The idea was to allow the party to reclaim the Presidency by moving toward the center.

Bill Clinton was eventually elected to five terms as governor of Arkansas. But 1990 was critical. Voters tend to get tired of the same face, and by 1990, he had served for the better part of the past dozen years. Knowing that he was getting ready to run for President in 1992, Clinton proclaimed the 1990 election to be crucial. Clinton reminded a campaign aide, "If I lose this race for Governor, I'll never get elected dog catcher." Clinton won again, easily.

The widely held belief among the peers he had met, from Washington to England and back to Little Rock, that one day they would all assist him run for President, was fast becoming a reality.

The Least You Need to Know

➤ Clinton had been repeatedly told, since he was a young boy, that someday he would be President.

➤ He impressed almost everyone who met him as he journeyed from Arkansas to the most elite institutions in the world.

➤ While he didn't quite "dodge" the draft, he didn't enlist, either.

➤ He isn't called the "Comeback Kid" for nothing.

Chapter 6

Family Matters

In This Chapter

➤ Hillary's childhood

➤ Off to college

➤ My daughter, the lawyer

➤ The man of her dreams

➤ Career woman

Some hate her. Others adore her. As the seeming power behind the throne, she commands respect, admiration, or denigration (depending upon your affiliation). Whatever the case, Hillary Rodham Clinton certainly makes an impression.

While her husband's history is well-known, few of us know much about the First Lady aside from the fact that she met Bill at Yale, seems to be a sharp lawyer (too sharp, for some), and she works a lot with children. Would it surprise you to know that she entered college as a Republican? Whatever you may think of this walking lightening-rod, she is an intriguing, perplexing, and fascinating woman.

Bill and Hillary Clinton.
Matthew Mendelsohn/
Corbis

Hillary's History

Hillary Diane Rodham, born in Chicago on October 26, 1947, was the first child in a Methodist family headed by a strong, Republican father, Hugh, and a mother, Dorothy, who kept her Democratic views mostly to herself. Although born in Chicago, Hillary grew up in Park Ridge, Illinois, a well-to-do suburb about as staunchly Republican as you'll find. In an ironic twist sure to amuse her detractors, young Hillary grew up surrounded by Republicans.

White House Confidential

Chicago was critical to the election of John F. Kennedy in 1960. Kennedy needed the densely populated metropolis to win Illinois' electoral votes and the Presidency. Legendary political boss Mayor Richard Daley assured Kennedy's father that young Jack would take the city, but talk of vote-buying threatened the entire campaign. "My father's not going to buy one more vote than is necessary," Kennedy quipped, and with that, silenced his critics. Kennedy took Chicago by the slimmest of margins, and thus Illinois, and the Presidency.

"You can do anything you want, even if you are a girl," she was continually told by her mother. But the primary influence on Hillary seems to have been Hugh Rodham and his more exacting nature. After looking at one of her many perfect report cards, he said, "You must have gone to an easy school." Pleasing her father, although difficult, was a challenge she gladly undertook. Hugh Rodham kept things to himself, mostly. A close friend of Hillary's described Mr. Rodham as "kind of a recluse."

Hillary's interchangeably abrasive and friendly personality was only one of her father's legacies. At the age of 17, she was well-known in high school as a banner-wearing Republican. She even supported Barry Goldwater during his 1964 Presidential race against Lyndon Johnson. One of the most well-known Democrats in modern history, she didn't begin her move left until after a few years in college.

Her ambition showed itself early. In high school, Hillary was everywhere. She participated in speech club, debate club, the newspaper, talent shows, and anything that allowed her to express herself.

The support of both parents, expressed as it was in almost opposing ways, made Hillary a woman of contradictions from the beginning. She played baseball after church every Sunday and baked chocolate-chip cookies with her two brothers, Hughie and Tony, every Christmas. By all accounts, she was popular from a very young age, even though some friends in high school nicknamed her "Sister Frigidaire."

Throughout high school Hillary was popular, outgoing, and capable. Already she was attracting attention as one of the best and the brightest. At her graduation she collected award after award—from the National Honor Society to a National Merit Scholarship.

Although not the valedictorian, Hillary Rodham was voted most likely to succeed. (Interestingly, this same award was received by her future husband, Bill Clinton, and her future nemesis, Kenneth Starr.) She graduated in the top 5 percent of her class.

Become a Pundit

Barry Goldwater is the father of the modern conservative movement in the United States. His statement during the 1964 campaign that "extremism in defense of liberty is no vice" galvanized the right wing of the Republican Party, including Ronald Reagan. Although Goldwater lost, the movement he created became stronger than ever in the Reagan-Era '80s.

Into the Fray

In the fall of 1965, the Rodham's Republican daughter entered distinguished, women-only Wellesley College, located just outside Boston. Wellesley seemed a perfect fit for the intense intelligent young woman. It was prestigious, rigorous, small, and well-respected.

The school also reflected the times, times about to undergo radical social and political change. There were only 10 black students in the entire school when Hillary entered. By the time she left, both she and the school would be very different.

White House Confidential

Only 10 First Ladies besides Hillary Clinton have graduated from college. Since 1960, all First Ladies have graduated from college except for Barbara Bush and Betty Ford.

"My world exploded when I got to Wellesley," Hillary said in a 1994 PBS documentary. As she had in high school (in fact, as she would her entire life) Hillary threw herself into the fray. She was very active on campus and with her studies, becoming, at one point, president of Wellesley's Young Republicans. John Lennon once said, "Life is what happens when you're busy making other plans." Life had other plans for Hillary besides young Republicanism.

Change was afoot, and for an independent, intelligent young woman on her own for the first time, that meant reviewing her own principles, not just those of society. The war in Vietnam, the civil-rights movement, the women's movement, and even the outdated traditions of Wellesley itself drove Hillary to change her loyalties. By her junior year at Wellesley, the young Republican had become a liberal Democrat. Hillary began working for Eugene McCarthy.

Become a Pundit

Eugene McCarthy was the anti-war candidate in 1968. Although very popular amongst the young, McCarthy was soon dwarfed by the Bobby Kennedy juggernaut. After Kennedy was killed at the Ambassador Hotel in Los Angeles, Hubert Humphrey became the Democratic front-runner. He eventually lost a close election to Richard Nixon.

Yet, not surprisingly, Hillary refused to fit the mold, a pattern that would return throughout her life. Things just weren't as black and white to Hillary as they were to many of her idealistic contemporaries. She was conflicted about just how far to go. In the words of one former student, "She was very anti-war, but she was a little more conservative than the others [and] unsure about how much campus life should be disrupted."

She was a radical to be sure, like any good student of the day, but she was also President of the student body. Hillary Rodham saw early that idealism alone was insufficient. To create any kind of significant change, the idealism had to be tempered in reality, it needed to be a bit more centered than some of her friends would have liked. She didn't know it at the time, but even then, Hillary Rodham was a Clinton Democrat.

She made history early, and not for the last time. Hillary became the first student commencement speaker in the history of Wellesley when she graduated in 1969. Watching her at the podium that day, fellow students were convinced that *she* might one day become President.

Hillary Rodham, Esq.

One thing about Hillary—she was no pie-in-the-sky hippie. Already well aware of how the world actually works, and embracing the belief held by many of her generation that government can make a positive difference, Hillary concluded that the next logical step for her was law school.

For Hillary, law was the perfect vehicle to create social change. In her perhaps overly intellectual way, she called it "the activist view of law as a function of power." In actuality, law was an opportunity to be taken seriously and have her ideas become reality.

She favored the smaller Yale. Harvard, she thought, was Yale's "closest competitor." A meeting with a Harvard professor helped her make her decision. She recalled that the professor "looked down at me and said, 'Well, first of all, we don't have any close competitors. Secondly we don't need any more women.'" Yale it was.

The mood around Yale at the time supported Hillary's future plans perfectly. According to alumnus Michael Medved, every Yale radical "wanted to be an anti-poverty lawyer or an environmental lawyer working for a cause." Hillary just wanted to change the world.

Become a Pundit

Seven current members of the Senate are Yale graduates. Twelve members of the House are also alumni of the institution.

Hippie Hillary

Not surprisingly, Hillary distinguished herself early and often among the students, and not just in the classroom. She is remembered as often being the most vocal protester at a demonstration, shouting on behalf of the Black Panthers, the Chicago Seven, and the anti-Vietnam movement, along with anything else she felt passionately about (which was practically everything.)

Hillary's appearance during these years was yet another political statement. She wore the hippie "uniform" of the day. One classmate thought she looked like "the serious, intense, long-haired girl who appears as Woody Allen's first girlfriend in all of his

1970s movies." Another remembers her as a student of the "look-like-s—t school of feminism." Yet despite her slightly dowdy appearance, Bill Clinton, already a well-known lady-killer on campus, was hooked from the moment he laid eyes on her.

Right from the start, the two of them, "basking in each other's admiration," saw in one another the perfect complement. Theirs was an acutely passionate relationship. They were passionate about everything—sex, politics, law, change, and most of all, each other. "Look at this," Medved recalls Hillary saying to him, "I'm in love. I am happy, and I have got this great guy who is going to change the whole world." They fell in love, and they fell in love hard.

After only one year, Hillary made the first, and certainly not the last, of many concessions in order to be with Bill. Instead of graduating with the class of 1972, she decided to spend an extra year at Yale so they could graduate together in 1973.

That extra year changed Hillary's life. She spent that year taking classes at Yale's child study center. It was here that an intense love for, and commitment to, children was born. This commitment would last into her adult life and eventually take up much of her time as First Lady. It was here too that she met Marian Wright Edeleman, founder of the Children's Defense Fund. Edeleman and her husband, Peter, would provide valuable early opportunities for both Hillary and Bill.

Also during that last year, Bill and Hillary worked together on George McGovern's Presidential campaign. Surprisingly, Hillary's political savvy got most of the attention at the time, not Bill's. Betsey Wright (later to be Clinton's chief of staff and head bimbo defuser in Arkansas—the Kathy Bates character in the film *Primary Colors*) remembers, "I was less interested in Bill's political future at this point than Hillary's." Wright would later tell *Vanity Fair* that she was "disappointed" when she learned that Hillary had married Bill. Bill was a bit of a cad, you see.

White House Confidential

LBJ was a legendary lover who liked to entertain guests at his ranch in Texas. He encouraged guests, especially attractive women, to stay the night. After a party, one of Johnson's aides once took the President up on his offer after having a bit too much to drink. She was awakened in her dark room in the middle of the night by Johnson and his flashlight. "Move over, this is your President," Johnson commanded.

After the McGovern campaign, Hillary worked at the National Women's Political Caucus. Wright was not the only one who thought seriously that it would be Hillary's first step on the way to the White House—not as First Lady, but as President. This was becoming a familiar tune.

But it was not to be. Ultimately, famously, Hillary decided to give up what could have been a glittering political future of her own to shape the rise of her lover. The driving force that was her ambition had finally met the immovable object it could not overcome: true love.

'Till Death Do Us Part

Certainly only love could have compelled Hillary to move to—gulp—Fayetteville, Arkansas. She could have gone anywhere—New York, back to Chicago, *anywhere*—but she chose Fayetteville. Such was her boyfriend Bill Clinton's intense pull on her.

Bill was running for Congress and he needed Hillary. She went down to Arkansas to see what the future would bring with this brilliant, exasperating man. Her constant support in the campaign was invaluable from the start. He came to rely on her and her sharp political instincts more and more, and she became the driving force behind Bill Clinton. Before the first election was even over, it set a precedent that would define their entire relationship. What they could do together seemed so much more than what they could do apart. They made a very good team, Bill and Hillary did.

But if Hillary thought she was the only one for Bill, she was mistaken. It was a lesson she would learn only too well. According to Clinton's campaign manager at the time, Paul Fray, virtually all of Clinton's female volunteers were smitten with the candidate: "Women who had met [him] while he was on the road were calling headquarters from all 21 counties in the district." What did Hillary do? She had taken to rummaging through Bill's clothes to tear up slips of paper with phone numbers on them.

Yet despite his philandering, their passion for each other was great, their respect immense, and their love intense. Neither was going anywhere. Even though Bill eventually lost his first election, he put himself on the map. This was solid evidence to Hillary that she was destined to realize her own success through this enigmatic, charismatic man. Any misgivings she may have had were set aside. She wanted to go to the top, and she wanted to get there with him. That she loved him strongly made it all the better. In October 1975, amid a swell of rumors and increasing, intoxicating attention, they married.

Sound Bites

I find it not an accident that every time he is on the verge of fulfilling his commitment to the American people and they respond … out comes yet a new round of these outrageous, terrible stories that people plant for political and financial reasons.

—Hillary Clinton on allegations that Arkansas state troopers helped her husband pick up women

It would not be long before Clinton tasted political success. They were on their way. Neither was sure where this new union was headed, but both felt that it could lead to something big.

Thoroughly Modern Hillary

In 1978, Bill was elected as Arkansas' attorney general and the Clintons moved to Little Rock, where Hillary soon went to work at the Rose Law Firm. With her credentials, commitment, and important husband, she quickly became a partner. Here she would meet long-time confidantes Vince Foster and Webster Hubbell. As her husband's fortunes grew, so did hers.

A Bull Market

Tyson Foods, as you may or may not know, is a huge company that produces chicken and is headquartered in Little Rock. Little Rock isn't a big city, and most of the important people know each other pretty well. One of the people in Little Rock who the Clintons knew from Fayetteville was an attorney who served as outside counsel for Tyson Foods by the name Jim Blair. The Blairs and the Clintons were very close friends.

Blair figured out a way to trade commodities to win big. It was nothing illegal; he just was a sharp money-man and understood how to analyze cattle futures correctly. Happy with his success, Blair encouraged several friends, not just Hillary, to join him. Blair had an account at the Refco brokerage house and his broker was another member of the Tyson network. Hillary opened an account with $1,000.

Hillary played the high-stakes, high-reward, very stressful cattle market for nine months, and definitely benefited from Blair's advice. At the end of her ride, she had made an extraordinary $99,357 profit. Why did she quit when she did? She was ahead, it was very intense, and she was pregnant.

Become a Pundit

Hillary was not alone in making a bundle trading commodities. Fortunes can be won and lost very quickly. At this time, some Refco brokers were making between $10,000 and $100,000 a month trading cattle futures.

Hillary did nothing illegal or even immoral in earning her hefty profit—the whole thing was more like two pals helping each other on a wild ride. But she did have one advantage. In commodities, the trader often plays with the brokerage's money. Sometimes the market turns against the trader and the house forces the trader to pay the difference between what the current value of the commodity and what the house has extended as credit to the trader. As many traders know, this is called a "margin call."

The one advantage Hillary had was that when a "margin call" may have been called against another trader, Hillary wasn't called in. Jim Blair had brought much business to Refco, was associated with Tyson Foods, was therefore safe, and those with Blair were safe too. He was a good customer and the house was not going to pinch him. "They weren't going to hassle me, and if I brought someone in, they weren't going to hassle them," Blair said. Again, it was nothing illegal; it is just the way of the world.

Hillary got out while the getting was good. Later that year, happy with her earlier investing success, she and Bill acquired 230.4 acres of undeveloped land along the White River with some friends, Jim and Susan McDougal.

Brighter Skies Ahead

Hillary's political fortunes were rising, too. During this time, she often took leaves of absence from the law firm to help her husband with his many political campaigns, ideas, and plans. She worked on her favorite cause—helping children—by heading Bill's effort to improve Arkansas state schools. She became a critical member of the firm's hierarchy.

As the 1980s were drawing to a close, her dreams seemed ever more close. She had a successful career and a beautiful child. She was committed to causes larger than herself and was taken seriously in her own right. She had a husband she loved, regardless of his wandering eye.

And Bill was more popular than ever. Despite whatever flaws their marriage may have had, it was now obvious that Hillary Clinton had hitched herself to someone who was on the verge of becoming a national star.

The Least You Need to Know

➤ Hillary grew up a Republican.

➤ College and the issues of the day had a profound political impact on her.

➤ Her goal was to make the world a better place; the law was her vehicle.

➤ She is a very smart woman who knows how to get what she wants.

Chapter 7

On the National Stage

In This Chapter

➤ A bad speech

➤ A good candidate

➤ Ross Perot

➤ It's the Economy, Stupid!

➤ The beginnings of the "right-wing conspiracy"

➤ President Clinton

➤ A Rocky Start

It had long been Bill Clinton's dream, and Hillary's dream for him, to be President of the United States. Now, everything was in place: the educational pedigree, the look, the personality, the brain, and now, with re-election to the Governorship almost guaranteed every two years, the experience. All he needed was to show the American people why he had become the darling of the Democratic Party. The national stage was beckoning.

The Not Ready for Prime-Time Player

When millions of Americans first saw Bill Clinton on television, he bored them silly. While nominating Michael Dukakis at the 1988 Democratic convention, Clinton talked so long the crowd started interrupting, yelling, "We want Mike!" This was surprising, because the "buzz" on Clinton was that he was an up-and-comer, and a gifted orator.

According to biographers Charles Allen and Jonathan Portis, "It was clear to television viewers that Clinton was confused and frightened." The Governor pleaded for patience, but when he said the words, "In conclusion," the conventioneers spontaneously erupted in cheers.

To those who had heard Clinton previously, his stiff delivery was a mystery. To those who had only heard about the energetic, young Governor, the speech was equally confusing. He was supposed to be bright, capable and, above all, articulate. He was still considered a young, rising star, 10 years after first being elected Governor of Arkansas.

The speech quickly became a national joke. Johnny Carson called Clinton a "windbag." Nevertheless, Clinton managed an invitation to *The Tonight Show* and proved to be a wonderful guest. When he played saxophone with Doc Severinson's orchestra, he foreshadowed things to come. He made everything all right. A minor comeback, but a comeback to be sure, for the self-proclaimed "Comeback Kid."

The Seven Dwarves

At the end of the war in the Persian Gulf in 1991, it seemed unlikely that anyone could legitimately challenge President George Bush and his sky-high approval rating. Bush's popularity was enough to frighten away all the major Democratic Presidential aspirants: Jesse Jackson, Dick Gephardt, Al Gore, Lloyd Bentsen, Sam Nunn, and Mario Cuomo. Bush's international bravado was also sufficient to send nearly all of his political opponents within his party packing.

Media Alert

At the end of the Gulf War, George Bush had an amazing 91 percent approval rating in the polls. A mere 13 months later, his approval rating was down to less than 50 percent.

Just one year later, Bush seemed poised to snatch defeat from the jaws of victory. The same George Bush who drew a line in the sand in Kuwait 1990 betrayed his famous "read my lips" promise just weeks later by signing the largest tax increase in history. As steam began to go out of the Reagan economy, Bush's approval rating began to decline and he began to look more and more vulnerable. Bush, a well-bred "Eastern elitist," seemed curiously out-of-touch with the American electorate.

Become a Pundit

The seven Democratic candidates were dubbed the "7 Dwarves" for their alleged lack of political stature.

Into this void stepped several Democratic candidates branded by the national press as lacking the stature necessary to really challenge a sitting President. Bill Clinton jumped in, as did Bob Kerry, Paul Tsongas, Jerry Brown, and a few others. Clinton blew them all away. Although Clinton was almost knocked out by the double-whammy of Gennifer Flowers and the "I did not inhale" fiasco, he still managed to come in first in the Iowa Caucus and second in the all-important New Hampshire primary.

Within a month, every Democratic challenger dropped out of the race except former California Governor Jerry Brown. Political commentators seemed not to know exactly what to make of Brown's candidacy. Every joke imaginable was lobbed in his direction in an attempt to ridicule his quixotic image and his 800 number. Brown's no-frills campaign slowed the Clinton inevitability, but that is about all it did.

Democrats were not the only politicians to jump on Bush's weakness. Conservative Pat Buchanan violated the Republican "11th Commandment" (thou shall not speak ill of another Republican) and challenged the sitting President for the Republican nomination. Buchanan's unexpectedly strong showing tilted the Republican Party ever more to the right.

In the end, Clinton ran away with the nomination and Bush was re-nominated. The stage was set for a classic two-man battle. Then H. Ross Perot came out of the blue.

The Perot Factor

The 1992 election was all about change. It was Clinton's mantra and the country seemed to eager to hear it after 12 years of Republican administration. But Bill Clinton wasn't the only person who was able to see and tap into this sentiment.

Ross Perot is a maverick gadfly multi-billionaire who announced his candidacy on *Larry King Live*. He was a unique candidate by any standard. His fortune was self-made, and the thrilling story of how he was able to privately rescue his own employees from Iran is the stuff of legend. He was outspoken, cranky, intelligent, opinionated, creative, and rich.

In less than three months, the Ross Perot phenomenon came out of nowhere to capture the imagination of a nation of disillusioned voters. With no party and no political experience, he still was able to quickly match Bill Clinton's nationwide popularity, while trailing not far behind George Bush. For many Americans, he was the only major candidate who was truly an outsider, in a year when the entire Washington establishment desperately tried to portray themselves as such.

And then, just as quickly, he quit the race. While his reasons remain unclear, his story that Bush's henchmen were planning on disrupting his daughter's wedding struck some as a bit nutty. Perot became a laughingstock, and although he soon re-entered the race, he never again had the same credibility or posed the same threat as he had before. In the end, Perot garnered 19 percent of the vote in the 1992 election.

In the meantime, the real race was between Bush and Clinton, or, as Clinton deftly put it, between the past and the future.

"It's The Economy, Stupid"

That was the sign that hung in the war room of Clinton's main campaign headquarters in Little Rock, Arkansas. The sign was intended to keep everyone focused on what people were worried about and what could get Clinton elected. Stay on message!

Mumbo Jumbo

In any political campaign, there is one place where all the main decisions are made, where the candidate and his advisers meet, where they review polls and strategies—the **war room**.

The campaign was run by two unknown men who would later gain much notoriety from their relationship with Clinton—the wunderkind George Stephanopoulos and the Cajun whip-cracker James Carville. Both were greatly impressed by Clinton's amazing intellect and grasp of the issues. Combined with his ability to reach voters better than any politician since the Gipper, Clinton seemed to have it all.

Yet, there were problems. Clinton had that annoying habit of shading the truth whenever he got in a jam. And of course, there were the so-called "bimbo eruptions." It was hard to figure out just where Clinton's actual womanizing ended and various women's desire to get rich off Clinton began. In any case, after the *60 Minutes* appearance with Hillary (see Chapter 8), that all seemed to be behind him. Clinton was worth the effort. Carville and Stephanopoulos knew that they had the best Democratic politician in a generation on their hands.

James Carville
AP/Wide World Photos

George Stephanopoulos
Reuters/Corbis-Bettmann

Stephanopoulos and Carville devised a brilliant campaign strategy:

➤ Position Clinton as a moderate.

➤ Paint Bush as an out-of-touch tool of the elite.

➤ Capitalize on Clinton's ability to empathize with people.

➤ Highlight Clinton's apparent ability to understand the new world economy.

Questions among the electorate remained. Was Clinton too slick? As the first baby-boomer with a legitimate chance to become President, was he sufficiently mature for the position?

The situation was the reverse of an election only a few years before. In 1984, when Ronald Reagan was in his 70s and running for reelection against Walter Mondale, a man in his 60s, Reagan stumbled badly in the first of two debates. He looked old, feeble, and confused. In comparison, Mondale looked young and vital. For the first time, it seemed like Mondale had a chance. Until the second debate. The charming, disarming, Reagan of old showed up again, solving the "age question" forever by saying, "Some people have been saying that age is an issue in this campaign .... Well, let me put an end to that. I'm not going to hold my opponent's youth and inexperience against him." The line got a big laugh, and the age issue dissolved.

In 1992, it was Clinton's youth that was at issue. After all, if elected, he would become President at the age of 46. Only John Kennedy (at the age of 43) and Teddy Roosevelt (at the age of 42) were younger when they became Chief Executive.

In the end, the country came to terms with Clinton—with both his strengths and his weaknesses. He seemed to be worth a gamble, despite whatever reservations some people had about him. His vitality, his awareness of people's fears, and his obvious grasp of the country's problems simply overwhelmed Bush, who seemed never to "get it."

Despite the amusing interference run by Perot, Clinton became the country's 42nd President, capturing 43 percent of the vote. As if to amplify the reason he was elected, the night after his election, Clinton said he would focus "like a laser" on the problems of the economy. It was just what people wanted to hear.

Become a Pundit

The President who was elected with the lowest percentage of the popular vote was John Quincy Adams, who received only 31 percent of the popular vote. In 1876, Rutherford B. Hayes won with 48 percent of the vote even though his opponent, Samuel Tilden, received 51 percent of the vote. Because of how the electoral college works, Hayes won more states and the Presidency.

Clinton Upsets the Right Wing

Clinton has always attracted both intense adoration as well as scathing hatred. Once he became a national figure, Clinton paved the way for his enemies to attack him on a national level. Clinton upset the conservative apple cart. He was called a draft-dodging coward. Conservatives, from Pat Buchanan to Bob Novak to Newt Gingrich to Rush Limbaugh were more than a little displeased that a dope-smoking, adulterating

Media Alert

Right after Clinton was elected, Rush Limbaugh began to open his nationally syndicated radio show everyday with the banner "America Held Hostage," in reference to the Clinton Presidency.

Mumbo Jumbo

A **conspiracy** is a group of two or more persons with a common design and common plan to achieve their goals.

"liberal" made it into the highest office in the land. To these people, the election of Clinton meant that they were losing the "cultural war" so many of them talked about.

Aside from the cultural issues, Clinton's election was a threat to the New Right politically as well:

➤ It threatened to turn women, already favoring Democrats generally, into a Democratic linchpin constituency.

➤ It threatened to take the Western states away from the Republicans. California voted for Clinton; the first time a Democrat had carried the state in decades.

➤ It threatened the South. As Clinton and Gore were both southerners, their election had pro-found long-term implications for the Right.

➤ Most of all, the election of the smooth talking, feel-your-pain, young Governor threatened to end the changes the "Reagan Revolution" had wrought.

That was unacceptable. It's not surprising that the Right viewed the election of Clinton with some fear. What was surprising is how vitriolic their denunciations of Clinton would become.

Hillary Clinton would later claim that a "vast right-wing conspiracy" intended to destroy her husband. Whether such a conspiracy exists or ever existed remains to be seen. What cannot be doubted however, is that Clinton's adversaries wanted him out of office, and were willing to commit the time and resources to achieve their goals.

President William Jefferson Clinton

With a speech of surprising brevity, Clinton began his Presidency—his inaugural address was only 14 minutes long. Clinton promised to be a "different kind of Demo-crat." He reiterated his campaign theme that with opportunity came responsibility. He spoke of reducing the deficit and creating a "third way" that was neither Democratic nor Republican. He promised change.

Despite that lofty rhetoric, the Clinton Presidency began with the new President looking much like an old-style liberal. Clinton's first act as President was to challenge the long-standing military policy against having gays serve in the armed forces.

Angering both the left (for not going far enough) and the right (for going too far) the new President's initial foray into policy was none too impressive.

The Price of Inexperience

Although not quite as focused as a laser beam, Clinton turned to the economy. His first budget faced a problem. The deficit was growing and it had to be tamed. Bill Clinton the candidate made contradictory promises to the American people. On one hand, he promised to halve the budget deficit in four years. To do so would take a tax hike. But candidate Clinton also promised a tax cut:

> *I want to make it very clear that this middle-class tax cut, in my view, is central to any attempt we're going to make to have a short-term economic strategy and a long-term fairness strategy, which is part of getting this country going again.*
> —Primary debate, Manchester, NH, January 1992

After much internal debate and disagreement, deficit reduction was deemed more important economically than a tax break. Clinton's first budget emphasized the former over the latter. But the fact that the oft-mentioned "middle-class tax cut" never made it into his initial budget fueled the inkling of belief that maybe, just maybe, Clinton was a liar. This belief would fester and grow as time went on.

While Clinton waited for his economic package to bear fruit, the economy continued to slide and his inexperience in national politics began to show. He had a hard time getting Cabinet nominees confirmed (Janet Reno was his third choice for attorney general.) He had his hair cut on a runway at Los Angeles International Airport, causing a small revolt (although it was never reported that Clinton twice asked whether the haircut would delay other planes and was assured that it would not). Then, more serious matters began to occur.

Become a Pundit

It's no secret that politicians make promises they can't keep. Voters like promises. Before the days of instant communication, it was much easier for a politician to get away with an unfulfilled promise because news wasn't as instantly and effectively reported. Today's instant global communications have changed that, though few politicians seem to have realized it.

Cracks in the Dike

Whitewater, as we will see, is a land deal the Clintons entered into with Jim and Susan McDougal. McDougal also took over a small savings and loan called Madison Guaranty. The charges that would later come out were that Madison money had been used to subsidize the Whitewater project. Like many S&Ls in the late 1980s, Madison Guaranty later went belly up. (You'll get a lot more detail on Whitewater in Chapter 15.)

The tsunami we now know of as Whitewater began with a trickle. In late 1993, the *Washington Post* reported that the federal government was beginning a criminal investigation of Madison.

The White House travel office was fired. The President hired his wife to introduce a massive overhaul of the country's health-care system, much to the consternation of many. The plan was a complete failure—it was probably too massive and centralized, and the Republicans outmaneuvered the Administration politically, labeling it a "government takeover" of health care tantamount to socialism.

Then things really got bad.

When Vince Foster killed himself, the anti-Clinton dam burst. The Right was convinced that Foster was murdered, and many accused the Clintons. A special prosecutor, Robert Fiske, was named to investigate Foster's suicide and the "Travelgate" affair (which you'll also read about in Chapter 15).

Although no one realized it at the time, a minor event that occurred during this era would likely turn out to be the most significant event of the Clinton Presidency. An ex-staffer from Clinton's Arkansas days by the name of Paula Jones filed suit against the President, alleging that he sexually harassed her (see Chapter 8). Paula Jones begat Monica Lewinsky, who begat Linda Tripp, who begat Kenneth Starr.

A Showdown and a Shutdown

But 1994 would also turn out to be the year of Clinton's redemption. The "Contract with America" convinced the public to vote Republican after the mid-term elections, and the House of Representatives was controlled by a Republican majority for the first time in many years.

The revolutionary House freshman, however, understood neither the game they were playing nor who they were playing with. Their stridence turned off many voters, and their showdown with Clinton over the budget and the subsequent government shutdown allowed Clinton to recast himself as the friend to the middle-class.

Become a Pundit

Prior to 1994, the House had been run by Democrats for 50 years.

Combined with a surging economy, both Clinton's stock as well as the stock market began to rise. Clinton's approval rating shot up and has yet to come back down. He easily won reelection in 1996.

But everything was not perfect. Little did the country know it, but Clinton had just started an affair with a young intern. The new special prosecutor, Ken Starr, was continuing his Whitewater investigation. Clinton's enemies were laying in wait. Vince Foster had predicted it. The last line in his suicide note read: "Here, ruining people is considered sport."

The Least You Need to Know

➤ Clinton's first national television appearance was memorable, only because it was so bad.

➤ Clinton easily took the Democratic nomination in 1992.

➤ His focus on the economy and easy charm convinced voters to take a chance on him.

➤ Clinton's election greatly upset the right wing.

➤ President Clinton got off to a rocky start but rebounded handsomely.

Chapter 8

Liar, Liar, Pants on Fire

In This Chapter

➤ Clinton's alleged history of infidelity

➤ Gennifer Flowers

➤ Kathleen Willey

➤ Paula Jones

➤ I did not inhale

➤ Promises, promises

➤ Are all lies alike?

As we all know, soon after Clinton was elected to the Presidency, a former state worker from Arkansas named Paula Jones claimed that Clinton propositioned her, while he was Governor, in a hotel room in Little Rock. With the assistance of right-wing backers, Jones filed and pursued a sexual-harassment suit against the President.

In late 1997, Paula Jones's attorneys took the deposition of President Clinton. His troubles now stem from the fact that he may have lied about his relationship with Monica Lewinsky in that deposition, and because he may have lied in his grand jury testimony as well.

It is not surprising that Clinton landed in hot water for lying about infidelity, as those two character flaws—lying and infidelity—have been his Achilles heel since his political career began. Indeed, the Jones case and Starr's grand jury examination were not the first time Bill Clinton lied, or cheated.

Mumbo Jumbo

In a civil lawsuit, each party needs to find out what the other party in the case knows about the facts of the case. This is called **discovery**. A main tool of discovery is the **deposition**. A deposition is the taking of someone's sworn testimony under oath outside of a courtroom.

Clinton's Alleged History of Infidelity

The American people voted for Clinton because they were able to separate the public and private Bill Clintons. The Monica Lewinsky scandal, wherein he ostensibly lied in a public proceeding (at a deposition and to the grand jury) about a private matter, forever intertwined the public and private Clinton. Ignoring the private Bill in favor of the public Clinton has become more and more difficult for many Americans.

A caveat: Gennifer Flowers claims she had a 12-year affair with Bill Clinton; the President, in his deposition in the Paula Jones case, says he slept with Ms. Flowers once. Kathleen Willey says the President clumsily groped her in the Oval Office. Clinton denies the encounter. Remember, when it comes to sex and Bill Clinton, people are apt to say just about anything. Nevertheless, there sure are a lot of women who say Clinton was their paramour.

Dolly Browning

One of the first women to claim that she had an extra-marital relationship with Bill Clinton is Arkansas resident Dolly Browning. Ms. Browning submitted an affidavit in support of Paula Jones in the *Jones v. Clinton* lawsuit. In that affidavit, Ms. Browning states:

> 1. I have known William Jefferson Clinton since I was eleven years old. I call him "Billy." We attended high school together. During the period from the mid-1970s until January 1992, we had a relationship that included sexual relations. The frequency of our contact with each other, and the frequency of our sexual encounters, varied over that time period, but we did have sexual relations many times during that time period.

> 2. Our relationship ended abruptly in January of 1992 when Billy would not return my telephone call. I told his secretary, Linda, that a tabloid had the story about me and Billy. I asked her to have him call me and he refused. Instead he had my brother, who was, at that time, working in the 1992 Clinton Presidential campaign, call me from Billy's New Hampshire apartment or office .... He said "we" think you should deny the story. He finally said: "If you cooperate with the media we will destroy you."

> 8. In the fall of 1994, through the intermediaries of Dorcy Kyle Corbin and Bruce Lindsey, Billy and I reached a "deal." The "deal" was that I agreed not to tell the

true story about our relationship if he would not tell any lies about me. I agreed not to use, in public, the "A words" which were defined as "adultery" and "affair." I was allowed to say that we had a thirty-three year relationship that, from time to time, included sex. If I needed to contact Billy, I would call Dorcy and she would call Bruce Lindsey. I used this method of communication several times over the years.

I declare under penalty of perjury that the foregoing is true and correct.

Executed on March 6, 1998
(signed)
Dolly Kyle Browning"

White House Confidential

In 1964, Lyndon Johnson aide Walter Jenkins was arrested in the men's room of a YMCA one block from the White House and charged with having sex with a man. Jenkins resigned his position.

What Did the Troopers Know and When Did They Know It?

Bill Clinton was Governor of Arkansas for 12 years. During that time, Arkansas state troopers were assigned as his security detail. Consistent rumors have come out of Arkansas that Clinton used the troopers for personal, as well as public, functions. While not really surprising, Clinton nonetheless denies the allegations made by the troopers.

In a sworn deposition, former Arkansas state trooper L.D. Brown tells of a story that allegedly occurred outside of Arkansas at a Southern Regional Education board meeting. Brown stated that:

> One night after Hillary ... went to bed, we went out to a club, a disco kind of club, dance club ... and there was a table of women across the room from us, young women, and the Governor asked me to go over and ask this particular woman if she wanted to meet the Governor from Arkansas.

And I did, I gave her one of my cards, and again, this was out of town as opposed to in-state where people knew who he was. And I think the girl said something, "Right, I'm the Queen of England, too," and someone at the table, which invariably would happen, actually noticed and knew who he was. And they said, "No, no, no. That's really Bill Clinton. I've seen him on television."

A couple of the girls came over, and when it was time to go and pay the bill, the Governor got in the car with the girl that I had given the card to, and we followed them to a remote area ... and pulled over, Ralph and I did. [The Governor then got out of the car with the woman.]

Q: When Bill Clinton got back in the car with you after he left the car where he had been with the woman, what did he say to you about what they had done in there?

A: Well, he indicated in so many words that she had performed oral sex on him.

Trooper Danny Ferguson also stated that Clinton was quite the womanizer. He relayed the story, in a deposition under oath, of a particular woman with whom Clinton had been flirting:

A: That's when he said, "She's got that come-hither look."

Q: What does that mean?

A: That's just a word he used.

Q: Did he use it a lot?

A: Yes, sir.

Q: Come hither?

A: Yes.

Gennifer Flowers

Of all of the sexual allegations that have threatened to undermine Clinton's political career, the allegations put forth by Gennifer Flowers were the first to rock the nation. On February 4, 1992, the tabloid newspaper the *Star* came out with a banner headline:

MY 12-YEAR AFFAIR WITH BILL CLINTON
Dem's Front-Runner Lied to America,
Says His Former Lover

Mistress Tells All:
We Were Lovers from 1977 to 1989

Why did Ms. Flowers make her claim in the *Star*? She had wanted to come forward in the *Washington Post*. *Star* writer Steven Edwards states: "I had a helluva time persuading her to go with us. I told her that unlike the *Star,* the *Post* would pay nothing. In the end … money was the deciding factor."

Gennifer Flowers.
AP/Wide World Photos

In the article, Flowers stated that she had audiotapes of her and her lover speaking over the phone. The *Star* called them "BILL CLINTON LOVE TAPES."

Ms. Flowers elaborated on her alleged affair with Clinton in an affidavit she submitted in the Paula Jones lawsuit:

My name is Gennifer G. Flowers.

1. I met Bill Clinton in 1977. Shortly after we met, we began a sexual relationship that lasted for twelve years.

2. In the late 1970s I moved away from Little Rock. Bill Clinton and I maintained our relationship during this time. I returned to Little Rock in the mid-1980s. We discussed my return to Little Rock and … he encouraged me to move into Quapaw Tower, a high-rise apartment building located in Little Rock. He told me that he had aides in the building and that it wouldn't be so noticeable for him to come to that building to visit me.

Media Alert

The *Arkansas Democratte-Gazette* of February 28, 1992, reported that Flowers had claimed to be the opening act for comedian Rich Little, but that her former agent, Jim Porter, stated he had no knowledge of her doing any such work.

3. Once I moved to the Quapaw Tower in Little Rock we continued our personal relationship on a more regular basis.

4. On several occasions, I discussed with Bill Clinton the subject of inquiries by the media about our relationship. He told me to continue to deny our relationship, that if we would stick together, everything would be okay. In one conversation which occurred while Bill Clinton was running for the Democratic Presidential nomination in 1991 [he said] "I expect them to look into it and interview you and everything, but I just think that if everybody is on the record denying it, you got no problem."

I declare under penalty of perjury that the foregoing is true and correct.

Executed on March 12, 1998
(signed)
Gennifer G. Flowers

Become a Pundit

When he came in second in the New Hampshire primary in 1992, Bill Clinton became the only person ever not to win that primary and still become President.

Despite her allegations and the subsequent hysteria, Clinton survived. After news of the affair became public, on the eve of the New Hampshire primary in 1992, Bill and Hillary went on *60 Minutes* to discuss the crisis that threatened his political career (definitely a recurring theme). Admitting that he had caused "pain" in his marriage, Clinton came off as sincere, apologetic, and human. Hillary also shone in that interview. Saying she was no Tammy Wynette, "Stand By Your Man" kind of woman, Mrs. Clinton seemed strong, intelligent, and dynamic. The interview worked, Clinton came in second in New Hampshire, and his candidacy was saved.

Kathleen Willey

Gennifer Flowers was certainly not the last woman to allege a sexual fling with Bill Clinton. One of the most recent is Kathleen Willey, although Willey's claim has less supporting documentation than the others.

Willey went to work in the White House in 1993. She worked in the Office of White House Counsel and in the White House Social Office. Willey and the President exchanged a few gifts and some personal notes. On November 22, 1993, Willey sent the President a note asking for a few minutes of his time. Although the meeting that occurred on November 29 was brief, the ramifications have been long-lasting.

Willey's husband was having business problems and had in fact been missing for a few days. One of the reasons Willey wanted to see the President was to ask for a paid position for herself, as she and her husband were having financial problems. On that fateful day, unbeknownst to her, Willey's husband committed suicide. Willey would state, almost five years later, that the President had groped her at that meeting, and that it had greatly upset her.

Yet, despite her allegations, Willey continued to fawn over the President, causing some people to doubt her claims. Only a month after the meeting took place, on December 20, 1993, Willey wrote the President, wished him a merry Christmas, and thanked him for the meeting. Similarly, on June 17th of that year, she wrote the President and stated: "I just wanted to take a moment to tell you how caring and heartfelt your speech was on D-Day … for me that was the proudest I have been that you are our President." She later wrote him and said that she was his number one fan, and worked for his reelection campaign in 1996.

In 1998, *Newsweek* learned of the alleged grope. Linda Tripp told *Newsweek* that she ran into Willey right after Willey allegedly was groped by Clinton in the Oval Office. Tripp said Willey was "disheveled, her face was red and her lipstick was off. She was flustered, happy, and joyful." Willey eventually went on *60 Minutes* and claimed again that the meeting was actually very horrible.

Media Alert

The first hint of any scandal involving Kathleen Willey was via the Internet, with Matt Drudge of the infamous *Drudge Report* taking the honors.

In her deposition in the Jones case, Willey had this to say:

> Q: Please describe [what happened] as fully as you can.
>
> A: He attempted to kiss me.
>
> Q: Mr. Clinton did?
>
> A: Yes.
>
> Q: On the lips?
>
> A: Yes.
>
> Q: Did you allow him to kiss you?
>
> A: I don't think so.
>
> Q: Was he successful in kissing you?
>
> A: I can't remember.
>
> …

Media Alert

In the Starr Report, Clinton denies to Lewinsky that he ever touched Willey. Clinton is said to have told Lewinsky that Willey's breasts were too small for him.

Mumbo Jumbo

Cross-examination is the process whereby the opposing lawyer asks leading, intense, and often confrontational questions of the witness in order to better reveal the truth. There is no cross-examination of witnesses in a grand jury. The Starr Report was based almost exclusively upon grand jury testimony.

Q: Did Mr. Clinton ever seek to take either of your hands and place it on his body anyplace?

A: Yes.

Q: Please describe that. …

A: He put his hands—he put my hands on his genitals.

Q: Did you resist?

A: Yes.

Q: Were you successful?

A: Yes.

Q: Could you tell whether he was aroused?

A: Yes.

Kathleen Willey leaving U.S. District Court following her testimony. Agence France Presse/ Corbis-Bettmann

Clinton's attorney Robert Bennett then had this exchange with Ms. Willey on cross-examination:

> Q: Following this incident, you've testified that you went and saw Mr. Clinton in the Oval Office on a few occasions; is that correct?
>
> A: Correct.
>
> Q: And after the incident you corresponded with him; isn't that correct?
>
> A: That's correct.
>
> Q: And on occasions you would communicate that you would request certain favors of him, such as your friend who was sick with the tumor?
>
> A: Right, yes.

In the end, given her inconsistent behavior, Kathleen Willey's allegations seemed to lead nowhere.

Paula Jones

The same cannot be said for Paula Jones. As we all know, Jones is the former Arkansas state employee who alleges that Clinton exposed himself to her, and she sued. Although her case was eventually dismissed, it sowed the seeds for Clinton's current crisis.

As you'll see in the next chapter, the inability of Clinton and his attorneys to settle the case or otherwise get rid of it sooner, created the opening that independent counsel Kenneth Starr needed to finally pin something on the President.

"I did not inhale."

It is not just that Clinton has lied about his infidelity that has caused him problems. It seems that whenever he is in a tight spot, Clinton lies, shades the truth, fudges, equivocates, chooses his words very carefully ... call it what you will. So eager is he to keep his reputation stain-free that he often cloaks himself in blanket denials that, when repudiated, cause him worse damage than the initial accusation. The current crisis is really nothing more than this pattern taken to its illogical extreme.

Go back to 1992. At the time, Governor Clinton, like all candidates that year, was asked whether he

Sound Bites

The President had a "Saturday night personality," where he gives in to his sexual desires, and a "Sunday personality," where he is remorseful and goes to church.

—Monica Lewinsky, as quoted by investigators for independent counsel Kenneth Starr

had ever smoked marijuana. Clinton answered that he had—sort of. "When I was in England I experimented with marijuana a time or two. But I didn't like it, and I didn't inhale"

Clinton compounded his problems by stating that he had broken no *American* laws, as he smoked marijuana while he was a student living outside of the United States.

The answer was remarkably inept for many reasons:

➤ **It was overly legalistic.** By confessing to smoking, but doing so overseas, and thereby making the action "legal," Clinton looked like the well-trained lawyer he was. The same sort of hair-splitting may bring down his Presidency.

➤ **It was too slick.** Clinton tried to have it both ways. While admitting the "truth" of his sin, he simultaneously tried to show that he had done nothing wrong.

➤ **It was a lie.** (At least we can surmise so.) To think that a draft-resisting, liberal, intelligent, curious, 1960s student took a joint but did not inhale is a little silly, to say the least.

At the time the answer seemed ridiculous, but not necessarily a character flaw. In light of the present controversy, it may turn out that such clever answers provide more evidence of the latter than of the former.

It was not long before Clinton's inability to lie without getting caught began to sully his reputation. Take a look at what *The New York Times* said about him in 1994:

> *The President's essential character flaw isn't dishonesty so much as a-honesty. It isn't that Clinton means to say things that are not true, or that he cannot make true, but that everything is true for him when he says it, because he says it. Clinton means what he says when he says it, but tomorrow he will mean what he says when he says the opposite. He is the existential President, living with absolute sincerity in the passing moment.*
> —Michael Kelly

Promises, Promises

Like all good politicians, Clinton made many, many promises, both while campaigning and while in office. What is remarkable is how many of Clinton's turned out to be false.

➤ **Running for President**
Question: "Will you guarantee to us that if re-elected, there is absolutely, positively no way that you'll run for any other office and that you'll serve out your term in full?
Answer: "You bet…. That's the job I want. That's the job I'll do the next two years."
—1990

"Today I am declaring my candidacy for President of the United States."
—Campaign kickoff, 1991

➤ **Middle class tax cut**
"I believe you deserve more than 30-second ads or vague promises. That's why I've offered a comprehensive plan to get our economy moving again. It starts with a tax cut for the middle class and asks the rich to pay their fair share again."
—Clinton's first campaign ad, January 1992

"From New Hampshire forward, for reasons that absolutely mystified me, the press thought the most important issue in the race was the middle class tax cut. I never did meet any voter who thought that."
—January 14, 1993

"To middle class Americans who have paid a great deal for the last 12 years and from whom I ask a contribution tonight ...."
—February 17, 1993

➤ **Tax burden**
"You know what my plan is, to raise taxes on people whose incomes are above $200,000 ...."
—July 13, 1992

In Clinton's first budget plan, he proposed a new 36 percent tax rate which would take effect on couples earning more than $140,000 and individuals making more than $115,000.

➤ **"100 Days"**
"I intend to have a legislative program ready on the desk of Congress on the day after I'm inaugurated. I intend to have an explosive 100-day action period."
—June 23, 1992

"People of the press are expecting [us] to have some 100-day program. We never, ever had one."
—Dee Dee Myers, January 12, 1993

➤ **China (Most Favored Nation trading status)**
"We will condition favorable trade terms with repressive regimes—such as China's Communist regime—on respect for human rights, political liberalization, and responsible international conduct."
—Putting People First, September 1992

"We will link China's trading privileges to its human rights record and its conduct on trade and weapon sales."
—August 13, 1992

Mumbo Jumbo

Most Favored Nation (MFN) status is a designation made by the federal government that allows certain countries, "most favored" countries, tax and tariff breaks when exporting to the U.S.

"I am moving, therefore, to delink human rights from the annual extension of most-favored nation trading status for China."
—May 26, 1994

➤ **Haitian refugees**

"I am appalled by the decision of the Bush administration to pick up fleeing Haitians on the high seas and forcibly return them to Haiti before considering their claim to political asylum .... If I were President, I would—in the absence of clear and compelling evidence that they weren't political refugees—give them temporary asylum until we restored the elected government of Haiti."
—May 27, 1992

"For Haitians who do seek to leave Haiti, boat departure is a terrible and dangerous choice .... For this reason, the practice of returning those who fled Haiti by boat will continue, for the time being, after I become President. Those who do leave Haiti ... by boat will be stopped and directly returned by the United States Coast Guard."
—January 14, 1993

➤ **Drug War**

"[President Bush] hasn't fought a real war on crime and drugs. I will."
—July 16, 1992

"I never thought I'd miss Nancy Reagan. There can't be a rating [on the Clinton drug policy] when there hasn't been a performance."
—Rep. Charles Rangel (D-NY), April 24, 1993

➤ **Government reform**

"It's long past time to clean up Washington. The last twelve years were nothing less than an extended hunting season for high-priced lobbyists and Washington influence peddlers. On streets where statesmen once strolled, a never-ending stream of money now changes hands — tying the hands of those elected to lead."
—Putting People First, September 1992

"But in a recognition of the fact that lobbyists constitute a fertile source of fundraising, Clinton will accept contributions [to his legal defense fund] of up to $1,000 annually from the Washington lobbyists whose activities he decried during the campaign and since taking office."
—*Washington Post*, June 29, 1994

➤ **Childhood**

"I have 'vivid and painful' memories of black churches being burned while I was growing up in Arkansas."
—1996

"I've never known of a black church being burned in Arkansas."
—The Director of the Arkansas History Commission, 1996

➤ Sex
"I am going to say this again. I want you to listen to me. I did not have sexual relations with that woman, Miss Lewinsky. I never told anyone to lie, not one time, never."
—January 1998

"Indeed, I did have a relationship with Miss Lewinsky that was not appropriate. In fact, it was wrong."
—August 17, 1998

Are All Lies Alike?

Democratic Senator Bob Kerry once said, "Clinton is an unusually good liar, unusually good." Just how serious are these lies and this serial infidelity? Not all lies are alike. Shading the truth is worse than a blatant whopper, and the law recognizes that not all lies are the same. For example, lying under oath is not necessarily perjury. Perjury only occurs when the lie is material to the case. Lying about one's age, for instance, would not normally be considered perjury.

This distinction is helpful in analyzing Clinton's fibbing. Breaking a campaign promise is akin to an insignificant lie. While wrong, no one expects a politician to keep every promise. Conversely, looking the nation in the eye and denying sexual relations with "that woman" was a bit more than a white lie. That was a lie about a material fact.

In her book *Lying*, Sissela Bok states:

> It has been thought worse to plan to lie than to do so on the spur of the moment; worse to induce others to lie … than to do so oneself; worse to lie to those with a right to truthful information than to lie to others; worse to lie to those who have entrusted you with their confidence about matters important to them than to your enemies.

Did Clinton do more than lie to his enemies? Yes. He lied to his enemies while under oath, twice. He lied to his family, his friends, his Cabinet, and his allies. He lied to the country. He lied to you.

It may be forgivable, and then again, it may not. Presidents have done worse. Much worse. They just weren't dumb enough to conspire to lie with a love-struck 22-year-old intern.

The Least You Need to Know

➤ Gennifer Flowers' allegations of a long-term affair threatened candidate Clinton's campaign, but failed to derail it.

➤ Kathleen Willey's allegations don't seem to have the same veracity as those of other sexual accusers.

➤ More than anything, the Paula Jones suit was the catalyst for the President's current crisis.

➤ Clinton's history of lying and breaking promises has come back to haunt him.

➤ While not all lies may be alike, breaching the public trust by lying to a whole nation may be unforgivable.

Chapter 9

Jones v. Clinton

In This Chapter

➤ What happened at that hotel in Little Rock

➤ The Supreme Court permits the case to proceed

➤ Case dismissed

➤ Why Paula Jones lost

➤ Paula and Monica

Little did he know it at the time, but that pesky sexual-harassment lawsuit filed by Paula Jones would serve to be President Clinton's undoing. Apparently, the case could have been settled long ago for several thousand dollars and an apology. Allegedly, in 1997, the President offered to settle for $700,000 and no apology. Although Jones's attorneys wanted to take the settlement, she did not, and the case never settled.

Had the case settled, history would have been different. The only reason Clinton is facing impeachment today is because Jones's attorneys found out about Monica Lewinsky and questioned the President about her in his deposition. Starr knew about the depositions—and learned of the relationship—and thus was able to expand his investigation. Had the Jones case settled, no-one would have ever heard of Monica Lewinsky.

The Background on the Jones Case

On May 6, 1994, Paula Jones filed a civil suit against President Clinton in U.S. District Court in Little Rock, Arkansas, seeking $700,000 in damages for "willful, outrageous, and malicious conduct" at the Excelsior Hotel in Little Rock on May 8, 1991. Her court papers accuse Clinton of "sexually harassing and assaulting" her, then defaming her with denials.

The first thing to understand is that Paula Jones may have had a much stronger case against Clinton had she filed her suit sooner. While she has maintained that she had other legitimate claims against Clinton (e.g., various personal injury claims), because she waited so long to file the suit, the statute of limitations on these claims expired. It can be legitimately asked: If Paula Jones was harmed as badly as she alleges she was by Clinton, why did she wait three full years before filing suit? If we were in court, the judge might instruct you to make a "reasonable inference" from that delay.

In 1993, a year and a half before she ever filed the suit, Paula Jones moved with her new husband Steve to California. In January 1994, a right-wing magazine called *American Spectator* (see Chapter 13) printed an article called "His Cheatin' Heart: Living With the Clintons." The article was written by David Brock. The article quoted four Arkansas state troopers who described, among other things, an incident with a woman named "Paula" in a hotel room in Little Rock.

Although this maze gets confusing, it is important to know exactly what happened. Jones read the story and then hired a Little Rock real-estate attorney named Danny Traylor to help her sue the President. Before ever filing suit, Traylor made contacts with a Little Rock businessman named George Cook who had contacts with the White House.

Sound Bites

I kill liberals for a living.

—David Brock

Cook would relay an offer to settle the case. In a later affidavit, Cook said Traylor told him the "case was a little bit weak." According to Cook, the Jones's also wanted the President to get Paula's husband Steve an acting job in California. The White House would not settle.

Jones's attorney Traylor then contacted long-time Clinton foe and Little Rock attorney Cliff Jackson for help. Jackson contacted *Washington Post* reporter Michael Isikoff and told him Paula's tale. The *Post* initially refused to run Isikoff's story without corroboration.

Jones reiterated her allegations at a press conference, but received little national attention. Traylor knew he needed help, and soon two trial attorneys, Gilbert Davis and Joseph Camarata, took over the case.

Media Alert

Michael Isikoff was outraged when the *Post* refused to run the Paula Jones story. He left and took a job at *Newsweek*, a sister publication of the *Post*, where he was instrumental in uncovering and reporting the Lewinsky drama.

In the meantime, Jones started making the rounds on those talk shows that would listen, Pat Robertson's *700 Club*, for example. She then repeated the story in a videotape called *The Clinton Chronicles*. You'll read more about that in the next chapter—suffice it to say that the video may not meet the highest standards of journalistic ethics and authenticity.

So, what actually happened that spring day in Little Rock? In her complaint, Paula Jones alleged that on the afternoon of May 8, 1991, in a suite at the Excelsior Hotel in Little Rock, Arkansas, Governor William

Jefferson Clinton exposed himself to her and requested oral sex.

According to the record, then-Governor Clinton was at the Excelsior Hotel on the day in question, delivering a speech. Jones stated that she and another state employee, Pamela Blackard, were working at a registration desk when a man approached, introducing himself as Trooper Danny Ferguson, the Governor's bodyguard.

Upon leaving the registration desk, Ferguson apparently had a conversation with the Governor about the possibility of meeting Ms. Jones. Ferguson said the Governor remarked that she had "that come-hither look." "Some time later," Ferguson said, the Governor asked him to "get him a room, that he was expecting a call from the White House and … had several phone calls that he needed to make." The Governor told him that if Jones wanted to meet him, she could "come up."

Mumbo Jumbo

All lawsuits begin when the party allegedly harmed (the "plaintiff") files a **complaint** against the defendant. The complaint alleges what the plaintiff thinks happened and how he was harmed as a result. It may or may not be true. That is the point of a trial. The trial determines what really happened; the complaint is unsubstantiated.

Paula Jones said that Ferguson later reappeared at the registration desk, handed her a piece of paper, and said that the Governor would like to meet with her in this suite number. Jones was honored, agreed to the meeting, and Ferguson escorted her to the Governor's suite.

Paula Corbin Jones.
Reuters/Corbis-Bettmann

In Paula Jones's complaint, she said that the Governor shook her hand, invited her in, and closed the door. She states that a few minutes of small talk ensued. The Governor then "unexpectedly reached over to [her], took her hand, and pulled her toward him, so that their bodies were close to each other." She states that she removed her hand from his and retreated several feet, but that the Governor approached her again and, while saying, "I love the way your hair flows down your back" and "I love your curves," put his hand on her leg, started sliding it toward her pelvic area, and bent down to attempt to kiss her on the neck, all without her consent. Jones states that she exclaimed, "What are you doing?" and told the Governor that she was "not that kind of girl."

Jones then says that she sat down at the end of the sofa nearest the door, but that the Governor approached the sofa where she had taken a seat and, as he sat down, "lowered his trousers and underwear, exposed his penis (which was erect) and told [her] to 'kiss it.'"

She states that the Governor, "while fondling his penis," said, "Well, I don't want to make you do anything you don't want to do," and then pulled up his pants and said, "If you get in trouble for leaving work, have Dave call me immediately and I'll take care of it." She states that she left the room, horrified and humiliated.

White House Confidential

In 1889, one-time Presidential hopeful, Representative William Taulbee was caught having sex with a patent clerk in a Capitol stairwell. Journalist Charles Kincaid exposed the matter in the *Louisville Times*, and Taulbee decided not to seek re-election. When he saw Kincaid at the Capitol the next year, he pounced on him. The fight was broken up, but two hours later, the journalist shot the House member dead.

Her Legal Claims

After much wrangling, Jones's complaint was pared down to three claims. The first alleges that Governor Clinton, acting under color of state law, sexually harassed her. The second alleges that Governor Clinton and Ferguson conspired against her to deprive her of her rights. The last asserts a claim of intentional infliction of emotional distress.

The Supreme Court Sets the Stage

From the outset, this was a dubious lawsuit, for a variety of reasons, but before the suit itself could even be addressed, there was a question that had never been decided before: Can a sitting President be sued in civil court while in office? The issue had to be decided before the case could even begin, and it went all the way up to the Supreme Court.

Justice Stevens delivered the opinion of the Court.

> *This case raises a constitutional and a prudential question concerning the Office of the President of the United States. Respondent [Jones], a private citizen, seeks to recover damages from the current occupant of that office based on actions allegedly taken before his term began. The President submits that in all but the most exceptional cases the Constitution requires federal courts to defer such litigation until his term ends and that, in any event, respect for the office warrants such a stay. Despite the force of the arguments supporting the President's submissions, we conclude that they must be rejected.*

> *As a starting premise, petitioner [Clinton] contends that he occupies a unique office with powers and responsibilities so vast and important that the public interest demands that he devote his undivided time and attention to his public duties.*

Become a Pundit

A federal case cannot be appealed directly to the Supreme Court. Only after the District Court has decided, and then the Appellate Court, can a party ask the Supreme Court to resolve a dispute. Even then the chances of being heard are remote. Only about 1 percent of all cases on appeal are ever accepted for hearing by the Supreme Court.

> *We have no dispute with the initial premise of the argument. Former presidents, from George Washington to George Bush, have consistently endorsed petitioner's characterization of the office. After serving his term, Lyndon Johnson observed: "Of all the 1,886 nights I was President, there were not many when I got to sleep before 1 or 2 a.m., and there were few mornings when I didn't wake up by 6 or 6:30.*

Yet, despite noting that the office of the President is unique, the Court somehow decides that a sitting President will not be hampered by a civil lawsuit. In fact, the Court seems to think that the suit would not take up much of the President's time at all.

> *If the past is any indicator, it seems unlikely that a deluge of such litigation will ever engulf the Presidency. As for the case at hand, if properly managed by the District Court, it appears to us highly unlikely to occupy any substantial amount of petitioner's time. (Emphasis added.)*

It may be hard to remember now, but before Jones's case was dismissed, it did indeed seem to take up a lot of the President's time. If nothing else, this decision certainly shows that it's been quite awhile since any of the current Justices of the Supreme Court have practiced law!

Whether you like or hate the President, this decision has really harmed the Presidency, for two reasons. First, defending a lawsuit is extraordinarily time-consuming and distracting for most people, let alone someone as busy the President of the United States. Protracted litigation is war (as the Jones case, once played out, proved). It is expensive and exasperating, time-consuming and emotionally draining. Do we really want our Chief Executive preoccupied when there is a dangerous world to contend with? Of course not. The President obviously occupies a unique position. He needs to devote his time to issues of state, not civil disputes.

Secondly, the decision paves the way for politically inspired suits to be filed against future Presidents. Lawsuits with the merest grain of truth behind them are difficult to get rid of (again, witness the Jones case). Given the success the Jones case had in distracting the Clinton Presidency, it should be no surprise if the next few Presidents face similar distractions, until this case is reversed.

The Case Goes Forward

Be that as it may, the Jones case continued. That is, until April 1, 1998, when the judge in the Jones case, Susan Webber Wright, dismissed Jones's suit as meritless.

As with any case, the bulk of the time is spent conducting *discovery*. Discovery is the process whereby each side finds out what the other knows about the facts of the case. Written questions, called *interrogatories*, are sent and must be answered. Depositions of possible witnesses are taken. In the Jones case, her lawyers spent most of their time trying to find other women who would back up Jones's allegations with incidents of their own.

(As you will see in the next section, it is obvious that Jones's attorneys spent too much time trying to prove Clinton was a philanderer and not enough time proving that their client was harmed as a result of his alleged actions.)

Clinton was bombarded with a ton of discovery requests. Among them were:

➤ A request to admit that the following statement is true: "On May 8, 1991, at the Excelsior Hotel in Little Rock, Arkansas, Defendant Clinton exposed his penis to Paula Jones (whose name at that time was Paula Rosalee Corbin)."

➤ A request to admit that the following statement is true: "After May 8, 1991, but while he was still Governor of the State of Arkansas, in the Rotunda of the Arkansas State Capitol, Defendant Clinton touched Paula Jones and said, "Don't we make a beautiful couple—beauty and the beast," (or words to that effect)." (The first set of these "Requests for Admissions" numbered 72 in all.)

➤ A request to turn over "each and every record of any surgery or other medical procedure performed after May 8, 1991, on the genitalia of Defendant Clinton."

➤ A request to turn over "each and every record of any treatment received by Defendant Clinton after May 8, 1991, for a disease or abnormality of the genitalia."

➤ A request to turn over "each and every videotape in which appears Paula Jones."

➤ A request to turn over "each and every document containing a reference to any individual who had, or who has claimed to have had, extramarital sexual relations with Defendant Clinton while he was Attorney General or Governor of the State of Arkansas." (In all, set one contained 60 document requests.)

Would this interfere with your concentration or ability to run the country?

Besides these discovery requests, the Jones lawyers contacted anyone who could corroborate their belief that Clinton was an adulterer. It was a mistake. The issue in the case was not whether Clinton was an adulterer. The issue was: Did he do what Paula Jones alleged, and if so, was she harmed? That is what they needed to prove. Nevertheless, here is what they did with their time:

➤ Obtained the affidavit of Gennifer Flowers.

➤ Obtained the affidavit of Dolly Browning.

➤ Deposed all the state troopers.

➤ Deposed Kathleen E. Willey.

➤ Obtained the affidavit of Julie Hiatt Steele (a friend of Kathleen E. Willey).

➤ Obtained the affidavit of "Jane Doe #5." The Jones legal team alleged this woman was raped by Bill Clinton 20 years ago. In the affidavit, the woman says allegations of unwelcome sexual advances are completely untrue.

Become a Pundit

Discovery is very broad. Parties may learn many unsavory facts about the other in discovery, but that does not mean that such evidence will necessarily be admitted at trial. Only if the evidence is relevant will it be admissible.

In November 1997, Linda Tripp anonymously called lawyers for Paula Jones and told them about Monica Lewinsky's relationship with the President. In the meantime, the President's sworn deposition was scheduled for January. What he didn't know was that Jones's lawyers now knew about Lewinsky and were feverishly preparing to ambush him with questions about the relationship at that deposition.

How Monica Lewinsky Fits In

On Friday, December 5, 1997, (five months before the case was dismissed) attorneys for Paula Jones identified Ms. Lewinsky as a potential witness in the Jones sexual-harassment suit. Ms. Lewinsky would not learn of that for another 12 days. At about

3:00 a.m. on December 17, the President called her and told her she may be called as a witness in the Jones case. He then reminded her of their established story: Lewinsky was coming to the White House to see Clinton's secretary, Betty Currie. In Chapter 19, you'll read what Monica said in her affidavit. Under oath, she denied her relationship with the President. In the meantime, Starr continued his investigation.

The Jones team took Clinton's deposition on January 17, which you'll also read more about in Chapter 19. (You can hardly wait to get there, can you?) Of relevance here is that, although Judge Wright allowed initial discovery and deposition questioning regarding the intern, eventually Judge Wright ruled that discovery related in any way to Monica Lewinsky would be permanently enjoined [stopped] because the judge would not admit that evidence at trial.

Judge Wright ruled that the Lewinsky allegations are "not essential to the core issues in this case. Admitting any evidence of the Lewinsky matter would frustrate the timely resolution of this case and would undoubtedly cause undue expense and delay." Judge Wright determined that a recent, consensual relationship, however improper it might be, could not help Paula Jones prove what she says happened seven years earlier. The Lewinsky information was deemed irrelevant.

In the meantime, Clinton's lawyers thought they could get the case tossed out. To them it was obvious: Jones could not prove her allegations. As attorney Traylor had known in 1994, the case was indeed "weak."

Mumbo Jumbo

When there is a **summary judgment** motion, the judge considers the evidence on both sides and determines whether a reasonable jury could conclude the contrary of the movant's evidence. Since a judge decides law, and a jury decides facts, when no evidence showing that facts are disputed are proffered by the non-movant, no trial is needed. The judge can then decide the case by this type of motion.

Judge Wright Tosses the Case Out

Jones's case was dismissed because Clinton's lawyers filed a successful summary judgment motion. Judge Wright agreed with Clinton's legal arguments.

The first thing Judge Wright did was examine Paula Jones's claim of sexual harassment. Judge Wright explained that there are two categories of sexual-harassment cases—quid pro quo cases and hostile work environment cases. A quid pro quo case is one where the victim is forced to have sex in exchange for a job benefit. That is what quid pro quo means—"this for that." A hostile work environment case is where the pervasive sexual attitudes, comments, and mores in an office make working there impossible. It is too "hostile." Jones was unable to prove either type of case.

To make a prima facie case of quid pro quo sexual harassment, this plaintiff must show, among other things, that her refusal to submit to unwelcome sexual advances or requests for sexual favors resulted in a tangible job detriment.

Jones listed several alleged job detriments in her suit, but to show just how flimsy they were, Judge Wright seized on the most absurd one. Apparently, Jones felt that she was singled out since she was "the only female employee not to be given flowers on Secretary's Day."

Reeking with sarcasm, Judge Wright declared

Mumbo Jumbo

In order to be awarded **damages,** a plaintiff in a lawsuit must be able to prove injury in some way. The injury could be physical, emotional, or economic. The dollar amount a jury awards for those injuries are the "damages."

> *Although it is not clear why plaintiff failed to receive flowers on Secretary's Day in 1992, such an omission does not give rise to a federal cause of action in the absence of evidence of some more tangible change in duties or working conditions that constitute a material employment disadvantage.*

> *The President essentially argues that aside from the alleged incident at the Excelsior Hotel, plaintiff alleges only two other contacts with him, alleges only a few additional contacts with Ferguson, and contains conclusory claims that plaintiff's supervisors were rude. He argues that taken individually or as a whole, these contacts do not in any way constitute the kind of pervasive, intimidating, abusive conduct that courts require to establish a hostile work environment claim. The Court agrees.*

How could there be a hostile work environment, concluded Judge Wright, when

> *Jones admits that she never missed a day of work following the alleged incident in the hotel, she continued to work at AIDC another nineteen months (leaving only because of her husband's job transfer), she continued to go on a daily basis to the Governor's Office to deliver items and never asked to be relieved of that duty, she never filed a formal complaint or told her supervisors of the incident while at AIDC, and she never consulted a psychiatrist, psychologist, or incurred medical bills as a result of the alleged incident.*

> *Considering the totality of the circumstances, it simply cannot be said that the conduct to which plaintiff was allegedly subjected was frequent, severe, or physically threatening.*

Become a Pundit

Once a judge makes an order, the decision carries the weight of the United States government behind it. Failure to follow a judge's order is called contempt of court, and is criminal.

The court then threw out the conspiracy claim as it, too, rested on nothing more than unsubstantiated allegation. It then considered the emotional distress claim:

> *Notwithstanding the offensive nature of the Governor's alleged conduct, plaintiff … acknowledges that her two subsequent contacts with the*

> *Governor involved comments made "in a light vein" and nonsexual contact that was done in a "friendly fashion.*

This claim too was deemed meritless.

> *For the foregoing reasons, the Court finds that the President's and Ferguson's motions for summary judgment should both be and hereby are granted. There being no remaining issues, the Court will enter judgment dismissing this case.*

> *IT IS SO ORDERED this 1st day of April 1998.*

The case was dismissed, but not before it did its damage.

Why Paula Jones Lost

Paula Jones lost because she had no evidence of damage. It had nothing to do with politics. The burden on the plaintiff in a lawsuit is to prove that someone has harmed you in a manner that the law determines is compensable. Not all injuries are compensable. For example:

➤ If someone insults you, you can't sue him. Well, you can, but you'll lose. The law doesn't compensate people for such "injuries."

➤ If you trip and break your ankle through no fault but your own, there is no one to sue.

➤ If someone tells your husband that you are a thief, and you are, no good lawyer would take your case. A person cannot be sued for telling the truth.

➤ If you are in a fender bender causing no damage to your car and you were not hurt, a suit would be pointless. You must be injured to sue someone.

Paula Jones's problem was that, despite her protestations to the contrary, she could not prove any damages resulting from Clinton's alleged behavior. She never went and saw a psychologist, psychiatrist, or any doctor for that matter. How else could she prove she was "emotionally distressed"? She never lost her job, and she failed to proffer evidence that anyone treated her differently.

The Damage Done

Regardless, Paula Jones's lawsuit managed, despite its lack of merit, to inflict a great deal of damage on its target. Before it was dismissed, the case permitted Linda Tripp to declare what she knew about Monica Lewinsky to both Jones's attorneys and Independent Counsel Kenneth Starr. They took it from there.

Furthermore, by forcing President Clinton to answer questions under oath in his deposition (as all deponents must), Jones's attorneys trapped the President. Knowing that he had had an "inappropriate relationship" (to say the least!) with Ms. Lewinsky, Clinton reverted to form and tried to finesse the issue.

Did he commit perjury? You'll learn much more about the definition of perjury—the primary "impeachable" offense of which the President is accused—in Chapter 23. Perjury is more than just lying under oath. For false testimony to be considered perjury, it must be material to the case in question. It is doubtful that Clinton's statements, truthful or not, meet this standard.

Beyond whether the President's testimony can be proven to be perjury, the question is, should a President's personal life ever be open to such scrutiny in a legal proceeding while he is still in office? Is any civil case serious enough? Beyond any risk to a sitting President's political reputation, is this not a risk to the nation as a whole?

The Least You Need to Know

➤ The Jones case took a long time before any serious litigation occurred due to appeals to determine whether a President could even be sued.

➤ The Supreme Court determined that a President would not be distracted by a pending, ongoing lawsuit.

➤ Monica Lewinsky became a key witness in the Jones case and filed an affidavit that falsely denied her sexual contacts with the President.

➤ Judge Wright tossed Paula Jones's case out because Jones could not prove that she was harmed by Clinton's alleged behavior.

Part 3
The Road to Impeachment?

The specter of scandal is no stranger in Washington—Clinton's isn't the first or the worst, and it certainly won't be the last. Before you look at attempts to make charges of wrongdoing stick to the Clintons, take a look back at a few of the most memorable crises in American politics, including the granddaddy of them all—the one that led to the current and controversial independent counsel statute—Watergate.

Then you'll look at the beginnings of Kenneth Starr's investigation, the beginnings of Starr himself, and the real or imagined "right-wing conspiracy." Since Starr began his investigation looking into the failed Whitewater real-estate deal of the Clintons' Arkansas days, we'll start there.

Tough luck, old bean...

Clinton

Jefferson

Chapter 10

Scandals of the Past

In This Chapter

➤ Credit Moblier

➤ The Whiskey Ring scandal

➤ The Teapot Dome scandal of 1922

➤ Abscam

➤ The Iran-Contra affair

Long before Richard Nixon resigned in shame, long before Monica Lewinsky was even born, scandal and corruption have been the norm rather than the exception when it comes to American politics. In fact, some of the most notorious scandals in our history make Watergate pale in comparison—and *greatly* overshadow the alleged crimes in the current scandal. Before we examine Watergate in detail, and then Clinton's predicament, let's look to the distant past for a few other precedents.

Money and Manifest Destiny

Greed and corruption became synonymous with government in the Credit Moblier scandal of 1872. With America expanding its real-estate holdings westward, the plan to link East with West gave a few opportunists the chance to make huge fortunes. To this end, an unaware Congress awarded a railroad construction contract to Credit Moblier of America. Credit Moblier was run by two brothers, one of whom, Oakes Ames, happened to be a Massachusetts congressman who voted on most railroad bills.

Credit Moblier's chief railroad engineer determined that they could lay the track for $30,000 a mile. But with the smell of money in the air, Credit Moblier told Congress it would cost $50,000, and then $60,000 a mile to build the railroad. In the end, Credit

Moblier charged nearly $94 million to build a $54-million railroad. The $44-million difference lined the pockets of the company's shareholders and officers, including Congressman Ames and other high government officials.

Word of these outrageous profits eventually reached Congress and began to raise questions. To quiet his colleagues, Congressman Ames decided to sell his fellow House members shares of stock in Credit Moblier at radically reduced rates. After all, he mused, "There is no difficulty in getting men to look after their own property." Knowing that opportunity was knocking, some congressmen agreed and emptied their wallets for Credit Moblier stock.

Soon the story was leaked and in 1872 the public was let in on the scandal. Immediately, the full Congress initiated an investigation which lead to a censure of Oakes Ames. Also implicated in the scandal were Congressman James A. Garfield, as well as former Vice President and Speaker of the House Schuyler Colfax. Neither man was tried for a crime, and James A. Garfield actually went on to become our nation's 20th President.

The Whiskey-Ring Scandal

After Ulysses S. Grant had been inaugurated for a second term as President, a financial panic struck the country. In an attempt to help restore faith in the economy, the President gave the job of secretary of the treasury to an old crony named Benjamin H. Bristow. Bristow was a go-getter and had the full confidence of Grant. In an aggressive move, Bristow uncovered the so-called "Whiskey Ring" affair.

It turned out that whiskey distillers in Chicago, New York, St. Louis, Peoria, Milwaukee, and elsewhere had been operating without trouble since the Civil War, bribing tax officials to either reduce or eliminate taxes on their product. This untaxed whiskey, sometimes known as "crooked whiskey," defrauded the United States government out of millions of tax dollars.

When President Grant got word of the scandal, he said, "Let no guilty man escape." But Grant spoke too soon. Shortly thereafter, a number of his own friends and family were implicated in the scandal, although the charges against his family seemed trumped up as there was no reliable evidence against them. Nevertheless, the President's son, brother, and his secretary, Orville Babcock, were implicated in the Whiskey-Ring affair.

Unwilling to believe anything bad about anyone close to him, Grant thought his brother, son, and Babcock were all being made scapegoats for the countless others who were truly guilty. His family members escaped charges, but Babcock did not. He was soon formally arrested along with 350 others involved in the Whiskey Ring tax scam.

At his trial, despite overwhelming evidence pointing towards guilt, Babcock was exonerated. His acquittal was, in part, due to the deposition that President Grant submitted on his behalf. But, regardless of his courtroom loyalty, Grant bowed to public pressure and fired Babcock before he had a chance to return to the President's side.

Notwithstanding Babcock's acquittal, Grant's Presidency was forever scarred with the Scarlet Letter: "S" for scandal.

White House Confidential

Actress Judy Garland was President Ulysses S. Grant's first cousin three times removed.

The Teapot-Dome Scandal

Teapot Dome is one the granddaddies in American scandal history. The scandal is one of several reasons that President Warren G. Harding, the 29th President, is consistently rated near the very bottom of the list of U.S. Presidents.

While traveling by boat in Alaska, on what was dubbed the "Voyage of Understanding," President Harding received news that made his heart sink: The secretary of the interior, Albert B. Fall, had secretly leased government-owned oil fields to some of his own personal friends. To make matters worse, the profits from the leases were apparently lining Fall's own pockets.

Albert Fall was a rancher and braggart from New Mexico. He had come to Harding's attention when the two served together in the United States Senate. They became poker-playing pals and, after Harding became President, he offered to make his poker buddy secretary of state. Instead, Fall lobbied to be secretary of the interior and Harding agreed.

In 1921, Fall quietly leased a government-owned oil field, at Elk Hills, California, to a friend of some 30 years. In exchange, his friend "loaned" the secretary of the interior $100,000. The dough was delivered in a little black bag. In 1922, Fall did it again; this time at an oil reserve just north of Casper, Wyoming, named Teapot Dome. In this instance, Fall received $308,000 for the lease as well as a sturdy herd of cattle.

Media Alert

Warren G. Harding had a longtime affair with Nan Britton, a woman 20 years his junior. Harding died in 1923. In 1927 Britton wrote a tell-all book entitled *The President's Daughter*, wherein she alleged that she was the mother of Harding's daughter. The book was a national bestseller that year, although it was sold under the counter at many book stores.

Become a Pundit

After being convicted of taking a bribe in the Teapot Dome scandal, Albert Fall gained the distinction of becoming the first Cabinet officer in American history to go to jail.

Upon hearing the news of Fall's misdeeds, Harding was said to have asked an aid, "What is a man supposed to do when all of his friends betrayed him?"

Fall claimed that the money he received had nothing to do with the granting of oil leases. He even wrote a letter to the Senate investigating committee stating flatly that he had never received a dime from either deal. Later, this was proven to be a bald-faced lie.

Although the Senate investigation began in 1924, Fall was not tried for his misdeeds until 1929. Fall was tried in court, found guilty of taking a bribe, and in 1931, served one year in jail.

Abscam

Abscam, short for Arab-scam, was an FBI sting operation which became public in 1980. The FBI's plan was to use phony Arab "sheiks" dressed in full chic sheik clothing to offer bribes to U.S. congressmen. The plot was reminiscent of a *Saturday Night Live* sketch, but that's where the joke stopped.

In exchange for cash, the legislators were asked to help the "sheik" obtain lucrative real estate deals, gambling licenses or federal grants. Some of the things witnessed were alarming: John Murphy (D-NY) and Raymond Lederer (D-PA) were caught taking $50,000 each. John Jenrette (D-SC) told an undercover FBI agent, "I've got larceny in my blood." Michael "Ozzie" Myers (D-PA) bragged to the FBI, "bulls—t walks and money talks." Richard Kelly (R-FL), after stuffing $25,000 into his suit and pants pocket, asked the undercover agents, "Does it show?"

Become a Pundit

As a consequence of the Abscam sting, Harrison Williams of New Jersey became only the fourth senator in American history to be convicted of a crime while serving in office.

All of this was caught on video. Abscam resulted in 19 congressmen, politicians, and businessmen being sentenced to jail.

The scandal did create one hero though: Senator Larry Pressler, a Republican from South Dakota, refused to take the bait. Pressler told the phony sheiks, "Wait a minute, what you're suggesting may be illegal."

Iran–Contra

If we lined up all past political scandals and pointed to the one that did the most to cripple the Constitution, the Iran-Contra affair may win hands down.

Iran-Contra revealed that a phantom government, operating out of the White House, had embarked on a plan to sell arms to Iran in return for the release of American hostages held in Lebanon, and then to secretly use the profits to fund the Contras of Nicaragua—all of this in violation of laws passed by Congress. This scandal violated America's long-standing policy never to negotiate with terrorists and, more importantly, it violated the Boland Amendment of 1981, which banned U.S. military aid to the Contras.

The scandal was born out of a problem that had bewildered the Carter Administration right up to the very moment of Ronald Reagan's inauguration: Americans were being held hostage in the Middle East. Unlike Carter's situation, where the whereabouts of the hostages were known, the predicament facing President Reagan was decidedly different. The hostages were held captive in the chaotic anarchy of Lebanon by mysterious parties believed to be allied with the Iranian government.

In the summer of 1985, National Security Advisor Robert McFarlane was approached with a plan that could possibly win the release of the American hostages. It involved an Iranian arms merchant who proposed that Iran could use its influence to free the hostages in return for a few hundred U.S. anti-tank missiles. Iran needed the missiles so they could continue fighting their jihad against neighboring Iraq.

President Reagan met with key staffers to discuss the arms-for-hostages deal, including Robert McFarlane, Secretary of State George Shultz, and Defense Secretary Casper Weinberger. Both Shultz and Weinberger remembered Vice President George Bush also being present at the meeting, but to this day, Bush continues to deny it. According to McFarlane, President Reagan signed off on the plan, but no formal record of his approval was ever made.

Nonetheless, a shipment of weapons was sent to Iran and one hostage was freed. Later, a second shipment was sent, but this time the deal went awry and no hostages were freed. By this time one of McFarlane's security council deputies was in charge of the shipments to Iran. The deputy was a Marine lieutenant colonel by the name of Oliver North.

Mumbo Jumbo

Jihad is a Muslim "holy war."

Become a Pundit

The Contras were right-wing guerrillas based in Honduras who opposed the freely elected Sandinista government in Nicaragua. The Reagan Administration and Republicans on the Hill wanted to support the Contras, but the Democrat-controlled Congress voted down resolutions to send them U.S. aid. Diverting profits from the sale of weapons to Iran gave the Administration and the CIA a way around Congress—and the law.

President Ronald Reagan and Vice President George Bush.
UWE Walz/Corbis

While the Reagan administration played "Let's Make a Deal" with Tehran, the President was involved in a power struggle with Congress over an unrelated foreign-policy issue. Reagan believed that the Contra rebels in Nicaragua deserved of America's aid. The Democratic Congress however, disagreed, and passed an amendment to cut off all U.S funds to them.

By overruling him, Congress put Reagan in a quandary. How to fund the Contras while still obeying the law? At some point, someone in the Administration came up with what they deemed a solution. They could make an end run around Congress by using the profits from the arms sales to Iran to fund their secret war in Nicaragua. Everyone would be happy. Reagan would achieve his goal of keeping the Contras funded, the hostages held captive in Lebanon could be freed, and Iran would continue to get missiles to use against Iraq. Hence the name, Iran-Contra.

No one in the Reagan Administration seemed to mind the fact that the plan meant negotiating with terrorists despite our official policy not to, and was a clear violation of the Boland amendment.

The job of funding the Contras was given to the same man who was in charge of the arms sales in Lebanon—Oliver North.

North and McFarlane went to Tehran to try and create some good will with the Ayatollah Khomeini. Shortly after McFarlane delivered a birthday cake to the Ayatollah, Reagan's roof fell in when an obscure Middle Eastern magazine broke the scandal. For Reagan, the best laid plans of mice and men had gone terribly awry.

Reagan denied everything. On November 12, 1986, he declared, "We did not—repeat—did not trade weapons or anything else for hostages—nor will we." Six days later, however, he relented and begrudgingly confessed that a secret project did exist involving a third country. On February 11, 1987, he contradicted himself again and said he had not approved of any arms for hostages deal. Nine days later, as the heat on the President intensified, Ronald Reagan declared, "I don't remember—Period!"

Become a Pundit

Two entrepreneurs lost a bundle of money when they began manufacturing Oliver North dolls. Their hope was to sell 450,000 dolls for $19.95 each, but they only managed to sell 230.

White House Confidential

On March 30, 1981, President Ronald Reagan survived an assassination attempt. The assailant, John W. Hinkley, Jr., was hoping to impress actress Jodie Foster by killing Reagan.

One immediate outcome of the scandal was the formation of a Presidential commission headed by Senator John Tower. The "Tower Report" was a stinging indictment of President Reagan. Congressional hearings followed.

Although Oliver North was convicted of a number of the Iran-Contra charges, he never served any time. North was tried on 12 charges, including obstruction of Congress and illegal destruction of government documents, and found not guilty of nine charges and guilty of three. He was given a three-year suspended sentence, a $150,000 fine, placed on probation for two years, and barred from ever holding federal office. His entire conviction was overturned on appeal.

Media Alert

Oliver North is now a radio talk-show host in Virginia. He ran for the Senate, but lost, in the early '90s.

Oliver North.
AP/Wide World Photos

Democrat Daniel K. Inouye from Hawaii was the Senate chairman to the Iran-Contra hearings. In his closing statement, he said, "The story has now been told. Speaking for myself, I see it as a chilling story." He went on to characterize Iran-Contra as "a story of deceit and duplicity and the arrogant disregard of the rule of law."

Iran-Contra was a far more serious breach of the law and Constitution than the current sex scandal now playing in Washington. It involved clear violations of Congressional intent, secret government agents operating outside the law, and trading arms for hostages. Nevertheless, few people were ever as remotely interested in that story as they are in today's headlines. Iran-Contra, like Whitewater, was confusing and boring. Monica is exciting and tawdry. Apparently, more Americans can relate to that.

The Least You Need to Know

➤ Scandals have been part of American politics for over 200 years.

➤ Many of the scandals have dealt with politicians who were trying to line their own pockets by using their power.

➤ Scandals often revolve around underlings more than Presidents.

➤ Iran-Contra was a blatant attempt to avoid a law passed by Congress.

Nixon

Chapter 11

Watergate and Its Aftermath

In This Chapter

➤ A bungled burglary

➤ A cover-up

➤ Secret tapes

➤ Secret allies

➤ Watergate changed everything

The most famous scandal in American political history began on a Saturday morning on June 17, 1972. A security guard at Washington's Watergate Hotel and apartment complex found a stairwell door lock had been taped in the open position. He called the police and three officers responded.

Five intruders were caught inside the headquarters of the Democratic National Committee. The burglars were there to monitor bugging equipment they had installed during a previous May break-in.

The investigation of the break-in led directly back to the reelection campaign of President Richard M. Nixon. As the story emerged, it turned out that the scandal that came to be known as Watergate was far more than the "third-rate burglary" it had been derisively dismissed as by Nixon supporters. Watergate came to include political spying, sabotage, bribery, and the illegal use of campaign funds. The disclosure of these activities, and the Administration's cover-up of them, resulted in Richard M. Nixon being the first President to resign under pressure of impeachment.

Deep Background

The *Washington Post* would become the paper of record in this amazing case. Its story that day began like this:

Become a Pundit

The break-in at the Watergate Hotel occurred right before the 1972 election. It had little effect on the outcome. Richard Nixon was re-elected with one of the largest landslides in American history—he won 49 of 50 states.

Media Alert

Daniel Ellsberg was a pro-war staffer in the Defense Department when he was asked to help prepare a secret, detailed account of the U.S. involvement in the Vietnam War. Writing the "Pentagon Papers" turned Ellsberg into an anti-war crusader. In 1971 he leaked the report to *The New York Times,* which published it in full. Nixon's henchmen were so infuriated that one of the first jobs for the plumbers unit was to break into the office of Ellsberg's psychiatrist to get dirt on Ellsberg.

5 Held in Plot to Bug Democrats' Office Here

Five men, one of whom said he is a former employee of the Central Intelligence Agency, were arrested at 2:30 a.m. yesterday in what authorities described as an elaborate plot to bug the offices of the Democratic National Committee here. Three of the men were native-born Cubans and another was said to have trained Cuban exiles for guerrilla activity after the 1961 Bay of Pigs invasion. They were surprised at gunpoint by three plain-clothes officers of the metropolitan police department in a sixth floor office at the plush Watergate, 2600 Virginia Ave., NW, where the Democratic National Committee occupies the entire floor.

There was no immediate explanation as to why the five suspects would want to bug the Democratic National Committee offices or whether or not they were working for any other individuals or organizations."

The *Post* reported that a GOP security aide was among the Watergate burglars. At the time, Attorney General John Mitchell, who was also head of the Nixon reelection campaign, denied any link to the operation. The Campaign to Re-elect the President was known by the acronym "CREEP" and things began to look suspicious when a $25,000 cashier's check, earmarked for CREEP, wound up in the bank account of one of the Watergate burglars. The burglars were also known as "plumbers," so called because their job was to stop information leaks. It turned out that two of the plumbers worked for CREEP. It was creepy.

Bob Woodward and Carl Bernstein were the two *Post* reporters who began to investigate the connection between the burglary and the President's re-election efforts. Woodward had a mysterious inside source who was known only by the pseudonym "Deep Throat." Meeting with Woodward late at night in parking garages and hidden passageways, Deep Throat would give

Woodward and Bernstein leads, they would confirm the lead with other sources, and more damaging revelations would appear in the paper.

According to Woodward:

> *The source known as Deep Throat (a name given to the source by the managing editor of The Washington Post) provided a kind of road map through the scandal. His one consistent message was that the Watergate burglary was just the tip of the iceberg, part of a scheme and a series of illegal activities that amounted to a subversion of government. The interlocking nature of the crimes gave it weight and provided the context, and in fact one of the incentives for us to continue our investigations.*

Woodward and Bernstein reported that John Mitchell, while serving as attorney general, controlled a secret Republican "slush-fund" used to finance widespread intelligence-gathering operations against the Democrats. Soon, the FBI began investigating the matter.

Nixon then turned what probably could have been contained as a small problem into a major scandal. He ordered his aide, H.R. "Bob" Haldeman to order the CIA to halt the FBI's investigation into the matter. This was a blatant abuse of power and attempt to use the government for personal gain. Then, the President and his men created a cover story, attempting to distance themselves from the break-in. The "cover-up" was in full swing.

Mumbo Jumbo

A **slush fund** is an informal name given to an account whose funds cannot easily be traced back to their original source.

President Richard M. Nixon.
AP/Wide World Photos

Media Alert

Watergate burglar G. Gordon Liddy refused to cooperate with authorities and was given the longest sentence of the five burglars. He served 52 months in jail. Liddy is now a conservative radio talk-show host in Washington, D.C.

The matter got even more complicated when, in March 1973, burglar James McCord admitted that he had previously lied under oath at the urging of John Dean (counsel to the President) and John Mitchell (attorney general).

The Waters Rise

As FBI agents established that the Watergate break-in stemmed from a widespread campaign of political spying and sabotage conducted on behalf of the Nixon reelection effort, the public began to turn on the President. Allegations of a cover-up and obstruction of justice by the highest law officers in the land made Watergate a national crisis. In February, the Senate voted (77-0) to establish a Select Committee on Presidential Campaign Activities, chaired by Senator Sam Ervin.

Things began to move rapidly. Nixon's top White House staffers, H.R. Haldeman and John Ehrlichman, and Attorney General Richard Kleindienst resigned over the scandal. White House counsel John Dean was fired.

Dean then turned-coats, and began to work with the Watergate investigators. As the entire public watched, Dean admitted that he had discussed the Watergate cover-up with President Nixon at least 35 times. They learned that the President had used the FBI to create an "Enemies List" and that he planned to use the IRS against these enemies. They learned that prominent businessmen were threatened with IRS audits if they did not contribute to CREEP.

Archibald Cox was then appointed as a special Watergate prosecutor. As the Senate hearings continued that summer, Nixon aide Alexander Butterfield dropped the biggest bombshell to date: Nixon had secretly been taping every conversation he had had in the Oval Office.

The existence of the Oval Office tapes began a protracted legal battle between the President and Congress. Nixon claimed "executive privilege" for the tapes and argued that he should not have to hand them over. Special Prosecutor Cox and the Senate Watergate committee requested that the Supreme Court instruct Nixon to surrender the tapes. In the meantime, Nixon offered only selected transcripts of the tapes, containing the soon-to-be-famous line "expletive deleted."

In October 1973, Vice President Spiro Agnew resigned due to charges of bribery and tax evasion. Gerald Ford, Republican minority leader in the House, became Vice President. At the same time, Nixon refused to turn over the Presidential tape recordings to the Senate Watergate committee or the special prosecutor.

October was significant for other reasons. Nixon ordered Attorney General Richardson to dismiss Special Prosecutor Cox. He refused and resigned. His deputy was fired for also refusing, and finally, Solicitor General Robert Bork sacked Special Prosecutor Cox. This came to be known as the "Saturday Night Massacre."

Finally, under immense pressure, Nixon released some of the tapes. One tape was found to have a $18^1/_2$ minute gap. Nixon's secretary, Rose Mary Woods, admitted erasing the tape but claimed she did it accidentally.

In November, during a press conference, Nixon told the nation, "I'm not a crook." By early 1974, the calls for Nixon to resign began. In July 1974, by a vote of 8-0, the Supreme Court ordered Nixon to release more tapes. Also in July, the House Judiciary Committee voted to recommend that Nixon be impeached on three charges, including obstruction of justice. (Ironically, Hillary Clinton served as a staffer on that committee.)

In August, under court order, Nixon released three more tapes that showed he ordered the cover-up of the Watergate burglary six days after the break-in. The tapes also showed that Nixon knew of the involvement of White House officials and CREEP in the Watergate affair. It also showed that Nixon had tried to use the CIA to block the FBI's investigation into the matter.

One of the tapes had Nixon clearly attempting to cover-up the break-in (or "plan" as he called it). "I don't give a [expletive deleted] what happens," Nixon is heard saying. "I want you to stonewall it. Let them plead the Fifth Amendment, cover up, or anything else if it will save the plan."

Finally, the House Judiciary Committee had its "smoking gun." The Republicans on the Judiciary Committee who previously voted against impeachment announced that they were going to change their votes. It was clear by this point that Nixon would be impeached, and convicted in the Senate.

Become a Pundit

Robert Bork later went on to serve on the Court of Appeals. He was nominated by President Reagan to be on the Supreme Court, but was lambasted by Democrats in the Senate. He was never confirmed. His ordeal spurred a colloquialism: When your name is trashed at a confirmation hearing in nation's capital now, it is called being "Borked."

Mumbo Jumbo

The Fifth Amendment of the Bill of Rights in the Constitution gives all citizens the right not to testify against themselves if they don't want to. **Pleading the Fifth** means you are using your right against self-incrimination. Juries are told that no inference, either positively or negatively, should be drawn when a person invokes this right.

On August 9, 1974, Nixon resigned. He is the first President ever to do so. Gerald Ford became the 38th President and he nominated Nelson Rockefeller to be his as Vice President. They became the nation's first unelected executive officers. On September 8, 1974, Ford granted Nixon a "full, free and absolute pardon."

All the President's Men

Watergate was far more than a bungled burglary. It showed abuse of power, a cover-up, and corruption at the very highest levels of our government. The President and his men were willing to use government agencies to hound their opponents, block investigations, deceive the public, and intimidate enemies.

The tally is staggering:

➤ One Presidential resignation.

➤ One Vice Presidential resignation.

➤ 40 government officials indicted or jailed.

➤ H.R. Haldeman (chief White House aide) resigned and was subsequently jailed.

➤ John Erlichman (chief White House aide) resigned and was subsequently jailed.

➤ John Dean, former White House counsel, was charged with obstruction of justice and spent four months in prison for his role in the Watergate cover-up.

➤ John Mitchell, attorney-general and chairman of the Committee to Re-elect the President, was jailed.

➤ Howard Hunt and G. Gordon Liddy, ex-White House staffers who planned the Watergate break-in, were both jailed.

➤ Charles Colson, special counsel to the President, was jailed.

➤ James McCord, security director of CREEP, was jailed.

In all, three top aides, two Cabinet officers, and 26 other members of the Nixon Administration were tried and sent to prison.

Who Was Deep Throat?

The identity of Bob Woodward's source during the Watergate investigation remains one of the best-kept secret in American politics and journalism. Only four people know his actual name—Woodward, Bernstein, the former executive editor of *The Washington Post*, Ben Bradlee, and of course, Deep Throat himself.

In *All the President's Men*, their 1974 book about the Watergate scandal, Woodward and Bernstein gave us some hints as to Deep Throat's identity. The person held an extremely sensitive position in the executive branch. He could be "contacted only on very important occasions." The source encouraged Woodward and Bernstein to "follow the money." He had access to information from the White House, Justice, the FBI, and CREEP.

A few more pieces of the puzzle have emerged over the years. Deep Throat is one person, not a composite of several. He is male and is still living. He was a smoker and drank Scotch. "Aware of his own weaknesses, he readily conceded his flaws," the reporters once wrote. "He was an incurable gossip, careful to label rumor for what it was, but fascinated by it.... He could be rowdy, drink too much, overreach. He was not good at concealing his feelings, hardly ideal for a man in his position." It's not much to go on.

Woodward has kept his promise to protect his source's privacy because Deep Throat wishes to remain anonymous.

The most-cited suspects include Nixon administration members Henry Kissinger and Alexander Haig, CIA officials Cord Meyer and William E. Colby, and FBI officials L. Patrick Gray, W. Mark Felt, Charles W. Bates, and Robert Kunkel.

Media Alert

All The President's Men was made into a movie starring Robert Redford and Dustin Hoffman as Woodward and Bernstein. The movie was nominated for an Oscar as Best Picture in 1976 but lost to ... *Rocky*.

Aftermath

Watergate changed everything. First of all, politics is far different today than before Watergate. Much of the intense partisanship that is so prevalent in the nation's capital today can be traced back to the aftermath of the 1972 break-in. Some Republican loyalists still hold resentments over Nixon's resignation.

Not only did Watergate change the way politics is played informally, but it changed the way it was played legally as well. The greatest changes ever made in our nation's campaign laws resulted from the Watergate affair.

➤ **Ethics rules**   The House and Senate adopted codes of conduct in 1977 that limited the privileges that allow members to send mail to constituents at taxpayers' expense. It imposed restrictions on outside income, including honoraria for speeches to interest groups. These rules also imposed limits on lobbying by former members of Congress and former Capitol Hill staff members.

➤ **Financial disclosure forms**   The congressional ethics rules passed in 1978 required senators, representatives and some close relatives to file annual reports detailing income and investments. The law requires congressional candidates and high-level officials in the executive and judiciary branches to disclose personal finances.

➤ **Special prosecutors**   The special prosecutor law that created Ken Starr came from the Nixon-ordered firing of Watergate prosecutor Archibald Cox.

➤ **Limits on political contributions**   The 1974 campaign finance law limited individual contributions to candidates for federal office to $1,000 for each primary, election and runoff. Contributions from political action committees (PACs) were limited to $5,000.

➤ **Donor and campaign expenditure reports**   Candidates and political parties who spend money in elections are now required to file periodic campaign finance reports with the Federal Election Commission. Campaigns must list expenditures and any contributor who gave $100 or more, including the donor's address, occupation and place of business.

➤ **Taxpayer campaign funding**   Public financing for Presidential campaigns was created. Presidential candidates began receiving federal funds for their campaigns under a system created in 1974. Third-party and independent candidates could collect taxpayer dollars if they received more than 5 percent of the vote in the general election. Money for all the candidates comes from a voluntary check-off on federal tax forms, but low public participation means the fund sometimes runs low.

Candidates complain the spending ceilings, which are based on each state's voting-age populations, are too low, especially in small but important states such as Iowa and New Hampshire. Third-party and independent candidates complain the system unfairly favors the two major parties. In 1996, the major party nominees each received $62 million from federal taxpayers, while third-party candidate Ross Perot received half that, based on his showing in the 1992 race.

➤ **Campaign spending limits**   The 1974 election law attempted to restrict independent expenditures on behalf of candidates to $1,000. The law also tried to limit the amounts individuals could spend on their own campaigns—$25,000 in House races, $35,000 in Senate races and $50,000 in Presidential contests. The Supreme Court overturned most of these limits in a 1976 decision, *Buckley v. Valeo.*

Besides politics, journalism too was revolutionized by Watergate. Investigative reporters are part of every local newscast in the country now because Woodward and Bernstein became stars. After Watergate, every young journalistic pup on the block wanted to expose a political scandal—and was more certain than ever that if they looked for one, they'd find one.

Furthermore, the media is now far more aggressive and daring, and much less respectful of privacy than before the Nixon debacle. Today's "gotcha" journalism is a direct result of Watergate.

Finally, we are different as a nation because of the scandal. Our standards have been lowered. Our expectations of politicians are far lower. We are much more cynical. Maybe most distressing is that we seem to have become immune to hearing about the private goings-on of public figures. Privacy is becoming a thing of the past. No-one would have tolerated the invasion of privacy and pornography contained in the Starr Report even a generation ago. The Watergate tape transcripts did not have the profane language deleted for nothing. Today, such a bow to civility would be taken as a cover-up.

We have also become numb to scandal at this point. Iran-Contra, while clearly an affront to the Constitution, barely registered on the nation's consciousness. From Billygate and Abscam (Carter Administration) to Whitewater and Travelgate, we have become jaded and tired of alleged corruption. Now, nothing less than a good sex scandal can get our blood boiling.

And let's not forget that all political scandals now have to end with "-gate."

How Does the Watergate Scandal Compare to Today's?

Watergate and the Monica Lewinsky mess are quite different. Watergate was about the abuse of power and the misuse of public institutions for private gain. Siccing the FBI and the IRS on one's enemies is a blatant abuse of public trust.

Starr's charges are different. There are no allegations here of misuse of public trust. The matters that Starr had been investigating prior to the issuance of his report on the President's affair with the intern would have been similar to Watergate. Travelgate and Filegate in particular seemed to revolve around the abuse and misuse of public trust. But Starr has issued no report on those matters.

As disheartening as it may be for some people to digest, the Starr report essentially boils down to allegations of perjury in a deposition in a highly partisan private case that was dismissed for lack of merit. That is just not the same as having 40 members of your Administration indicted or jailed for criminal activity.

The Least You Need to Know

➤ A simple break-in of the Democratic headquarters began a series of events that would topple a President.

➤ Nixon tried to cover-up the role of his White House and reelection effort.

➤ Nixon's secret tapes proved to be his undoing.

➤ We still don't know who Deep Throat was.

➤ Watergate and the Lewinsky scandal are fundamentally different.

Chapter 12

The Independent Counsel

In This Chapter

➤ The history of the independent counsel statute

➤ What the statute says

➤ How the statute really works

➤ Secrets of an independent counsel

➤ Independent counsel investigations since 1978

The framers had a great plan—there would be three branches of government, each of which would counter-balance the other. They say "if it ain't broke, don't fix it," and for 200 years, no one thought our government was broken. That is, until Watergate.

Watergate convinced lawmakers that a new office was needed to investigate the executive branch, and the special prosecutor (later called the independent counsel) was born. For the first time in the history of the country, a new position was created especially for the purpose of "checking" the executive branch, even though the original blueprint had Congress and the courts performing that duty. Was this a wise move? Look at the seven-year Iran-Contra investigation, and the Starr investigation, and decide for yourself.

The Office of the Independent Counsel is under much scrutiny today. In fact, there's a good chance that when the current independent counsel statute expires in 1999, it will not be renewed. And if it is renewed, you can rest assured that it will be far different than what we have today.

The reason is Kenneth Starr. Republicans on Capitol Hill have been dissatisfied with the statute since Lawrence Walsh concluded his seven-year investigation into the Reagan Administration. Now many Democrats believe—perhaps rightly so—that Starr's four-year, $40-million investigation has been too broad, too long, and too political. Starr's investigation has now made both sides of the aisle equally unhappy with the statute.

This was not how a well-intentioned law was meant to turn out.

The History of the Independent Counsel Statute

The position now known as an independent counsel used to be called a "special prosecutor." Presidents have long had the authority to appoint special prosecutors to root out high-level official corruption. Prior to the enactment of the current law, special prosecutors were appointed by the executive branch, normally by the attorney general, and often upon the recommendation of the President.

Special prosecutors have investigated such cases as the 1920s Teapot Dome scandal and the tax scandals of the early 1950s. But the investigations into the Watergate break-in and the Nixon Administration convinced legislators and the public of the need for someone *independent* of the executive branch to be able to investigate the executive branch. (You read about the specifics of Watergate in Chapter 11.)

Become a Pundit

Richard Nixon is the first, and only, President to ever resign.

Mumbo Jumbo

The **attorney general** is the highest-ranking law-enforcement person in the country. Appointed by the President, the attorney general is charged with enforcing federal laws.

Watergate Sets the Stage

As the *Washington Post* investigation of the 1972 break-in of the Democratic National Committee's Watergate offices began to reveal a deeper level of corruption, many in Congress pushed for the Administration to appoint a special prosecutor—to investigate itself. After President Nixon's top aides and attorney general either resigned or were dismissed due to allegations of corruption and cover-up, Nixon suggested he might allow the new attorney general to name a special prosecutor to investigate the scandal. Newly appointed Attorney General Elliot Richardson responded by naming Harvard University law professor Archibald Cox to the position, and then publicly guaranteed that the Justice Department would not interfere in the case.

This promise was put to the test in October 1973, after Cox had pressed hard for full release of the President's secret Oval Office tapes. During the so-called "Saturday Night Massacre," the President, feeling the heat of Cox's investigation, ordered Attorney General Richardson to fire Special Prosecutor Cox. Richardson refused and resigned in protest. Nixon then demanded that Deputy Attorney General William Ruckelshaus fire Cox. He, too, refused and resigned.

Finally, the next in command, Solicitor General Robert Bork (later to be nominated to the Supreme Court by Ronald Reagan), removed Cox on October 20. The public outcry convinced Congress to initiate impeachment proceedings and begin searching for ways to appoint a new prosecutor with greater independence.

By the time Nixon resigned on August 9, 1974, Archibald Cox and his successor Leon Jaworski had created a new space in the public mind for the special prosecutor's role in investigating official corruption. Clearly, if the President had the power to force the termination of his investigator, that investigator would have little success uncovering wrongdoing among the President or his executive staff. Many in Washington began to push for an institution that would ensure a prosecutor's independence in the future.

A Law Is Born

In 1978, President Jimmy Carter signed a group of reforms collectively known as the Ethics in Government Act. The Act aimed to clean up American politics by creating a new ethics watchdog organization and by instituting new controls on the executive branch. These controls included:

➤ All high-ranking members of the executive branch must make yearly financial statements public.

➤ Lobbying restrictions.

➤ Creation of a new position—an independent special prosecutor.

Originally passed in 1978, the law is up for review every few years, as part of the budget process. It has been periodically amended as part of that process, and even lapsed in 1991 when it was not funded. Revived in 1992, the current law is set to expire in 1999.

What the Statute Says

The law requires that the attorney general recommend the appointment of a special prosecutor whenever he or she receives specific charges of misconduct on the part of a wide range of executive-branch officials, unless the charges are so unsubstantiated as to not warrant further investigation. This is a very easy standard to meet. Today, instead of the attorney general appointing the prosecutor as in years past, the independent counsel is appointed and overseen by a three-judge

Become a Pundit

There are nine United States Courts of Appeals, each for a different area of the country.

panel, based at the U.S. Court of Appeals in the District of Columbia, based upon a recommendation by the attorney general.

Entitled 28 USC (United States Code) section 49, subsections 591-98, the independent counsel law has many interesting aspects. The first thing it does is require an initial investigation by the attorney general.

> *The Attorney General shall conduct a preliminary investigation in accordance with section 592 whenever the Attorney General receives information sufficient to constitute grounds to investigate whether any [member of the executive branch] may have violated any Federal criminal law.*

The law gives the attorney general guidelines to consider in her initial investigation. She has 30 days to consider only the basis of the information received. At first, the "Attorney General shall consider only the specificity of the information received, and the credibility of the source of the information...."

Once the attorney general concludes that the information is "specific and credible" then "the Attorney General shall, at the end of that 30-day period, commence a preliminary investigation with respect to the substance of information received." This begins a 60-day review process. If the attorney general determines that the information is basically meritless, the matter will be dropped. If not—if the attorney general has "reasonable grounds to believe that further investigation is warranted"—the law requires the attorney general to "apply to the division of the court for the appointment of an Independent Counsel." The three judges then appoint an independent counsel.

One of the obvious flaws in the law is that it contains no provision for limiting the scope of inquiry. Everything is fair game—from allegations of wrongdoing many years ago to present accusations of possible misconduct.

What if Congress disagrees with a decision not to investigate further? The law provides that members of Congress may request in writing that the attorney general apply for the appointment of an independent counsel.

Become a Pundit

The very first special prosecutor was appointed to look into allegations that Jimmy Carter's chief of staff, Hamilton Jordan, used cocaine at Studio 54. The charges proved false and no indictments were ever issued.

Powers of the Prosecutor

Much has been made of Independent Counsel Starr's broad authority. Initially, however, the independent counsel is authorized to investigate only "the subject matter with respect to which the attorney general has requested the appointment of the independent counsel, and all matters related to that subject matter."

Each time the Clinton Administration has allegedly broken the law, Starr has gone back to Attorney General Janet Reno to expand the scope of his authority. He could only have done so after presenting her with "specific and credible" evidence of wrongdoing. The statute says: "Upon the request of the Attorney General, [the judges] may expand the prosecutorial jurisdiction of an Independent Counsel." This is not a difficult standard to meet. An accusation coupled with a few specifics is all that is currently required to expand an inquiry.

All of this commotion has been caused by section 595 of the law. It states that

> *[an] Independent Counsel shall advise the House of Representatives of any substantial and credible information which such Independent Counsel receives, in carrying out the Independent Counsel's responsibilities under this chapter, that may constitute grounds for an impeachment.*

The independent counsel's work is done when "the independent counsel notifies the attorney general that the investigation of all matters within the prosecutorial jurisdiction of such independent counsel have been completed." (Or when the independent counsel decides to teach law beside the Pacific Ocean at Pepperdine University. See Chapter 14.)

Become a Pundit

One of Ken Starr's so-called "Whitewater convictions" relates to a gentleman who was, at best, tangentially involved in the Whitewater development. When Starr investigated his records, he found a mistake on the man's (completely unrelated) previous bankruptcy filing. Starr charged and convicted the man for bankruptcy fraud.

How the Statute Works in Reality

The law sounds great. The attorney general conducts two separate investigations, one to see if the evidence is specific and credible, and another into whether the allegations themselves are significant.
If so, an independent panel of judges appoints an independent investigator. Everything's hunky-dory, right? Wrong.

A lawyer arrives at his or her new independent counsel office with orders to investigate a specific charge. But since the law covers powerful figures who inevitably have made enemies, the probe quickly turns political. Old rumors surface, old charges appear anew. The independent counsel
must then expand the scope of his work. And,
once substantive criminal accusations disintegrate, independent counsels then turn their attentions to technical violations. Get that aide who forgot to fill out that form correctly! In the end, innocent people spend hundreds of thousands of dollars to clear their names, knowing they can never really do so.

But the independent counsels themselves are not all to blame. The law requires the courts to appoint hired guns at the slightest hint of suspicion. If the attorney general receives specific information from credible sources about a "potential violation, or allegation of a violation, of criminal law" and concludes "there are reasonable grounds to believe that further investigation is warranted," then he or she is *required by law* to ask for an independent counsel.

Should an attorney general choose not to investigate, she can be hauled into a Congressional Committee and potentially grilled on national television, have investigation records subpoenaed by Congress, and more. We saw this in Janet Reno's refusals to appoint independent counsels in cases such as Gore's fundraising, and the Waco, Texas, assault. A vague suspicion, backed up by a tad of circumstantial evidence, is sufficient to begin an investigation that, once underway, may have no limits.

This is not to say that all independent counsel investigations exponentially explode as Starr's seemed to. Most are confined to the original area of inquest. The problem is, the way the law is currently written, expanding a probe is too darn easy.

The Ghosts of Prosecutors Past

There have been 20 investigations arising from this law since 1978 (see the following table).

The Special Prosecutors' Top Twenty

Target	Charge	Indictment?
Hamilton Jordan Carter chief of staff	Drug use	No
Timothy Kraft Carter campaign mgr.	Drug use	No
Raymond Donovan, Reagan sec. of labor	Connections to organized crime	No
Edwin Meese, Reagan attorney general	Financial impropriety	No
Theodore Olson Reagan counsel	Obstruction of investigation	No
Michael Deaver, et al Reagan Admin.	Conflict of interest	Yes
Oliver North, Caspar Weinberger et al Reagan Admin.	Iran-Contra	Yes
Lawrence Wallace Reagan asst. attorney general	Tax	No
Lyn Nofziger, Ed Meese Reagan Admin.	Lobbying violations	Yes
Samuel Pierce Reagan HUD sec.	Fraud	Yes
Under Seal	Under seal	No
Under Seal	Under seal	No

Target	Charge	Indictment?
Bush Admin. officials	Clinton passport file search	No
Bill Clinton et al	Whitewater	Yes
Mike Espy Clinton sec. of ag.	Gratuity violations	Yes
Henry Cisneros Clinton sec. Of HUD	False statements	Yes
Ron Brown Clinton sec. of commerce	Financial	No
Eli Segal Clinton Americorps chief	Conflict of interest	No
Bruce Babbitt Clinton sec. of interior	False statements	No
Alexis Herman Clinton sec. of labor	Influence Peddling	Pending

Only one-third of these investigations have ended with criminal convictions; the rest ended with the individual's reputation at least tarnished, his career in government perhaps over, and, in many cases, his legal fees perilously high.

The cost of becoming a target of one of these investigations is often extraordinarily high, financially and emotionally. Financially, the prosecutor has an almost unlimited budget, whereas most targets do not. If they fight, the targets spend hundreds of thousands of dollars. If they can't afford to fight, they face the cost of a tarnished reputation. And remember, only about a third of the time has an independent-counsel investigation even led to an indictment, let alone a conviction. Nevertheless, defending oneself is extraordinarily time consuming, draining, and frightening, and the effect on a career can be devastating.

Yet, what are our options? Certainly there are plenty of illegal activities going on in government that necessitate investigation. There must be a way to accomplish that goal without inflicting such harm on the innocent. (See Chapter 25 for a discussion on the future of this law.)

Upon Further Review...

The original special prosecutor law was set to expire in October 1983. By the summer of 1981, Congress began reviewing the law for its effectiveness. Several reforms were incorporated into the statute during the reauthorization process:

➤ The 1983 law reduced the overall number of individuals covered by the special prosecutor provisions.

➤ The law was tightened, and the attorney general was given more responsibility in calling for a special prosecutor.

➤ The title "special prosecutor" was dropped in favor of the seemingly less prejudicial "independent counsel."

Already, the law was under attack for its alleged unconstitutionality. Nowhere in the Constitution did the framers foresee the possibility of a free-wheeling prosecutor looking over the shoulder of the executive branch. Nevertheless, Reagan signed the reauthorization bill.

In 1987, with the Iran-Contra investigation underway, the statute again came up for reauthorization. (You read about Iran-Contra in Chapter 10.) Congress introduced several provisions placing new limits on the attorney general's discretion and powers under the law. In December 1987, President Reagan again reluctantly signed the law. He noted however, the continuing Justice Department opposition to the law on constitutional grounds.

Sound Bites

I told the American people that I did not trade arms for hostages. My heart and my best intentions tell me that's true. But the facts and the evidence tell me it is not.

—Ronald Reagan, on March 4, 1987, after initially denying that his Administration traded arms for hostages

In 1988, the Supreme Court heard the long-awaited challenge to the law's constitutionality. The opponents of the law argued that it was unconstitutional as it infringed upon the powers of the executive branch. The argument was two-fold. First, it was alleged that by passing the law, Congress was attempting to increase its own powers at the expense of the executive branch. Given that our three branches of government are considered equal, this would have been impermissible. Second, it was argued that the office of the independent prosecutor interfered with the ability of the executive branch to conduct business.

The court rejected both arguments. In its ruling, the Supreme Court upheld the law, finding that Congress did not seek to increase its own powers by passing the law, and held that it did not interfere "unduly" or "impermissibly" with the executive branch's powers.

Building a Better Bill-Trap

In December of 1992, the independent counsel law expired as a result of a Republican filibuster. Soon however, Congressional critics of the new Clinton Administration began to suggest that a revived independent counsel law might be a pretty good idea. Republicans hoped to invoke the law in the newly emerging Whitewater case.

Vowing to head up an Administration with the highest ethical standards, President Bill Clinton signed the reauthorization bill soon after he was inaugurated, and called the law "a foundation stone for the trust between the government and our citizens." In an ironic twist, he dismissed charges that it had been a "tool of partisan attack ... and a waste of taxpayer funds."

By 1998, seven separate investigations of the Clinton Administration were underway:

➤ Robert Fiske was appointed to investigate the Whitewater affair and the suicide of Vince Foster. Kenneth Starr was then appointed to replace Fiske.

➤ Donald Smaltz, who was charged with looking into Mike Espy's alleged acceptance of gratuities while secretary of agriculture. Espy was indicted as a result.

➤ David Barrett was charged with investigating charges that Housing and Urban Development Secretary Henry Cisneros had lied to government investigators. Cisneros was indicted.

➤ Daniel S. Pearson began examining Commerce Secretary Ron Brown's financial dealings. Brown died in a plane crash before the investigation was completed.

➤ Curtis Von Kann declined to prosecute Americorps chief Eli Segal of conflict of interest charges.

➤ Carol Elder Bruce was appointed to investigate allegations that Interior Secretary Bruce Babbitt made false statements to Congress. No indictment.

➤ Finally, on May 11, 1998, Attorney General Reno called for the appointment of an independent counsel to look into charges of influence peddling and campaign finance improprieties concerning Labor Secretary Alexis Herman.

Attorney General Janet Reno.
Agence France Presse/
Corbis-Bettmann

Republicans have been after Attorney General Reno to request another independent counsel be appointed to investigate alleged campaign fund-raising violations by Clinton and Gore in 1996. To date, she has refused.

Tactics of an Independent Counsel

Like all prosecutors, an independent counsel can call on a number of tactics to win indictments and cooperation.

➤ **"Squeezing and flipping"** This is the prosecutor's classic method of targeting underlings and insiders and securing their cooperation. Little fish are often traded for big fish. Monica Lewinsky is a little fish.

➤ **"Driving a wedge"** Similar to the squeeze-and-flip, here a family member is threatened with indictment to win guilty pleas or cooperation from a target. See Lewinsky's mother, Marcia Lewis.

➤ **"Charging lesser offenses"** This is how the government got Al Capone. The prosecutor prosecutes for an offense that is easier to prove than the primary allegations. For example, charging a President for lying under oath about an affair when you really wanted to prove he committed fraud in a real estate deal.

➤ **"Identifying adversaries"** Here, the independent counsel searches for whistleblowers and others willing to offer information about a target. Does the name Linda Tripp ring a bell?

➤ **"Multiplying minor charges"** Adding minor but related counts to an indictment to increase pressure on a target. For example, an official's allegedly corrupt telephone conversations may be treated as "wire fraud."

➤ **"Building subpoena pressure"** In this scenario, the prosecutor brings numerous witnesses before a grand jury in order to create uncertainty about who is and is not cooperating with government prosecutors. This encourages everyone to talk, even a President.

➤ **"Collateral consequences"** Here, the prosecutor reminds the potential witness that corruption convictions can severely and negatively impact all aspects of one's private and professional life. Just ask Monica.

Mumbo Jumbo

When a prosecutor believes he has enough evidence to charge a defendant with a crime, he does so by issuing an **indictment**. The indictment lists the charges.

These tactics may not be pretty, but they work. The question is, do we want to subject a sitting President to the indignity of such treatment, regardless of the cost to the nation, or should he be exempt from certain penalties of civil law while in office?

What Choice Do We Have?

It seems clear that the law as it stands today is flawed. It is too easy to expand a probe. Probes are permitted into allegations of corruption that occurred well before a President took office, and too many people are subjected to financial, professional, and emotional ruin. It is also counter to the original design of the framers of the Constitution, which alone should be a cause for concern.

There are no easy answers. We need to be able to investigate government corruption while respecting individual liberties. Illegalities must be uncovered but lives should not be ruined. A law that can balance both needs would be a step in the right direction.

The Least You Need to Know

➤ The independent counsel statute was borne out of Watergate with the intention of providing an effective remedy against corruption in the Executive branch.

➤ The statute is intended to counterbalance an attorney general's reluctance to investigate the Executive who appointed her.

➤ Once investigations are launched, they may spin quickly out of control in terms of scope and budget, because the current law practically requires an independent counsel to investigate any charge, no matter how baseless.

➤ Independent counsels, like all prosecutors, have a lot of tools at their disposal.

➤ Although Independent counsel investigations since 1978 have mostly been a remarkable waste of time and money, several, such as the Iran–Contra investigation and even the Starr investigation, have uncovered serious wrongdoings.

Chapter 13

A "Vast Right-Wing Conspiracy"?

In This Chapter

➤ Conspiracy defined

➤ Ken Starr's role

➤ The Money Man

➤ Linda Tripp, Lucianne Goldberg, and Paula Jones

➤ The Rutherford Institute

It was a dark and stormy morning late in January. The powerful woman entered the cold room. Coming here was a risk, and she new it. Her enemies had been after her and her partner for months—years—and it was time for revenge. At last the veil of secrecy would be lifted and the cold underbelly of her sneaky, rich foes would be brought to the light of day. It was a risk she was gladly willing to take. The her future, and that of her partner, was literally at stake.

Hillary spoke to NBC's Matt Lauer a few days after the Monica Lewinsky story broke. The President, according to Hillary, was the victim of a "vast right-wing conspiracy" determined to undo the results of the past two elections. She explained that her husband has many political enemies who have been dogging him since his days in Arkansas, and they were still trying to take Bill Clinton down.

There may yet be some proof in Hillary's pudding. Is there a conspiracy? If so, who are the conspirators and what kind of conspiracies have they concocted?

Media Alert

One of the best conspiracy movies of all time is *The Manchurian Candidate*. In it, Lawrence Harvey plays a man named Raymond Shaw. Shaw has been brainwashed by communists, and his mission is to assassinate a presidential candidate at the command of his mother. Frank Sinatra is the good guy who tries to foil their evil plans.

Become a Pundit

Who shot JFK? Joseph Milteer was the head of a right-wing organization under investigation by the Miami police. Three weeks before Kennedy was assassinated, Milteer was caught on tape telling a wired informant that there was a plan to kill Kennedy during a motorcade. According to Milteer, the plan was to shoot the President with a high-powered rifle and have a stooge take the fall. The FBI and CIA were made aware of this alleged plot, but the information was never passed along to law enforcement in Dallas.

What Is a Conspiracy?

Before we untangle this alleged web of deceit and trickery, it might be a good idea to understand the legal definition of conspiracy. The commonly held belief—that a conspiracy is a group of people acting in concert to achieve their nefarious ends—is fairly accurate. In legal terms, a conspiracy is a very specific crime with identifiable elements. Normally, to be able to prove a conspiracy, a prosecutor must prove that two or more persons have agreed with one another to engage in criminal conduct, or at least attempt a crime, even if it is unsuccessful.

Actors in the conspiracy may drop in or out. The details of the conspiracy may change from time to time. While members need not know of each other to be part of the conspiracy, all must know the purpose of the conspiracy and agree to be part of a plan to effect its illicit purpose.

It is indisputable that a lot of people hate Bill Clinton. He seems to be a lightening rod of innuendo, hearsay, lies, and distortions for the far-right. Some powerful and influential people see in Clinton all that is wrong with this country. Many of them know each other well. Some of them even work together.

But are they co-conspirators scheming to drive "Billary" (as some self-styled patriots derisively refer to the President and First Lady) from office? Uncovering a conspiracy is a difficult task probably best left to law enforcement. But take a gander at the connections for yourself and draw your own conclusions. Some of the groups and actors are so intertwined and cross-connected as to give one serious pause. It can get confusing, but there is a common thread—they all seem to know each other and all seem to hate Clinton. Conspirators, or just good friends with lots in common? You be the judge.

The "Ringleader": Ken Starr

We all know Ken Starr's official duty. He is the independent counsel charged with investigating the President. He has headed a four-year investigation that has exam-

130

ined everything from a failed land deal to Hillary's old billing records to the death of Vince Foster to the President's preference for fellatio.

But what do we discover when we investigate Ken Starr? You'll learn more about his background in the next chapter, but let's first see how he's connected with the supposed players in the "conspiracy." Begin with his law practice. Instead of giving it up in deference to his supposed independence, Starr has continued to practice law. Alone, that would seem tolerable, save for the fact that his clients tend to be right-wing groups who oppose the President and his policies. Understand too that the independent counsel statute requires the prosecutor to be free of any "political conflict of interest."

The first sign of a right-wing conspiracy may be that one of Starr's largest clients is "big tobacco." By some estimates, tobacco companies have paid Starr over $1 million in legal fees. Concurrently, it is no secret that the President has been a vocal opponent of tobacco. Damage to the President helps the tobacco companies. While Starr was investigating the President, he also found time to defend one of the largest of these tobacco manufacturers, Brown & Williamson Tobacco Co., in an appeals-court case involving class-action lawsuits. Apparently, Starr does not see his association with tobacco as a conflict of interest. One wonders what he might charge Clinton with if the tables were turned.

Mumbo Jumbo

A **conflict of interest** is a clash between the public interest and the private financial gain of the person involved.

Pop quiz! Which is probably the largest tobacco-growing state in the Union? If you answered North Carolina, you are correct sir. Who is the senior Senator from North Carolina? Correct again: Republican Jesse Helms. What Senator met with Judge David Sentelle (one of three judges who pick the independent counsel) right before former Whitewater Independent Counsel Robert Fiske was fired for being too soft on Clinton? Correct, tobacco Senator Jesse Helms. Who was named to take over for Fiske? Yep, tobacco attorney Ken Starr. It's not what you know, it's who you know.

People question Starr's impartiality for more than his continued representation of tobacco. He represented the state of Wisconsin in a case underwritten by the conservative Bradley Foundation, upholding the use of school vouchers, a program Clinton opposes. He continued to serve on the

Become a Pundit

Senator William Proxmire gave out monthly "Golden Fleece Awards" for what he believed to be the most egregious misuse of taxpayer money. Among his favorites are: $97,000 to the National Institute of Mental Health to study Peruvian brothels, $2,500 to the National Endowment for the Humanities to study why people cheat in tennis games, and $84,000 to the National Science Foundation to study why people fall in love.

board of advisers of the Washington Legal Foundation, a conservative group that has been critical of Clinton administration policies. In 1996, Starr spoke at a law school run by religious broadcaster Pat Robertson, who has been highly critical of Clinton.

Starr's continued association with conservative institutions that vehemently oppose Clinton are legitimate reason for concern, if not an accusation of conspiracy.

Starr is also associated with a right-wing billionaire who has funded many of Clinton's most vocal critics. In 1996, with Whitewater apparently dry-docked, Starr accepted, then quickly rejected, an offer to become the dean of the Pepperdine Law School in Malibu, California. Interestingly, and maybe not coincidentally, one of Pepperdine's largest financial contributors is reclusive right-wing billionaire Richard Mellon Scafie.

Who's Richard Mellon Scafie?!

Richard Mellon Scafie is a fourth-generation heir to the Mellon Bank fortune. His personal wealth has been estimated to be between $800 million and $1.5 billion. He was thrown out of Yale twice, and it is difficult to find a photograph of him that is less than 25 years old. He is a large financial backer of many conservative groups and causes but has also given $1 million each to the Salvation Army and the Pittsburgh Symphony.

How rich is Scafie? In 1972, Scafie was the second largest donor to the Committee to Re-elect the President (CREEP.) He gave CREEP more than $1 million. As Watergate dragged on, one Nixon aide came up with an ingenious plan to muzzle the *Washington Post*. "Scafie will offer to buy it," said a note in John Ehrlichman's handwriting found in the Nixon Archives.

White House Confidential

Nixon's infamous "enemies list" also contained several organizations. Among those on the list were the National Welfare Rights Organization, *The New York Times*, the *St. Louis Post-Dispatch*, and the *Washington Post.*

Scafie funds many of the most visible right-wing groups aligned against Clinton. One of those groups is Accuracy in Media (AIM). According to *Rolling Stone*, AIM was beating the Paula Jones drum well ahead of the pack. Long before anyone had ever heard of her, AIM placed ads in mainstream newspapers asking

WHO IS PAULA JONES AND WHY IS THE MEDIA SUPPRESSING HER CHARGE OF SEXUAL HARASSMENT?

But Scafie's association with the Jones case is deeper than that. Another of Scafie's beneficiaries, the Landmark Legal Fund, offered to assist Paula Jones' attorneys. Conspiracy alert! The Landmark Legal Fund teamed up with Ken Starr in the aforementioned school-voucher case. Furthermore, Landmark has links to attorney James Moody, the man who represents … Linda Tripp!

There are even more connections between Starr, Scafie, and Jones. The Independent Women's Forum, which according to *Rolling Stone* received its very first grant, $100,000, from Scafie, consulted with an attorney about various issues in the Paula Jones case. That attorney was Ken Starr (prior to Starr becoming independent counsel.) In fact, Starr advised Jones' attorneys on at least three different occasions about various aspects of *Jones v. Clinton*. At one point, Starr even considered writing a "friend of the court" brief supporting Jones' case against Clinton.

Another beneficiary of Scafie's largesse is Judicial Watch. Judicial Watch is headed by Larry Klayman. Among other clients, Klayman represents Republicans whose FBI files were given to the White House (Filegate). Klayman has brought 18 civil lawsuits against the Clinton Administration (you heard right: 18). Klayman is also suing his mother to recover money he spent caring for his grandmother.

Besides organizations like Judicial Watch, Scafie also assists media sources of his liking, many of which have ties to conservative organizations and Clinton accusers. For example, one of Scafie's favorite benefactors is the *American Spectator*. *American Spectator* is the magazine that first told the story of an anonymous woman who alleged that Governor Clinton had exposed himself to her. That's right, it was Paula Jones.

Mumbo Jumbo

Sometimes people or organizations beyond the two parties directly involved may be interested in a particular case because of the precedent the case may set. In these circumstances, the court allows those interested entities to lobby on behalf of one side or another. These arguments are called **friend of the court** briefs.

Become a Pundit

Judicial Watch challenged Clinton's use of insurance payments to help cover his costs in defending the *Jones v. Clinton* lawsuit.

Lucianne Goldberg, Linda Tripp, Paula Jones …

Scafie is not the only modern Republican with ties to Nixon. Lucianne Goldberg, Linda Tripp's confidante and erstwhile literary agent, worked for Nixon in 1972 as an undercover spy aboard McGovern's airplane. In recent years, she has represented Mark Furhman and Gary Aldrich.

Aldrich is another person who is aligned against Clinton. Aldrich worked at the Clinton White House at the beginning of the first term and left "deeply troubled." The ex-FBI agent then wrote an anti-Clinton book entitled *Unlimited Access*. Among his more outrageous accusations: Hillary Clinton's Blue Room Christmas tree was decorated with ornaments of drug and sexual paraphernalia.

Here's a connection: Aldrich's book was published by Regnery. Regnery has also published books by R. Emmett Tyrell. Tyrell is the editor of the *American Spectator*. *American Spectator* first broke the Jones story and is funded by Scafie!

It's no secret that Aldrich and Tripp know one another, but Aldrich denies that Tripp was the main source for his book about the White House. Tripp, by the way, got her first job in the Bush White House with the help of Bill Hecht, a lobbyist for … the tobacco industry. After Tripp was shuffled off to the Pentagon, she met Monica Lewinsky. Alarmed (possibly excited) about the tales Lewinsky told, Tripp went to see, not her priest, but her … literary agent! Lucianne Goldberg suggested that Tripp illicitly tape Lewinsky. Tripp was so enamoured with this idea that she let the tape roll for 20 hours.

Now, when you think about whether any conspiracy exists, consider the following: Before Linda Tripp made her now-legendary first call to Starr's office, it turns out that they had already known about Lewinsky and the President. How did the Office of the Independent Counsel find out? Jerome Marcus, a lawyer with ties to the Jones legal team called a friend of his in Starr's office to make sure that Starr's people knew of the affair. The Jones lawyers were tipping off the Starr lawyers.

It became clear to Marcus and others on the Jones legal team that Tripp needed legal help. Two other lawyers helped Marcus find a new lawyer for Tripp and formally bring her accusations to Starr's office, and one of the lawyers was Ken Starr's law partner, James Moody, a member of a conservative legal association called the Federalist Society. Another member of the group is—Ken Starr. And who helped these lawyers find Moody? Literary agent Lucianne Goldberg.

Tripp took the tapes to Starr, who wanted the goods on Clinton in the Jones case. Although Jones's case was first handled by her private attorneys (Gilbert and Camarata), when she refused a settlement offer of $700,000, they quit and filed a lien against any future settlement. (Jones steadfastly maintains, however, that the case "is not about money.")

Sound Bites

After a careful reading of the Starr Report, I am impressed by the salacious and voyeuristic nature of your work. The quality and quantity of material you have assembled … contains more pornographic references than Hustler Online this month.

—*Hustler* magazine publisher Larry Flynt offered Starr a job as "pornographic advisor." According to Flynt, the Starr Report contained 69 references to genitalia while Hustler Online contained only 44.

The Clinton Chronicles

Now we are deep in any "conspiracy." Jones hired new attorneys, and the bills for the case were picked up by the conservative Rutherford Institute. At one time, the Institute defended the right of football players at Jerry Falwell's Liberty University to pray in the end zone after touchdowns. Falwell has peddled an outrageous anti-Clinton video called *The Clinton Chronicles*.

The Rutherford Institute is headed by John Whitehead. Whitehead once wrote an article for the Institute's newsletter. Discussing the Clinton health-care overhaul, he said "The Clintons will now decide who can provide medical care for our children. If a parent attempts to go against their decision, he or she may be sent to jail."

Besides Falwell, the Rutherford Institute too has promoted *The Clinton Chronicles*. The tape sells for $19.95 and is estimated to have sold almost 300,000 copies. The video depicts Clinton as a drug-smuggling murderer. The narrator says, "At the time of his election in 1992, most Americans were not aware of the extent of Clinton's criminal background." Apparently, the real Bill Clinton has 52 murders to his name, a $100 million per month drug-running operation, a state trooper claiming to have arranged more than 100 sexual encounters for him, and a criminal empire called "Arkansas." Not surprisingly, *The Clinton Chronicles* ends with a call for Clinton's impeachment.

Now that's what we call "high crimes and misdemeanors!"

Become a Pundit

Jerry Falwell disbanded the Moral Majority in 1989. At the time, Falwell said that his work would be taken up by other groups and other people. Falwell specifically named Whitehead as an heir to the throne.

Untangle This Mess, Please

In all likelihood, the First Lady probably picked a poor choice of words that day on the *Today* show. What she likely meant, and what is likely true, is that there are many people who would love to see Clinton out of office sooner rather than later. That they all run in the same circles is probably more "birds of a feather cooperate together" than "birds of a feather conspire together."

While not conspiring to commit a crime, they certainly would not mind using their influence, power, money, and connections to see that Clinton is ousted legally and quickly.

The Least You Need to Know

➤ While not a conspiracy in the strict legal sense of the word, powerful forces are aligned against Bill Clinton.

➤ Ken Starr is associated with many of the right-wing causes opposing Clinton.

➤ Richard Mellon Scaife finances many of these ventures.

➤ Many of the people in the Jones and the Starr cases are associated with these right-wing organizations.

➤ Some amazingly absurd things have been said about the Clintons.

Chapter 14

The Report on Starr

In This Chapter

➤ A Texas childhood

➤ Ken Starr: conspirator or prosecutor?

➤ Things get personal

➤ The Pepperdine job

➤ The investigator is investigated

It was not easy, but he did it. Ken Starr salvaged his reputation, somewhat. Prior to the release of the report bearing his name, Independent Counsel Kenneth Starr was just about the most unpopular man in the country. Polls consistently showed that the American public thought that he was biased and ineffective. But, whether you like him or not, whether you agree with his tactics or not, the fact remains that he came up with something substantive. No longer could the well-worn phrase "4 years and 40 million dollars" be used in a derisive way implying that Starr's entire investigation was much ado about nothing. It may not be over *Whitewater*, but Starr may yet topple the President.

But at what cost? Indeed, the President lied while under oath. However, he lied about a sexual affair, which is understandable, if not acceptable to some. It takes a certain kind of man to charge a President with the impeachable offense of perjuring himself in a deposition deemed irrelevant to a case that was deemed meritless and later dismissed. That man is Ken Starr.

The Son of a Preacherman

Kenneth Winston Starr posseses the moral certainty of a son of a conservative minister, which he is. His zeal in investigating the President, some call it overzealousness, is entirely in keeping with his upbringing and personality. Like Clinton, he has always excelled. The roots of his work today can be found in his Texas childhood.

Ken Starr first went to church when he was $2^1/_2$ weeks old. He has never smoked or drank or been heard to curse. Even now, he still teaches Sunday school whenever he can in suburban Virginia. He was a straight-A student involved in everything. Unlike his nemesis Bill Clinton, he was never flashy, but he knew how to get what he wanted.

His hometown of Thalia, Texas, is isolated and nondescript. His parents drummed into him their view of how good people should behave. Starr's mother, Vannie Starr, has said that her boy "was just not raised up to be familiar with anything like" what Clinton has been accused of—cheating on one's wife. Starr's "daddy was not that kind of man."

By the time Kenny entered elementary school, the family had moved to Centerville, population 800, not far from Palestine, Texas. Religion was central to the family's life and, like other members of the Church of Christ, they believed in the saving grace of baptism and were steeped in the New Testament teachings of Jesus Christ.

At school, he easily excelled. "I didn't have to help him with his lessons," his mother says. "We were real proud of his report cards." By 1960, when Starr entered high school, the family had moved to southeast San Antonio. Vannie Starr still lives there; her husband Willie died of a heart attack in 1989, not long after the couple celebrated their 60th wedding anniversary.

At Sam Houston High School, Ken Starr was a big man on campus. He was junior class president, senior class president, and a member of the National Honor Society and the journalism club. He was on the yearbook staff and a photographer for the school newspaper. He was voted, not surprisingly, "Most Likely to Succeed."

Ken Starr attended George Washington University. During the summers, he sold Bibles door-to-door. He then went to Duke University Law School. Starr graduated near the top of his class and was hired to clerk for Supreme Court Justice Warren Burger; a prestigious position, difficult to obtain.

Upon conclusion of his clerkship, he joined the Washington office of the Gibson Dunn & Crutcher law firm. He married Alice Jean Mendell, a public relations executive, and together they had two daughters and a son.

Friends say that Starr is a sensitive, deeply religious man, who likes to read the Bible every morning. His manner is

Become a Pundit

Texas Governor George W. Bush is the son of ex-president George Bush. Bush the son is now a top-tier candidate for the Republican nomination for President in the year 2000. His brother, Jeb Bush, is Governor of Florida.

genteel and distinguished. While at Gibson Dunn & Crutcher, ironically, he helped draft the Reagan Administration's opposition to the independent counsel statute. (It failed.)

In 1994, he was appointed to investigate the Clintons' involvement in a failed Arkansas real estate development called Whitewater.

Starr's long-standing ties to conservatives are well-known. His entry into government came when his boss at the law firm, William French Smith, became President Reagan's first attorney general. Starr followed him to Washington as his chief of staff. Ronald Reagan appointed Starr to the federal Court of Appeals in Washington, considered by many as second in importance only to the U.S. Supreme Court. George Bush chose Starr as his solicitor general; a partisan appointment, but also an esteemed one.

Mumbo Jumbo

The **solicitor general** of the United States is in charge of representing the government before the Supreme Court. He decides what cases the government should ask the Court to review and what position the government should take in cases before the Court.

Right-Wing Conspirator or Tough Prosecutor?

The way Starr has gone about his job has caused a groundswell of criticism against an investigation that began with Arkansas land deals and has ended up with a inquisition-like investigation into the President's sex life. Hillary Clinton stated on the *Today* show that Starr's hunt was part of a "vast right-wing conspiracy." (You read about his connections in Chapter 13.)

Mumbo Jumbo

A **conspiracy** is a group of two or more persons who act with a common purpose and scheme to effectuate their illegal plans.

Besides the seemingly single-minded zeal of his investigation, Starr has also taken flak for the incessant leaks from his office, for his lack of prosecutorial experience, and even for the way he was appointed to his post.

"His personal behavior is undermining the perception this is an objective investigation," said former Independent Counsel Michael Zeldin, who with Joseph Di Genova led a 1992 investigation of the Bush Administration's alleged misuse of passport files. "He has given his critics the ammunition to make that claim."

Become a Pundit

While Starr worked under Bush, his name came up twice as a potential Supreme Court nominee. Ultimately David Souter and Clarence Thomas were handed the posts.

Kenneth Starr.
Reuters/Jeff Mitchell/
Archive Photos

Besides his right-wing credentials (or perhaps because of them), critics also focused on the method of Starr's selection as independent counsel. Recall that after a 30- and 90-day review, a three-judge panel appoints the independent counsel. In Starr's case, Robert Fiske was already the independent counsel in the Whitewater case. Having decided that Vince Foster did in fact commit suicide, Fiske was under attack by the right. In 1994, one of the three judges on the panel had lunch with Senators Jesse Helms and Lauch Faircloth. Days later, the panel appointed Ken Starr. Starr had never prosecuted a single criminal case prior that day.

Yet many defend Starr. According to several former independent counsels, Starr is going by the book. "Starr really has not done anything to abuse the kind of latitude that the system grants him," said a Justice Department official. After all, he is a prosecutor, and the job of a prosecutor is to get a conviction. If Starr looks ugly in the process, it is only because few people have seen an actual prosecution before.

John D. Bates, Starr's former deputy, took issue with accusations of a partisan witch hunt.

> *The independent counsel's office has been staffed over the last several years by professional prosecutors with enormous experience who have diligently and properly followed relevant leads in an attempt to discover the truth. These individuals are not partisans who are on a mission but rather professionals who take their jobs and obligations seriously.*

An Unhealthy Obsession

Be that as it may, it is difficult not to conclude that this has become personal for Starr himself, that whatever objectivity he had is gone. Starr is not alone in this personal vendetta; the White House is as much to blame as he is for the antipathy that exists between the two camps. Both sides seemed to be locked into some sort of strange death match.

Evidence of this obsession can be seen in the Starr report itself, replete as it is with pornographic detail that goes so far beyond what is needed to prove perjury and obstruction of justice that it would be laughable if it weren't so destructive. Some inclusions, such as Clinton's alleged statement that he might be "alone" in a few years, seem intended to do nothing more than hurt the President and his family and inflame moral sentiments against the President. Certainly there was no legal or prosecutorial need to include such a statement.

It is as if he has become Victor Hugo's Inspector Javert in pursuit of Jean Valjean. The unprecedented appearance of Hillary Clinton before a grand jury in 1996 illustrates this point. The White House sought desperately to avoid what officials viewed as a public humiliation, arguing that Starr could obtain whatever testimony he needed with a private interview at the White House. Yet Starr not only demanded she show up, but he made sure the cameras were present and rolling when she did.

Many leading legal authorities and other analysts have come to question Starr's motivations:

Sound Bites

Public media should not contain explicit or implied descriptions of sex acts. Our society should be purged of the perverts who provide the media with pornographic material while pretending it has some redeeming social value under the public's "right to know." Pornography is pornography, regardless of the source.

—Kenneth Starr, in a 1987 interview with Dianne Sawyer

I think there certainly is at least a hint of a political motivation, if not more. I think he clearly wants a conviction in this case. You cannot spend the amount of time and the amount of money that he has spent in this case … without wanting to win. He wants to win. He wants to get the President.
—CNN legal analyst Roger Cossack

There are so many other lawyers in this country. Why in the world did we have to select someone to investigate the President of the United States who has such a strong Republican agenda? Huge mistake to pick Ken Starr, so it certainly has the appearance that, indeed, it is political.
—CNN legal analyst Greta Van Sustern

White House Confidential

At the turn of the 19th century, Maria Reynolds claimed to have had an affair with Alexander Hamilton. The revelations derailed Hamilton's Presidential ambitions. In 1804, Hamilton and Aaron Burr dueled over the story and Burr's part in it. Hamilton was shot to death.

I think that it was ill advised that after 30-odd million dollars spent investigating Whitewater, he ends up policing the Paula Jones private litigation …. It's beyond his jurisdiction. He had no duty.
—Former Independent Counsel Lawrence Walsh

During his years as independent counsel, Mr. Starr continued private legal practice. He has also donated to Republican candidates and made speeches before groups antagonistic to Mr. Clinton, including one in 1996 sponsored by the evangelist Pat Robertson.
—The New York Times

Beyond suggestions of a moral crusade, Ken Starr's other problem is critics who think his agenda is political. He was a Reagan Justice Department official who helped write the Reagan opposition to the independent counsel law. Starr went on to the Court of Appeals, but gave up his lifetime appointment to become George Bush's solicitor general.
—CNN's Candy Crowley

He carries a lot of baggage. He's somebody who has been accused, with some justification, of partisan politics.
—Newsweek's Evan Thomas

[W]e may wonder how an investigation launched some three years ago to delve into Whitewater turned into one concerning the President's sex life. Starr's charter has been so broad, and his funding so rich (more than $30 million spent so far), that he has been able to keep going when other prosecutors would have turned to more urgent matters. He is supervised by a friendly three-man appellate panel that appointed him in the first place. They are all, like Starr himself, staunch Republicans.
—Richard Cohen, syndicated columnist

Mr. Starr's zeal [to take down Clinton] … raises questions about his partisanship.
— Scott Turow, lawyer and author, *The New York Times*

Surf's Up!

By late 1996, it seemed as if Starr's investigation would quietly wind down. Having spent three years investigating the President, he clearly had no "substantial and credible" evidence that the President had committed any impeachable offenses. If he had, he would have surely brought out all the bells and whistles he used to deliver the report on Lewinsky.

Starr accepted a position at Pepperdine University, a fine law school with an incredible view of the Pacific Ocean. Under any other circumstances, it would have been a great job. But these were not any other circumstances.

It is unclear why Starr simply did not close up shop, tell the attorney general that he had nothing (as he is required to do if that's the case), and move on. The best guess is that the Whitewater investigations were incomplete at that point; he cannot submit a final report until they are complete and indictments brought or targets cleared. The fact that he was ready to jump ship certainly seems to indicate that he didn't think he had much, at least at that point.

Become a Pundit

The woman who ran Michael Dukakis' unsuccessful Presidential campaign, Susan Estrich, also took a job teaching law in Southern California. She is a professor at the USC School of Law.

Critics had a field day. They said Starr was leaving because he had nothing on the Clintons. They called him a quitter. They said it just reinforced his reputation as a right-wing hatchet man, since one of Pepperdine's big benefactors is dedicated Clinton-hater Richard Melon Scafie, who took out ads suggesting the late Vince Foster had been murdered (see Chapter 13). The heat and embarrassment was too much. Starr did an about-face and stayed on.

In Conclusion...

There can be no denying that Ken Starr is an intelligent lawyer committed to his case. It is also true that he has taken a lot of heat for his apparent partisanship throughout the Whitewater investigation. That is too bad. Had he appeared less a right-wing attack dog and more a judicious independent prosecutor, his investigation and its results would have been given more credit by the American people.

The Least You Need to Know

➤ Like Bill Clinton, Ken Starr shone early in life.

➤ While he certainly has his right-wing credentials, Starr is a well qualified, tough, competent attorney.

➤ Unfortunately, his obsession with getting the President has tarnished his reputation.

➤ When it seemed that Whitewater was leading nowhere, Ken Starr tried to jump ship to Malibu.

Chapter 15

Whitewatergate

In This Chapter

➤ Whitewater starts the ball rolling

➤ Ken Starr

➤ Travelgate and Filegate

➤ The death of Vince Foster

Just what is Whitewater? It's become an umbrella term for a variety of sins allegedly committed by the President and First Lady. Their foes would have you believe they are murderers, drug runners, embezzlers, and thieves. The Clintons would have you believe it is all the imaginings of a "right-wing conspiracy" intent on destroying them.

While the truth is elusive, the fact remains: Neither of them has yet been charged with, let alone convicted of, any crime arising out of the Whitewater investigation—although associates of theirs have been.

Ken Starr was supposed to investigate the Whitewater land deal. As we have seen, one of the most legitimate criticisms of him has been that he abandoned that original charter to spy on the President's sex life instead. But Whitewater is not over. There is a very good chance that it, and the other scandals that have plagued this administration, will become part of the impeachment proceedings against the President. The House Judiciary Committee put no limit as to what it may eventually investigate, so everything is fair game.

Whitewater

Let's try and make this as simple as possible. In 1978, then-Arkansas Attorney General Bill Clinton and his wife, Hillary, joined with James and Susan McDougal to buy 220 acres of riverfront land and form the Whitewater Development Corp. The idea was to sell lots for vacation homes. The investment did poorly and finally dissolved in 1992, leaving the Clintons reporting a net loss of more than $40,000.

At the same time, James McDougal also owned Madison Guaranty Savings and Loan, for which Hillary Clinton did legal work. Due in part to several fraudulent loans, McDougal's S & L was one of many thrifts that went bust at taxpayer expense in the 1980s.

Media Alert

In an anti-Clinton videotape entitled *The Clinton Chronicles*, peddled by Jerry Falwell and others, the narrator accuses Bill Clinton of running a drug-laundering operation that netted "$100 million a month."

On March 8, 1992, *New York Times* reporter Jeff Gerth wrote an article that alleged that Whitewater was a "sweetheart" real-estate deal for the Clintons. The story alleges that the Clintons put up very little money and had no risk in the deal.

According to Clinton's critics, the Whitewater land deal was a money-loser from the start. They allege that the Clintons misappropriated bank money to prop up their failing investment. The main issue was a $300,000 loan from Madison to Susan McDougal, some of which went to prop up the Whitewater development. It is also said that the Clintons took improper tax deductions from the development and that Mrs. Clinton was retained by Madison to prevent it from being closed down after it had been found insolvent.

As a result of all of this, the Clintons are said to have assisted in the bank's failure. The Clintons have maintained that Whitewater was nothing more than a failed land deal.

Here are the facts:

➤ The Whitewater investment occurred 20 years ago.

➤ The Clintons lost $40,000 on the deal.

➤ If the deal had panned out (it didn't) the Clintons would have made $47,500.

➤ The Clintons personally borrowed nothing from Madison Guaranty Savings & Loan. Their business associates James and Susan McDougal borrowed $300,000 for the Whitewater Development Corporation.

Fraudulent Transactions

This doesn't mean the deal didn't have problems. Ken Starr has been investigating the complex deal for four years, and has had some success, including several convictions over the course of two trials relating to Whitewater.

The first trial ended in May 1996. Jim and Susan McDougal and former Arkansas Governor Jim Guy Tucker (another player in the deal), were convicted of most of the fraud and conspiracy charges Starr brought against them. The charges related to the multiple loan-swapping schemes that ultimately helped destroy Madison Guaranty. President Clinton testified at that trial on videotape but was not accused of any wrongdoing.

James McDougal received a reduced sentence of three years in return for his future cooperation with Starr after the trial. McDougal died of a heart attack in March 1998, while in prison.

Susan McDougal was convicted of much lesser charges. She was sentenced to two years in prison. However, she only started serving that sentence in May 1998, because she was already serving 18 months in jail on a contempt of court citation. That related to her refusal to testify before Starr's Little Rock grand jury. She has steadfastly maintained that Starr wanted her to testify to matters she could not honestly testify to before that grand jury. Starr had her thrown in jail for her failure to cooperate.

On July 30, 1997, she was moved into a federal detention facility after seven months in two Los Angeles jails, much of the time locked in a windowless cell 23 hours a day. The move to the better facility came a week after the American Civil Liberties Union (ACLU) filed a lawsuit alleging that Starr was holding McDougal in "barbaric" conditions in an attempt to coerce her to testify. She was eventually indicted for criminal contempt of court and obstructing Starr's investigation.

Jim Guy Tucker, who succeeded Clinton as governor, was convicted of conspiracy and mail-fraud charges. He was sentenced to 18 months of home detention because of his poor health. Tucker resigned as Governor after the verdicts.

The second Whitewater trial ended in August 1996. At that trial, a federal jury cleared two Arkansas bankers of four felony counts involving their bank and donations to Clinton's 1990 Arkansas Governor campaign. The jury deadlocked on the seven other counts.

The real problem here seems to be the Clintons' business partner, Jim McDougal. He put up $300,000 and the Clintons put up $45,000. He had a lot more to lose. McDougal is said to have called Madison his "candy store." But just because McDougal was a crook, such labels cannot automatically be placed on the Clintons without proof. To date, there has simply been no proof of wrongdoing on their part. Now, if they knew of McDougal's book-cooking or knowingly participated in it, they would be guilty in their own right.

Sound Bites

I think the office of independent counsel has made him [Starr] nutty and I don't understand it. This kind of fishing expedition makes him not a Whitewater special prosecutor, but a general persecutor of the President.

—Former Justice Dept. Adviser Cass Sunstein

Without proof of that, McDougal's crimes are not their crimes. Guilt by association is not guilt under law.

Web Hubbell and Hillary Clinton, Attorneys at Law

The final item with regard to the Clintons and Whitewater relates to the legal work done for the corporation by Hillary Clinton and former Assistant Attorney General and former Rose Law firm partner, Webster Hubbell.

Begin with Mrs. Clinton. In 1995, the Senate began what would be a 13-month investigation into Whitewater. Concurrently, Ken Starr subpoenaed Mrs. Clinton's billing records from the deal. The White House responded to the subpoena by stating that the records could not be located.

Two years later, the records somehow showed up in the Clintons' private quarters at the White House. Despite that strange occurrence and the wrongdoing that it seems to indicate, the records provided little new evidence against Mrs. Clinton. In fact, the documents included copies of bills showing she performed 60 hours of legal work for Madison in 1985 and 1986. (If you've ever hired an attorney, you know that a two-year average of two and a half hours of work per month is a pittance.)

The Senate Whitewater hearings ended in June 1996 and accomplished little. Republicans, in their majority report, accused the Clinton White House of stonewalling but uncovered no clear evidence of illegal conduct. The Democrats claimed the Clintons had been vindicated once again.

The conclusion? That's right. In 1995, a Republican by the name of Jay Stevens completed an investigation of the matter at the behest of the federal bank overseer—the Resolution Trust Corporation. Forty-five witnesses were interviewed, 200,000 documents examined, and two years and $4 million were spent on the investigation. It concluded that the Clintons had done nothing wrong and had been telling the truth the whole time.

Furthermore, on August Aug. 10, 1995, the House Banking Committee, chaired by Republican Jim Leach of Iowa, finished its examination of the Whitewater deal. Its conclusion? No illegalities were found.

Now consider the actions of First Friend Webster Hubbell. In 1994, Hubbell abruptly resigned as associate attorney general after allegations were raised about his conduct at the Rose Law Firm. The issue Starr is investigating relates to alleged hush money Hubbell received after he resigned.

Become a Pundit

The Rose Law Firm is the oldest law firm in Arkansas.

Former Associate Attorney General Webster Hubbell. AP/Wide World Photos

Soon after Hubbell quit government work, he received some lucrative consulting contracts, allegedly obtained at the behest of Clinton friends Mickey Kantor and Vernon Jordan. Starr is investigating whether Jordan and Kantor helped Hubbell get the contracts in payment for keeping quiet about whatever he knew about Whitewater. Hillary Clinton denies that any hush money was arranged for her former law partner. She says Whitewater reminds her "of some people's obsession with UFOs and the Hale-Bopp comet."

Yet the records of the House Government Reform and Oversight Committee show Hubbell did little or no work for most of the $593,442 he received from 18 companies and individuals after he resigned. This included $61,667 he received from HarperCollins for a book that was never completed. Three trust accounts were also established, with $110,710 to pay for the Hubbell family's living expenses, education costs, and legal bills.

Hubbell was found guilty of defrauding the Rose Law Firm and of income-tax evasion, and he served 18 months in jail. He has yet to be convicted of a crime relating to the Whitewater development, however.

Mumbo Jumbo

In a criminal case, **guilt** means that the defendant was found to have committed the acts alleged by the prosecution "beyond a reasonable doubt." In most jurisdictions, guilt must be agreed upon by a unanimous verdict of all jurors.

149

White House Confidential

Pat Robertson, the Republican preacher, activist, and host of the nationally syndicated *700 Club* told the *Washington Post* that running for President was "embarrassing" and "painful." One reason was that *The Wall Street Journal* reported that Robertson's son was born 10 weeks after Robertson and his wife DeDe were married.

Travelgate

The White House travel operation got its start during the Administration of President Andrew Jackson, when aides helped reporters following the President book train tickets. Today, the small operation in the Old Executive Office Building consists of seven employees who handle about $7 million a year in travel arrangements for the White House press corps.

White House Confidential

When Andrew Jackson married his wife Rachel, she believed she was divorced, but actually was not. During the 1828 Presidential election, she was the target of a smear campaign which accused her of being a bigamist. Jackson still won, but Rachel died shortly after he was elected.

In 1993, all seven, all long-term government employees, were fired by the Clinton Administration. It's a complicated series of events, so maybe a timeline will help explain:

➤ **1982:** Billy R. Dale, a 20-year veteran of the White House Travel Office, is appointed as its head. Several years later, during the Bush Administration, he is urged to take steps to control escalating costs of press travel.

➤ **1992:** Commercial travel for Clinton campaign staff and the Clinton-Gore transition is handled by Catherine A. Cornelius, a distant cousin of Clinton's. Cornelius begins efforts to take over the travel office before Inauguration Day, meeting with representatives of World Wide Travel Inc., a Little Rock agency that handled campaign travel, and David Watkins, a campaign official who became a White House transition aide in charge of administrative matters. (World Wide Travel was the nation's 24th largest travel agency, counting the Democratic National Committee among its clients.)

Cornelius soon goes to work for Watkins and in three memos, outlines a plan to take over the travel operation and install World Wide as the White House's travel agent. Her memos, according to a later General Accounting Office (GAO) investigation into the matter, falsely projected the savings that could be realized by replacing the existing staff. The GAO said she overestimated ticket sales and inaccurately described travel-industry commission and rebate practices. Cornelius said that under her plan the White House could earn $210,000 in rebates; the GAO later placed the figure at about $10,000.

➤ **1993:** It turns out everybody wants a piece of the Travel Office pie. In February, Darnell Martens, a partner of Hollywood producer and Clinton friend Harry Thomason, contacts Dale to learn how to bid for the press air-charter business. Thomason, as a Clinton friend, really has no official business in the White House, yet amazingly had Cornelius "keep her eyes and ears open," according to White House and GAO reports. After Cornelius produced records she had secretly taken home, White House lawyers Vince Foster and William Kennedy recommend an audit but are told the White House did not have the capability to do one.

➤ **Early May, 1993:** Cornelius, who has been assigned to the travel office, meets with Thomason at the White House and reports her observations regarding how the office is run. They meet with Watkins and Martens.

Thomason then meets with First Lady Hillary Clinton. Watkins then brings in White House Deputy Counsel Vincent Foster and Associate Counsel William Kennedy to meet with Cornelius and Thomason on alleged travel-office problems.

Media Alert

Harry Thomason and his wife, Linda Bloodworth Thomason, produced the television shows *Designing Women* and *Evening Shade.* They were also responsible for the feel-good movie about Clinton that ended the 1992 Democratic Convention, "A Place Called Hope."

151

OK. All we have so far are some unsubstantiated rumors of potential mismanagement and possible corruption in the travel office, combined with two Clinton cronies who know a potential financial goldmine when they see one. What they needed was actual proof of wrongdoings in order to get their mitts on the office. What happens next is where things get a bit fishy:

➤ White House attorney Kennedy asks the FBI to investigate the travel-office allegations. FBI agents initially tell Kennedy that they believed there was insufficient evidence to investigate.

When the agents hesitated, critics contend that Kennedy told them that the White House would use the Internal Revenue Service to investigate the matter instead (the old inter-agency power play). In the end, Cornelius convinced the agents that an investigation was necessary, telling them about suspected kickbacks and petty cash discrepancies. The agents later told the GAO that they did not know of her interest in running the office. We continue....

➤ **May 13:** Hillary Clinton meets with Foster on another matter, asks him about the travel office, and he tells her Kennedy is looking into the matter. Later, Foster tells her the accounting firm of KPMG Peat Marwick will conduct a review.

➤ **May 17:** The accounting firm reports to Kennedy problems regarding travel-office operations, including an $18,200 discrepancy. Watkins decides to fire the employees and White House Chief of Staff Mack McLarty approves, apparently with Hillary Clinton's knowledge.

➤ **May 19:** All seven travel office employees are fired. As they packed, the employees watch press secretary Dee Dee Myers reveal during a news conference that they are being investigated by the FBI.

➤ **May 25:** When news of the firing hit the press, a new storm of criticism crashes upon Camp Clinton. It is alleged that the firings are nepotistic and that the FBI investigation is the blatant misuse of an investigatory agency for personal use. The White House reconsiders the firings and five of the employees are placed on administrative leave.

➤ **October 27:** The five travel-office employees on administrative leave receive new government jobs.

➤ **December 7, 1994:** A federal grand jury charges former travel-office head Billy Dale with embezzling $68,000 paid by news organizations for expenses incurred traveling with the President. The two-count indictment alleges that between 1988 and 1991 (before Clinton ever took office) Dale took $54,000 in refund payments and embezzled about $14,000 in petty cash.

The longtime Clinton supporters brought in to run the travel office were removed.

The allegation is that the firing of seven members of the White House travel office in 1993 was possibly done to make room for Clinton friends. It was done in conjunction with an FBI investigation of the office, allegedly opened under pressure from the White House to justify the firings.

The Death of Vince Foster

On July 20, 1993, around 5:30 p.m. White House Deputy Counsel Vince Foster Jr. was found dead in northern Virginia. The death was reported as a suicide, but many Clinton bashers still don't believe it, even though numerous investigations have so concluded.

Even Ken Starr has ruled it a suicide. His report on Foster's death concludes that Foster was severely depressed about his work at the White House, specifically the blossoming Travelgate "crisis," took a revolver from a closet in his home, placed it in an oven mitt, and on the afternoon of July 20, drove to a Virginia park and shot himself.

Media Alert

Reed Irvine is chairman of the so-called Accuracy in Media (AIM). AIM released reports and produced television shows about Foster's alleged murder. One of its theories is that Vince Foster was lured into a "sex trap" from which he escaped to the park, where he was found dead. Irvine said that the Foster case is "the biggest scandal in postwar history."

White House Deputy Counsel Vince Foster. AP/Wide World Photos

The report contained new forensic details that refuted the conspiracy theories that surrounded Foster's death (more on those in a bit). As part of its investigation, Starr's office consulted renowned medical and forensic experts, including Henry C. Lee, a crime scene expert made famous in the O.J. Simpson trial, who determined that the condition of the body and other physical evidence unequivocally demonstrated that Foster shot himself. Alan L. Berman, an expert in the field on suicide, found that "to a 100-percent degree of medical certainty, the death of Vincent Foster was a suicide."

What upsets people concerned with obstruction of a criminal investigation is that the White House admittedly removed documents from Foster's office immediately after learning of his death. Foster had worked at the Rose Law Firm in Little Rock with Hillary Clinton, and was involved with the affairs of the Whitewater S & L—Madison Guaranty.

As Ann Coulter states in her book *High Crimes and Misdemeanors*:

> The President and First Lady, it seems, wanted to obscure something about Foster's work on Whitewater … or [his] work on the travel office firings, which may have revealed Presidential abuse of power.

Starr will have the final say.

Filegate

Another doozy, but again, likely a case where Clinton did nothing wrong. Clinton aides collected hundreds of sensitive FBI files on Republicans and past administration staffers. The files were stored in a walk-in vault that had a photocopying machine. Some of the FBI reports were on prominent Republicans, but most were little-known staffers from the Reagan and Bush administrations who would make unlikely targets for a Nixon-style "enemies list."

Mumbo Jumbo

In 1973, the American public learned of President Nixon's so-called "**enemies list**" of people who opposed him. Names on that list included Bill Cosby, Paul Newman, and then-CBS newsman Daniel Schorr. The administration planned on having these people audited by the IRS and investigated by the FBI.

At the time of the discovery of the illegal files, the White House called it a "a bureaucratic mistake," albeit an inexcusable one. Republicans voiced concerns of "a darker motive," especially in light of the two men linked to the acquisition of the files, personnel security director Craig Livingstone and investigator Anthony B. Marceca.

One person whose FBI file was found at the White House was Billy R. Dale, the fired director of the White House travel office. This fueled suspicions that Livingstone's actions were anything but a mistake. Marceca claimed that the files were required because the individuals listed needed access to the White House complex. Livingstone soon quit the White House.

So, serious breach of security protocol and violation of civil rights by two underlings—or honest mistake? You be the judge.

How Ken Starr Entered the Picture

It is interesting to learn how Ken Starr came to investigate Whitewater in the first place. Because there were so many allegations of wrongdoing swirling around the Clintons relating to Whitewater early in the first administration, Attorney General Janet Reno named New York lawyer and former U.S. attorney Robert B. Fiske Jr. as independent counsel to investigate the matter, in 1994. As you know, the independent prosecutor is normally chosen by a three-judge panel. But at the time of the appointment, funding for the job had run out due to a budget impasse. As a result, there was no panel at that time with the legal authority to name the independent counsel, so Reno did it herself.

Farewell to Fiske

Upon his appointment, Fiske announced that he would also explore a potential link between the Vince Foster suicide and Foster's knowledge of the Whitewater deal, since Foster also worked on the project back at the Rose Law Firm in Arkansas.

Fiske eventually concluded that Foster did commit suicide and it had nothing to do with Whitewater. The right were outraged and Fiske was immediately under fire. Clinton-haters were convinced that the President and First Lady had Foster murdered.

For example, on March 9, 1994, the Washington, D.C., consulting firm of Johnson Smick International put out a small newsletter that stated that "investigators" believed Vince Foster died in a "safe house" in suburban Virginia, not in a park near the Capitol. According to the investigators, the house had been a rented retreat for Clinton officials. It charged that Foster died there and was then transported to Ft. Mercy Park.

White House Confidential

One night, Warren G. Harding was visiting his mistress when he heard a siren and panicked. Convinced that he would be caught in the middle of a police raid, the then–Senator and future President hid in his mistress' wardrobe closet until the coast was clear.

The next day, Rush Limbaugh read this account to his national radio audience, and added that the "secret hideaway" where Foster was killed was an apartment belonging to Hillary Clinton. The same rumor had been floating around the Internet for a year.

As a result of all of this speculation, criticism of Special Counsel Robert Fiske was mounting, and there was a lot of pressure on prominent Republicans to get someone more ideologically aligned with the right to investigate the Clintons. By late 1994, the government was back in business, and this gave the Republicans the opportunity they needed.

Because Janet Reno initially appointed Fiske, and because formal funding for the position was now back in place, Fiske now had to be approved by the three-judge panel, which refused to renew his appointment. The panel officially cited a possible conflict of interest because Fiske was appointed by Clinton's attorney general. There has been much speculation that the real reason is that right-wing Clinton opponents were able to get Republican Senator Jesse Helms to talk to one of his friends who happened to be one of the panel judges. Whatever the real reason, Kenneth W. Starr succeeded Fiske as the independent counsel.

The terms of Fiske's removal as independent counsel are under review again due to further evidence of Starr's close association with Paula Jones's lawyers in her lawsuit against the President. Starr failed to disclose to Janet Reno his association with the Jones case when he requested permission to expand his investigation to include the Lewinsky allegations. In essence, he was covering up a bias as likely to compromise his "independence" as any bias of Fiske's.

Starr Wars

As the Clintons' time in the White House grew, so too did Starr's investigations. When the White House travel office was fired, Starr expanded his investigation. When FBI files were found in the basement of the White House, Starr expanded his investigation. By the time he learned of the President's relationship with Monica Lewinsky, Starr had spent four years and $40 million investigating the President and his wife without producing a single indictment of either. He was getting desperate.

Starr's aggressive tactics have fueled the belief that his investigations of Clinton has taken on an increasingly partisan tone. States Rep. Eliot Engel, a New York Democrat, after Starr's whistle-stop delivery of the report: "If I had any doubt that this was a partisan thing, I don't now."

Nevertheless, there was certainly no shortage of things for Starr to investigate. The independent counsel's office had evidence that Vernon Jordan and other friends of the Clintons were helping Assistant Attorney General Webster Hubbell, an Arkansas friend of the Clintons, get consulting contracts while he was a potential witness and/or subject in the Whitewater investigation. Hubbell was also the target of a separate criminal investigation into his own conduct. There was also evidence that the President and the First Lady knew and approved of the assistance to Hubbell.

After resigning from the Justice Department in April 1994, Hubbell launched a private consulting practice in Washington, D.C. He received substantial aid from important public and private figures. The day before Hubbell announced his resignation, White House Chief of Staff Thomas "Mack" McLarty attended a meeting at the White House with the President, First Lady, and others, where they discussed Hubbell's resignation.

Some time after that meeting, McLarty spoke with Vernon Jordan about the possibility of assisting Hubbell. Jordan introduced Hubbell to executives at MacAndrews & Forbes Holding Co. in New York. Jordan is a director of Revlon, Inc., which is controlled by MacAndrews & Forbes. The introduction was successful; MacAndrews & Forbes retained Mr. Hubbell at a rate of $25,000 per quarter. Vernon Jordan informed President Clinton that he was helping Mr. Hubbell.

By late 1997, Starr was investigating whether there was any connection between consulting payments to Mr. Hubbell and his "incomplete testimony" in the Whitewater investigation. Starr was particularly concerned with whether Hubbell concealed information about certain critical Arkansas matters, namely, the much-publicized Castle Grande real-estate project and related legal work by the Rose Law Firm, including the First Lady—the issues that led to the infamous missing files controversy.

All of this laid the groundwork for one of Starr's rationales for expanding his jurisdiction to include the President's affair with Monica Lewinsky: If, as is alleged, the President and Vernon Jordan arranged a job for Monica Lewinsky, it would be a close parallel to what Starr hopes to prove they did for Web Hubbell. Proving one helps prove the other.

Criminal Incompetence?

For an administration that came into office promising to be the most ethical in history, the list of matters under the title Whitewater is shameful. Even if it all can somehow be explained away and no proof of illegality can be shown, there still should have never been such mismanagement and lack of accountability.

On the other hand, the potential for criminal wrongdoing is also real. While the Whitewater development deal seems a moot non-issue, what about the potential siccing of the FBI on innocent travel office staff? What about the people whose privacy was invaded when their FBI files were improperly requested? Was Web Hubbell paid off with lucrative contracts? Were incriminating documents seized from Vince Foster's office?

We deserve a believable answer to all of these questions.

The Least You Need to Know

➤ Whitewater was a failed land deal in Arkansas. Investigation has proven wrongdoing by past associates of the Clintons, but not by the Clintons themselves.

➤ Clinton pals tried unsuccessfully to take over the White House travel office.

➤ Vince Foster committed suicide, and the White House removed key documents out of Foster's office immediately thereafter.

➤ The White House was found to be in unlawful possession of secret FBI files of Republicans.

Part 4
A Scandalous Affair

Bill Clinton's philandering ways became legendary at almost the same time he burst onto the national political scene. His enemies and opponents have been trying to make political hay from his penchant for pulchritude since 1992, and they've almost succeeded several times. But it took an unknown intern named Monica Lewinsky to finally reveal his Achilles' heel for all the world to see.

It's all here: the "sexual encounters," the illicit tape recordings, the desperate pleas for attention from a spurned lover, the behind-the-scenes maneuvers by a desperate prosecutor, the slippery schemes and half-truths of a cornered President, and the glee and shock of the media and the nation as a President self-destructs in the glare of the spotlight.

But first, let's take a look at some of Bill Clinton's predecessors in office, and see if any past Presidents were as imperfect in private as Mr. Clinton is in public.

Chapter 16

Sex in the White House

In This Chapter

➤ Thomas Jefferson's slave to love

➤ James Buchanan and his special friend

➤ Grover Cleveland's love child

➤ Warren G. Harding: Love on the sly

➤ FDR: They both loved women

➤ JFK: Insatiable

➤ LBJ and the secretarial pool

William Jefferson Clinton is not our first President to have a sexual scandal disrupt his Presidency. Throughout history, many of our most revered, renowned, and influential Presidents have engaged in "improper relationships" with companions who were not their wives. A political sex scandal never fails to hold our collective voyeuristic attention. Before we get to the chapters containing the raw materials of this most recent Presidential crisis, let's look at some of our nation's other merely human leaders.

White House Confidential

According to a Harvard historian, George Washington died by catching a chill after leaping out a back window with his trousers in hand "after an assignation with an overseer's wife."

Jefferson's "Black Venus"

To this day, there remains a controversy involving one of the first well-known scandals involved the father of the Declaration of Independence and our nation's third President, Thomas Jefferson. The belief was that Jefferson was involved in a long-time romance with one of his slaves named Sally Hemings, dubbed his "Black Venus." The *Richmond Recorder*, a Federalist, anti-Jefferson newspaper, accused Jefferson of seducing the young slave girl and fathering several mulatto children with her.

President Thomas Jefferson.
AP/Wide World Photos

Sally Hemings was characterized by Jefferson's grandson as being "light colored and decidedly good looking." Historians report that Sally Hemings became Jefferson's concubine while he was acting United States Ambassador to France. Hemings had traveled with one of Jefferson's young daughters over to France in order to be her maid. While there, at the age of 16, Sally Hemings became pregnant with Thomas Jefferson's baby.

Hemings gave birth to four more children. These mulatto children joined the white society, a very unusual occurrence for that time, which only served to increase speculation that they were Jefferson's children.

Upon her death, an editorial recounting Jefferson's love for Sally was printed in the *Boston Gazette*. It read;

> *Thou Sally, thou my house shall keep,*
> *My widower's tears shall dry!*
> *My virgin daughters—See! They weep -*
> *Their Mother's place supply.*
> *Oh, Sally. Hearken to my vows.*
> *Yield up thy sooty charms -*
> *My best beloved! My more than spouse,*
> *Oh, take me to thy arms.*

Today, historians are fairly convinced that Jefferson was indeed the father to Hemings' five mulatto children, and descendents of those children claim the Founding Father as their ancestor.

James Buchanan and His "Better Half"

Before becoming America's 15th President, James Buchanan was both a rising young lawyer and a swinging single. While his friends would drink the night away in local taverns, Buchanan spent his evenings in fashionable homes making himself agreeable to the parents of rich families. His hope was to ensnare a rich, young, unmarried daughter as his own wife.

To no one's surprise, he fell in love with Anne Coleman, the daughter of the ironmaster Robert Coleman, who was one of the country's first millionaires. In 1819, they became engaged to be married. But, neither her father, nor Lancaster society, approved of the union. Most concluded that Buchanan was more interested in the Coleman fortune than Anne.

Nonetheless, the couple maintained their courtship. But, in a fit of jealousy over a visit that Buchanan had made to another woman, Anne called off the engagement in a huff. She left to stay with her sister, and, before the lovers could be reconciled, Anne died of mysterious causes, possibly a suicide.

Become a Pundit

Like Bill Clinton, James Buchanan was also elected without winning a majority of the votes cast. In 1856, when he was elected President, Buchanan received only 45 percent of the popular vote. In 1992, Clinton won with 43 percent of the vote.

Become a Pundit

In 1990, after Republicans spread a rumor that House Speaker Tom Foley was gay, Representative Barney Frank, the only openly gay member of the House, threatened to go on the floor of Congress and out every gay Republican unless the rumor stopped. The rumor stopped.

At the age of 65, still a single man, James Buchanan became President of the United States. Though he was always known as a careless flirt to the wives of his Cabinet ministers, Buchanan was unusually close to a male companion named William Rufus De Vane King of Alabama, who became Vice President under Franklin Pierce.

The friendship between Buchanan and King lasted for 23 years and prompted never-ending rumors that the President was a homosexual. For a time, the two men were roommates in Washington, and King's fastidious habits and obvious intimacy with bachelor Buchanan gave rise to some cruel jokes. Andrew Jackson called King "Aunt Fancy" and James Buchanan's "better half."

King wrote long and intimate letters to Buchanan. After King was appointed minister to France, he wrote, "I am selfish enough to hope you will not be able to procure an associate who will cause you to feel no regret at our separation."

Buchanan was America's only unmarried President; William Rufus De Vane King of Alabama was our only unmarried Vice President.

Grover Cleveland: Ma, Ma, Where's My Pa?

Known as a gambler, a drinker, a scoundrel, a draft dodger, and the father of an illegitimate child, Grover Cleveland overcame huge odds to become the 22nd President of the United States.

In the bid for the 1884 Presidency, the battle between Republican candidate James G. Blaine and Democrat Grover Cleveland became known as one of the dirtiest campaigns in history. Democratic newspapers ran feature articles that showed how Blaine accepted bribes while a Congressman. The Republicans countered with rumors about Cleveland fathering an illegitimate child with a widow named Mrs. Maria Halpin.

Rather than deny the story, Cleveland took the bold step of admitting his indiscretion. He announced to the public that he had once formed an "illicit connection with a woman and the child had been born." Cleveland also volunteered that he gave the child his name and dutifully maintained an interest in the child's welfare. His strategy paid off handsomely. The more information that came out about the Halpin affair, the better Cleveland appeared.

Meanwhile, the Democrats learned that James G. Blaine's first child had been born just three months after his marriage. Instead of coming clean like Cleveland, Blaine back-pedaled and floated a story about a mix-up involving the death of his father and another about two different marriage services. No one bought his explanations, and the contrast between the two candidates could not have been more clearly drawn.

From there, the Presidential campaign of 1884 dissolved into a classic mud fight. Democrats would chant: "James G. Blaine, the continental liar from the state of Maine." Republican's would counter with: "Ma, Ma, where's my pa?" The Democrats, gloating at a probable Cleveland victory, would answer: "Gone to the White House, ha, ha, ha."

Grover Cleveland won the Presidency by 219 electoral votes to Blaine's 182, notwithstanding the fact that he was only ahead in the popular count by 1,100 votes.

Become a Pundit

To win the Presidency today, a candidate must obtain 270 electoral votes. In fact, it's possible to lose the popular vote and still become President.

Warren G. Harding: Sex in the White House Coatroom

President Warren G. Harding was known more for his extramarital affairs than affairs of State. While running the country, Harding kept two mistresses and had constant sex under the First Lady's nose in a White House coatroom—an accomplishment unequaled until John F. Kennedy occupied the White House.

The love of Harding's life was not his wife Florence. Instead, it was a young girl who was just 13 years old when they met. Nan Britton was described as an "overly developed child who wore extremely short dresses above the knees," who was always doing things to attract the already-married Harding's attention.

After graduating from secretarial school, Nan contacted Harding on the premise of looking for a job and from that point on their passion erupted. While campaigning for the Senate, he and Nan made love from one end of the country to the other. After becoming a senator, Warren Harding would pen 30-, 40-, 50-page love letters to Nan during boring debates in the Senate. He also sent her regular boxes of her favorite candy. On her 21st birthday, Harding gave her a gold watch.

After his election as the 28th President, his distress over his sham marriage to Florence grew even more problematic. He had a strong appetite for sex and love, and in the Oval Office he was getting neither. Throwing caution to the wind, Harding summoned his mistress to the White House.

According to Nan,

> *He introduced me to the one place where, he said, he thought we might share kisses in safety. This was a small closet in the anteroom, evidently a place for hats and coats, but entirely empty most of the time we used it, for we repaired there many times in the course of my visits to the White House, and in the darkness of a space not more than five feet square, the President of the United States and his adoring sweetheart made love.*

Harding and Nan would regularly have sex in that White House coatroom. Once, Nan and Harding were almost caught by the First Lady. They were in the coatroom making love when Mrs. Harding turned up at the door to the President's office. The Secret Service man barred her way. She demanded that he stand aside, but he said that it was a Secret Service regulation that no one was allowed in when Harding had asked not to be disturbed.

The First Lady quickly made off so she could get into the President's office via his secretary's. The Secret Service man banged on the coatroom door. Harding hurried Nan out of a side door before the First Lady could catch them.

President Harding often complained about this sort of inconsiderate behavior by his wife. "She makes my life hell for me," he told Nan.

Franklin and Eleanor: They Had a "New Deal"

Franklin D. Roosevelt was a debonair, martini-sipping politician whose New Deal put America back to work. He also ran one of the most sexually indiscriminate White Houses in history.

During his time at college, FDR fell under the tutelage of his distant relative, President Theodore Roosevelt, and met his niece Eleanor. Eleanor was an ugly duckling and was delighted that such a suave man as Franklin Roosevelt would be interested in her. After swearing to be faithful (apparently, with his fingers crossed behind his back), they married in 1905.

FDR couldn't keep his promise. After he was appointed Assistant Secretary of the Navy, Eleanor discovered love letters written between her husband and her social secretary, Lucy Page Mercer. Lucy represented everything Eleanor wasn't: youth, beauty, sexiness. Eleanor threatened divorce but Roosevelt replied, "Don't be a goose."

Eleanor agreed to stay married under two conditions. One, that he understood that she would never share his bed again. And two, that he agree to end the affair with Lucy Mercer.

FDR consented, but as soon as Eleanor turned her back, he started up where he had left off. First with Lucy, and then, after she married, with a new secretary, Marguerite "Missy" LeHand. In time, Eleanor learned to tolerate her husband's liaisons and their marriage became more of a working partnership than a romantic relationship.

Unloved by her husband, Eleanor Roosevelt eventually turned to women for companionship and took a lover of her own named Lorena Hickok. Lorena was an Associated Press reporter who was a well-known lesbian. She smoked cigars and cigarettes, drank bourbon and was very much "one of the boys."

President Franklin Delano Roosevelt and Eleanor Roosevelt.
Archive Photos

Eleanor wrote to Hickok, saying: "I wish I could lie down beside you tonight and take you in my arms"; "I ache to hold you close"; and "Most clearly I remember your eyes, with a kind of teasing smile to them, and the feeling of that soft spot just northeast of the corner of your mouth against my lips …." She and Hickok exchanged rings and Hickok took up residence across the hall from Eleanor in the White House.

White House Confidential

Eleanor Roosevelt wrote an article for *Photoplay* in July 1938 entitled "Why We Roosevelts Are Movie Fans." Some of the First Family's favorite films included: *Arsene Lupin Returns* (1938), *The Buccaneer* (1938), *The Hurricane* (1937), *The Life of Emile Zola* (1937), *Snow White and the Seven Dwarves* (1937), *The Adventures of Tom Sawyer* (1938).

Concurrently, FDR's mistress, Missy LeHand, became sick and was moved out of the White House and died three years later. Lucy Mercer returned as Roosevelt's mistress. In fact, Roosevelt had kept in touch with her over the years without Eleanor's knowledge.

With his longtime love Lucy Mercer at his side, the President died of a massive cerebral hemorrhage in Warm Springs, Arkansas, less than a month before the end of WWII in Europe and four months before the fall of Japan.

JFK: Some Like It Hot

John F. Kennedy's reputation as a womanizer is peppered with many famous names: Marilyn Monroe, Angie Dickinson, Jayne Mansfield, stripper Blaze Starr. It's also peppered with women who just had titles: hookers, stewardesses, showgirls, baby-sitters, hostesses, secretaries. If you were a woman, you were fair game to our Nation's 34th President.

JFK married "the classic virgin," Jacqueline Bouvier, but, in the Kennedy tradition, never had any intention of keeping his vows to her. Jackie did not expect fidelity, as she had witnessed her father's many affairs, but depression over Jack's sexual dalliances sometimes proved unavoidable. Jackie tried to stay one step in front of Jack. At White House receptions, she would always seat one of his lovers on either side of him. This way, at least, Kennedy would have no access to fresh talent.

President John F. Kennedy
UPI/Corbis-Bettmann

The night of his inaugural, JFK attended a party and the first thing he asked was, "Where are the broads?" The place was packed with Hollywood starlets and young girls. His brother-in-law, actor Peter Lawford, provided Kennedy with six candidates. JFK lined them up, picked two of them, and off they went to the bedroom to celebrate in style.

One visitor of the President tells of a time that she was kissing and hugging the President to the musical *Camelot*. She went to the bathroom to undress and when she returned, the President was already in bed waiting for her in his favorite position, on his back. He told her that they would have to have sex with her on top, which eased the pressure on his sore back.

Besides tryst's in the Lincoln bedroom and beyond, Kennedy used the White House swimming pool to host nude pool parties. At one party, JFK and a beautiful blonde were joined by attorney general and brother Bobby Kennedy, a male friend, and several other gorgeous naked girls. Suddenly, they got a message that the First Lady, who had left for Virginia, was on her way back to the White House. Everyone scrambled. But after the First Lady gathered the things she had forgotten and left again, the festivities in the pool resumed.

Kennedy had his White House staff comb the living quarters for dropped hairpins, lipsticks, and other incriminating remnants of his philandering. Unfortunately, they were not always thorough enough. One time, Jackie found a pair of women's panties stuck in a pillow case. Holding them between her thumb and forefinger, she said to her husband, "Would you please shop around and see who these belong to? They are not my size."

Kennedy loved blondes best, and the best blond was Marilyn Monroe. In 1954, while recuperating from back surgery, he pinned her picture to his wall and fantasized about bedding her. His affair with her lasted from the late '50s to March of 1962.

But Marilyn was not the only woman he was dreaming about. Even during the Cuban Missile Crisis, his mind was on sex. During a tense meeting when the fate of the world hung in the balance, Kennedy eyeballed an attractive secretary. He told Secretary of Defense Robert McNamara: "I want her name and number. We may avert war tonight."

Lyndon Baines Johnson: No Cows Please

Lyndon Baines Johnson was a rival of John F. Kennedy's in every way and considered it unfair that JFK's reputation as a womanizer usurped his own. Johnson boasted, "I have had more women by accident than he has had on purpose." One aid said, "He would screw anything that would crawl." But Johnson claimed he held himself to a higher standard, "I put high marks on beauty" he exclaimed. "I can't stand an ugly woman or a fat one who looks like a cow that's gonna sit on her own udder."

President Lyndon Johnson and Lady Bird Johnson.
Archive Photos

Like Kennedy, Johnson used the White House secretaries to his own sexual end. He would spot the ones that attracted him, make an advance on them, and if they had sex with him, place them on his personal staff. It was said that of the eight secretaries around him, only three were not having sex with him. One especially attractive secretary had sex with Johnson on his desk in the Oval Office.

Become a Pundit

Former Senator John Tower was nominated by President Bush to be his secretary of defense. The Senate rejected the nomination in part because Tower had been accused of chasing a secretary around a desk.

Another time, he and a secretary got caught by Lady Bird having sex on the President's sofa. Johnson blamed the Secret Service for not warning him. To ensure never getting caught with his pants down again, Johnson ordered the Secret Service to install a buzzer system so that the agents stationed in the Presidential residence could warn him when the First Lady was approaching. The Secret Service reported, "If we saw Lady Bird heading for the elevator or stairs, we were to ring the bell."

The White House secretaries were not only entertained in the Oval Office. Johnson also had sex with them on

Air Force One and on the presidential yacht, *Sequoia*. "He may have been just a country boy from Texas," explained press secretary George Reedy, "but he had the instincts of a Turkish sultan."

The Gentlemen's Agreement

Of course, America at large was none the wiser. Even though rumors abounded among the journalists who covered the White House, few outside the President's inner circle knew of these affairs, and certainly the general public—in Kansas, Vermont, Wyoming—had no idea what Roosevelt was up to after they switched off his fireside chat. It was deemed unseemly to report on such matters—beneath the dignity of any respectable newspaper, and unimportant to the national discourse. (You'll read more about the change in media standards in Chapter 20.)

Obviously, things have changed. Are we better off knowing? It's hard to say. Of course we don't want to be kept in the dark about our President's true nature; but how relevant is the President's "nature" to how well he does his job? It would be hard to conceive of how our national story would have played out had the contributions of George Washington, Thomas Jefferson, and John F. Kennedy been eliminated because their character behind closed doors was ruled impeachable.

The Least You Need to Know

➤ Sex in the White House is as old as the Republic.

➤ Men considered to be great presidents have done far worse than what Clinton is accused of doing.

➤ Letting our Presidents' human failings overshadow their capabilities and accomplishments may do the country more harm than good.

Chapter 17

Enter the Intern

> **In This Chapter**
>
> ➤ Monica Lewinsky eyes the President
>
> ➤ The affair begins
>
> ➤ People get suspicious
>
> ➤ Lewinsky is transferred to the Pentagon
>
> ➤ Monica refuses to give up
>
> ➤ The Blue Dress
>
> ➤ We can still be friends

Is Bill Clinton so obsessed with sex and power that he is willing to undermine both national respect and his focus on policy and statesmanship? Was Monica Lewinsky a big flirt who the President just found simply irresistible, or did she have her sights set on a relationship with the President before she ever got a job at the White House? Given that Monica supposedly told a friend that she was going to Washington to get her "Presidential kneepads," it seems that she indeed had an agenda, and it certainly wasn't "good government." Whatever the case, Monica got her man, and consequently, Kenneth Starr finally got his.

Initial Contacts with the President

In June 1995, at the ripe age of 21, Monica Lewinsky began work as a White House intern. She was assigned to work on correspondence in the office of Chief of Staff Leon Panetta in the Old Executive Office Building.

Monica Lewinsky.
AP/Wide World Photos

The very month after her internship began, Monica and the President began what she characterized as "intense flirting." At White House functions and departure ceremonies, she made eye contact with him, shook his hand, and above all, made sure she introduced herself. Later, she ran into the President in the West Wing basement and introduced herself again. She was delighted that the President told her that he already knew who she was.

Monica told her aunt that the President seemed attracted to her. She then confided in a friend that she had a big crush on Clinton. She was sure she'd gotten his attention.

Mumbo Jumbo

An **internship** is a non-paying position similar to an apprenticeship where an inexperienced person gains experience.

Sex with the Commander in Chief

In late 1995, Congress and the President could not agree on a budget. As a result, the government "shut down" until a compromise could be reached. Only essential federal employees worked during the furlough, and the White House staff shrank for the week. The interns kept working and took on extra duties, because they were unpaid.

November 15, 1995, the second day of the government shutdown, marked the beginning of the sexual relationship between the President of the United States and the intern. Ms. Lewinsky worked in Chief of Staff Panetta's West Wing office, where she answered phones and ran errands. On that day, the flirting between the President and Monica Lewinsky began when they were alone in the Chief of Staff's office. In the course of their conversation, a brazen Monica lifted her jacket and showed the President the straps of her thong underwear.

This must have piqued Clinton's interest because they rendezvoused again later that same night. Monica says that while she was en route to a restroom, which just happened to be in the West Wing, she passed George Stephanopoulos' office, where she saw the President. He beckoned her to come in. Once inside, she let on that she had a crush on him. The President chuckled and then asked if she'd like to see his private office. Of course she would!

They went through the President's private dining room and toward the study off the Oval Office. Monica said, "We talked briefly and sort of acknowledged that there had been a chemistry that was there before and that we were both attracted to each other." Clinton then asked if he could kiss her. Without hesitation, Monica puckered up.

Later that same evening, she and the President met for a third time. In the hallway, just off the Oval Office, she and the President started kissing again. Monica then unbuttoned her jacket, her bra came off, and Clinton kissed and massaged her breasts.

Their fun was interrupted by the phone. So the President could take the call, they moved from the hallway and into the back office. Clinton spoke to the caller while he "put his hand down my pants and stimulated me manually in the genital area." Lewinsky said she thinks the call was from a senator or a congressman. While he talked, she started performing oral sex on him.

The President finished the phone call, but before Monica could finish, he made her stop. She was hurt. She said, "I told him that I wanted … to complete that. And he said … that he needed to

Sound Bites

When you catch his eye, you must give him the most inviting and receptive look you can manage ….

—Dr. Patricia Allen, *Getting to "I Do" The Secret to Doing Relationships Right*

Media Alert

Clinton and Lewinsky's first sexual encounter took place on the same day that Clinton signed a "Family Week" proclamation. *The New York Times* notes: The Family Week proclamation cited a "shared commitment to the importance of family life."

Become a Pundit

Prior to going to work for the Clinton campaign in 1992, George Stephanopoulos was chief of Staff for Speaker of the House Tom Foley.

wait until he trusted me more." The President then joked that he "hadn't had that in a long time." (Ken Starr's inclusion of this quote seems unnecessarily cruel.)

On November 17, Monica went to the Oval Office and told the President's secretary, Betty Currie, that she was there because the President had asked her to get him some pizza. Once inside, all thoughts of Italian food went out the window as she and the President went at it once again.

At some point, Betty Currie approached the door leading to the Oval Office and said the President had a telephone call. Monica remembers the caller being a member of Congress. She then said that while the President was on the phone "he unzipped his pants and exposed himself." She took the hint and performed oral sex on him while he spoke on the phone. Again, he stopped her before he ejaculated.

During this visit, the President told her that he liked her smile and her energy. He also said, "I'm usually around on weekends, no one else is around, and you can come see me."

White House Confidential

Ninety minutes before airtime of the first televised debate with Republican Presidential candidate Richard Nixon, John F. Kennedy disappeared into a hotel room with a prostitute. He was so pleased with his relaxed on-air performance that he had hookers lined up for each of the subsequent debates.

President Clinton called Monica Lewinsky early on the afternoon of Sunday, January 7. She was thrilled because it was the first time he had called her at home. "I asked him what he was doing?" The President told her that he was going to the office soon. She replied, "Oh, do you want some company?" Clinton said, "That would be great!"

Here was their plan: He would leave the door to his office open and she would pass by with some papers. He would then notice her in the hall and invite her in for a visit. The plan worked perfectly. Monica walked by and he said, "Oh, hi Monica, come on in." Once inside, they managed to contain their passion for about 10 minutes before they retired to the Oval Office bathroom to be intimate.

During the bathroom encounter, Monica and the President kissed, and he touched her breasts with his hands and his mouth. The President, according to Monica, "was talking about performing oral sex on me." She stopped him because she was having her period, but she did perform fellatio on him.

Afterward, she and the President moved to the Oval Office and talked. Monica said, "He was chewing on a cigar. And then he had the cigar in his hand and he was kind of looking at the cigar in … sort of a naughty way. And so … I looked at the cigar and I looked at him and I said, we can do that, too, sometime."

"We need to talk about our relationship …"

On Sunday, January 21, 1996, she and the President got together again. By now, Lewinsky was developing what could only be described as a schoolgirl crush on Clinton, and, typically, she made more of their "relationship" than he did.

She told the grand jury, "We had … had phone sex for the first time the week prior, and I was feeling a little bit insecure …. I didn't know if this was sort of developing into some kind of a longer-term relationship than what I thought it initially might have been …." In the course of conversation, she asked the President why he didn't ask her any questions about herself. "Is this just about sex … or do you have some interest in trying to get to know me as a person?" The President replied that "he cherished the time that he had with me."

Pleased that he was mirroring her feelings, Monica nevertheless thought that his statement was a little odd since he didn't really even know her yet. Then, in mid-sentence, "he just started kissing me," said Monica. The President then unzipped his pants. She knew what to do.

While she was giving him oral sex someone walked into the Oval Office. She said, "[The President] zipped up real quickly and went out and came back in …. I just remember laughing because he walked out there and was visibly aroused, and I just thought it was funny."

At her suggestion, they continued in their devilish plan to bump into each other in the hallway, because, according to Monica, "when it happened accidentally, that seemed to work really well." Once back in the privacy of his study, she and the President went back to their routine. They kissed, he touched her breasts, he kissed her breasts, he touched her genitals, and then she performed oral sex.

After their sexual encounter they sat in the Oval Office and talked for about 45 minutes. It was during this conversation, according to Monica, that their friendship "started to blossom."

Sound Bites

I've looked on a lot of women with lust. I've committed adultery in my heart many times.

—Candidate Jimmy Carter in a 1976 *Playboy* magazine interview

Breaking Up Is Hard to Do

On President's Day 1996, President Clinton broke off (albeit only temporarily) his affair with Monica Lewinsky. The President told her that "he no longer felt right about their relationship, and he had to put a stop to it." Monica was informed that she was still welcome to visit him, but "only as a friend." When they parted, he hugged her, but would not kiss her.

Though her spirit was broken, her will remained. Monica said, "there continued to be sort of this flirtation … when we'd see each other." She passed him often in the halls of the White House (accidentally on purpose) because she knew that whenever the President saw her it reminded him to call her. Monica Lewinsky was no dummy. She was a woman with a mission. A month and a half after the February 19th breakup, the President resumed their affair.

On March 31, 1996, the President telephoned Monica at her desk and suggested that she come to see him on the pretext of delivering papers. With glee that he was interested in her again, Monica did exactly that. She went to the Oval Office with a folder containing Presidential papers under her arm and was admitted by a plainclothes Secret Service Agent. In her folder was a gift for Clinton, a Hugo Boss necktie.

Clinton allegedly wearing a tie bought for him by Monica Lewinsky.
Agence France Presse/ Corbis-Bettmann

On this occasion, according to Monica, "he focused on me pretty exclusively." The President kissed her breasts and fondled her. At one point, Clinton inserted a cigar into her vagina and then put it in his mouth and told her "it tastes good"—another detail that seems included in this legal document for no other reason than to outrage or amuse.

Secret Service Suspicions

The relationship was heating up. Clinton was hooked and Monica was loving it. Everything was fine except for one minor detail—people were starting to notice. Officer John Muskett testified, "If the President was known to be coming into the Diplomatic Reception Room, a lot of times [Lewinsky] just happened to be walking down the corridor, you know, maybe just to see the President."

Secret Service Officer Lewis Fox testified, "It was pretty commonly known that she did frequent the West Wing on the weekends." Officers would even wager with each other that the President would arrive from the Residential Wing within 10 minutes whenever Lewinsky was admitted to the White House.

Deeming her frequent visits "a nuisance," one Secret Service officer complained to Evelyn Lieberman, the deputy chief of staff for operations. In December 1995, according to Monica, Lieberman chided her for being in the West Wing and told her that interns are not permitted around the Oval Office. Monica, who had begun a new job at the Office of Legislative Affairs, told Lieberman that she was not an intern anymore. After expressing surprise that she'd been hired by Legislative Affairs, Lieberman said she must have her confused with someone else.

Become a Pundit

Before President Kennedy instituted an embargo against Cuba in 1963, he had his aides buy him several hundred Cuban cigars for his own personal use.

Become a Pundit

The Clinton Administration fought vigorously against having the Secret Service testify against the President. It was only after a district Court judge, and then nine unanimous D.C. circuit judges, ruled against them, that the President's bodyguards testified.

White House Confidential

There have been six Congressmen who have admitted to, or have been convicted of, having sex with a teenager.

In Monica's view, some White House staff members seemed to think that she was to blame for the President's interest in her. "People were wary of his weaknesses," she said. "Maybe they didn't want to look at him and think that he could be responsible for anything, so it had to all be my fault …. I was stalking him or I was making advances towards him."

Lewinsky's Transfer to the Pentagon

With the White House staff and Secret Service employees whispering about Lewinsky's constant presence in the West Wing, Lieberman decided that Monica had to go. The threat to the Presidency was too great. Without fanfare, Lieberman took the initiative and had Lewinsky transferred to the Pentagon.

Though she was out of sight, apparently she wasn't out of mind. On Easter Sunday, April 7, 1996, the President telephoned Monica at home. She told him of her dismissal and said, "I was crying and I asked him if I could come see him, and he said that that was fine."

Once at the White House, the President told her that he thought her transfer had something to do with him. He said, "Why do they have to take you away from me?" He continued, "I promise you if I win in November I'll bring you back." Clinton promised Monica something that would never be.

The President and Monica then had another sexual encounter in their favorite hallway. Monica said, "I think he unzipped [his pants] … because it was sort of this running joke that I could never unbutton his pants, that I just had trouble with it." During this encounter, someone called out from the Oval Office that the President had a phone call. He went back to the Oval Office for a moment, then took the call in the study. The President indicated that Monica should perform oral sex while he talked on the phone, and she obliged.

The telephone conversation was about politics, and Monica thought the caller might have been from the President's advisor Dick Morris. She was correct. White House records confirmed that the President had one telephone call during her visit: from "Mr. Richard Morris," to whom he talked from 5:11 to 5:20 p.m.

White House Confidential

In 1996, Dick Morris was caught on videotape having sex with a prostitute and was forced to resign as a Clinton confidante.

It was great that he was inviting her over again, but what Monica really wanted was the job she thought he'd promised her. White House job offers were not forthcoming. In an unsent letter to Clinton she wrote:

> *I was so sure that you would call me to come visit and you would kiss me passionately and tell me you couldn't wait to have me back. You'd ask me where I wanted to work and say something akin to "Consider it done" and it would be. Instead I didn't hear from you for weeks ….*

The hope amongst White House staffers was that Lewinsky's relationship with the President would fade away. Monica however, would not be deterred. She was love-struck. Now she wanted what she saw as rightfully hers—the Leader of the Free World.

Playful Monica

Like a child who refuses to go to bed when told, Lewinsky refused to give up the role of seductress. Her problem, though, was access. She no longer worked at the White House so she had no business wandering the West Wing. "Bumping" into Clinton wasn't as easy as it used to be.

For his part, President Clinton must have breathed a little easier. By not putting up a fight about her transfer to the Pentagon, the temptation of a quickie in the Oval Office had been eliminated. If he wanted to see her, he could do it on his terms.

White House Confidential

Lady Bird Johnson knew of her husband's philandering. She explained it away this way: "My husband loves people. All people. And half the people in the world are women. You don't think I could have kept my husband away from half the people?"

After Monica began her Pentagon job on April 16, 1996, she had no further physical contact with the President for the remainder of the year. But they did talk by phone, especially in her first weeks at the new job. The President sometimes called from trips when the First Lady was not accompanying him. During at least seven calls, Monica and the President had phone sex. In fact, on the day the President was to leave for the

Olympics in Atlanta, he and Monica had phone sex at 6:30 in the morning. After it was over, the President exclaimed, "Good morning!" and then said, "What a way to start a day!"

Phone sex was okay, but it wasn't the kind of up-close-and-personal relationship Monica yearned for. With this is mind, she went to great lengths to position herself at events that she knew the President would be attending. Though her private access to Clinton had been blocked by her transfer to the Pentagon, she was determined to play the temptress in public. By putting on the charm when he walked by, she was often able to remind Clinton that she was still a good-time gal.

On August 18, Monica attended the President's 50th birthday party at Radio City Music Hall, where she decided to have a little public fun with him. When he reached past her at the rope line to shake hands with another guest, she reached out and touched his crotch in a "playful" fashion. It's likely she got his attention.

White House Confidential

When he was a young boy, George Washington copied pages of a popular etiquette book of the time. One piece of advice he heeded: "When in company, put not your hands to any part of the body not usually discovered."

Betty Currie's Role

After the 1996 election, the President and Monica resumed their sexual relationship face to face. But with more suspicious eyes watching their every move, they needed help.

Enter Clinton's secretary, Betty Currie. Monica would often call Currie and ask to see the President. From there, Currie would then ask Clinton if he wanted to see Monica. If he did, Currie arranged the meeting and the sexcapades continued.

The President and Monica got together usually when his life was less hectic and the mansion less crowded. When Monica would arrive at the White House, Betty Currie generally would be the one to authorize her entry and take her to the West Wing. Sometimes Betty came to the White House on the weekends to accomplish only one task: to take Monica in to see the President.

President Clinton's personal secretary, Betty Currie.
AP/Wide World Photos

Currie suspected impropriety in Clinton's relationship. In her words:

> *He was spending a lot of time with a 24-year-old young lady. I know he said that young people keep him involved in what's happening in the world, so I knew that was one reason, but there was a concern of mine that she was spending more time than most.*

In actuality, Betty Currie truly understood that the President's meetings with Monica were "more personal in nature as opposed to business," and she did what she could to avoid learning the sordid details. One exchange between Betty and Monica explained her position:

> *Lewinsky: As long as no one saw—and no one did—then nothing happened.*

> *Currie: Don't want to hear it. Don't say any more. I don't want to hear any more ….*

Become a Pundit

When Clinton wanted to talk to Lewinsky, Betty Currie would dial the phone herself rather than going through the White House operators. This way, evidence of the call was kept off the switchboard log books, and, at least for a while, no one at the White House was none the wiser.

183

The Blue Dress

Like most lovers, Monica and the President shared pet-names. She called him "the Big Guy" and "Handsome" (and later, the "big creep"). Sometimes she was "Sweetie," sometimes "Dear," other times "Baby."

On Valentines Day 1997, Monica's "Handsome" was the recipient of a public love note published in the *Washington Post*. The ad read:

> *HANDSOME*
>
> *With love's light wings did*
> *I o'er perch these walls*
> *For stony limits cannot hold love out,*
> *And what love can do that dares love attempt.*
> *—Romeo and Juliet 2:2*
>
> *Happy Valentine's Day.*
> *M*

Shakespeare's magic worked. Within two weeks of posting her message, the President called and invited her to come see him at his weekly radio address. Wearing a navy-blue dress from the Gap, Monica went to the White House thinking she'd be playing Juliet to Clinton's Romeo. She watched as he delivered his speech, then they had their photo taken together. Afterwards, the President asked her to walk with him and Betty towards his office. Once there, Currie excused herself, and left them alone.

After 11 long months, Monica was once again in the arms of her President. She said, "The President started to say something to me and I was pestering him to kiss me, because … it had been a long time since we had been alone." But Clinton showed some self-restraint and told her to wait a minute because he had some presents for her.

He gave her a hat pin and a special edition of Walt Whitman's *Leaves of Grass* as belated Christmas presents. Monica described it as "the most sentimental gift he had given me … it's beautiful and it means a lot to me."

Media Alert

At the height of the Depression, Franklin Delano Roosevelt used the radio to speak to the nation. FDR's "Fireside Chats" served to bolster the country's flagging confidence.

After the President gave her the gifts, Monica said, "we went back over by the bathroom in the hallway, and we kissed. We were kissing and he unbuttoned my dress and fondled my breasts with my bra on, and then took them out of my bra and was kissing them and touching them with his hands and with his mouth." As they kissed, she massaged him through his pants. She then unbuttoned his shirt and started kissing his chest. She said, "I wanted to perform oral sex on him … and so I did." Moments later, he thought he heard someone approaching so they moved into the bathroom.

White House Confidential

Bill Clinton also romanced Hillary Rodham with Walt Whitman's *Leaves of Grass.*

Monica continued giving the President oral sex but before he had an orgasm he pushed her away. Monica stood up and said, "I care about you so much; … I don't understand why you won't let me … it's important to me; I mean, it just doesn't feel complete. It doesn't seem right."

Monica and the President hugged and he told her that he didn't want to get addicted to her and didn't want her to get addicted to him. They look at each other for a moment. Then, saying, "I don't want to disappoint you," the President consented. For the first time in their relationship, she performed oral sex to completion.

When Monica next took the navy-blue Gap dress from her closet to wear it, she noticed stains near one hip and on the chest.

Much later, the President explained, "I was sick after it was over and I, I was pleased at that time that it had been nearly a year since any inappropriate contact had occurred with Ms. Lewinsky. I promised myself it wasn't going to happen again. The facts are complicated about what did happen and how it happened. But nonetheless, I'm responsible for it."

Sound Bites

Yes, Mr. President, of course we can get that stain out.

—Slogan for Meurice Garment Care, New York, New York, as seen in 9/21/98 New York Observer

Sound Bites

I don't think there is a fancy way to say I have sinned.

—President Clinton, September 11, 1998

The President added, referring to the evening of the radio address: "I do believe that I was alone with her from 15 to 20 minutes. I do believe that things happened then which were inappropriate." He continued, "I never should have started it, and I certainly shouldn't have started it back after I resolved not to in 1996."

Can We Still Be Friends?

On Saturday, May 24, 1997, Clinton ended their affair for good. He was now firm in his resolve. On that day, Monica received a phone call from their go-between, Betty Currie, passing on an invitation for her to see the President. She arrived at the White House soon thereafter bearing gifts.

She gave him a puzzle and a Banana Republic shirt while visiting in the dining room. From there they moved to the President's private study. For Monica, the meeting now held new promise. The study was to them as the bedroom is to most couples. President Clinton, however, had different plans. He wanted a new world order.

The President broke the sad news and told her he was ending their affair for good. Earlier in his marriage, he told Monica, he had had hundreds of affairs, but since turning 40, he had made a concerted effort to be faithful. Clinton told Monica that he was attracted to her, considered her to be a great person, and hoped they would remain friends. Clinton explained that it was not her fault.

Sound Bites

I invented "it's not you, it's me"!
—George Costanza

Weeping, Monica begged Clinton not to end their affair, but the President was steadfast in his resolve. They kissed and hugged but that was it. For Monica, the truth was hard to take. The party was over.

Three days after this meeting, on May 27, 1997, the Supreme Court unanimously rejected President Clinton's claim that the Constitution immunized him from civil lawsuits. The Court allowed the sexual-harassment case of *Jones v. Clinton* to proceed.

The Least You Need to Know

➤ Monica Lewinsky made a concerted effort to catch the eye of the President.

➤ Their sexual relationship began shortly after she came to the White House.

➤ As time went by, Monica became emotionally attached to the President.

➤ Clinton, worried about possible ramifications from the affair, tried unsuccessfully to end the relationship with Lewinsky.

➤ White House staffers became suspicious of the relationship and had Monica transferred to the Pentagon.

➤ Clinton finally did end the affair, but it was too late.

Chapter 18

"It's Illegal to Threaten the President..."

In This Chapter

➤ Monica demands the President's attention

➤ Fatal attraction

➤ "I am not a moron"

➤ Vernon Jordan to the rescue

Working at the Pentagon would be a dream job for many young people just starting their careers—exciting, challenging, and intellectually stimulating. For Monica Lewinksy, however, her heart just wasn't in it. She longed to be back at the White House. There, she could roam the West Wing, pop in on the Big Guy, and, frankly, remind the President of what he'd been missing.

Her New Friend, Linda

Linda Tripp worked at the Pentagon, a floor below Lewinsky. Tripp had worked at the White House during the Bush Administration, and had been one of the few to stay on after the transition to work with Clinton's staff. The two were drawn together by their experiences at the White House and a shared love of gossip.

Tripp played the role of love adviser to Lewinsky. Lewinsky told Tripp that she was engaged in a dangerous liaison with an older married man whom, at first, she did not name. Pressed by Tripp, Lewinsky confessed that the man was the President of the United States.

Tripp disapproved of the relationship. She had a strong sense of morality—"Things like this would never happen in the Bush days," she declared more than once. She began referring to Clinton as "the big creep." Nevertheless, she was eager for details, and Monica began to confide more and more in her new friend.

Linda R. Tripp.
AP/Wide World Photos

Monica's Job Search

While going through the motions at the Pentagon, Lewinsky lobbied hard for a transfer back to the White House. The President, for his part, felt strong in his resolve to resist her sexual advances. He was sure he could stay out of trouble if she returned, and he agreed to do what he could to bring her back. Starr reported, "According to Betty Currie, President Clinton instructed her and [Deputy Assistant to the President] Marsha Scott to help secure Lewinsky a new White House job."

Betty Currie resisted this request. She later told Starr's office that her opinion of Monica had shifted over time. At first she said, she considered Lewinsky "a friend," someone who "had been wronged" and "maligned improperly."

But, as time went on, Currie started considering her a "pain in the neck." Starr explained, "The change of heart resulted in part from Ms. Currie's many phone calls in 1997 from Ms. Lewinsky, who was often distraught and sometimes in tears over her inability to get in touch with the President."

Deeming her "a little bit pushy," Currie expressed these concerns to the President and argued against bringing Monica back to work at the White House. But still the President was, according to Ms. Currie, "pushing us hard" on the matter. As far as Ms. Currie could recall, it was the only time the President instructed her to try to get someone a White House job.

Even though he was the world's most powerful man, Clinton was apparently helpless in orchestrating Monica's return. Time marched on and there was no White House job for Monica Lewinsky in sight. Not believing that the President really wanted her back, she blamed him for her troubles. She recounted a conversation to Starr that she had had with a girlfriend:

> *I don't know what I will do now but I can't wait any more and I can't go through all of this crap anymore. In some ways, I hope I never hear from him again because he'll just lead me on because he doesn't have the b—ls to tell me the truth.*

In a desperate note addressed to the President, Lewinsky expressed her escalating frustration:

> *I believe the time has finally come for me throw in the towel …. The only explanation I can reason for your not bringing me back is that you just plain didn't want to enough or care about me enough. … I just loved you— wanted to spend time with you, kiss you, listen to you laugh—and I wanted you to love me back. … As I said in my last letter to you I've waited long enough …. I give up. You let me down, but I shouldn't have trusted you in the first place."*

In one of their phone conversations when Monica made complaints about not getting to see him anymore, the President replied, "Every day can't be sunshine."

The truth was that Betty Currie and other White House staffers knew best. By keeping Monica Lewinsky away from the President, they could help the President avoid another damaging scandal.

Media Alert

As of midnight on the day the Starr report became public, pathfinder.com reported that the text was viewed on 61,863 different Web pages. Conversely, the President's rebuttal to the Starr report was viewed on only 3,177 Web pages.

Fatal Attraction

But Monica did not give up, and besides, Clinton had the free world to look after. Months passed, countless calls and messages from her went unreturned, and Monica once again turned into the ex-girlfriend from hell.

Very frustrated over her inability to get in touch with the President to discuss her job situation, Monica wrote him an angry letter on July 3, 1997. Opening, "Dear Sir," the letter took the President to task for breaking his promise to get her another White House job. Monica then pulled out the big guns. She obliquely threatened to disclose their relationship. According to the Starr report, "If she was not going to return to work at the White House, she wrote, then she would 'need to explain to my parents exactly why that wasn't happening.'"

Fireworks

Become a Pundit

Starr left nothing to chance in his report. He even hired a professional to write it. Starr report author Stephen Bates is a Harvard-trained lawyer and literary editor of the cerebral journal *The Wilson Quarterly*.

On the 4th of July, 1997, Lewinsky and Clinton set off some fireworks of their own. After reading her threatening letter from the day before, the President called Lewinsky to the White House. Lewinsky characterized it as a "very emotional" visit.

The Starr report said, "[T]heir meeting began contentiously, with the President scolding her: '[I]t's illegal to threaten the President of the United States.' He then told her he had not read her July 3 letter beyond the "Dear Sir" line; he surmised that it was threatening because Ms. Currie looked upset when she had brought it to him."

Among other things, Monica complained about Clinton's failure to get her a White House job after her long wait. Although the President claimed he wanted to be her friend, she said, he was not acting like it. Monica started weeping. In turn, the President tried to calm her by taking her in his arms to console her.

According to Starr, the President, "stroked her arm, toyed with her hair, kissed her on the neck, praised her intellect and her beauty." In Ms. Lewinsky's recollection:

> [H]e remarked … that he wished he had more time for me. And so I said, well, maybe you will have more time in three years. And I was … thinking just when he wasn't President, he was going to have more time on his hands. And he said, well, I don't know, I might be alone in three years. And then I said something about … us sort of being together. I think I kind of said, oh, I think we'd be a good team, or something like that. And he … jokingly said, well, what are we going to do when I'm 75 and I have to pee 25 times a day? And … I told him that we'd deal with that ….

Monica Lewinsky left the White House that day "sort of emotionally stunned." The depth of her naiveté can best be seen in her statement to the independent counsel. She told Starr, "I just knew he was in love with me."

White House Confidential

The judge overseeing the Paula Jones Sexual Harassment case ruled that Clinton had to answer a written interrogatory naming every state and federal employee since 1986 with whom he had sex or with whom he proposed having sex with. On December 23, 1997, the President answered the interrogatory: "None."

Vernon Jordan: Super Lawyer!

On October 6, 1997, Monica Lewinsky was told in a phone call from Linda Tripp that she would never work at the White House again. Tripp had heard the news from a friend who worked at the White House. For Monica this call was the "straw that broke the camel's back." Desperate and distraught over this awful news, Monica decided that the President owed her. In a conversation that Linda Tripp secretly recorded on October 6, Monica said she wanted two things from Clinton.

The first was contrition: He needed to "acknowledge that he helped f—k up my life." The second was a job, one that she could obtain without much effort: As she put it in a letter to the President later, "I don't want to have to work for this position ... I just want it to be given to me."

She then wrote the President a note saying that they should "get together and work on some way that I can come out of this situation not feeling the way I do." After composing the letter, she told Tripp, "I want him to feel a little guilty, and I hope that this letter did that."

After receiving that letter, Clinton telephoned Monica to discuss the matter. Lewinsky said that they spent most of the 90 minute call arguing. According to Monica, "[H]e got so mad at me, he must have turned purple." Lewinsky told him that she wanted a job in New York by the end of October, and the President promised to do what he could.

With friendship once again in the air, Lewinsky sent the President a packet, that included a "wish list" detailing the types of jobs that interested her. "She also included a pair of sunglasses and ... some jokes, a card and a postcard ... [which] featured a 'very erotic' Egon Schiele painting." The report dryly concludes, "[She] also enclosed a note with her thoughts on education reform."

In November 1997, Lewinsky asked Clinton whether Vernon Jordan might be able to help her get a job. Vernon Jordan was a well-known Washington attorney who was a close friend of Mr. Clinton's. He had many business contacts and, according to Lewinsky, might be able to help her. According to Monica, the President was receptive to the idea.

White House Confidential

In 1969, a drunk Senator Ted Kennedy drove his car off a bridge on Chappaquiddick Island. The Senator survived but his companion, Mary Jo Kopechne drowned. Kennedy did not report the accident for 10 hours. Thereafter, any Presidential aspirations he harbored drowned, too.

Pleased that the President of the United States was once again willing to help with her job hunt, she called Betty Currie at the White House to arrange a meeting between her and Vernon Jordan. Lewinsky said to Currie, "I don't think I told you that in my conversation last Thursday night with him [President Clinton] that he said that he would ask you to set up a meeting between VJ and myself, once VJ got back. I assume he'll mention this to you at some point—hopefully sooner rather than later!"

Currie told Lewinsky to call Vernon Jordan's secretary and set up a meeting. Monica did just that and scheduled a meeting with Vernon Jordan for November 5, 1997. Starr reported that,

> *Mr. Jordan and Ms. Lewinsky met in his office for about 20 minutes. She told him that she intended to move to New York, and she named several companies where she hoped to work. She showed him the "wish list" that she had sent the President. Mr. Jordan said that he had spoken with the President about her and she came "highly recommended."*

On the day after meeting with Mr. Jordan, Monica wrote Jordan a thank-you letter: "It made me happy to know that our friend has such a wonderful confidant in you."

Attorney Vernon Jordan after testifying for the fifth time before Starr's grand jury. AP/Wide World Photos

Though Jordan seemed eager to help her, Starr explained that "Mr. Jordan took no steps to help Ms. Lewinsky until early December, after she appeared on the witness list in the Jones case." In fact, Vernon Jordan couldn't even recall meeting with Monica on November 5. Starr mused, "Mr. Jordan's failure to remember his meeting with Ms. Lewinsky may indicate the low priority he attached to it at the time."

But Monica Lewinsky was about to go way up on everyone's priority list.

White House Confidential

Vernon Jordan has been compared to fabled Washington attorney Clark Clifford. While a noted statesman, Clifford was also said to have helped soothe Jack Kennedy's many girlfriends.

"I Am Not a Moron"

The rollercoaster that was Monica Lewinsky's life continued to race up and down. In the fall of '97 it was on a downward slope. A job at the White House was out. Vernon Jordan talked a good game but had yet to deliver the goods. The President was as evasive as ever. Monica tried to organize another meeting with Clinton to make sense of it all.

She had hoped to see him on November 11, Veteran's Day, but he did not respond. By courier, she sent the President another letter:

> *I asked you three weeks ago to please be sensitive to what I am going through right now and to keep in contact with me, and yet I'm still left writing notes in vain. I am not a moron. I know that what is going on in the world takes precedence, but I don't think what I have asked you for is unreasonable. … This is so hard for me, I am trying to deal with so much emotionally, and I have nobody to talk to about it. I need you right now not as President, but as a man, PLEASE be my friend.*

Her cries for help were answered. That evening, according to Monica, the President called and invited her to the White House the following day. Monica described this meeting in an e-mail as a "hysterical escapade," the culmination of days of phone calls and notes to Betty Currie and the President.

The next day, after the President returned from the Army-Navy Golf Course, Lewinksy met the President in the Oval Office study for only a minute or two. Starr explained, "Ms. Lewinsky gave him an antique paperweight In the shape of the White House. She also showed him an e-mail describing the effect of chewing Altoid mints before performing oral sex." Monica then pointed out that she just happened to be chewing Altoid mints. Showing great restraint, Clinton replied that he did not have enough time for oral sex. They kissed, and the President rushed off for a State Dinner with Mexican President Ernesto Zedillo.

Pent-up and upset after this brief visit, Monica did not see the President again until the first week in December. Hoping to arrange a longer rendezvous, she sent the President several notes, as well as a cassette with a recorded message.

In draft letters to the President, which were recovered from her Pentagon computer, Lewinsky reflected on the change in her relationship with the President: "[B]oth professionally and personally, … our personal relationship has caused me more pain. Do you realize that?" She begged for the President's understanding: "I don't want you to think that I am not grateful for what you are

Become a Pundit

Monica Lewinsky lived at the Watergate Apartment complex. Her nextdoor neighbor was Bob Dole. It was at the Watergate that a "third-rate burglary" took place which lead to the Watergate scandal and the eventual resignation of the 37th President, Richard M. Nixon.

doing for me now—I'd probably be in a mental institute without it—but I am consumed with disappointment, frustration, and anger."

Ms. Lewinsky rued the brevity of her November 13 visit with the President: "All you … ever have to do to pacify me is see me and hold me," she wrote. "Maybe that's asking too much."

On Friday, December 5, Monica got herself an invitation to attend a Christmas party at the White House with a Defense Department colleague. The closest she could get to the President was exchanging a few words in a reception line. This encounter heightened her sense of frustration. That evening Monica drafted yet another anguished letter to the President.

"[Y]ou want me out of your life," she wrote. "I guess the signs have been made clear for a while—not wanting to see me and rarely calling. I used to think it was you putting up walls."

She had purchased several gifts for him, and wrote, "I wanted to give them to you in person, but that is obviously not going to happen. I will never forget what you said that night we fought on the phone—if you had known what I was really like you would never have gotten involved with me. I'm sure you're not the first person to have felt that way about me. I am sorry that this has been such a bad experience."

She concluded: "I knew it would hurt to say goodbye to you; I just never thought it would have to be on paper. Take care."

White House Confidential

John F. Kennedy had affairs with dozens of women, including two secretaries, a blonde and a brunette, known as Fiddle and Faddle. He was said to have had threesomes with them and they often swam nude in the White House pool.

Advice from Uncle Vernon

Monica Lewinsky didn't know that since March 1997, Michael Isikoff, a reporter for *Newsweek*, had been in contact with her friend Linda Tripp. In January, one of Jones's lawyers told Isikoff that he had been given a tip about a sexual incident between

Clinton and a female staffer at the White House. The name of the woman in question was Kathleen Willey. Isikoff also got a lead on a possible witness: Linda Tripp. Isikoff met with her at the Pentagon in March.

In late 1997, Lewinsky was subpoenaed to testify in the Jones case. She panicked. She told Tripp that she called the President, who told her not to worry. He would call Vernon Jordan again.

With Lewinksy now a potential witness in the Jones civil case against the President, making Monica happy took on new importance. Vernon Jordan understood this and he and Monica met for a second time on Thursday, December 11.

> *Ms. Lewinsky testified that they discussed her job search, and Mr. Jordan told her to send letters to three business contacts that he provided her. Mr. Jordan testified that Ms. Lewinsky was anxious to get a job as quickly as possible, and he took action. Mr. Jordan told Ms. Lewinsky to keep him informed of the progress of her job search.*

At one point in the conversation, Jordan said, "[Y]ou're a friend of the President." This prompted Monica to reveal that she "didn't really look at him as the President." Rather, she "reacted to him more as a man and got angry at him like a man." When Jordan asked why Lewinsky got angry at the President, she replied that she became upset "when he doesn't call me enough or see me enough."

Like a knight acting as a second in battle for his king, Vernon Jordan told Monica that she should take out her frustrations on him rather than the President. He elaborated, "You're in love, that's what your problem is."

In actuality, Monica's problems were just beginning.

The Least You Need to Know

➤ Monica Lewinsky tried in vain to get a job back at the White House after her expulsion to the Pentagon.

➤ Clinton did little to assist her in her attempts to get back into the White House fold.

➤ Like Ken Starr, Monica became obsessed with the President.

➤ Once Monica became a potential witness in the Paula Jones case, Vernon Jordan offered his assistance.

Chapter 19

Sex, Lies, and Audiotape

In This Chapter

➤ Linda Tripp's secret tapes

➤ Monica encourages Tripp to commit perjury

➤ Monica does commit perjury

➤ Enter Ken Starr

➤ The President's deposition in the Jones case

As 1997 drew to a close, when Clinton and Lewinsky were just winding down their ill-fated affair, the Paula Jones case was just heating up. The case was getting closer to trial, and Jones' attorneys were getting closer to finding more women who, they thought, could substantiate Jones' claims.

Among the people they had learned of was Monica Lewinsky, now at the Pentagon but looking for a new job, and Linda Tripp, whose curious friendship with Monica may eventually change history.

Secret Tapes: A Washington Cliché

Linda Tripp may not have been the best new friend for naive Monica. Monica didn't know it, but Tripp had a history of trying to blow the whistle on Bill Clinton.

Tripp had explored another potential source of income—a "tell-all" book about the Clinton White House. Tripp had been approached by a New York literary agent,

Media Alert

Tripp denies that she was the source for renegade, ex-FBI agent Gary Aldrich's Clinton-bashing book, "*Unlimited Access.*"

Lucianne Goldberg, who was shopping for just such a book and had heard about Tripp from an old friend in the Bush Administration. Goldberg immediately hit it off with Tripp. The book idea they discussed was about the alleged illicit culture of the Clinton White House. But Goldberg couldn't find an interested publisher, and the project died.

Goldberg herself has a political background. She was an undercover operator for the Nixon White House in 1972. Posing as a reporter, Goldberg had been a Nixon spy on the George McGovern press plane.

Lucianne Goldberg
AP/Wide World Photos

Monica's Motives

By the time she was served with her subpoena, Monica Lewinsky was well on her way to getting a job in the private sector. It's important to understand she enlisted the President's help well before being named as a potential witness in the Jones case, because one of the charges being leveled at the President is that he obstructed justice by trying to get Lewinsky a job, in order to keep her quiet. Although Clinton had called Vernon Jordan once prior to Lewinsky's subpoena, it is the President's help after the subpoena that is under scrutiny.

Not only that, but in Linda Tripp's tapes, Monica is said to have said that the President encouraged her to lie about the affair in her Jones affidavit. Yet, in her grand jury testimony Lewinsky says "no one ever told me to lie." Which Monica is telling the truth? If it can be shown that Clinton did in fact encourage Lewinsky to lie, his job is in deep peril.

For her part, it seems that Monica just wanted to get a job in New York and get the heck out of Dodge. Her lover had left her and Washington was a sad place for her. It also seems clear that Lewinsky sincerely wanted to keep the relationship a secret. Doing so would cause her less aggravation, and would certainly enhance her chances of further assistance from the President and his powerful friend Vernon Jordan. Handy job references to be sure.

To that end, Lewinsky began to encourage Tripp to lie about what she knew, if and when Tripp was called to testify in the Jones case. Tripp knew two pieces of potentially damaging evidence that could help the Jones lawyers. The first had nothing to do with Monica Lewinsky at all: The main reason the Jones attorneys were after her was that Tripp allegedly had seen Kathleen Willey just after Willey exited the Oval Office after the supposed Presidential grope. Further, the Jones attorneys knew that Tripp knew about Lewinsky (they had already received an anonymous phone call informing them of that fact.)

Tripp's Trepidation

For good reason, this made Linda Tripp nervous. Although Monica had lots to gain by keeping quiet, there was nothing in it for Linda Tripp but potential criminal conduct. Worse, from Tripp's perspective, she had knowledge that could bring down the President. This weighed heavy on Linda Tripp. It cannot be discounted that it also may have thrilled her, given her past proclivities.

In December 1997, both Tripp and Lewinsky were served with subpoenas in the case of *Jones v. Clinton*. Jones's lawyers knew about Tripp from *Newsweek*'s story about Kathleen Willey in August. They had heard rumors about Lewinsky's alleged affair sometime in the fall.

Tripp had a dilemma. She feared being asked whether she knew any other women who had sexual relations with Clinton, and she did not want to perjure herself. But if she told the truth, she would be savaged by Clinton's lawyer Bob Bennett. She would probably lose her $88,000-a-year job at the Pentagon.

Tripp decided that she needed to protect herself. She bought a tape recorder and, over the course of several months, secretly taped her "friend" telling all about her relationship with the President. Undoubtedly, this is a strange way to protect

Become a Pundit

Clinton's lawyer in the Jones case, Robert Bennett, is the brother of conservative author and former Bush Cabinet member, William Bennett.

oneself. Tripp obviously wanted the tapes in case it ever came down to a case of her word about what Lewinsky had told her versus Lewinsky's potentially perjurous version. In that case, secretly taping Lewinsky was probably smart.

However, the sheer quantity of taping Tripp would undertake, eventually some 20 hours' worth, seems to indicate that Linda Tripp had more on her mind than just self-defense. In fact, it would later come out that literary agent Lucianne Goldberg had also encouraged Tripp to begin taping her conversations with the President's young mistress, perhaps for reasons more lucrative than legal.

Right before Christmas, with tape recorder running, and Monica not knowing, Tripp and Lewinsky talked about the upcoming legal battle: Tripp, foreshadowing the future, said to Monica:

> *I am being a sh—ty friend and that's the last thing I want to do because I won't lie. How do you think that makes me feel? I can make you stop crying and I could make your life so much easier if I could just f——g lie …. I feel like I'm sticking a knife in your back, and I know at the end of this, if I have to go forward, you will never speak to me again and I will lose a dear friend.*

White House Confidential

No one knew that Richard Nixon was secretly taping every conversation he had in the White House. It never came out until Presidential aide Alexander Butterfield was called before the House Watergate Committee and asked if there was a taping device in the Oval Office. "I was hoping you guys wouldn't ask me that," Butterfield replied. The rest, as they say, is history.

The Talking Points

On the way home from work one day, Lewinsky handed Tripp a sheet of paper entitled "Points to Make in an Affidavit." These "talking points" were intended to "help" Tripp, should she make a sworn affidavit in the Jones case. It remains a mystery as to who wrote them, although Lewinsky insists that she did herself.

The talking points start with a description of what the beginning of the affidavit should state:

> *Your first few paragraphs should be about yourself—what you do now, what you did at the White House and for how many years you were there as a career person and as a political appointee.*

This already is interesting. Unless you'd given an affidavit (also known as a declaration) in a case before, you wouldn't know that most affidavits begin this way—with some general background. If Lewinsky wrote it, how did she know it should start this way? If she didn't write it, then the person who did may be engaging in witness tampering (trying to influence what a witness will say) or suborning perjury (trying to get a witness to lie.)

The paper then asks Tripp to describe in the best light possible, what Tripp saw that day when she saw Willey emerge from the Oval Office:

> *You and Kathleen were friends. At around the time of her husband's death (The President has claimed it was after her husband died. Do you really want to contradict him?), she came to you after she allegedly came out of the oval and looked (however she looked), you don't recall her exact words, but she claimed at the time (whatever she claimed) and was very happy.*

Indeed, that is what Tripp had later claimed. The points then ask Ms. Tripp to elaborate on what she knew about the situation following the incident:

> *You spoke with [Willey] that evening, etc., and she relayed to you a sequence of events that was very dissimilar from what you remembered happening. As a result of your conversation with her ... you now do not believe that what she claimed happened really happened. You now find it completely plausible that she herself smeared her lipstick, untucked her blouse, etc.*

Maybe it's not perjury, but this section certainly depicts the incident in the best light possible. The document then asks Tripp to come across as "neutral" in the matter, since that is "better for credibility."

It then tells Tripp to explain why she cannot be deposed on December 18, 1997. (A deposition would open Tripp up to all sorts of questions that could lead to Lewinsky. An affidavit, since it is simply a document filed with the court, has the advantage of preventing follow-up questions.)

> *Your livelihood is dependent on the success of [a program that keeps you busy that day.] Therefore, you want to provide an affidavit laying out all of the facts in lieu of a deposition.*

The document then asks Tripp to state: "I never saw her go into the Oval Office, or come out of the Oval Office. I have never observed the President behave inappropriately with anybody." Again, literally true (Tripp did not actually see Willey "come out of the office," she saw her a very short time later.)

This is a very clever document. It never asks Tripp to directly lie, instead, it wants her to cast the whole situation in the best possible manner for the President. Therefore, it likely would not be considered suborning perjury per se. It could possibly be witness tampering, but again, it skirts very close to the line of the law. If Monica Lewinsky wrote it, she is one sharp lawyer!

Monica's Affidavit in the Jones Case

Lewinsky herself did in fact file a false affidavit in the Jones case on January 7, 1998. Here is what she said (attorneys for Jones referred to Lewinsky as a "Jane Doe"):

She begins with a brief overview of herself:

> *1. My name is Jane Doe #6. I am 24 years old and I currently reside at 700 New Hampshire Avenue, N.W. Washington, D.C. 20037.*

Lewinsky's affidavit then proffers her first whopper:

> *3. I cannot fathom any reason that the plaintiff would seek information from me for her case.*

It then goes on to state some true facts:

> *6. In the course of my employment at the White House I met President Clinton several times. I also saw the President at a number of social functions held at the White House. When I worked as an intern, he appeared at occasional functions attended by me and several other interns. The correspondence I drafted while I worked at the Office of Legislative Affairs was seen and edited by supervisors who either had the President's signature affixed by mechanism or, I believe, had the President sign the correspondence itself.*
>
> *7. I have the utmost respect for the President who has always behaved appropriately in my presence.* [This may or may not be true in her mind.]

It is in the next section that Monica really concocts some doozies, and is a main reason she had to accept an immunity deal from the independent counsel, lest she be charged with perjury:

> *8. I have never had a sexual relationship with the President, he did not propose that we have a sexual relationship, he did not offer me employment or other benefits in exchange for a sexual relationship, he did not deny me employment or other benefits for rejecting a sexual relationship. I do not know of any other person who had a sexual relationship with the President, was offered employment or other benefits in exchange for a sexual relationship, or was denied employment or other benefits for rejecting a sexual relationship. The occasions that I saw the President after I left employment at the White House*

in April, 1996, were official receptions, formal functions or events related to the U.S. Department of Defense, where I was working at the time. There were other people present on those occasions.

I declare under the penalty of perjury that the foregoing is true and correct.

(signed)
Monica S. Lewinsky

Feeling safe that no one she had told of her relationship with the President, except Linda Tripp, would be asked to testify in the Jones case, and certain, of course, that the President would not divulge their affair, Monica Lewinsky signed this affidavit, swearing under penalty of perjury that she had had no sexual relationship with the President.

Media Alert

Time magazine reports that Monica Lewinsky refused to cooperate with Ken Starr until he agreed to grant her mother immunity also. Lewinsky's mother, Marcia Lewis, was the keeper of the infamous blue dress.

The Big Payoff

By no coincidence, the day after she signed the affidavit, January 8, 1998, Ms. Lewinsky interviewed in New York at MacAndrews & Forbes Holdings, Inc. Ms. Lewinsky called Vernon Jordan and reported that she felt that the interview had gone "very poorly." Mr. Jordan indicated in response that "he'd call the chairman."

That day, Mr. Jordan called Ronald Perlman, chairman and chief executive officer of MFH. Asked why he chose to call Mr. Perlman, Mr. Jordan responded: "I have spent a good part of my life learning institutions and people, and in that process, I have learned how to make things happen. And the call to Ronald Perlman was a call to make things happen."

According to Mr. Perelman, Mr. Jordan spoke of "this bright young girl, who I think is terrific," and he wanted to make sure somebody took a look at her. Mr. Perelman testified to the Starr grand jury that Mr. Jordan had been on Revlon's Board of Directors, he did not recall Mr. Jordan ever calling to recommend someone.

After he spoke with Mr. Perelman, Mr. Jordan telephoned Ms. Lewinsky and told her, "I'm doing the best I can to help you out." On the morning of Friday, January 9, 1998, Ms. Lewinsky interviewed

Media Alert

Monica Lewinsky's mother, Marcia Lewis, wrote a book entitled *The Private Lives of Three Tenors*, which was, in part, a tell-all account of her own love affair with famed opera singer Placido Domingo.

a second time at Revlon and was informally offered a job. Mr. Jordan testified: "I have to assume that if she got the job and … the day before I had talked to the chairman [Ronald Perelman], I have to assume the Jordan magic worked."

Ms. Lewinsky then called Mr. Jordan and told him the good news. According to Mr. Jordan, he believed that he notified Ms. Currie and the President as soon as he learned that Ms. Lewinsky had obtained an offer: "I am certain that at some point I told Betty Currie, 'Mission Accomplished.' Mr. Jordan also testified that he also told the President directly that "Monica Lewinsky was going to work for Revlon,'" and his response was, 'Thank you very much.'"

Starr's Circuitous Path from Whitewater to Sex

It was all too much for Linda Tripp. Five days after Lewinsky filed her false affidavit in the Jones case, on Monday, January 12, Tripp placed a call to the office of Whitewater Independent Counsel Kenneth Starr.

Here is what she told Starr's office over the phone: The President was having an affair with a government employee who had been subpoenaed in the Paula Jones case. Clinton and Vernon Jordan had told the woman to lie. The woman then signed an affidavit denying the affair. Tripp had 20 hours of tapes to back her up. Within an hour, a half-dozen federal prosecutors and an FBI agent were sitting in Tripp's living room.

This was not the first Starr heard of the false affidavit. Just a few days before, he had been tipped off by lawyers knowledgeable with the case about Lewinsky's denial. The call from Tripp was welcome nonetheless.

After four years and $40 million (as the familiar refrain goes), the Starr investigation was stalled; Tripp's call was more than welcome. If Tripp was telling the truth, this was a chance to finally pin something on the President. Starr's men were also particularly interested in Jordan. For months, Starr had been investigating whether Webster Hubbell had been given hush money to buy his silence in Whitewater (see Chapter 13). Jordan was one of Clinton's best friends, and he had arranged lucrative consulting contracts for Hubbell. If Starr could prove that Jordan had done favors for Monica Lewinsky in return for helpful testimony in the Jones case, it might help him prove Jordan had done it for Webster Hubbell in the Whitewater case—and then maybe he could get at whatever Hubbell might be hiding!

Yet Starr's team knew that following Tripp's leads would be risky. The tapes themselves would not be worth much as evidence. But the information on them, if true, could wind up impeaching the President.

Sound Bites

I'm you. I'm just like you. I'm an average American who found herself in a situation not of her own making.

—Linda Tripp

To develop more solid leads, Starr decided to set up a sting operation. The next morning, FBI agents wired Linda Tripp with a secret listening device. Over lunch, while hidden tapes turned, Tripp again walked her unwitting friend through the whole story. As they listened in an upstairs room at the hotel, the prosecutors were stunned. Somebody could go to jail, and it wasn't just Monica Lewinsky. Starr finally had a piece of solid evidence.

FBI agents were dispatched to the dining room of the hotel, and Monica Lewinsky's life turned upside down. She was escorted to the room from which the agents had been listening, and for two hours was interrogated, coaxed, pressured, and threatened before she was finally released. She was allowed to call her parents, but refused to speak without talking to her lawyer.

Become a Pundit

It is against state law in Maryland to tape someone without their knowledge and consent.

Starr now needed to get permission to expand his probe. Remember that under the independent counsel act, the attorney general and a three-judge panel from the federal court of appeals must sign off on any expansion of an investigation. After presenting his new evidence, Starr was given permission to expand his probe.

This too is cause for concern regarding Starr's tactics. Starr had no authority to wire Linda Tripp since his authority, at that time, was limited to Whitewater. The President's attorneys claim that Starr could never have expanded his probe to include Lewinsky without the FBI tapes, yet Starr had no authority to create those tapes, and thus the entire case made to the three-judge panel was based on evidence he obtained "illegally." Nevertheless, the genie is out of the bottle. The probe was expanded, and however that was done is now a moot point.

The President's Deposition in the Jones Case

In the meantime, the Jones case was continuing. On January 17, 1998, Jones' attorney took the deposition of President Bill Clinton. Armed with Lewinsky's denial of the affair, the President approached the deposition confident that he could keep it under wraps. What he did not know was that Paula Jones' attorneys already knew about Lewinsky. How did they know? Linda Tripp had told them, and in fact met with them the night before they took the President's deposition.

Here is why Clinton is in trouble: The Jones legal team submitted the following "Definition of Sexual Relations" to the court:

> *For the purposes of this deposition, a person engages in "sexual relations" when the person knowingly engages in or causes—*
>
> *(1) contact with the genitalia, anus, groin, breast, inner thigh, or buttocks of any person with an intent to arouse or gratify the sexual desire of any person;*

(2) contact between any part of the person's body or an object and the genitals or anus of another person; or

(3) contact between the genitals or anus of the person and any part of another person's body. "Contact" means intentional touching, either directly or through clothing.

On the piece of paper shown to Clinton, the first definition was circled. At this point in the deposition the questioning about sex between Clinton and Lewinsky was interrupted by Clinton lawyer Bennett. Judge Wright interceded and allowed questioning along the lines of "definition number one."

Wright was referring to the first, circled definition on the sheet shown to the President. While there have been reports that Wright made modifications to the definition, no such modification is recorded in publicly available transcripts of the deposition. It seems likely that Wright had already struck out the second and third definitions provided to the President when he answered the question: "Did you have 'sexual relations' with Ms. Lewinsky?"

Clinton read the definition carefully, very, very, carefully. And he discovered that receiving oral sex did not exactly fit the definition provided to him by his enemies. Accordingly, he denied having "sexual relations" (their term) with the intern. Any other lawyer caught in the same predicament probably would have done the same thing.

However, it must be said that much of Clinton's behavior falls into the category of "intent to gratify," if proving his "intention" is possible. If the President is to evade an impeachment for perjury, at least as far as the deposition issue goes, it will likely come down to these wrangling between Jones' lawyers, Clinton's lawyers and the court over the definition of sexual relations.

Media Alert

In 1997 Clinton said "I haven't eaten at McDonald's a single time since I've been President." Incredulous reporters were later told by Clinton aides that the key words were "eaten at." He had McDonald's to-go many times.

Here are the relevant portions of Clinton's deposition:

Q: Now, do you know a woman named Monica Lewinsky?

A: I do.

Q: How do you know her?

A: She worked in the White House for a while, first as an intern, and then in the legislative affairs office.

Q: Well, you also saw her at a number of social functions at the White House, didn't you?

A: Could you be specific? I'm not sure.

Q: At any time were you and Monica Lewinsky alone together in the Oval Office?

A: I don't recall, but … it seems to me she brought things to me once or twice on the weekends.

Q: Do you recall ever walking with Lewinsky down the hallway from the Oval Office to your private kitchen there in the White House?

A: Well … it's a little cubbyhole, and these guys keep the door open. [W]hen Ms. Lewinsky was still an intern, [she] was working in the chief of staff's office. And my recollection is that on a couple of occasions after that she was there but my secretary Betty Currie was there with her. She and Betty are friends. That's my, that's my recollection. And I have no other recollection of that.

Q: At any time were you and Monica Lewinsky alone in the hallway between the Oval Office and this kitchen area?

A: I don't believe we were alone in the hallway, no.

Q: At any time have you and Monica Lewinsky ever been alone together in any room in the White House?

A: I don't think so, no.

Q: Have you ever met with Monica Lewinsky in the White House between the hours of midnight and six a.m.?

A: I certainly don't think so.

Q: Well, have you ever given any gifts to Monica Lewinsky?

A: I don't recall. Do you know what they were?

Q: A book about Walt Whitman?

White House Confidential

As President, George Washington faced continuous rumors of illicit sexual liaisons and illegitimate children.

A: I give—let me just say, I give people a lot of gifts, and when people are around I give a lot of things I have at the White House away, so I could have given her a gift, but I don't remember a specific gift.

Q: Has Monica Lewinsky ever given you any gifts?

A: Once or twice. I think she's given me a book or two.

Q: Did she give you a tie?

A: Yes, she had given me a tie before. I believe that's right.

Q: Did you have an extramarital sexual affair with Monica Lewinsky?

A: No.

Q: If she told someone that she had a sexual affair with you beginning in November of 1995, would that be a lie?

A: It's certainly not the truth. It would not be the truth.

Q: Have you ever had sexual relations with Monica Lewinsky?

A: I have never had sexual relations with Monica Lewinsky. I've never had an affair with her.

Media Alert

The first newspaper to report the story was the *Washington Post,* which said:

Starr Investigates Whether Clinton Told Intern to Deny Affair—Independent counsel Kenneth W. Starr has expanded his investigation of President Clinton to examine whether Clinton and his close friend Vernon Jordan encouraged a 24-year-old former White House intern to lie to lawyers for Paula Jones about whether the intern had an affair with the president, sources close to the investigation said yesterday.

Extra, Extra, Read All About It!

About a week after the President's deposition, news of the entire affair broke. It would be impossible to overstate just how explosive the discovery of the President's affair with the intern and Starr's investigation thereof was. *Newsweek* and its intrepid investigative reporter, Michael Isikoff, had been gathering the story for months. But *Newsweek* editors decided to delay reporting what would be the story of the decade, at the behest of Independent Counsel Starr.

Matt Drudge and the *Drudge Report* had no such druthers. As soon as he heard about the story, he posted it on his Web site. All hell then broke loose.

The day that the Lewinsky story broke was historic for other reasons as well. The Pope was visiting Cuba for the first time ever under communist rule, and all major television networks had sent their news anchors to Havana. ABC's Peter Jennings broke into regular programming at 3:32 p.m. to pick up a live feed of Clinton's interview with PBS's Jim Lehrer. Jennings was followed two minutes later by NBC's Tom Brokaw. CBS's Dan Rather did not get on the air until more than 20 minutes later. Ted Koppel returned from Havana to anchor *Nightline* and soon all three network anchors followed suit.

January 26, 1998: Clinton issues his strongest denial of the Lewinsky allegations.
Reuters/Win McNamee/ Archive Photos

CNN, MSNBC, and Fox News Channel provided live coverage of White House spokesman Mike McCurry's grilling at his daily briefing. ABC's Sam Donaldson asked whether Clinton would cooperate with an impeachment inquiry. Rush Limbaugh read listeners the latest Drudge update.

The press pounced on the story, hardly able to conceal its glee that they were back in O.J. mode. Pundits filled the airwaves with dire predictions of impending resignation— or worse. Viewers tuned in in droves, desperate for more information. Ratings soared. Leaks, gossip, innuendo, and hard news all mixed and viewers and readers had a difficult time determining fact from fantasy. *Could there really be a stained dress?*

And so the stage was set. Monica Lewinsky lied under oath. President Clinton certainly *seems* to have lied under oath. As Clinton was said to have told his many paramours, "If we both deny it, they can't prove it." His problem this time was that more than two people knew of the liaison, and the others were out to get him.

Sound Bites

You poor son of a bitch.

—Dick Morris to Bill Clinton on the day the Lewinsky story broke

The Least You Need to Know

➤ While taping your friends is inexcusable, Monica Lewinsky's insistence that Tripp commit perjury almost makes Tripp into a sympathetic figure.

➤ Monica's false affidavit created the need, later, to take an immunity deal offered by Starr.

➤ Actual proof of a potential real crime resurrected a moribund investigation.

➤ Clinton had little choice but to step gingerly when confronted about Lewinsky in his deposition; it was either that or admit to infidelity.

Chapter 20

The Role of the New Media

In This Chapter

➤ O.J. Simpson and the new media

➤ Cable TV and sensationalism

➤ Matt Drudge and the Internet

➤ Not everyone is happy

The culture of political drama that now consumes Washington is not just of one or two persons' making. Many different parties must take the responsibility or the blame for what the country is now going through. High on that list is a group that exists outside of government altogether, but is important enough to be called the "Fourth Estate," due to its critical relationship to the other three branches of government.

The feeding frenzies that took place on the days that the Lewinsky story broke and the Starr report became public were something to behold. Radio stations read excerpts from the report live over the air. Television stations had reporters spend all day doing nothing but reading the 455-page report so they could report the salacious details live at 6:00. Cable television ran the story around the clock, even though there was nothing new after the first 10 minutes. Magazines had complete analysis of the report and the President's response within days. The Internet, heretofore a bastion of generally unreliable gossip, sleaze, and advertising, became the chosen vehicle for dissemination of information that may yet bring down a President.

That a new age of media is upon us is no secret, but not everyone is happy about it. Whereas more media could mean a more informed and intelligent national discourse, it seems to have had an opposite effect. The cacophony of talking heads often plays to the lowest-common denominator and has become overwhelming to many.

The Good Old Days

Old-timers say there was a time when we didn't know everything about everybody. We didn't know that John F. Kennedy liked women—lots of 'em. We didn't know that Eisenhower had a mistress. We weren't told that LBJ slept with the White House secretarial pool. We didn't even know that our President for 16 years, Franklin Delano Roosevelt, was crippled and confined to a wheelchair.

Media Alert

In 1982, the *Chicago Tribune* asked 49 distinguished historians to rank the Presidents. Eisenhower was ranked 9th best of all time. The top 5 were, from best on: Abraham Lincoln, Franklin Roosevelt, George Washington, Theodore Roosevelt, and Thomas Jefferson. The bottom five were, from least worst to worst: Richard Nixon, Franklin Pierce, James Buchanan, Warren Harding, and William Henry Harrison.

Now, maybe that's too much discretion. Yet for many people, discretion is the better part of valor. It may be preferable not to know that your President was a victim of polio, or to know that your President has "distinguishing characteristics" on certain parts of his body. Certainly many people feel that the publication of the Starr report is the epitome of a media run amok.

Yes, there was a time when an "old boy" network allowed Presidents and other public officials to have a private life that went unreported. This unspoken "gentlemen's agreement" began to change with Watergate. Woodward and Bernstein showed that maybe it is necessary to dig in and report some unsavory details of the private lives of public figures. After the revelations about Nixon, Pandora's box was open. What we are seeing today is the logical, albeit alarming, conclusion of 20 years of an open box.

White House Confidential

Nixon Secretary of State and National Security Advisor Henry Kissinger was quite the ladies man. He once said "power is the ultimate aphrodisiac." In his heyday, he dated many famous women, including Candice Bergen (*Murphy Brown*), Judy Brown (star of the X-rated film *Threesome*) Shirley MacLaine, Jill St. John, Diane Sawyer, Marlo Thomas, and Liv Ullman.

In the '70s, we learned that Betty Ford was an alcoholic and had breast cancer. In 1976, it was reported that our soon-to-be President had "lust in his heart." At the time, it was a shockingly honest revelation (how naive we were). By 1992, Clinton all but admitted to being an adulterer.

But none of those revelations prepared us for what we see today—graphic portrayals of sex, news being reported over the Internet one day and being run on NBC the next. CNN reported that the government used nerve gas on its own soldiers, and then retracting the story, admitting that it was incorrect and unverified.

Journalistic standards have certainly diminished. The question is why, how has it effected the Clinton story, and what can we do about it?

Dawn of a New Age

When Congress voted to release Starr's report to the public without having even read it, people were outraged. When Congress then permitted Clinton's taped grand-jury testimony to be released, even though grand jury secrecy is one of the benchmarks of the American judicial system, and then when almost every television and radio station in the country played it sight unseen, even more people began to think that something was seriously amiss.

White House Confidential

Although many in the press knew it, they never publicly reported that Eleanor Roosevelt's lesbian lover Lorena Hickock lived in the White House with Mrs. Roosevelt for many years.

One of the people who was angry was Arthur Gilbert, a man who had the resources to have his feelings heard. Gilbert took out a half page ad in the *L.A. Times* that read, in part:

> *The newspaper and television media are acting like vultures and ghouls when reporting on the current situation in the White House. THEY ARE INEBRIATED BY THEIR INTIMATIONS AND INSINUATIONS. In America I have been told a man is innocent until proven guilty, however, this does not seem to be the case with the press … THIS MUST BE STOPPED … we must wait until all the facts are in.*

Facts, shmacts. What counts now are ratings, and the reason is O.J. Simpson. The new era for the media really began along the San Diego freeway in Los Angeles during the O.J. Simpson Bronco chase.

Media Alert

Many of television's well-known legal talking heads can thank O.J. Simpson for the boost his trial gave their career. Appearing on Geraldo Rivera's cable gabfest *Rivera Live*, lawyers such as Gerry Spence, Alan Dershowitz, Joseph Di Genova, Victoria Tensing, and Leo Terrell became household names.

Sound Bites

You know, if it happend to you or me, what the President is going through, we'd probably have jumped in the Potomac a long time ago.

—Leon Panetta, former White House Chief of Staff

The Simpson case, with its soap opera-like storyline, was a never-ending saga that drove ratings through the roof. When ratings go up, stations can charge more money to advertisers, and thereby make more money. The new media is all about money. The Clinton sex scandal has become just one more money-making venture that brings in high ratings.

In terms of media mania, the comparisons between the Simpson and Clinton cases are eerie. A few years ago, all we heard about was the bloody gloves; now it's the stained dress. In both cases, previously unknown people (Kato Kaelin, Linda Tripp) have become household names. And, just as in the Simpson case, there is a sporting-event quality to this story. Who's winning and who's losing everyday becomes part of the national discussion.

But of even greater importance is the sheer amount of coverage. With both Simpson and Clinton, we see sustained attention to a continuing story involving a well-known personality. But since everyone already knows basic plot elements of the show, coverage must revolve around something else. "Experts" are needed to discuss the conflict of the day. In both the Simpson and Clinton cases, these analysts add to the unfolding drama by creating conflict of their own. Alan Derschowitz fights with Charles Grodin who disagrees with Chris Matthews who contradicts Tim Russert. In so doing, issues that in another time might have been relegated to the back pages of the paper become grist for the pundit mill. Why? There's time to fill and money to be made.

Stand By for News!

One reason there is so much, never-ending news is that there are far more stations than ever. In television, the creation of CNBC, MSNBC, and Fox News Channel, in addition to CNN and the traditional networks has created greater competition to get that big story. Except that there really aren't that many stories. So, given the ever-growing competition, news has become more and more sensationalized. (How much did you hear about the Jon-Benet Ramsey murder?) In the Simpson case, the *National*

Enquirer became one of the main sources of information on the case. This trend has filtered down to the media as a whole.

Bill Clinton and Monica Lewinsky, May 8, 1996. AP/Wide World Photos

Consider the following headlines from major news sources:

➤ *The New York Times*: "President weighs admitting he had sexual contacts"

➤ Reuters: "Clinton wins machismo prize"

➤ Reuters: "Penthouse offers Lewinsky $2 million"

➤ AP: "Lewinsky's mother to wed N.Y. man"

Respected journalist Judy Woodruff has complained that the new sensationalism is making it ever more difficult to run a democracy. According to Woodruff, the news media have traditionally functioned to inform voters of current events so that they can make educated choices in their social and public lives. But, she has wondered, can Americans continue to make educated choices if the news media increasingly caters only to the sensational?

Media Alert

Cable television jumped all over the story that Bill Clinton "rented out" the Lincoln Bedroom. Among the people who were reported to have spent the night there are Chevy Chase, Ted Danson, Richard Dreyfus, Jane Fonda, Billy Graham, Tom Hanks, Steve Jobs, Dr. Dean Ornish, Steven Spielberg, and Marianne Williamson.

Mumbo Jumbo

A **zine** is an Internet magazine. As such, it can only be read online and cannot be found in bookracks.

Become a Pundit

When Henry Hyde was confronted with his previous affair with Cherie Snodgrass, he chalked it up to a "youthful indiscretion." (Hyde was 41 at the time.) The affair broke up the Snodgrass marriage. When asked about Mr. Hyde chairing the impeachment hearings against President Clinton, ex-husband Fred Snodgrass said, "All I can think of is, here is this man, this hypocrite, who broke up my family."

Some of us in the media … have gotten caught up in the size of our audience, the profits to be made, catering to short attention spans, and seeking the sensational. Consequently, we seem to have forgotten something basic—that we are here to serve the public, to bring them informed judgments about their community, the nation, and the planet."

Oh, if that were only so. Just ask Matt Drudge.

Birth of a New Medium

The Internet is an amazing thing. With its ability to link millions of people around the globe, it's a new form of media unlike anything the world has ever seen. And it too can take some of the blame and/or responsibility for making the Lewinsky scandal as big as it has become and for disseminating news that may or may not be accurate.

Several analysts said that the Internet became a legitimate media outlet that day that the Starr report was made available online to millions of people simultaneously. Since there was some fear that the Net would be unable to handle the torrent of interest and simultaneous download of Starr's magnum opus, many rejoiced when it failed to crash.

According to Ken Bode of PBS's *Washington Week in Review,* the Starr report elevated the Internet from an information service to a national news source. The story that House Judiciary Chairman Henry Hyde had had an affair was first reported by an Internet zine called *Salon.*

That is the good news. The bad news is that the Net continues to be an unreliable outlet for news. Unlike traditional media sources, which back in the days of Watergate would routinely make sure that all stories had two sources of authentication, journalists on the Internet have no such tradition or requirements.

One of these new cyber-reporters is the man who broke the Lewinsky story—Matt Drudge. His Web page is called *The Drudge Report,* a site full of gossip and innuendo as well as fact. But which is which? In January, 1998, Drudge revealed that *Newsweek* magazine had decided to sit on a story "destined to shake official Washington to its foundation! A White House intern carried on a sexual affair with the President of the

United States!" Working from his $600-a-month Hollywood apartment equipped with four cheap computers, Drudge scored one of the most stunning journalistic coups in history with his disclosure of the Monica Lewinsky scandal.

The fact that he was able to make the story instantly available to millions of people via the Internet shook up the establishment media. With his story available through America Online to as many as 11 million subscribers, there was no way to ignore it. Every major media organization in the country clambered to confirm Drudge's report. Within 72 hours, lurid tales about fellatio, a semen-stained dress, and Clinton's views on sex filled the headlines.

Sound Bites

I never imagined that in America I would be hauled before a federal grand jury to answer questions about my conversations with members of the media.

—Sidney Blumenthal, former White House Communications Strategist

Matt Drudge of the Internet's Drudge Report. *AP/Wide World Photos*

Journalism professor Craig T. Wolff of Columbia University has cautioned that this new era of Internet journalism may be more of a curse than a blessing.

Media Alert

One of Drudge's first big exclusives came when a stagehand at NBC told him Jerry Seinfeld was demanding $1 million an episode for his TV show. Other early breaks included CBS firing Connie Chung and Bob Dole's choice of Jack Kemp as a running mate.

As we move into a technological stage in journalism, it's important that we should not forsake basic virtues. To see journalists approach everything in this breathless, unmoderated tone—I think we are absolutely going to look back on this time as a very sorry day in the history of the media.

An Unhappy Populace

Not everyone is happy with all of these changes in the media, or how it has affected the reporting of the Clinton-Lewinsky story. There is ample evidence now of a populace weary, both of the explicitness of the information being disseminated, as well as the manner in which the story is being told. The sense is that the presidency is being treated the same way supermarket tabloids treat "news" of alien abductions and troubled celebrities.

Many people think that the media is in as much of a moral quandary as the President—the graphic details, the language, the gossip. For some people, it shows disrespect for the presidency and a sense that the pursuit of this story has gone way beyond any rational limit.

Many would just rather not know all of the details of the President's sex life. Even more troubling is the fact that our children are hearing about things many parents would rather they know nothing about for some time, thank you very much.

Despite it all, despite a new sensationalism no one seems to like, despite the lack of credibility, despite the anger over details too graphic and unnecessary, the media continues to tell the story with as much gusto as ever. And we, apparently, can't help watching.

A Return to Civility

There is a way out of this media mess. Journalists could adopt some basic rules for their profession, just as most other professions (doctors, lawyers, accountants) have. If the rules are broken by a reporter, the group can penalize the offender. Some of the most common rules that have been bandied about among journalists include these:

1. **No publication of unsourced reports.** Journalistic institutions should report only verifiable factual information or analysis and opinion clearly labeled as such.

   Matt Drudge will not be confused with *The New York Times*, and the public will seek and find reputable news organizations that set and stick by high standards.

2. **Respect privacy.** The private lives of public people should no longer be acceptable as news, except as it pertains to their public life. For example, drug or alcohol abuse raises questions about an officeholder's competence on the job.

3. **Create a set of standards for all reporters to adhere to.** Journalists can create internal guidelines regarding standards and ethics. Alleged violation of these standards would be cause for removal from the profession.

The First Amendment can still be respected without every salacious story making its way into print. We have 200 years of proof of that.

The Least You Need to Know

➤ There used to be a "gentlemen's agreement" forbidding the reporting of private matters.

➤ Watergate and the O.J. Simpson trial changed that agreement.

➤ Sex and sensational details *always* sell.

➤ The Internet has made it even more difficult for traditional news sources to retain journalistic standards.

Chapter 21

Stand by Your Man

In This Chapter

➤ Public Hillary

➤ Private Hillary

➤ Hurt Hillary

➤ Love-struck Hillary

Sometimes it's hard to be a woman
Giving all your love to just one man
You'll have bad times, he'll have good times
Doin' things you don't understand

It would be a safe bet to say that Bill Clinton has done a host of things that Hillary just doesn't understand.

But if you love him, you'll forgive him
Even though he's hard to understand
And if you love him, oh be proud of him
'Cause after all he's just a man

She did forgive him, but the demons reappeared. This time dressed as a 22-year-old intern. The very public debate about when, and where, and how, her husband received oral sex from Monica Lewinsky would have shattered most marriages. The Clintons' is not most marriages. Their marriage has remained intact even though her husband has been chronically unfaithful from the day he took his vows.

Stand by your man, give him two arms to cling to
And something warm to come to
When nights are cold and lonely
Stand by your man, and show the world you love him
Keep giving all the love you can
Stand by your man.

So why, we ask, does Hillary Rodham Clinton continue to stand by her man? Is it for love? Is it for power? Is it because she made a Faustian bargain many years ago? The reason may be all of the above.

Hillary Puts On a Good Face

After the Lewinsky story broke, Hillary Clinton went on the *Today* show to defend her husband. She seemed so sincere in her belief that the entire story was yet another baseless accusation planted by right-wing conspirators. The rest of us sensed viscerally that there must be some accuracy to the story. But what was the truth? We couldn't be sure. Was Hillary a victim or co-conspirator?

Hillary Clinton's appearance on the Today show.
AP/Wide World Photos

If she was a victim, then we all did (and do) feel sorry for her; her husband had lied to her as he did to us, "I did not have sex with that woman, Ms. Lewinsky!" But, if she was a co-conspirator, and she knew about the Lewinsky affair all along, how could she defend him with a straight face? This question has kept many talk-radio listeners up way past their bedtimes.

Hillary Clinton is a complicated woman. To be sure, she loves her husband. But she loves being First Lady too, and would be loathe to give it up. The Clintons plotted and planned and worked and fought very hard to get to where they are. She wants Bill to fight, not just for his sake, but for hers too.

One of the reasons that their relationship endures is that they make a good team. His weaknesses are her strengths, and vice versa. He creates a crisis and she manages it. Indeed, crisis management is her forte. During these times she's determined to come across as strong, poised, and confidant. In fact, one insider remarked, "If anyone in the White House is acting Presidential these days, … it's the First Lady."

Throughout this sex scandal, Hillary has refused to be portrayed as a victim. "She reminds me of the commander of Apollo 13," said one long-time friend. "Very cool under pressure." In fact, Hillary relishes that role. The perception she gives is that even if the President is down, she will not be forgotten. In '92 many hated her for that. Today, it's a trait people embrace and admire.

At these critical marital junctures (when she finds out he's cheating again) Mrs. Clinton becomes committed to looking and acting the best she can. For example, on the day the President said that he did not have "sexual relations" with Lewinsky, most other spouses may have looked bedraggled or upset. Not Hillary Clinton. She was described by one leading magazine as "radiant." Her hair had just been done, she wore a crisp canary-yellow suit, and her face was poised and untroubled. The message? She is a woman to be reckoned with. If dishes were flying in the private residence, the public sure couldn't tell.

A similar situation arose in the '92 Presidential bid. The 1992 election wasn't easy. Clinton was a threat to established interests, and every possible negative rumor that had been following him for 20 years made it into print. During one of many crises, one campaign aide recalls the staff walking around looking like they'd all been beaten with clubs. Hillary changed all that. She came into the office dressed to the nines. She wore a beautiful dark pants suit with brass buttons. Her makeup was perfect and her hair was done meticulously. Hillary was determined to send the campaign a message: "Stop moping. We are professionals. The worse you feel the better you should look."

Media Alert

In one poll, only 20 percent of those polled believed Hillary was an unknowing victim in the Presidential sex scandal; 68 percent believed that she knew about the President's affair and looked the other way.

Sound Bites

I hate to see the leader of the free world go through a perpetual 12-step program.

—Republican Representative Peter King of New York

Media Alert

The book *Primary Colors* is the thinly veiled inside story of the 1992 Clinton Campaign. It was written by "Anonymous" and became an instant bestseller. Periodicals and talk shows spent a great amount of time speculating about just who "Anonymous" was. Finally, journalist Joe Klein admitted that he wrote the book and it was based upon his coverage of the '92 Clinton campaign.

Sound Bites

All things considered, actually, it wasn't too bad.

—Hillary Clinton, responding to the question, "Did you have a nice summer?"

Author Joe Klein says, "She looks good at such times because she's invigorated." He goes on to note that "in times of crisis, Hillary becomes a key White House player …. Her husband needs her desperately. She is the essential element in his defense."

A Private Woman in a Public World

Who is this private Hillary? She is who she has always been: a strong, capable, intelligent, no-B.S. woman. She enjoys intellectual stimulation and vigorous debate. She is passionate and committed. She is a loving mother to their daughter, Chelsea.

When scandal is not consuming her, the First Lady is actually most comfortable traveling. She loves shuttling from one adoring crowd to another without the pomp and circumstance found in Washington. She loves sitting in her swivel chair on her Air Force jet, surrounded by her staff (nearly all of whom are women) cracking jokes, talking about the kids, and discussing politics. Her aides have a word for such times: "Hillaryland." This is when she seems least guarded and most at ease.

Hillary Rodham Clinton also happens to be a wife whose husband has cheated on her many, many times. By the time the Lewinsky story made news, she knew the drill. Except that this time was different. While she knew how to behave in, and react to, a bimbo-eruption, she was unprepared for the explicit details associated with this one. The spectacle that is the Lewinsky affair has been an unprecedented invasion of her privacy.

Hillary's anger at her husband is two-fold. First and foremost, she is mad at him for betraying her, again. Secondly, and maybe more importantly, she is mad that he has again jeopardized everything that they've worked for. How could he be so stupid?

Her private agony could be witnessed on Martha's Vineyard where the First Family vacationed after the President's unprecedented grand-jury testimony. At a party, newsman Mike Wallace, in a conversation about a friend's medical status politely asked Mrs. Clinton if she'd ever had a stress test. "I'm having one now," she deadpanned.

White House Confidential

President Millard Fillmore's wife, Abagail, hated Washington society life and did not want to serve as hostess for White House functions, as First Ladies normally do. In fact she refused every invitation to host White House dinners, parties, State Dinners, etc. Finally, an exasperated Fillmore asked his daughter, Mary Abagail, to be the White House hostess, a role she performed throughout the Fillmore presidency.

A photographer who regularly follows the First Couple has noted that now, when the Clintons think they're no longer in range of telephoto lenses, they stop holding hands and tend to keep a distance from each other. One friend described the current status of their marriage as "brittle."

For the most part, Hillary has kept her private hurt to herself. Democratic pollster Geoff Garin explains, "What people see in her response is a quiet dignity." It is not her way to show weakness.

A Woman Scorned

As for the Starr report, Hillary is said to be livid and sad about the "gratuitous" details of her husband's trysts with the intern. She believes that Starr wrote the report intending to hurt her, damage the President, drive a wedge between them, and undermine their marriage.

Become a Pundit

Since the Lewinsky scandal broke, Hillary has been the recipient of sustained and emotional standing ovations wherever she has gone.

Mrs. Clinton was especially upset about Starr's references to the state of the marriage. In one section of the report, Starr has an account of Clinton telling Lewinsky that he had "hundreds of affairs" earlier in his marriage. To what purpose, the First Lady has wondered, would this inclusion serve?

What grieved her the most was Starr's vivid description of an emotional meeting between the President and a weeping Lewinsky on the 4th of July, 1997. Clinton is quoted as telling Monica that he wished he had more time for her and adding that when he was no longer President, he might be "alone." Clinton supporters have maintained that that quote was gratuitous, unprofessional, intentionally hurtful, and completely unnecessary to prove any of the charges outlined in the report. Certainly, it does nothing to prove obstruction of justice, perjury, witness tampering, or abuse of power.

White House Confidential

Before he married Mary Todd, Abraham Lincoln courted Mary Owens, the daughter of a wealthy Kentucky farmer. After several years, the relationship fizzled. Mary Owens, it was said, was turned off by Lincoln's "rough manners." For his part, the future President disliked the fact that Miss Owens had gained too much weight and lost too many teeth.

A Woman in Love

So why has she stayed? Many have argued that it's a marriage of convenience, a business relationship, not a romantic union. The evidence suggests otherwise.

On a recent Super Bowl Sunday, a day when the country turned to football, the President and his wife went to church. As the Clintons sat in their place of worship, the minister read from the New Testament. The words seemed to be aimed at Mrs. Clinton: "Love is patient, love is kind … love does not rejoice in evil but rejoices with truth." At its conclusion, the First Lady called the service, "inspirational."

Sound Bites

She has to forgive him. Basically he's a good man. He made a very stupid mistake. He loves her. But you know men.

—Actress Zsa Zsa Gabor, veteran of nine marriages

Why does she stay, we ask? One reason is because of her faith. Her Methodist upbringing taught Hillary the value of forgiveness. But her forgiveness is not like that of an abused wife; it's more like a muscular Christianity. Her church has reminded her that in faith, there is forgiveness, and in forgiveness, there is love.

That is the other reason she stays: for love. Since meeting at Yale, Hillary Rodham has been deeply in love with Bill Clinton and vice versa. One friend recalled bumping in to the couple when they were first courting, "I was walking back from a movie when I ran into Hillary on the street. She was walking with Bill. It startled me to see the two of them together and so obviously in love … they were basking in each other's glow, taking pride in their mutual possession. It struck me that these two had real physical chemistry." He continued, "These two people unequivocally had the hots for each other. She was so in love and he looked like he had just swallowed the canary." It is that passion for one another that has fueled Hillary's commitment.

One aide has said, "He can't stop touching her." Another expanded, "They don't kiss, they devour each other." And still another told a tale of spending an evening with the Clintons and stumbling upon the First Couple locked in a passionate embrace in the White House Solarium. The fire he witnessed was so real, he said he felt like a voyeur watching them.

Of course, their marriage, like all marriages, is a tangled psychological web with terrain known only to them. Hillary defended her union on television recently, "The only people who count in any marriage are the two that are in it." She went on to say, "We know everything there is to know about each other, and we understand and accept and love each other." Friends and observers have never doubted that for a second.

Media Alert

How much of an advisor to the President is Hillary? In a meeting in July of 1992, the Clinton team was trying to figure out what Clinton needed to end his acceptance speech with a bang. It was Hillary who came up with the last line in the speech: "I still believe in a place called Hope."

President and Mrs. Clinton and their daughter, Chelsea.
Reuters/Gary Cameron/ Archive Photos

What emerges from all this is a couple that genuinely seems to love, and like, one another. They show respect to each other, even if they are sometimes exasperated by their partner. The Clintons are married, for better or worse. Predicting the future of a marriage is an impossible task. Theirs has been very durable, and by all accounts, very close. Yet, who among us could withstand such public humiliation? It is difficult to imagine what she has gone through and what she now feels. Whatever she does, she will have good reason.

"When I think about them," Neel Lattimore, the First Lady's former deputy press secretary, says, "I think about the two of them sitting on a couch on Air Force One, holding hands, telling some old political story and arguing about who's going to tell which part—and finishing each other's sentences. The chemistry is just out there—they're such great friends!"

The Least You Need to Know

➤ Hillary Clinton will not permit her enemies any victory by being anything but dignified in public.

➤ In private, she is admired for her strength.

➤ She was very hurt by the personal nature of the Starr report.

➤ Hill loves Bill and Bill loves Hill.

Part 5
The President on Trial

So how does it end? Will it ever end? Speculation abounds as to whether Bill Clinton will survive the latest, greatest threat to his Presidency—and his legacy. Congress and the nation must investigate the real charges leveled at the President, then consider whether they actually warrant impeachment and perhaps driving a Chief Executive from office.

Are Starr's charges worthy of impeaching Bill Clinton? How will the Congress conduct the investigation and, if the investigation demands it, the impeachment? And what will happen then?

Perhaps more importantly, what effects will this national soap opera have on our political systems in the future, on the quality of candidates willing to open every aspect of their private lives, and on the extent to which political vendettas can be played out in the courts?

Read on for some educated speculation, then keep reading for some extended reading, including excerpts from Starr's report to the Congress, a timeline to put the scandalous events in perspective, a list of the major players, a bibliography of further reading, and a glossary of all those legal terms.

Chapter 22

Starr Chambers

> ## In This Chapter
>
> ➤ Hell hath no fury like a prosecutor scorned
>
> ➤ Monica cops a plea
>
> ➤ Vernon Jordan's legal problems
>
> ➤ Tripp's troubles
>
> ➤ Investigating Kenneth Starr
>
> ➤ Hillary Clinton handles the whitewater

At long last, Independent Counsel Kenneth Starr delivered 18 boxes of information to Congress's doorstep, amid much fanfare and a cavalcade of automobiles, press, and public. It was as if, as one pundit put it, Starr was trying to prove "guilt by volume."

But the President is not the only one likely to be damaged by the legal fallout of the investigation and its progeny. Like the smell of rotting fish, potential legal liability from the investigation permeates everyone who has come in contact with it, including Prosecutor Starr himself.

The Risks of Angering a Prosecutor

The report, filled with graphic, tawdry details, seems to be personal as well as professional for the independent counsel. While it is not hard to understand why, it is also improper.

Originally commissioned to investigate Whitewater, the Starr report only mentioned the failed Arkansas land deal four times. Instead, the 445-page manifesto focused on the President's private sex life. The report is graphic, personal, incriminating, and embarrassing. It is the work of a prosecutor trying to prove his case. The evidence (contained in the appendix to the report) is based almost entirely upon one-sided grand-jury testimony.

Grand juries are tools for prosecutors. Cross-examination is not permitted and exculpatory evidence is not allowed. Any prosecutor worth his salt can, as the saying goes, "indict a cheese sandwich" by using a grand jury. A document based upon such evidence simply cannot be even-handed, and is not supposed to be. So take the Starr report with a grain of salt. It's akin to being a judge in a divorce case and hearing only one side of the story.

Mumbo Jumbo

Exculpatory evidence shows the innocence of the accused and thereby contradicts the charges alleged.

Starr has been investigating Clinton under the penumbra of Whitewater for four years. In that time, Clinton has turned over volumes of material to the Office of the Independent Counsel, and yet Starr apparently could make nothing stick. If he could, his report would have contained evidence of wrongdoing in Whitewater or some other alleged Clinton misdeed. He also would not have tried to escape to Malibu a year and a half ago (see Chapter 14).

Over the course of his investigation, Starr became increasingly criticized by the American people. It seemed as if he had a highly personal vendetta against the President—but he was unable to prove anything until the Lewinsky story broke.

Become a Pundit

James Carville, Clinton's 1992 campaign manager, is married to George Bush's 1992 campaign manager, Mary Matalin. Their daughter is named Matalin Carville.

All of a sudden, charges of an actual crime appeared (forget for a moment that the crime was lying about an affair). Clinton loyalists, led by his 1992 campaign manager, James Carville, declared "war" on the independent counsel, and thereafter did all they could to deflect the charges against Clinton and instead smear Starr's already tattered name.

What the Democrats forgot was that Starr would be writing the report. It's not really surprising that it was written in the worst possible light. Clintonites asked for it.

Legal Ramifications of the Investigation

The report will reverberate for years to come. The most obvious legal ramification of the Starr Whitewater investigation is upon the President. Starr lists 11 counts for impeachment. Whether Starr is simply trying to shore-up whatever credibility remains after his investigation, or whether the President actually committed "treason, bribery or other high crimes and misdemeanors" will be discussed in the next chapter.

Although the others involved in this saga face potential criminal prosecution, Starr focused on impeachment as a penalty for Clinton. The reason is that a President is in a unique position recognized by the Constitution and the only legal remedy for a President's high crime is impeachment. If a President were to be impeached and ousted, only then could he face a criminal indictment. Most constitutional scholars believe that the Constitution forbids the criminal indictment of a sitting President.

Definition of Terms

The ramifications from the report will be felt by all of the major players, from Linda Tripp to Vernon Jordan to Hillary Clinton and beyond. The potential crimes being tossed about range from perjury to obstruction of justice to conspiracy, and on. You better know what these terms mean.

Sound Bites

This is personal, and not impeachable. The salacious allegations in this referral are simply intended to humiliate, embarrass, and politically damage the President.
—David Kendall, Bill Clinton's attorney

David Kendall is not the one who will decide what is impeachable and what isn't. It's the House of Representatives.
—Orrin Hatch, Senate Judiciary Committee Chairman

White House Confidential

The Clintons are not the first members of the Executive branch to be accused of shady land deals. James Buchanan's Secretary of War, John Floyd, was accused of the same, and much worse. Buchanan ordered Vice President Breckinridge to fire Floyd, but he couldn't. Floyd refused to be fired!

Perjury is the crime of lying under oath about a material matter. It is important to understand that perjury is a two-part crime; most people think of it only as lying under oath. That is incorrect. It is *knowingly* lying under oath about something that is *material* in the underlying case.

If you are called as a witness in a criminal trial and you lie about your address, and your address is irrelevant to the proceedings, you have not committed perjury. If you lie and say that you did not see the defendant kill someone, and you did, that's perjury. The lie must be about something significant to be perjurous.

Perjury is a highly technical legal term. Remember this when people tell you that Clinton committed perjury in the Jones case. The fact is, Judge Wright deemed Clinton's affair with Lewinsky irrelevant to the Jones matter—and then she threw out Jones's entire case. It is hard to say that Clinton committed perjury when his testimony was deemed insignificant. (Not only that, but it is debatable whether Clinton actually lied, from a legal standpoint, in the Jones case. Again, this is a topic for the next chapter.)

Subornation of perjury is the crime of asking or forcing another person to lie under oath. And again, the lie must be about a material matter. If Clinton asked Monica Lewinsky to deny her sexual relationship in Lewinsky's Jones affidavit, that is subornation of perjury. It would have been a lie about a material matter.

Obstruction of justice means impeding or obstructing those who seek justice in court or those who are conducting an official investigation. For example, if you lie to a prosecutor to protect a friend of yours who committed a crime, you are obstructing justice.

Conspiracy is a crime that may be committed when two or more persons agree to do something unlawful (or to do something lawful by unlawful means). The agreement doesn't have to be in writing to be proven; it can be inferred from the persons' actions.

If you and your friend rob a bank, you can be guilty of both conspiring to rob the bank as well as robbing it. However, certain crimes that, by their very nature, require more than one person (such as bribery) are not usually charged as conspiracy as well.

A *wiretap* is information that is obtained by intercepting messages by wiretapping, radio surveillance, and other means. In some states, it is illegal to tape conversations without both parties' consent. For instance, if you tap into and tape your neighbor's cordless-phone telephone calls, you may be guilty of illegal wiretapping.

Contempt of court is any act which is calculated to embarrass, hinder, or obstruct court administration of justice, or which is calculated to lessen its authority or dignity. If a judge orders you to pay child support and you don't, you can be found guilty of contempt of court. Your actions show disrespect for the court and its authority.

Kenneth Starr: Yep, Him Too

Starr has continued to have one small problem—he's still losing the battle of public relations. Since the scandal, with all its gripping details, burst onto the national agenda, Starr and his office have been accused by Clinton lawyer David Kendall of numerous leaks to the news media. Kendall filed a motion in federal court in Washington on February 9, 1998, accusing Starr of contempt of court and calling for the independent counsel's office to be investigated.

Grand-jury proceedings are supposed to be sealed. Only the prosecutors, the jurors, and the witness are allowed to be in the jury room. Lawyers for witnesses are not even allowed in. Neither the prosecution nor the jurors are allowed to discuss testimony before the grand jury with anyone. If Starr or his office spoke to any member of the media about the proceedings of the grand jury, it is possible they could be found in violation of the laws surrounding grand juries.

It would be the ultimate irony if Starr, in the course of his protracted attempt to prove that Clinton broke the law, has broken the law himself. Kendall claimed that Starr violated rule 6(e) of the Federal Rules of Criminal Procedure. Rule 6(e) specifies the circumstances under which evidence and testimony before grand juries can or cannot be revealed.

The difficulty in proving these charges is in determining where the leaks came from. But Judge Norma Holloway Johnson has reportedly forced members of Starr's office to testify about the leaks during a contempt hearing. Johnson has oversight of Starr's grand jury, and any possible abuses of the grand jury would need to be brought before her.

"If a prosecutor violates [the grand jury laws], they can be punished," says Thomas Sargentich of American University's Washington College of Law. "They can be removed, and I think it would be grounds for a judge to fine or even criminally go after an independent counsel."

Although, according to Judge Johnson, Starr maintains that his office has operated fully inside the law, Kendall documented dozens of news reports from organizations from the *New York Times* to *NBC News* to the *New York Post* that he claimed were based on information given out by Starr's office. Some reports directly mentioned that they came from "sources in Starr's office" while others were more oblique in their references, using phrases like "people familiar with the investigation":

➤ *NBC Nightly News*, February 4, 1998   A report directly identifies Starr's office as the source of information regarding Lewinsky's potential testimony.

➤ *New York Times*, February 2, 1998   An article identifies Starr's prosecutors as the source of information about Lewinsky's investigative interviews.

Become a Pundit

The independent counsel statute does not cover investigations of independent counsels. There is no precedent for the investigation of an independent counsel. In all likelihood, an investigator assigned by the attorney general would look into the matter.

Media Alert

Starr is not the only person who has had a problem with media leaks. Clinton had many problems with press leaks, especially early in his first term. According to a former Clinton aide, the problem seemed to get out of hand when a story was leaked to the press that Mrs. Clinton had thrown a lamp at the President. The President says the incident never occurred.

Become a Pundit

Nixon attempted to forestall the release of the Watergate tapes by claiming they were made as part of his duties as President, and therefore were covered by Executive privilege. The Supreme Court disagreed and forced Nixon to turn over the tapes.

Mumbo Jumbo

Transactional immunity is a sort of blanket immunity. It prevents any prosecution relating to any matter surrounding the testimony. **Use immunity** is much more narrow. It only prevents prosecution from the testimony itself. Any other matter surrounding the testimony would still be a potential cause for criminal prosecution.

➤ *CBS News*, May 8, 1998   Scott Pel simply admitted a year ago that this was a case of an independent counsel gone astray, packing his bags and going to California.

Monica Is Almost Out of the Woods

Monica Lewinsky cut a deal with Independent Counsel Starr for a very good reason: If she hadn't, he was going to charge her with several crimes. Monica had two big legal problems before she copped the immunity deal:

➤ **Perjury:** Lewinsky lied about her affair with Clinton in her sworn affidavit in the Jones case.

➤ **Obstruction of justice:** This relates to the anonymously written "talking points" given to Linda Tripp by Lewinsky on January 14. Recall that this document outlined how Tripp should give testimony about Kathleen Willey, who Tripp said received unwanted sexual advances from Clinton. The document told Tripp to contradict herself and deny any such actions by Clinton. Passing the document along to Tripp could easily have qualified as the more serious charge of obstruction of justice.

But the transactional immunity deal negotiated between Lewinsky's new lawyers, Jacob Stein and Plato Cacheris, and Starr's office gave her protection from any criminal act she might have committed in relation to this case.

Monica's immunity came after months of negotiations, first by Los Angeles lawyer William Ginsburg, and then by Stein and Cacheris, two Washington veterans. (Stein is himself a former independent counsel.) The problem with the deals proposed to Ginsburg was that Lewinsky would have received "use immunity" only, instead of the preferred "transactional immunity" she finally received. Use immunity would have left her vulnerable to future prosecution by Starr. Now, with transactional immunity, that is not possible.

However, if Monica lied to Starr's grand jury, she could still face new criminal perjury charges.

Vernon Jordan Had Better Be a Superlawyer

Jordan has admitted that he helped Monica Lewinsky get interviews at American Express, Revlon, and Young & Rubicam in New York. He also said he introduced her to Washington attorney Frank Carter when she came to him after being subpoenaed by Starr. Jordan also said Lewinsky told him that she "absolutely and unequivocally" did not have an affair with the President.

Jordan is, and has been, one of Starr's prime targets, and Starr is playing hardball. Jordan has been under suspicion by Starr's office for some time because of previous allegations that he helped former assistant attorney general and Clinton pal Web Hubbell obtain lucrative consulting contracts in return for Hubbell's silence in the Whitewater matter. These charges remain unproven. Jordan has maintained that he had no knowledge of any sort of potential deal between the President and Lewinsky in exchange for her false affidavit, and was not trying to buy her silence by helping her find a job in New York.

Sound Bites

I'm not talking about anything.

—Dr. Bernard Lewinsky after the Starr report was released.

White House Confidential

Ronald Reagan's Secretary of the Interior, James Watt, was forced to resign after he identified some members of an Interior Department panel as "a black, a woman, two Jews, and a cripple."

Another suspicion is that Jordan tried to coerce Lewinsky to lie about the affair or tried to keep her from giving testimony to Starr or to Paula Jones's attorneys. The day after Lewinsky submitted an affidavit in the Jones case, Jordan reportedly called officials at Revlon, where he is a board member, and Lewinsky was soon offered a job. Revlon has since withdrawn the offer. Jordan claims he helps many young people get jobs.

Jordan has said that he was not aware at the time that Lewinsky was going to be called in the Jones case. When he found out, he reportedly claimed he confronted Clinton and the President told him that "never, no way" did he have a sexual relationship with Lewinsky. However, logs of the phone calls made to and from Jordan, in the days immediately following the discovery that Lewinsky was on the Paula Jones witness list, seem to betray Jordan's claim of innocence. The many phone calls to and from the White House suggest that the Lewinsky matter may have been discussed, and in some detail.

The lowdown on Vernon Jordan's legal problems:

➤ **Obstruction of justice:** If Jordan tried to keep Lewinsky from telling the truth under oath in the Paula Jones case an obstruction charge could be brought against him.

➤ **Subornation of perjury:** On these same facts, if Jordan did assist Lewinsky in her false affidavit, this charge is likely.

➤ **Conspiracy:** If Jordan and Lewinsky, or Jordan and Clinton, discussed the possibility of obstructing Lewinsky from testifying or telling the truth in the Jones case, or if they tried to get her a job to keep her quiet, it is a potential conspiracy charge.

In order to indict Jordan, Starr's grand jury would need to show evidence that Jordan did more than attempt to help Lewinsky find a new job and a lawyer at the behest of Clinton's personal secretary, Betty Currie. If they find an adequate link between Jordan, the President, and Lewinsky's false affidavit, they might be able to indict him. On the other hand, Jordan is likely too smart to have broken the law.

It is important to note that buried in the Starr evidence is a quote from Ms. Lewinsky insisting that no one asked her to lie and no one promised her a job if she did. This will surely go a long way in getting Vernon Jordan off any legal hook he may be on.

Linda Tripp May Reap What She's Sown

Tripp recorded 17 tapes of phone conversations between herself and Lewinsky from her home in Columbia, MD. She made these recordings without the consent of Lewinsky.

She told Starr's office on January 13 about the existence of the tapes. She also told them that she was meeting Lewinsky the next day for lunch. When Tripp met Lewinsky in the bar of the Ritz-Carlton Hotel in Virginia, the FBI had wired Tripp with listening devices. Tripp was brought before Starr's grand jury in July and provided several days of testimony. But she has no immunity from Starr, and she has legal concerns of her own.

Maryland wiretap laws require that all people being recorded consent to the recording. Violation of that law is punishable by up to five years in jail and a fine of $10,000. If Tripp's tapes are shown to have been recorded in Maryland (which would be the case if she recorded them at home) she could be prosecuted under the Maryland statutes.

White House Confidential

People often wonder why Nixon never destroyed the Watergate tapes before they had a chance to ruin him. One Secret Service agent has said "Nixon wanted to destroy the tapes, but Haldeman talked him out of it."

Maryland's law requires proof that the person doing the taping know that one-way recording is illegal. In order to be charged, the statute requires that the person making the recording understand that he or she is breaking state law. "It's contrary to the maxim that ignorance of the law is no excuse," says University of Baltimore law professor Lynn McLain.

But they may still have the goods on her. The Maryland grand jury reportedly heard testimony from an employee at the Radio Shack where Tripp bought the recording equipment to tape Lewinsky. The employee reportedly told the grand jury that Tripp was informed when she bought the equipment of the Maryland requirements for recording telephone calls.

Maryland prosecutors have said they were going to take their time deciding whether to prosecute Tripp. There is no statute of limitations in the wiretap law in Maryland.

Besides potential criminal liability, Tripp may face a civil lawsuit as well. Lewinsky's lawyer said he was prepared to sue Tripp for entrapping his client and exposing her to potential criminal prosecution.

Hillary Clinton: What, She Didn't Kill Vince Foster?

Starr began his investigation with a broad-based inquiry into several White House missteps—Travelgate, Filegate, the Foster suicide, and so on. It has been widely believed that a main target of Starr has been First Lady Hillary Rodham Clinton. Her many foes have alleged that she broke the law by committing fraud in the Whitewater affair, abused her power in the Travelgate mess, and may have been behind the Filegate fiasco. These allegations, if true, would find the First Lady facing criminal charges.

That seems increasingly unlikely, however. The Starr report barely mentions Whitewater and fails to mention the other "-gates" altogether. If Starr had substantial and credible evidence that Hillary Clinton broke the law, it would have been as newsworthy as Monica. Given that he has almost completed his investigations without charging her with any crime, it seems ever more unlikely that he ever will.

The Least You Need to Know

➤ While legal turmoil abounds for most major players, Monica's immunity deal will protect her.

➤ Vernon Jordan should also make it through this ordeal without a criminal conviction.

➤ This just leaked! The independent counsel's office is in trouble.

➤ Hillary Clinton, despite all the horrible things that have been said about her, should also emerge unscathed.

Chapter 23

Is Sex an Impeachable Offense?

In This Chapter

➤ Starr's 11 charges

➤ The House of Representatives' 15 counts

➤ Perjury

➤ Obstruction of justice

➤ Witness tampering

➤ Abuse of power

➤ A process out of control

The Starr report accuses President Clinton of some very serious offenses, including perjury and obstruction of justice. In the report, the prosecutor does two things. First he lays out, in seemingly unnecessary pornographic detail, the events as he thinks they occurred between Clinton and Monica Lewinsky. Second, Starr applies those facts to the law and sets forth 11 different counts for impeachment.

The House will surely use Starr's report as the springboard for its investigation. The offenses charged by Starr against the President will certainly parallel those that will be eventually voted upon by the House. The articles of impeachment voted by the House are somewhat different than the "impeachable offenses" alleged by Starr, but by and large, they will be roughly the same. Understand what Starr alleges and you will be ahead of the game.

The Charges

Once the Starr report was delivered to the House Judiciary Committee, the committee had its own lawyers examine the charges. In a report made to the committee, David P. Schippers, chief investigative counsel for the House Judiciary Committee's Republican majority, outlined 15 events "directly involving" President Clinton that could constitute felonies and be grounds for impeachment. Schippers repackaged the Starr evidence, dropping some counts while adding others charging the President with conspiracy to obstruct justice and allowing Lewinsky to file a false affidavit. These 15 charges will likely be pared down to between three and five, the evidence of which will be the focus of the investigation the House is about to begin.

As evidence of a conspiracy, Schippers highlighted three days of phone calls to and from Clinton and Vernon Jordan, after Clinton denied a sexual relationship with Ms. Lewinsky during his Jones deposition. The calls then show Betty Currie trying to find Ms. Lewinsky, instructing her in code to "Call Kay."

On the possible charges of perjury, Schippers chose to refer to those acts as making false statements, not perjury. As you will see in this chapter, it is easier to prove that someone made a false statement under oath than to prove they committed legal perjury. By changing the wording Schippers sought to neutralize the argument that the President's testimony in the Jones case and before the Starr grand jury, while misleading, did not fit the legal definition of perjury.

It should also be noted that the committee dropped Starr's last count of "abuse of power." As you will see, that charge is an embarrassment that the committee chose not to share with Starr. By dropping Starr's charge that Clinton abused his power in asserting executive privilege, the committee abandoned the count that most analysts considered weakest.

In a rebuttal, Abbe Lowell, the counsel for the minority Democrats, stated that impeachment is reserved only for high crimes against the state and that no matter how the Republicans had altered Starr's case, "one basic allegation—the President was engaged in an improper relationship which he did not want disclosed—is the core charge."

Lowell said that Judge Susan Webber Wright called evidence about Ms. Lewinsky immaterial to Paula Jones's case against the President. She ultimately dismissed Mrs. Jones's lawsuit, ruling that Mrs. Jones had not proved that she had suffered any harm after her alleged encounter with Clinton. Lowell used this as evidence of any high crime or misdemeanor: "The judge was giving the committee the ability to determine that the President's statements, whether truthful or not, were not of the legal importance suggested by Starr, let alone grave constitutional significance to support impeachment."

"This was not an attempt [by the President] to organize his staff to spread misinformation about the progress of the war in Vietnam," Lowell said, referring to the Watergate era. "Or about a break-in of the Democratic headquarters at the Watergate, or even about how funds from arms sales in Iran were diverted to aid the Contras in Nicaragua.

This was a President repeating to his staff the same denial of an inappropriate and extremely embarrassing relationship that he had already denied to the public directly."

After hearing the evidence and arguments of both lawyers, the House Judiciary Committee passed the following resolution:

> *Resolved, that the Committee on the Judiciary ... is authorized and directed to investigate fully and completely whether sufficient grounds exist for the House of Representatives to exercise its constitutional power to impeach William Jefferson Clinton, President of the United States of America.*

Does the Judiciary Committee actually have substantial and credible evidence to prove these charges against the President? In order to make that determination, we'll have to analyze each of Starr's 11 and the committee's additional counts, translate it into English, see what the President says, and then decide.

Perjury (Counts 1, 2, 3, 4, and 8)

The first salvo against the President relates to various allegations of perjury in the Paula Jones deposition and Clinton's grand-jury testimony. Remember what perjury actually is. Not every lie is a perjurous lie. Perjury is a specific crime, and the burden is upon the prosecutor to prove the elements of the crime. In the case of perjury, a prosecutor must prove that a witness 1) knowingly lied, and 2) about a material fact.

Perjury convictions in criminal matters are notoriously difficult to obtain. That is because of a 1973 Supreme Court case called *United States v. Bronston*. In that case, the Court determined that for a lie under oath to be perjury it must be specific and uncategorical. According to the Court, an unresponsive answer is not perjury, nor is a misleading statement, or even a half-truth. None of those are enough to get a criminal conviction. Therefore, the law now makes it clear that a lie is not perjury if the answers are literally truthful but misleading. Without a specific lie about a material fact made in response to a completely unambiguous question, there is no perjury as a matter of law, no matter how misleading the testimony is or is intended to be.

Many courts of appeals have broadly interpreted this Supreme Court decision. Among their conclusions are:

➤ "Literally true answers by definition are non-perjurous even if the answers were designed to mislead."
—*United States v. Light*, 1986

➤ "Perjury is not to be invoked because a 'wily witness succeeds in derailing the questioner.'"
—*United States v. Tonelli*, 1978

➤ "Unambiguous and literally true answers are not perjury, even if there was intent to mislead."
—*United States v. Abroms*, 1991

➤ "An answer to a question may be non-responsive, or may be subject to conflicting interpretations, or may even be false by implication. Nevertheless, if the answer is literally true, it is not perjury."
—*United States v. Shotts,* 1998

Now look at Starr's first charge:

> *I. There is substantial and credible information that President Clinton lied under oath as a defendant in Jones v. Clinton regarding his sexual relationship with Monica Lewinsky.*

Starr alleges in his report that President Clinton committed perjury in his civil case when he denied a sexual relationship, a sexual affair, or having had sexual relations with Monica Lewinsky. As has been discussed (ad nauseum), the term "sexual relations" was given a very specific meaning in the Jones case. Denying a "sexual affair" is more problematic for the President.

Not surprisingly, the White House responded to Starr's allegation that this warrants impeachment by saying that the President's answers on these subjects do not fall within the legal definition of perjury because:

1. His answers were "literally true."
2. President Clinton did not "knowingly" make any false responses.
3. "Answers to inherently ambiguous questions cannot constitute perjury."
4. "The perjury prosecution cannot rest on the testimony of a single witness."

The President is therefore probably right on this point. Each of Clinton attorney David Kendall's arguments are legally accurate, especially as they relate to the "sexual relations" matter. Denying a "sexual affair" with Lewinsky is more of a problem for the President. "Sexual affair" was not narrowly defined, and he and Lewinsky seem to have had one. Now, Clinton can always maintain that he considers a "sexual affair" to mean intercourse; therefore the term was ambiguous, and therefore he didn't commit perjury. If so, he may be get off. (By the way, who says this isn't about sex?)

You are the jury. Now you have been given the law and you know the facts. Did he commit perjury or not? If his answers were literally true, even if misleading, he did not. The law simply does not require the witness to aid his interrogators.

> *II. There is substantial and credible information that President Clinton lied under oath to the grand jury about his sexual relationship with Monica Lewinsky.*

This could potentially be very serious, except that Clinton doesn't seem to have lied about this matter to the grand jury. The fact is, the President tried to avoid going into specifics about the details of his relationship with the intern. That is not perjury. Here is what Clinton did: At the beginning of his grand-jury testimony, he read a statement to the jurors. Whenever Starr's prosecutors endeavored to get Clinton to get graphic, the President would "fall back on his opening statement."

Here is that statement:

> *When I was alone with Ms. Lewinsky on certain occasions in early 1996 and once in early 1997, I engaged in conduct that was wrong. These encounters did not consist of sexual intercourse. They did not constitute sexual relations as I understood that term to be defined at my January 17th, 1998, deposition. But they did involve inappropriate intimate contact.*
>
> *These inappropriate encounters ended at my insistence in early 1997. I also had occasional telephone conversations with Ms. Lewinsky that included inappropriate sexual banter.*
>
> *I regret that what began as friendship came to include this conduct, and I take full responsibility for my actions.*
>
> *While I will provide the grand jury whatever other information I can, because of privacy considerations affecting my family, myself, and others, and in an effort to preserve the dignity of the office I hold, this is all I will say about the specifics of these particular matters.*
>
> *I will try to answer, to the best of my ability other questions including questions about my relationship with Ms. Lewinsky, questions about my understanding of the term "sexual relations" as I understood it to be defined at my January 17, 1998, deposition, a questions concerning alleged subornation of perjury, obstruction of justice, and intimidation of witnesses.*

And that was it. While Clinton refused to go into details, he certainly did not lie about his relationship with Lewinsky, and he certainly did not commit legal perjury. Starr was probably fit to be tied.

The White House responded to Count II by saying even if the President and Lewinsky's testimony differ on the scope of their sexual contact or the duration of the relationship, that still does not prove that the President "knowingly and intentionally gave false testimony."

Count III poses more of a problem for Clinton.

> *There is substantial and credible information that President Clinton lied under oath during his civil deposition when he stated that he could not recall being alone with Monica Lewinsky and when he minimized the number of gifts they had exchanged.*

Here, Starr asserts that President Clinton lied under oath in his deposition. The alleged lie was three-fold. First, in order to support his false statement about the sexual relationship with Lewinsky, he

Sound Bites

It depends upon what your definition of "alone" is.

—President Clinton during his grand-jury testimony

lied. Next, he also allegedly lied about being alone with Lewinsky. Finally, he may have lied about the number of gifts exchanged between the two of them.

Sound Bites

What's the big deal? So she lied and tried to convince someone else to lie?

—Marcia Lewis, Monica Lewinsky's mother, to Ken Starr's prosecutors

The White House responded by saying that the President "did not deny meeting alone" with Monica Lewinksy, nor did he "deny that they exchanged gifts." His answers were legally accurate, and as Kendall asserts and as you no know, Clinton was under no legal obligation to help the prosecution by volunteering additional information. However, if Clinton did deny being alone with Lewinsky, that could be a knowingly made false statement.

IV. There is substantial and credible information that the President lied under oath during his civil deposition concerning conversations he had with Monica Lewinsky about her involvement in the Jones case.

Starr said President Clinton also lied under oath in his deposition about discussions he had with Monica about the Jones case. The White House responded that Clinton recalled joking with Monica about being subpoenaed, but this was before he ever saw a witness list for the Jones case. Just because Lewinsky testified to additional conversation on this subject after Clinton had seen the list "does not establish the President's answers were inaccurate."

Indeed. Starr would need more than "he said-she said" if this count is to be proven.

The final perjury charge is Count VIII.

> *There is substantial and credible information that the President lied under oath in describing his conversations with Vernon Jordan about Ms. Lewinsky.*

Starr accuses the President of lying at his deposition about his discussions with Jordan. Did they conspire to shut Lewinsky up by getting her a job in New York? Starr says that Clinton denies even talking to Jordan about Lewinsky.

The White House responded to this charge, saying that the OIC's [Office of the Independent Counsel's] "account of the question and answer is simply false." They argued that portions of the President's testimony that didn't rule out the President having ever spoken to Vernon Jordan were left out of the Starr report.

That wouldn't be the first time it has been alleged that the prosecutor picked what he put in his report with particularity. It wouldn't be surprising if Starr did leave out of the report plenty of exculpatory evidence favorable to Clinton. Lawyers do that all the time.

Before we leave the "perjury" charges altogether, it would be wise to consider one seemingly small but very critical point: Each of the charges in Starr's report specifically allege that there is "substantial and credible evidence that the President lied under oath" during his deposition or his grand-jury testimony. That's an interesting choice of words: "lied under oath."

White House Confidential

Paula Jones claimed that she could substantiate her sexual-harassment allegations by describing distinguishing characteristics on the President's genitals. The President's attorney countered saying, "in terms of size, shape, and direction, the President is a normal man."

Starr is a lawyer. His assistants are lawyers. The author of his report is a lawyer. Why didn't they allege that there was substantial and credible evidence that Clinton "committed perjury" at his deposition or before the grand jury? There is a world of difference between lying under oath and committing actual, legal perjury. Lying under oath is not a crime, perjury is.

It seems that the inference to draw from his choice of words is that Starr himself knows the President's lying didn't rise to the level of criminal perjury. If he did, he would have used the word. Can non-criminal lying be deemed impeachable?

Obstruction of Justice (Counts 5, 6, 7, and 10)

Starr's next set of allegations are more serious, and easier to prove, than the perjury charges. Here, Starr lays out his theory that the President tried to conceal evidence of his relationship with Lewinsky.

> *V. There is substantial and credible information that President Clinton endeavored to obstruct justice by engaging in a pattern of activity to conceal evidence regarding his relationship with Monica Lewinsky from the judicial process in the Jones case. The pattern included concealment of gifts that the President had given Ms. Lewinsky and that were subpoenaed from Ms. Lewinsky in the Jones case; and concealment of a note sent by Ms. Lewinsky to the President on January 5, 1998.*

Starr asserts that during the Paula Jones sexual-harassment lawsuit, the President obstructed justice and had an understanding with Lewinsky to jointly conceal the truth about their relationship by concealing gifts subpoenaed by Paula Jones's attorneys.

If the President did in fact suggest to Lewinsky that she get rid of gifts he had given her, or if he agreed with her suggestion to do the same, and if in fact Clinton told his secretary Betty Currie to retrieve some of those gifts from Lewinsky, then Clinton is in a lot of trouble. That would be obstruction of justice, that would be criminal, and it would be impeachable.

The White House responded that Lewinsky's testimony that the President's reaction to her suggestion that she get rid of gifts was "I don't know" or "hmmm" does not constitute obstruction of justice. Furthermore, Clinton was not worried about the gifts and did not instruct Betty Currie to pick them up. Clinton may yet have a large problem with this charge.

Become a Pundit

In the late 1970s, the judge in the Paula Jones case, Judge Susan Webber Wright, was a law student. Her constitutional law professor was Bill Clinton. Clinton lost her final exam that year, and offered her a B+ as a grade anyway. She refused his offer, took the exam again, and got an A.

VI. There is substantial and credible information that President Clinton endeavored to obstruct justice by suggesting that Ms. Lewinsky file an affidavit so that she would not be deposed, she would not contradict his testimony, and he could attempt to avoid questions about Ms. Lewinsky at his deposition.

Starr alleges, and Congress will too, that during the Paula Jones case, the President obstructed justice and had an understanding with Lewinsky to jointly conceal the truth of their relationship. Their scheme allegedly included the following means:

1. Both the President and Lewinsky understood that they would lie under oath in the Paula Jones case about their sexual relationship.

2. The President suggested to Monica that she prepare an affidavit that, for the President's purposes, would memorialize her testimony under oath and could be used to prevent questioning of both of them about their relationship.

3. Lewinsky signed and filed the false affidavit.

4. The President used Lewinsky's false affidavit at his deposition in an attempt to head off questions about her.

5. When that failed, President Clinton lied under oath at his civil deposition about the nature of his relationship with her.

This is by far the most serious of Starr's charges. If the President and Lewinsky did in fact conspire to have her file a false affidavit, impeachment is very possible. The actions, if true, are clearly criminal.

The White House responded to this charge by noting that the President and Lewinsky did try to keep their relationship a secret, but this is not obstruction of justice. The White House then came up with an even better defense, one that could create serious doubts about much of Starr's report, and would throw a monkey-wrench into Congressional impeachment allegations.

248

At the end of her August 20 grand-jury testimony, Lewinsky said,

> *I think because of the public nature of how this investigation has been and what the charges aired [sic], that I would just like to say that no one ever asked me to lie and I was never promised a job for my silence.*

This critical comment was not made part of the Starr report. Clinton attorneys David Kendall and Charles Ruff were quick to latch on to the omission of this statement. Kendall and Ruff sent a letter to the House Judiciary Committee, contending that the report "distorted" Lewinsky's testimony, quoting it only when it suited the independent counsel.

It is a glaring admission, even by Starr's standards. The statement seems to contradict this charge completely. It is difficult to see how Clinton could obstruct justice by getting Lewinsky to file a false affidavit if, according to the prime witness herself, he never asked her to lie.

By the same token, charge VII is also completely contradicted by the former White House intern's omitted statement.

> *VII. "There is substantial and credible information that President Clinton endeavored to obstruct justice by helping Ms. Lewinsky obtain a job in New York at a time when she would have been a witness against him were she to tell the truth during the Jones case.*

Starr said President Clinton tried to obstruct justice by helping Monica obtain a job in New York. But Lewinsky's own testimony seems to say otherwise. Read again what she said: "No one ever asked me to lie and I was never promised a job for my silence." We can't believe everything else Monica has said and ignore this, can we?

> *X. There is substantial and credible information that President Clinton endeavored to obstruct justice during the federal grand jury investigation. While refusing to testify for seven months, he simultaneously lied to potential grand jury witnesses knowing that they would relay the falsehoods to the grand jury.*

Starr thinks that President Clinton tried to obstruct justice during the grand-jury investigation by his refusal to testify and by lying to senior White House aides. By doing so, he allegedly deceived, obstructed, and impeded the grand jury's investigation.

The issue of lying is significant and could be a serious charge if it could be proven. However,

Media Alert

When the Lewinsky story broke, fact and fiction merged in the film *Wag the Dog*. Robert DeNiro played a White House spin doctor who hired movie producer Dustin Hoffman to create the appearance of a war so the White House could deflect the country's attention away from a presidential sex scandal. Hoffman said, "It's not a war, it's a pageant!"

Clinton is a "very good liar," to quote Bob Kerry. If Clinton told his aides, "There is not relationship between myself and Ms. Lewinsky," it would not be a lie in Clinton-speak. There *was* a relationship, but there *is* not one now.

And in any case, even if he did lie to his aides, he obviously did not do so to obstruct justice, he did it because he was cheating on his wife and didn't want to get caught. Unethical for sure, but hardly impeachable.

Now, the issue regarding failure to testify is another matter. Kendall said that the fact that the President declined to testify to the grand jury "absent compulsion" was prudent and in no way illegal. That is very true. Clinton was invited to testify before the grand jury, but declined to do so. He was never subpoenaed, and he has a constitutional 5th-amendment right not to incriminate himself.

Alleging that Clinton committed an impeachable offense for this would be an embarrassment to most prosecutors. Starr's arguments begin to look specious at this point—he seems desperate to pin something, anything, on the President. "He didn't accept my invitation!"

By the way, targets of grand juries are seldom called to testify to those grand juries. A potential defendant's refusal, absent court order, is smart, not impeachable.

Witness Tampering (Count 9)

> IX. There is substantial and credible information that President Clinton endeavored to obstruct justice by attempting to influence the testimony of Betty Currie.

Starr accuses the President of improperly attempting to influence the testimony of his personal secretary, Betty Currie, in days just after his civil deposition in the Jones case.

The problem here is, it is difficult to tamper with a witness when the individual is not actually a witness. As the White House pointed out, Betty Currie was never a witness in the Jones case. Furthermore, the OIC's probe had not yet been extended to cover the Lewinsky matter at the time Clinton allegedly spoke with Currie, so she was not a witness in the OIC probe either. Any discussions the President may have had with her would therefore not fall under the rule of witness tampering or obstruction of justice. If Clinton wiggles out of this one, it will be because of good timing and dumb luck.

Abuse of Power (Count 11)

This is Starr's final allegation. Remember, it was tossed out by the Judiciary Committee, but is interesting nonetheless.

> XI. There is substantial and credible information that President Clinton's actions since January 17, 1998, regarding his relationship with Monica Lewinsky have been inconsistent with the President's constitutional duty to faithfully execute the laws.

Starr said President Clinton abused his constitutional power by:

1. Lying to the Congress and the American people in January 1998 about his relationship with Monica Lewinsky.

2. Promising at that time to cooperate fully with the grand-jury investigation.

3. Later refusing six invitations to testify willingly to the grand jury.

4. Invoking executive privilege.

5. Lying to the grand jury in August 1998.

6. Lying again to the American people and the Congress on August 17, 1998—all as part of an effort to hinder, impede and deflect a possible investigation by the Congress of the United States.

If this is all Starr could come up with in four years, he has wasted everyone's time and money. Yes, the charge sounds bad—abuse of power. But examine closely what Starr is saying. It is an affront to the American judicial system and to Americans themselves. It is unlikely Congress will follow Starr's lead on this one.

Here's why: Starr says that Clinton's private relationship with Lewinsky interfered with his constitutional obligation to carry out the laws of the country. Is there proof of that?

Starr said President Clinton abused his constitutional power by lying to the Congress and the American people in January 1998 about his relationship with Monica Lewinsky. Yes, he did lie. He looked us all in the face and wagged his finger and lied. To quote his own words, "It was wrong." But did that really violate the Constitution? It is difficult to conceive that Clinton's bald-faced lie somehow interfered with his ability to faithfully execute that the laws of this country are carried out. Wrong, yes. Unconstitutional, no.

Remember too, that all Presidents lie, most just don't get caught. In 1960, the Russians shot down Gary Powers' U2 spy plane. Eisenhower had the secretary of state tell the country that a weather-research plane had gone off-course. At the Kennedy-Nixon debates, JFK told the country, "I do not have Addison's disease." He did. Roosevelt promised the country it would not be dragged into WWII, while planning to drag the country into the war. If lying to the country is impeachable, we would have no President serve out his term.

Starr also alleges that Clinton promised to cooperate fully with the grand-jury investigation. You are hereby challenged to find one person in this country who is obliged to assist a grand jury that is investigating potential criminal wrongdoing by that person. The Fifth Amendment protects individuals from incriminating themselves. Even Presidents.

Starr also believes that Clinton should be impeached because he refused six invitations to testify willingly before the grand jury. Forget for a moment that no President has ever testified before a grand jury before and focus instead on the delusions of grandeur that must accompany such an allegation.

Starr asserts that the President abused his power by invoking executive privilege. Nixon invoked executive privilege, and although he was rebuked by the courts (as was Clinton), the Watergate Committee never contemplated impeaching Nixon for it. Apparently, Mr. Starr thinks that mounting a vigorous defense in a criminal investigation is worthy of impeachment. Suffice to say that many constitutional-law scholars and criminal defense attorneys disagree with the independent counsel's analysis.

Media Alert

In a *Time*/CNN poll taken on September 16-17, 1998, 71 percent of those polled believed that Clinton's relationship with Monica Lewinsky should be a private matter between Clinton and his family; 27 percent said that it was a legal matter that needed to be explored further in public.

Finally, Starr asserts that Clinton abused his power by lying to the grand jury and again to the American people and the Congress on August 17, 1998—all as part of an effort to hinder, impede and deflect a possible investigation by the Congress of the United States.

Starr may not agree with Clinton's use of the English language, but parsing words and defending oneself is not be considered abuse of power to most people. And then again, maybe it is to others. That is the beauty of a democracy.

The New House Charges

The House added four new allegations of wrongdoing that it will be investigating. These revolve primarily around Clinton's failure to disclose that Ms. Lewinsky had filed a false affidavit, and a charge that Clinton, Jordan, and Betty Currie may have conspired to obstruct justice.

Of the two, the conspiracy charges are far more serious, and may be the most serious of all of the impeachment allegations against the President. The charge that Clinton knowingly allowed Lewinsky to file a false affidavit can likely be dismissed via the President's fractured language. In Clinton-speak, they may not have had an affair or sexual relations because he and Lewinsky never engaged in sexual intercourse. Clinton has even said that he believes that most Americans agree with his definition. If that is what he thought, then he can probably get away with arguing that he thought Lewinsky's affidavit, while misleading, was legally accurate, to quote Clinton himself.

On the other hand, the conspiracy to obstruct justice charges will be very difficult for the President. As shown by majority counsel Schippers, Clinton, Jordan, and Currie were in heavy communication with one another immediately after Clinton's deposition. If they did in fact have some sort of plan to keep Lewinsky quiet or otherwise prevent the truth from coming out, Clinton edges ever closer to the high crimes threshold.

So, What Does It All Mean?

Starr made things worse for himself by alleging that everything but the kitchen sink was an impeachable offense. That is not to say he does not have some substantial charges aimed at the President. He has a couple. But he denigrates this important process when he declares, for example, that Clinton's refusal to testify before the grand jury constitutes an impeachable action. That is just plain silly.

The Judiciary Committee resolved many of Starr's problems by paring down his worst excesses. If anything positive can be gleaned from this mess, it is that political vendettas have no place in a constitutional process. Clinton treated Starr like the enemy and Starr treated the President like a traitor. A pox on both their houses.

The Least You Need to Know

➤ Starr charged the President with five counts of lying under oath. Clinton denies the charges.

➤ Starr charged the President with four counts of obstruction of justice. Clinton denies the charges.

➤ Starr's witness-tampering allegation is faulty.

➤ His abuse of power allegation is ill-conceived.

➤ There are no good guys here.

Chapter 24

The Impeachment Scenario

In This Chapter

➤ Political considerations

➤ The role of the House Judiciary Committee

➤ The role of the House

➤ Trial in the Senate

➤ President Gore?

The charges leveled against the President by the independent counsel are exceedingly serious. Whether you think this is "just about sex" or is about perjury and obstruction of justice, the fact remains that very few Presidents have faced charges serious enough to warrant a full-blown House impeachment inquiry. And that is exactly where we are headed.

Our Course Is Clear?

All of us, the country, the Congress, and the President, have several stark choices now. These are relatively uncharted waters, and the key players will be considering the legal and political issues with great care. An impeachment overturns an election and the will of the people. It should not be undertaken lightly.

First of all, the country has to decide what it wants done with the Deceiver-in-Chief. By and large, people seem to think that Clinton should be allowed to stay in office. We might question his personal morals, but we seem to appreciate his skill and results.

Media Alert

Ex-actor Ronald Reagan was the oldest man ever to take the oath of office. When he was first elected in 1980, he was 69 years old.

Become a Pundit

Former Speaker of the House Thomas P. "Tip" O'Neil from Boston had a political motto that has become the maxim of many a politician. "All politics is local," Tip taught.

This bodes well for the President. It will be very difficult for Congress to oust the President if he continues to have 60-percent approval ratings—a very high number, historically. Most Presidents do not have approval ratings in that neighborhood. The last President to have such consistently high ratings was Ronald Reagan. Prior to Reagan, the last President to be so consistently popular was Eisenhower. Truman, Kennedy, Johnson, Nixon, Ford, and Carter all missed that mark.

The House of Representatives and the Senate have their own decisions to make, both individually and collectively. Each member must decide what to say and do about Clinton. Call for his impeachment? Ask him to resign? Vote against impeachment? There are no easy answers here.

By and large, each representative will make his or her decision based more upon their own political situation than the good of the country, however unpalatable that may be. A Democrat from a safe district, like Jerrold Nadler from Manhattan's West Side for example, will have a far easier time defending the President than a Democrat in a district that is 50 percent Republican. Self-interest will trump national interest.

But, Republicans especially must consider the political fallout from having Clinton removed, be it by resignation or impeachment. If Clinton were to resign or be impeached after January of 1999, Vice President Al Gore would become President, and would be able to run for reelection twice. Gore could conceivably serve another 10 years as President. Republicans might well decide they are better served by allowing a damaged Clinton to stay in office rather than allow a healthy Gore to take the mantle of Clinton's popular domestic agenda into the next millennium.

Several censure scenarios have been put forth. One includes censure with a fine (Clinton would have to pay the $4.4 million cost of Starr's Lewinsky investigation). Another plan has Clinton being censured and agreeing to a trial on perjury charges after he leaves office. Still another has Clinton censured and pleading guilty to misdemeanor perjury charges.

Vice President Al Gore. Reuters/Chris Kleponis/ Archive Photos

Clinton's in the House

While the country and the Congress will have plenty to say, the ball really is in Bill Clinton's court, and he has several choices. He could broker a deal with Congress for some sort of "super-censure." He could resign. Or, he could take his chances and risk it all in a trial in the Senate. Which one sounds like Clinton?

As a young boy, Clinton dreamed of being President someday. He wanted to be like his heroes John Kennedy or Franklin Roosevelt. As a middle-aged man, Clinton knows that his choices are more limited. He will not be President like JFK or FDR; instead, he will be President like Richard Nixon or Andrew Johnson. It's either resignation or impeachment for him.

For Clinton, censure would be preferable, but it is highly unlikely to happen. Although it would allow him to stay in office, remember that for the past few years, Clinton has consistently outmaneuvered, outthought, and outfoxed his adversaries in

Mumbo Jumbo

A **misdemeanor** is an offense lower than a felony and generally punishable by fine, or imprisonment other than in a penitentiary.

Mumbo Jumbo

Censure is the formal resolution of a legislative body reprimanding and condemning a person, normally a member, for specified conduct.

Become a Pundit

In 1973, the year before Nixon resigned, National Security Advisor Henry Kissinger won the Nobel Peace Prize for negotiating a cease-fire in Vietnam.

Congress. Now he is on the ropes. It's hard to imagine the Republican-controlled Congress permitting Clinton to get out of this debacle until they have wrung every drop of political blood possible.

Bill Clinton is not going to resign. Not only is he a politician, he is a political animal. You don't become President by the age of 46 without being incredibly driven and capable. He spent his whole life preparing and planning to become Chief Executive, and he is not going to give it up easily.

He is also a political survivor. Clinton is not called the "Comeback Kid" for nothing. He has been counted out so many times that it is difficult to keep track of every reincarnation. Surely he thinks he has one last grand comeback up his sleeve.

Resignation Situation

Clinton need only look to Nixon to see the demerits of the resignation option. Rather than risk an impeachment trial in the Senate, Nixon became the only President to resign his office. It took years to rehabilitate his name, and even then, he was only moderately successful. The stench of resignation will likely be too strong for Clinton.

Another reason Nixon resigned was that he was able to retain the perks of the office by foregoing impeachment. Impeached officials lose their government pension and benefits. An impeached Clinton would lose his annual $151,000 stipend, as well as his Secret Service protection. Such considerations will not assuage Clinton, though, because:

➤ Once out of office, he will be paid millions to write his autobiography.

➤ If he serves out his second term, he will be only 53. He will be at his peak earning potential and will make millions if he wants to. A Presidential pension will be peanuts, comparatively.

White House Confidential

Our sixth President, John Quincy Adams, was the son of our second President, John Adams. When John Quincy Adams was voted out of office after only one term in 1829, he was not done. He went back to Massachusetts, ran again, and served in the House of Representatives for another 17 years. It is said that his last words were, "This is the last of earth! I am content."

Playing the Impeachment Odds

Clinton is a risk-taker by nature. Indeed, he would never be in this predicament in the first place if he were not. So, what will he do? The betting here is that Bill Clinton will take his chances and gamble that the Senate will be unable to muster 67 votes necessary to toss him from office.

This strategy has three things going for it. First, Clinton is still quite popular. Voting to impeach a popular President will be a difficult proposition for many members of Congress. Moreover, the citizenry is already suspicious about Congress' motives. The release of the Starr report, Clinton's grand-jury testimony, Linda Tripp's tapes, and other seemingly partisan actions puts the Republican Congress at a disadvantage. Clinton will bet that his popularity will outweigh his sexual peccadilloes. Although if the economy turns, all bets are off.

Next, by taking this to the Congress, Clinton will effectively be challenging Congress to a game of "sexual roulette." We already know what's in Clinton's closet, and we have learned what is in House Judiciary Chairman Henry Hyde's closet. But what about the other members of Congress? Who among them is pure enough to go to the floor of Congress and cast the first stone calling for Clinton's impeachment? If you think the Democrats haven't been gathering this information for months, then you don't realize how intensely political this "nonpartisan" process has become.

This is all the more true since *Hustler* magazine publisher Larry Flynt is now offering $1 million for anyone who can document an extra-marital affair with a member of Congress or other high ranking government official. His belief is that we are now in an era of "sexual McCarthyism" and he wants to root out the hypocrites.

White House Confidential

Serious efforts were launched to impeach President John Tyler in 1843 and President Herbert Hoover in 1932, but the House rejected both impeachments.

What's Impeachable?

Finally, Clinton will be betting that Congress will be unable to solve the "high crimes and misdemeanors" riddle. The impeachment standard the Constitution sets is high and not easily reached. Impeachment was never intended to be simple; it is an option of last resort.

Become a Pundit

In 1792, Treasury Secretary Alexander Hamilton was under investigation by three members of Congress for allegedly using treasury money to pay off one James Reynolds for a stock-market swindle. Hamilton confessed to paying Reynolds out of his own pocket to keep Reynolds quiet about an affair Hamilton had with his wife, Maria. The Congressmen determined that the matter was strictly personal, not relevant to Hamilton's public duties, and that no impeachable offenses occurred.

Alexander Hamilton said "The Framers borrowed the phrase 'High Crimes and Misdemeanors,' [to] denote the gravest wrongs—offenses against the Constitution itself." Clinton is going to bet that Congress will be unable to prove that lying, even under oath, about sex, is an offense against the Constitution itself.

The fact that we are even debating whether Starr's case is about sex or an actual crime might prove that Clinton's actions don't rise to the level of high crimes and misdemeanors. Think about this: If Clinton sold military secrets to the Chinese, there would be no debate as to whether he should be impeached. Treason is impeachable. But what about lying about sex? That the case against Clinton is even debatable breaks in the President's favor.

Let the Courts Decide

Maybe it has crossed your mind that the Supreme Court could simply decide what constitutes a "high crime or misdemeanor"—either because Clinton's lawyers ask the court to intervene, or the President appeals any future conviction in the Senate. This is highly unlikely.

It is true that the Supreme Court has the final say on all matters constitutional. However, there are matters that the court believes are outside its authority to adjudicate (also known as jurisdiction). The idea goes like this: If you commit a crime in New York, you could not be tried in California, because California lacks jurisdiction over you. By the same token, if the Supreme Court finds that an issue that it is asked to resolve is "moot," or that the issue is not yet "ripe," it will conclude that it lacks jurisdiction over the matter. Another of these jurisdictional issues relates to so-called "political questions."

The Court has consistently held that it lacks the authority to resolve issues that come before it that are primarily political questions. The reasoning behind this doctrine, which is quite sound, is that there are certain matters that the Court believes are constitutionally given to another branch of government. A respect for the separation of powers demands that the court bow out of these matters. (Look, we've come full circle!)

Political questions are to be resolved by the political branches of government, not the judiciary. Whether a certain action would constitute a high crime or misdemeanor is just the sort of political question that the Constitution empowered to Congress to determine, not the courts. Indeed, Congress, not the courts, is given the power to remove officers who commit these high crimes. The Supreme Court will stay out of this battle.

Will the Witness Please Rise?

The 37-member House Judiciary Committee is already doing its part in this Constitutional process. It is investigating to see if articles of impeachment should be brought to the entire House of Representatives. While the committee is relying on the Starr report, it is not bound to accept the recommendations found in the report, although it does give them a head start on the investigation. Thus, although the Nixon impeachment investigation by the House Judiciary Committee took eight months, the current investigation will likely be much shorter.

The Judiciary Committee is made up of 21 Republicans and 15 Democrats. Certainly the spirited debate and vote will be partisan, even if all members tip their hat to bipartisan cooperation. Among the key players are:

➤ **Bob Barr** This Republican has been calling for Clinton's impeachment for years.

➤ **John Conyers** The committee's ranking Democrat will be one of Clinton's staunchest defenders.

Become a Pundit

Luther Patick served in the House for eight years, up until 1947. The first rule he lists in his "Rules for a Congressman" is "Entertain with a smile constituents, their wives, their sons, etc. Go with them to the White House and show good reason why you are unable to personally have them meet the President; take daughters to meet midshipmen at Annapolis."

➤ **Barney Frank** The liberal Democrat will be Clinton's alter-ego on the committee.

➤ **Newt Gingrich** Although not a member of the committee, the Speaker will be pulling plenty of strings behind the scenes.

➤ **Henry Hyde** The Republican chairman of the committee normally gets very good press for a reason—he is genial and judicious.

➤ **Bob Inglis** Inglis, a Republican, has already called for the President to resign.

➤ **Zoe Lofgren** This Democrat believes that impeachable offenses are only those that seriously undermine the functioning of the government.

➤ **Bill McCollum** A key Republican who has already argued forcefully that perjury is an impeachable offense.

➤ **Maxine Waters** This Democrat is partisan and outspoken.

House Speaker Newt Gingrich (R-GA). AP/Wide World Photos

Other prominent Republican committee members include:

➤ **Mary Bono** (R-CA) The widow of Representative Sonny Bono, an extra seat on the panel was created especially for her.

➤ **Ed Bryant** (R-TN) Bryant is not a vocal member of the often boisterous panel.

➤ **Charles Canaday** (R-FL) Canady is one of the most active members of the House Judiciary Committee.

➤ **George Gekas** (R-PA) Gekas participated in impeachment proceedings against former federal judge Alcee Hastings.

➤ **Lindsey Graham** (R-SC)   Graham's comments about impeachment have impressed some Democrats.

➤ **Asa Hutchinson** (R-AR)   Hutchinson, a former federal prosecutor, is a newcomer to the Judiciary Committee who often participates in committee debate and usually votes with his party.

➤ **William Jenkins** (R-TN)   Jenkins is a former circuit court judge and a conservative committee back-bencher.

Sound Bites

He is a sanctioned, adjudicated, and confessed liar.

—James Carville on Newt Gingrich, September 27, 1998 on Meet the Press

➤ **James Rogan** (R-CA)   Rogan was handpicked by Speaker Newt Gingrich to study possible impeachment proceedings even before the completion of the Starr report and assumed the late Sonny Bono's seat on the Judiciary Committee in 1998.

➤ **James Sensenbrenner** (R-WI)   The *1998 Almanac of American Politics* describes him as a "stickler for rules and ethics," who "has insisted on impeachment action against federal judges convicted of crimes."

Notable Democrats include:

➤ **Thomas Barrett** (D-WI)   Barrett is the newest member of the committee, having the distinction of being named by Democratic leaders on the same day the Starr report became public.

➤ **Howard Berman** (D-CA)   Berman is a quiet, behind-the-scenes deal-maker.

➤ **Willaim Delahunt** (D-MA)   Delahunt is a former district attorney in Massachusetts and is well-equipped to debate the finer points of law confronting the panel.

➤ **Jerrold Nadler** (D-NY)   The New York congressman has amassed a solidly liberal voting record.

➤ **Charles Schumer** (D-NY)   The Brooklyn congressman is in a tough campaign to unseat Republican Senator Al D'Amato in 1998.

➤ **Bobby Scott** (D-VA)   Scott is a graduate of Harvard University and Boston College Law School and was the first African American to be elected to Congress from Virginia since Reconstruction.

➤ **Melvin Watt** (D-NC)   Watt is a frequent foe of Republicans in the full committee on most issues. Like the President, he earned his law degree from Yale University.

➤ **Robert Wexler** (D-FL)   Wexler has said he believes the President's testimony was not truthful, but that fact alone is not grounds for impeachment.

Become a Pundit

Sam Dash is widely considered to be the father of the current independent counsel law. Dash was the counsel for the Judiciary Committee during Watergate. He is currently Ken Starr's ethics advisor.

Mumbo Jumbo

A **simple majority** is more than half of the voting members of any group. In the 435 member House of Representatives, 218 members make up a simple majority. Republicans alone number more than that figure.

If the committee finds adequate cause, it will pass articles of impeachment against the President. The best guess? The Republican-controlled committee will likely find cause for impeachment. It is doubtful, however, that they will find 15 counts for impeachment. During Watergate, the Judiciary Committee seriously considered sending five articles of impeachment to the full House, but ended-up only forwarding the strongest three. (Articles relating to tax evasion and the secret war in Cambodia were dropped.) This committee will forward only the very strongest case to the entire body of the House.

The Role of the House

The House is free to accept or reject the Judiciary Committee's findings. In 1993, the committee found insufficient cause to impeach federal judge Harold Lauderback, but the House impeached him anyway. (The Senate found Lauderback not guilty.) Once the articles from the committee make it to the House floor, the full House can add or drop articles as it sees fit. In the case of President Andrew Johnson, the House added two articles to the bill of impeachment it had received from the Judiciary Committee.

Each separate article is then put to a vote, and only a simple majority is needed for passage. Once even a single article of impeachment is approved, Clinton will be "impeached." Again, given the makeup of the House and the partisanship evident in Washington today, it is difficult to conceive of a scenario where Clinton would not be impeached if things proceed to this point.

It will be interesting to see how the mid-term elections of 1998 affect the process. Prior to the election, the Republican edge in the House was only 21 seats, the smallest margin for the majority party in more than 40 years. If, as a result of the elections, the Republican margin increases, as it is expected to, the prospects for impeachment will be greater.

If the Republicans cannot expand their majority, impeachment is less likely. In 1974, during the Nixon impeachment inquiry, Democrats held a 50-seat majority in the House. Although President Nixon resigned before the full House could vote on the impeachment articles approved by the Judiciary Committee, the widely held belief at the time was that the House would have easily impeached Nixon.

"The chair recognizes the Senator from..."

The House acts sort of like a grand jury. Evidence is gathered and submitted and forwarded on for trial. The trial takes place in the Senate.

The Senate adopted impeachment procedures after much debate during the impeachment of Andrew Johnson. Those procedures are largely still in use today. It is likely that whatever impeachment articles are forwarded to the Senate will land first in the lap of Senator Orrin Hatch (R-UT). Hatch, as chairman of the Senate Judiciary Committee, would hold hearings in review of the articles of impeachment.

White House Confidential

Andrew Johnson became President just after the Civil War. The President just before the war was James Buchanan. Buchanan did little to keep the Union together in his one term. Upon leaving the White House, he said to incoming President Abraham Lincoln, "If you are as happy, my dear sir, on entering this house as I am leaving it and returning home, you are the happiest man in this country!"

After the Senate Judiciary Committee concludes its review, the matter would be set for trial. Pursuant to the Constitution, Chief Justice of the Supreme Court William Rehnquist would preside. The President would be present, sitting aside his counsel at a table in the well of the Senate usually reserved for Senate clerks. As the prosecutors, members of the House Judiciary Committee would sit at the opposing table and would present the case against the President.

Following the Johnson precedent, the Senate would hear arguments from both the House prosecutors and the President's lawyers. Witnesses subject to cross-examination will be called (as opposed to the witnesses who testified before Starr's grand jury). Other forms of evidence would also be introduced.

If you thought the O.J. Simpson trial was a spectacle, you ain't seen nothin' yet! It is highly likely that any trial would be televised. C-SPAN already carries House and Senate debates live, and given the importance of this trial, it is hard to imagine it not being televised. If the unread Starr report can be released on the Internet because the public has a "right to know," the impeachment trial of President William Jefferson Clinton would be hard to keep off the airwaves.

White House Confidential

Q: Which Presidents allegedly have fathered illegitimate children?

A: Thomas Jefferson, Grover Cleveland, John F. Kennedy, and Lyndon B. Johnson.

This entire process will likely be very drawn out. The House investigation can take months. The House impeachment vote would be quicker. The Senate review will take time, and the trial of the President, unprecedented in our lifetime, would likely take many more months. No member of Congress will let it pass without having his or her say in the matter.

At the end of the trial, the Senate would go into secret session and deliberate. Each Senator is restricted to 15 minutes to make his views known. Upon termination of deliberations, they would adjourn to an open session where they would vote on each separate article of impeachment.

The Constitution requires a two-thirds vote of the Senate to convict the President. If Clinton banks on surviving a Senate trial, this is his ace-in-the-hole. While it would be relatively easy for the Republican House to find a majority willing to vote articles of impeachment, garnering 67 votes in the Senate will be difficult.

Sound Bites

This is not politics ... this is not polling ... this is not a witch hunt .... This is a constitutional test.

—House Democratic leader Richard Gephart, who voted to release Starr's report to the public without letting Clinton see it beforehand

The Senate, as judge and jury in the process, must be neutral; members should, if they wish to abide by the letter and spirit of the Constitution, be publicly silent about not only their view of whether or not Clinton engaged in impeachable offenses, but even what exactly an impeachable offense is. Their views on what constitutes high crimes and misdemeanors should be discussed in private until all evidence is presented. Currently, this is not happening—senators are speaking at length into any microphone thrust in front of them.

No matter your political affiliation, it is a fact that the charges essentially stem from a foolish attempt to conceal a petty sexual affair. There likely will be 34 Senators (the number of votes Clinton would need to remain in office) who don't think Clinton's stupidity amounts to "treason, bribery, or other high crimes and misdemeanors." Secondly, the manner in which Starr conducted his inquiry convinced many Democrats that this was nothing but a partisan witch-hunt. As such, a vote along party lines is possible.

Therein lies the rub. To remove Clinton from office, the Republicans would need Democrats to defect and turn on the President. Removing a President can't be done along party lines. In Nixon's case, only when his Republican allies began to abandon him did he realize he would have to resign or face impeachment.

Become a Pundit

In 1902, during a debate about the fate of the Philippines, Senator Tillman apparently impugned the integrity of Senator McLaurin, or so McLaurin thought. A fight broke out on the floor of the Senate. McLaurin bopped Tillman in the nose and Tillman gave McLaurin a shiner. Both were found in contempt of Senate and censured.

The same should hold true here. When the time comes, if the time comes, that Democrats think the President has in fact committed a high crime or misdemeanor and should therefore be removed from office, then we will be engaged in process that we all can be proud of. Because then, the grand plan of the framers will have been realized.

Impeachment is designed to be a bipartisan process that removes someone who has committed an offense against the Constitution itself. To do so requires a two-thirds vote of all Senators. That is the genius of this process: By requiring a two-thirds vote of the Senate, the framers of the Constitution ensured that the vote must be nonpartisan to succeed.

Then What?

Once impeached and removed from office, the President would be subject to a regular trial in criminal court and "liable and subject to indictment, trial and punishment, according to law." The Senate trial "merely" removes a President from office. A criminal trial would still be needed for the offenses that drove him from office. That is why Ford pardoned Nixon.

If Clinton is driven from office, Al Gore would immediately assume the Presidency. He would then pick a new Vice President who would need to be confirmed by both houses of Congress.

It's not difficult to speculate what a President Gore might be like. Even more than Clinton, Gore was born and raised to someday assume the mantle of Commander in Chief.

Born in 1948, Al Gore Jr. is the son of former Senator Albert Gore and Pauline Gore. He was born in Carthage, Tennessee, but spent his formative years in Washington, D.C., attending dinner parties with his father and meeting the famous Democrats of the era.

He attended Harvard University, where he received a degree in government; after college, he volunteered to join the U.S. Army, serving in Vietnam.

When he returned from duty, he was, for the first time in his life, unsure of what to do next. Turning on his government background, Gore decided to go to work for the enemy—he became a reporter for the *Tennessean* newspaper in Nashville. He soon abandoned this and went on to attended Vanderbilt Divinity School. He then went to the Vanderbilt Law School.

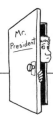

White House Confidential

Fourteen Vice Presidents have eventually gone on to become President. The last one was George Bush.

In 1976, a congressional seat in Gore's home district opened up, and a light went on in the head of the perplexed young man. He was supposed to run for office! Politics made sense. Gore ran, won, and served in the House that will decide his boss' fate for eight years. He was elected to the U.S. Senate in 1984. In 1988, Gore ran for President, but lost, after garnering about 3 million votes in the seven primaries he entered. Gore was re-elected to the Senate in 1990. During the 1996 Presidential race, Gore was involved in heavy fundraising activities on behalf of the party and his own re-election. Those activities have since come under much scrutiny.

The main problem has to do with money he received from some Buddhist Monks in Los Angeles. Not only have there been questions about the location of the fundraising (occurring at a temple), but the source of the money received is also under investigation. If it turns out that Gore received campaign donations from money that originated in China (and that is one of the allegations) his once bright political prospects certainly will be dimmed, if not extinguished.

And what if Gore was unable to serve, because of his potential fund-raising or other problems? Then the order of succession would go like this:

➤ Newt Gingrich, Speaker of the House of Representatives

➤ Strom Thurmond, President pro tempore of the Senate

➤ Madeline Albright, Secretary of State

➤ Robert Rubin, Secretary of the Treasury

➤ Janet Reno, Attorney General

From there it continues on through the Cabinet. President Gingrich? We better do this right.

The Least You Need to Know

➤ Clinton will likely risk a trial in the Senate than resign.

➤ The House Judiciary Committee would investigate and recommend articles of impeachment.

➤ The House would likely pass an impeachment article bill.

➤ Clinton would probably win in a Senate trial.

Chapter 25

What Does the Future Hold?

In This Chapter

➤ The prosecutor

➤ The statute

➤ The Presidency

➤ The parties

➤ The Comeback Kid

The President stands accused, and his accusers stand ready. The clash before us will be remarkable, probably unlike anything we have ever witnessed. With stakes so high and hostility in abundance, no one will come away from this struggle unscathed—not the President, not the independent counsel, not the Congress, and not the country.

Prosecutor or Persecutor?

Consider first of all the independent counsel, Kenneth Starr. Prior to this debacle, Starr was a star on the Republican stage. He had toiled in the Bush White House, on the Court of Appeals, and in private practice. He had made the rounds, knew the players, and was ready for more.

Prior to this appointment, Ken Starr was considered Mr. Clean in Washington. He was selected by both parties to review Bob Packwood's diaries. He was recognized throughout the country as an outstanding solicitor general, and was known as a very fine judge. Starr had been prominently mentioned as a possible Justice for the Supreme Court, which is about impressive as it gets. Just about anything seemed possible for the sharp son of a Texas preacher.

White House Confidential

Edmund Randolph, George Washington's secretary of state, was forced to resign when it was learned that he had solicited bribes from the French.

But that was yesterday. Today, he is a much different man in a much different place. His integrity has been assailed, as has his honesty, character, and capabilities. While friends of Bill are certainly to blame for much of the name-calling and bad publicity, he, like Bill Clinton, has no one to blame for his long fall but himself.

Much of what Starr stands accused of is legitimate, and some is not. He should have been able to discharge his duties with less grandstanding and more prudence. While he might actually be an impartial independent prosecutor bent on getting the facts, his apparent bias created legitimate cause for alarm. A professional investigation should never descend into a personal vendetta. A prosecutor investigating the President for wrongdoing should not be accused of wrongdoing himself. With his talent and ability, it is shameful that his investigation ended with such controversy.

His report was shocking in its content because he wanted it to be. It contains news of the President's actions that are upsetting, disheartening, wrong, and possibly even impeachable. But his case is not a strong one. We had a right to expect more or to expect him to bow out.

One does not go through what Ken Starr has gone through, been called the names Ken Starr has been called, without consequences. One result of his investigation is that it is unlikely Starr will again be the top-tier player he was previously, at least for a while. Why?

Become a Pundit

The Clintons and the Starrs both have daughters who currently attend Stanford University.

➤ He is too politicized. His name is synonymous with partisanship to many people now.

➤ His reputation is tarnished. It will be some time before he gets his erstwhile good name back.

➤ Confirmation to any appointed governmental office would be unlikely, given the propensity of politicians to extract revenge.

➤ He may not want it. After this high-profile case, Starr may want a break.

Starr's tenure as independent counsel is not yet over. His investigations continue. At some point he will have to report what he learned about the many "gates" that followed the Clintons. Maybe he will find more "impeachable" offenses. It seems unlikely, though, that anything remotely resembling the Lewinsky sexplosion will again be coming out of his office.

Starr is required by statute to complete the charge he was originally given. That means he must, at some point, wrap up his many Whitewater investigations and either indict the allegedly guilty or report to Attorney General Janet Reno that there have been no criminal wrongdoings. It took Lawrence Walsh seven years to conclude his Iran-Contra investigation. This, however, is likely to end sooner. With Congress already considering impeachment, all cards will need to be laid on the table fairly soon.

No More Independent Counsels, Ever!

Not really. The law, in theory at least, seems clear: It sets up a process for impartial investigation of the most powerful people in the federal government. But the statute that gave rise to Prosecutor Starr will be vastly revised if not eliminated completely as a result of this investigation. Republicans have been clamoring for years to discard the law, and suddenly Democrats see the problem as well.

There are several problems with the law as it stands today. First, the prosecutor, appointed by a three-judge panel, is supposed to be "independent." But the law doesn't state the prosecutor has to be nonpartisan. That is a loophole that must be fixed.

Another problem in both the Whitewater and Iran-Contra investigations is that the investigations were just too long. Serious business of the country gets lost amid often flimsy accusations that must be taken seriously and investigated. Along with that, it is currently too easy to expand an investigation. Even some Republicans fail to see any link between Whitewater and Lewinsky. Many lawmakers, including the law's author, Michigan Democratic Senator Carl Levin, want to see major revisions that would restrict independent-counsel investigations so they cannot stray far from their original purpose.

If the law does stay, it will be radically restricted. Currently, any member of the executive branch (from the President down through all lower level Cabinet posts) is subject to the law. One option under careful consideration currently is to have any new law apply only to the President and Vice President. By the same token, any new law would likely apply only to crimes committed *while in office*. That would allow for Watergate-style investigations but prevent those of the Whitewater variety.

Become a Pundit

Eight Congressmen have been reprimanded by the House of Representatives since reprimand was introduced as a punishment in 1976. The most recent was Speaker of the House Newt Gingrich in 1997, for putting tax-exempt funds to political use and submitting false information to the House Ethics Committee.

Some people want to get rid of the law altogether. Several experts believe that other parts of the government have the capacity to root out criminal impropriety and that an independent counsel is just not needed.

One idea that has received some backing is to vest the attorney general and the Justice Department with the authority to conduct such investigations. The problem with that idea is that the Justice Department is part of the executive branch. It seems a conflict of interest for it to investigate its own. In fact, the genesis for the current independent counsel law is that the Justice Department used to handle these matters. That is why Nixon was able to have Special Prosecutor Archibald Cox fired. That incident was the impetus for the current law. If it didn't work the first time, it is unlikely to work the second time.

Become a Pundit

How do you become a pundit? Become an independent counsel first. Joseph diGenova is a regular on the legal talk show circuit. In another life, he was the independent prosecutor looking into whether former Bush Administration officials searched Clinton's passport files when Clinton was a candidate for the Presidency.

One other option is to let Congress undertake these types of investigations. "I'm not sure it's worth having government mechanisms planning for the John Mitchells of the world," said Kathleen Clark, a former counsel for the Senate Judiciary Committee, referring to the former attorney general forced into resignation by Richard Nixon and later convicted for his role in Watergate. "The Senate Judiciary Committee has power right now [to investigate], but it doesn't currently use it."

Whatever changes are made will likely occur soon. Expect to see a very serious, spirited, and acrimonious debate about the statute.

A Disturbing Legal Legacy

Another valid criticism of Starr is that in his zeal to get the President he has forever harmed the Presidency. Never before has an independent counsel sought to use Secret Service testimony against the President. Never before has a President had grand-jury testimony made public. And never before have so many Presidential aides been forced to testify against their boss.

The Presidency is a less effective, less trusting institution today because of Ken Starr. Starr has subpoenaed so many Presidential aides and so many documents once thought confidential that by 1997, Presidential aides stopped taking notes while meeting with the President, lest Starr subpoena them. In the future, says old-hand and former Carter counsel Lloyd Cutler, "People in the White House are not going to write memos. They are going to be very circumspect in the advice they give." When you have a person running the country and already isolated by the nature of the office, you don't want his aides to be wary of giving honest advice. Yet that is what we now have.

This is all the more true since the Supreme Court has determined in its wisdom that sitting Presidents must defend civil lawsuits while they are in office. Given the success of the Jones case in politically damaging President Clinton, civil suits may become a new tool in Washington's political arsenal. Consider what will happen if a politically motivated lawsuit against a future President comes along. The Jones precedent will force future political aides to the President to be very guarded in the advice they give in case they are later deposed in the case. It's tough to be candid when your advice may later become public.

White House Confidential

President Jimmy Carter is widely considered the most successful ex-President ever. Many people know that he builds homes for the homeless and monitors elections worldwide. Carter is also an avid writer, having published many books since 1980, including a book of poetry. Among his poems are "Of Possum and Fatback," "The Day No One Came to the Peanut Picker," and "Why We Get Cheaper Tires from Liberia."

Legal advice for future Presidents will be poorer too. Normally, conversations between a lawyer and a client are sacrosanct; they are to be kept completely confidential—a lawyer's failure to do so is cause for disbarment—and for good reason. People tell their lawyers many secrets, things they obviously want to remain confidential. Lawyers, in return, provide needed advice about those matters. Clients would be very reluctant to divulge their secrets if they knew that the lawyer was under no legal obligation to keep these matters private.

So the rule is: Lawyer/client conversations are completely confidential. That is the rule everywhere in the country ... except the White House.

Here's why: Presidents have many advisors, many of them lawyers by trade. Many of these aides give both legal and political advice. Some give nothing but legal advice. In his determination to prove his case against Clinton, Starr subpoenaed every one of Clinton's lawyers. The President opposed this, claiming his conversations with those aides were protected by "executive privilege" and/or "lawyer-client privilege." These disagreements went before the judiciary, and in the end, the courts determined that the only person in the White House covered by the "lawyer-client privilege" was the President's personal lawyer. That means any attorney who works for the government and gives the President advice is subject to divulging that advice at some point in the future.

Because of Starr's zeal and Clinton's stonewalling, we now have a legal precedent stating that the only persons with whom the President can speak freely, secure in the knowledge that their testimony cannot be subpoenaed, are the President's spouse (spousal privilege) and personal lawyer. No one else can speak or advise future Presidents in complete confidence.

By the same token, Starr's fervor took him in the realm of questioning Secret Service agents. No one had ever considered taking the extraordinary step of issuing a subpoena to a Secret Service agent; it was assumed that their knowledge was confidential. Not anymore. The White House tried to prevent their testimony, asserting the unheard-of "protective function privilege." The Secret Service itself, as well as other law-enforcement agencies and former President George Bush agreed with the Clinton Administration that it sets a bad precedent to have the Secret Service testify against the President. Bad precedent is what we have.

White House Confidential

The Secret Service was established in 1865 by Abraham Lincoln. Originally intended to investigate counterfeiting, the Secret Service is a division of the Department of the Treasury. It began protecting Presidents and their families in 1901 after President William McKinley was assassinated. The Secret Service routinely assigns code names to Presidents and their family members. Among the most interesting are: Ronald Reagan—"Rawhide," Barbara Bush—"Tranquility," Bill Clinton—"Eagle," and Amy Carter—"Dynamo."

Forget for a moment what you think of this President and think about what this means for future Presidents. As a result of these legal skirmishes, the Presidency itself is weakened. However, Starr did not do this alone. Clinton could have given more rather than less information, sooner rather than later, to Starr, but did not. There is plenty of blame to go around, and we are all the worse for it.

Democrats, Republicans, Citizens, and Voters

Whatever the outcome of this historic event, it is not just the President, the Presidency, and the law that will be affected. The political parties, and in turn, we ourselves, will feel the brunt of this quagmire for years to come.

After Watergate and the resignation of Republican President Nixon, the Democrats were on the ascendancy and the Republicans were in deep decline. The 1974 elections were a banner year for the Demos. That mid-term election brought in a slew of new, young, energetic, Democratic "Watergate Freshman" House members. Eager to participate in good, moral governance, these Democrats were largely responsible for many of the campaign financing laws that are still around today.

Two years later, still in reaction to Watergate, the country voted for probably our most moral President ever: Jimmy Carter. An intelligent, honest man who nevertheless had a difficult time governing effectively.

Will this crisis have similar results? Mid-term elections are notoriously good for the out-of-office party. 1998 was no exception. Just as the Watergate Democrats came to see it as their job to clean up government, maybe these Republicans will see it as their job to purify Washington. Expect to see high-mindedness and moral virtue become the rule rather than the exception in our nations Capitol. At least for a little while.

The Democrats will surely be licking their wounds for some time to come. Their President has disgraced them, and the voters will remember it. Especially in light of the fact that Clinton called himself a "New Democrat," it will be harder for old Democrats to reclaim the legitimacy that Clinton's pre-Lewinsky popularity provided.

The country will certainly be different too. Politics, already at a low ebb, will somehow touch lower in people's minds and hearts. The Lewinsky saga has disheartened many and will turn many more people off to government.

If any good can come of this, it might be that a line can be drawn between acceptable and unacceptable intrusion into the private lives of public figures. The national discourse is not well-served, and the people really do not have a right to know the truth about every sexual or otherwise intimate secret a public person may have.

The Supreme Court has consistently held that the right of privacy is a "fundamental right." That doctrine holds true for all of our citizens, even Presidents. As the court said in its seminal (excuse the pun) opinion regarding the right to privacy, *Griswold v. Connecticut*:

> *We deal with a right of privacy older than the Bill of Rights—older than our political parties, older than our school system. Marriage is a coming together for better or for worse, hopefully enduring, and intimate to the degree of being sacred.*

Somewhere along the way, some of us seemed to have forgotten that notion.

The Comeback Kid

He better have one more comeback in his bag of tricks. But even if Clinton does come back from the brink, once again, his triumph will be short-lived. Surviving a trial in the Senate or a Congressional censure is not the stuff of greatness.

There is no delicate way around this. Clinton had it all and threw it away. He was first elected with 43 percent of the vote. Hard work, luck, and a skyrocketing stock-market catapulted him into the rarified 60-percent range. Coupled with a booming economy, that translated into loads of political capital.

Second terms are times for Presidents to create a legacy. Clinton, ever the student of history in general and Presidential history in particular, was keenly aware that his opportunity was golden. He could have used his political capital on most anything that impassioned him—race relations, Social Security, health care, anything. The chance to be considered more than a caretaker President during good times was his for the asking.

Clinton asked for fellatio instead. It would be unforgivable if it were not so blatantly self-destructive. It is all the more inconceivable considering he was the defendant in a sexual-harassment lawsuit; a lawsuit he believed to be politically inspired. His enemies were gunning for him and yet he couldn't help himself. This was not 1960, and he knew it; he tried to end his relationship with the intern a full year before it became public, but he couldn't help himself. It calls into question not just his morals and ethics, but his judgment.

Clinton disappointed himself, his family, his friends, his advisors, and even some of his detractors. He disappointed a country that had slowly come to trust him. To squander such promise and opportunity is the stuff of Shakespeare.

There will be no simple solutions for Bill Clinton. All scenarios seem to lead down the same sad path. It seems unlikely that he will get off with only a Congressional censure. That is the best he can hope for. If that were to happen, he will be weak, but he could still lead. The question is, will anyone follow? With a Republican Congress and an exhausted nation, no matter what initiatives he undertakes, there will be few loyalists left to carry the banner.

Presidents usually have at their disposal what Teddy Roosevelt called the "bully pulpit." It is that unique power held by Presidents only, because of the nature of their office, to alter the public debate. The bully pulpit will be of little use to Bill Clinton. He already lacks moral authority. It will be difficult for him to harness and shape public opinion in his favor as he has in the past.

And that's the best-case scenario. What happens if he clings to power and ends up being tried in the Senate?

Sound Bites

When once the woman has tempted us and we have tasted the forbidden fruit, there is no such thing as checking our appetites, whatever the consequences may be.

—George Washington

Sound Bites

I was not contrite enough ... I have repented.

—President Bill Clinton at a prayer breakfast

278

He will have no choice but to mount a vigorous defense. He will need to convince 34 Senators that his actions were insipid, but not impeachable. Whatever political capital he has will be expended fighting the charges and retaining office. Those 34 Senators are not going to save him without extracting demands.

Whether he is censured or he survives a trial in the Senate, most second-term Presidents are considered "lame ducks" by their last year in office. New elections are on the horizon, a new President will be coming into office soon, and the sitting President becomes old news. In Clinton's last year, should he survive, this would be all the more true. Humiliated even more (if that were possible) by a trial in the Senate or even a censure, Clinton will likely become fairly irrelevant.

What is the worst-case scenario? It isn't pretty. The House finds evidence that Clinton broke the law. The matter is referred to the Senate. The real trial of the century occurs, and the juror-Senators vote to oust Clinton. He becomes the only President in the history of the republic to be removed from office via impeachment. He will live on in history, although not how he ever imagined.

Become a Pundit

Members of Congress can be expelled by a two-thirds vote of the body they serve in. Since the founding of the country, only nineteen members of Congress have been expelled. Seventeen of those were kicked out for "supporting the Confederacy."

However, Clinton is at his best when he is at his worst. His knack for political revival is as real as it is legendary. If anyone could salvage something from this, if anyone could help people remember why they voted for him twice and still like him despite his buffoonery, it is Bill Clinton. It would not be an easy task, but it's not an inconceivable one either.

This is the man who was booted out of the Governor's mansion after one term and came back to become the most popular Governor in Arkansas state history. This is the candidate who survived the "did not inhale"/Gennifer Flowers double-whammy in the same week and became the Democratic nominee for President a few months later. This is the President whose party was kicked out of Congress as the majority for the first time in 50 years and became more popular than ever as a result.

Sound Bites

I don't anticipate anything. I just show up for work and see what happens.

—Mike McCurry, White House press secretary

Count Bill Clinton out? Don't count on it. He is the Comeback Kid.

Afterglow

When we elect Presidents, we are electing humans and leaders of men, not saints and paragons of virtue. It is indisputable that George Washington, Thomas Jefferson, and Franklin Roosevelt were great Presidents. They were also all adulterers. That fact does not lessen their accomplishments.

A theocracy is a government lead by those who are said to be divinely guided; men and women of unquestioned moral and religious authority. But we don't live in a theocracy, we live in a democracy. A democracy is a government of men and women whom we know are not angels and is a system designed to take into account that fact. We elect a President to be a democratic leader, not a theocratic one.

We have tried electing a moral leader as President, and it didn't work. Remember Jimmy Carter? To expect a President, any President, to be as moral as he or she is intelligent, strong, creative, and effective is missing the point. Great Presidents are great because they are both passionate and driven. It is those very qualities that permits them to rise to the top of a very dirty political game. Moral decency and political effectiveness tend to be mutually exclusive; that is the nature of the democratic beast.

Sure it would be nice to have an effective President who is also a very moral one, but it is not, and never has been, a job requirement. What you want, what the job requires, is a person who listens, who leads, who fights, and who can get things done.

What we are witnessing today is nothing less than sexual McCarthyism. None of the Presidents mentioned in this chapter could have accomplished what they did if they too were pursued by enemies with a political agenda, subpoena power, and deposition demands. What would have become of this country if Thomas Jefferson was forced to admit or deny, under oath, his adulterous relationship with his black slave? And if he denied it, as he would have, is that reason to charge him with an impeachable offense? We have sunk too low.

There is nothing wrong with expecting a President to follow the law. It is a given. But to trap a President in a political lawsuit, force him to admit an infidelity under oath, and then use that answer as a cause for impeachment, is wrong, and sets a frightening precedent. Whether you are a Democrat, a Republican, or an independent, the use of a civil suit as a partisan political tool should be viewed with great concern. It may be your guy next time.

And Now, the End Is Near

And so it goes. This so-called "bold experiment in self-governance" that is our country and Constitution marches on. But what is it really? Not so long ago, some middle-class land owners were angered about their tax situation. They tried to talk to city hall, but government bureaucrats turned a deaf ear. What to do? These men, these bold men, started a new country, "conceived in liberty, and dedicated to the proposition that all men are created equal."

Among those who are created equal is the President of the United States. He is neither above nor below the law. This President now stands accused of breaking that very law. What will become of him, his accuser, and the nation is sure to be an extraordinary chapter in the bold experiment. It's a chapter we are, in some ways, fortunate enough to witness.

The Least You Need to Know

➤ Ken Starr's wounds are largely self-inflicted, but he is too talented not to come back from this.

➤ The independent counsel statute will be radically reformed as a result of this affair.

➤ Starr seemed to care more about getting the President than he did about the Presidency.

➤ They don't call Clinton the Comeback Kid for nothing.

Excerpts from the Starr Report

The Starr report itself is divided up into 6 sections: Key dates, table of names, introduction, narrative, acts that may constitute grounds for impeachment and conclusion. The introduction draws a picture of the report to come. The narrative is the most-talked-about part of the report because it provides the well-footnoted details of the President's activities, from the points of view of many of those subpoenaed by the grand jury. The last section included here is the "acts" section, which outlines why the Independent Counsel believes the President should be impeached.

These excerpts include some of the original headings from the report. Some of them are labelled with numbers or letters that don't quite follow in this excerpted version of the report. We have included symbols and ellipses points to indicate material that has been left out.

Introduction

As required by Section 595(c) of Title 28 of the United States Code, the Office of the Independent Counsel ("OIC" or "Office") hereby submits substantial and credible information that President William Jefferson Clinton committed acts that may constitute grounds for an impeachment.(1)

The information reveals that President Clinton:

➤ lied under oath at a civil deposition while he was a defendant in a sexual harassment lawsuit;

➤ lied under oath to a grand jury;

➤ attempted to influence the testimony of a potential witness who had direct knowledge of facts that would reveal the falsity of his deposition testimony;

➤ attempted to obstruct justice by facilitating a witness's plan to refuse to comply with a subpoena;

➤ attempted to obstruct justice by encouraging a witness to file an affidavit that the President knew would be false, and then by making use of that false affidavit at his own deposition;

> ➤ lied to potential grand jury witnesses, knowing that they would repeat those lies before the grand jury; and

> ➤ engaged in a pattern of conduct that was inconsistent with his constitutional duty to faithfully execute the laws.

The evidence shows that these acts, and others, were part of a pattern that began as an effort to prevent the disclosure of information about the President's relationship with a former White House intern and employee, Monica S. Lewinsky, and continued as an effort to prevent the information from being disclosed in an ongoing criminal investigation.

Factual Background

In May 1994, Paula Corbin Jones filed a lawsuit against William Jefferson Clinton in the United States District Court for the Eastern District of Arkansas.(2) Ms. Jones alleged that while he was the Governor of Arkansas, President Clinton sexually harassed her during an incident in a Little Rock hotel room.(3) President Clinton denied the allegations. He also challenged the ability of a private litigant to pursue a lawsuit against a sitting President. In May 1997, the Supreme Court unanimously rejected the President's legal argument. The Court concluded that Ms. Jones, "[l]ike every other citizen who properly invokes [the District Court's] jurisdiction ... has a right to an orderly disposition of her claims," and that therefore Ms. Jones was entitled to pursue her claims while the President was in office.(4) A few months later, the pretrial discovery process began.(5)

One sharply disputed issue in the Jones litigation was the extent to which the President would be required to disclose information about sexual relationships he may have had with "other women." Ms. Jones's attorneys sought disclosure of this information, arguing that it was relevant to proving that the President had propositioned Ms. Jones. The President resisted the discovery requests, arguing that evidence of relationships with other women (if any) was irrelevant.

In late 1997, the issue was presented to United States District Judge Susan Webber Wright for resolution. Judge Wright's decision was unambiguous. For purposes of pretrial discovery, President Clinton was required to provide certain information about his alleged relationships with other women. In an order dated December 11, 1997, for example, Judge Wright said: "The Court finds, therefore, that the plaintiff is entitled to information regarding any individuals with whom the President had sexual relations or proposed or sought to have sexual relations and who were during the relevant time frame state or federal employees."(6) Judge Wright left for another day the issue whether any information of this type would be admissible were the case to go to trial. But for purposes of answering the written questions served on the President, and for purposes of answering questions at a deposition, the District Court ruled that the President must respond.

In mid-December 1997, the President answered one of the written discovery questions posed by Ms. Jones on this issue. When asked to identify all women who were state or federal employees and with whom he had had "sexual relations" since 1986,(7) the President answered under oath: "None."(8) For purposes of this interrogatory, the term "sexual relations" was not defined.

On January 17, 1998, President Clinton was questioned under oath about his relationships with other women in the workplace, this time at a deposition. Judge Wright presided over the deposition. The President was asked numerous questions about his relationship with Monica Lewinsky, by then a 24-year-old former White House intern, White House employee, and Pentagon employee. Under oath and in the presence of Judge Wright, the President deniedthat he had engaged in a "sexual affair," a "sexual relationship," or "sexual relations" with Ms. Lewinsky. The President also stated that he had no specific memory of having been alone with Ms. Lewinsky, that he remembered few details of any gifts they might have exchanged, and indicated that no one except his attorneys had kept him informed of Ms. Lewinsky's status as a potential witness in the Jones case.

The Investigation

On January 12, 1998, this Office received information that Monica Lewinsky was attempting to influence the testimony of one of the witnesses in the Jones litigation, and that Ms. Lewinsky herself was prepared to provide false information under oath in that lawsuit. The OIC was also informed that Ms. Lewinsky had spoken to the President and the President's close friend Vernon Jordan about being subpoenaed to testify in the Jones suit, and that Vernon Jordan and others were helping her find a job. The allegations with respect to Mr.Jordan and the job search were similar to ones already under review in the ongoing Whitewater investigation.(9)

After gathering preliminary evidence to test the information's reliability, the OIC presented the evidence to Attorney General Janet Reno. Based on her review of the information, the Attorney General determined that a further investigation by the Independent Counsel was required.

On the following day, Attorney General Reno petitioned the Special Division of the United States Court of Appeals for the District of Columbia Circuit, on an expedited basis, to expand the jurisdiction of Independent Counsel Kenneth W. Starr. On January 16, 1998, in response to the Attorney General's request, the Special Division issued an order that provides in pertinent part:

> *The Independent Counsel shall have jurisdiction and authority to investigate to the maximum extent authorized by the Independent Counsel Reauthorization Act of 1994 whether Monica Lewinsky or others suborned perjury, obstructed justice, intimidated witnesses, or otherwise violated federal law other than a Class B or C misdemeanor or infraction in dealing with witnesses, potential witnesses, attorneys, or others concerning the civil case Jones v. Clinton.(10)*

On January 28, 1998, after the allegations about the President's relationship with Ms. Lewinsky became public, the OIC filed a Motion for Limited Intervention and a Stay of

Discovery in *Jones v. Clinton*. The OIC argued that the civil discovery process should be halted because it was having a negative effect on the criminal investigation. The OIC represented to the Court that numerous individuals then under subpoena in the Jones case, including Monica Lewinsky, were integral to the OIC's investigation, and that courts routinely stayed discovery in such circumstances.(11)

The next day Judge Wright responded to the OIC's motion. The Court ruled that discovery would be permitted to continue, except to the extent that it sought information about Monica Lewinsky. The Court acknowledged that "evidence concerning Monica Lewinsky might be relevant to the issues in [the *Jones*] case."(12) It concluded, however, that this evidence was not "essential to the core issues in this case," and that some of that evidence "might even be inadmissible."(13) The Court found that the potential value of this evidence was outweighed by the potential delay to the Jones case in continuing to seek discovery about Ms. Lewinsky.(14) The Court also was concerned that the OIC's investigation "could be impaired and prejudiced were the Court to permit inquiry into the Lewinsky matter by the parties in this civil case."(15)

On March 9, 1998, Judge Wright denied Ms. Jones's motion for reconsideration of the decision regarding Monica Lewinsky. The order states:

> The Court readily acknowledges that evidence of the Lewinsky matter might have been relevant to plaintiff's case and, as she argues, that such evidence might possibly have helped her establish, among other things, intent, absence of mistake, motive, and habit on the part of the President. ... Nevertheless, whatever relevance such evidence may otherwise have ... it simply is not essential to the core issues in this case.... (16)

On April 1, 1998, Judge Wright granted President Clinton's motion for summary judgment, concluding that even if the facts alleged by Paula Jones were true, her claims failed as a matter of law.(17) Ms. Jones has filed an appeal, and as of the date of this Referral, the matter remains under consideration by the United States Court of Appeals for the Eighth Circuit.

After the dismissal of Ms. Jones's lawsuit, the criminal investigation continued. It was (and is) the view of this Office that any attempt to obstruct the proper functioning of the judicial system, regardless of the perceived merits of the underlying case, is a serious matter that warrants further inquiry. After careful consideration of all the evidence, the OIC has concluded that the evidence of wrongdoing is substantial and credible, and that the wrongdoing is of sufficient gravity that it warrants referral to Congress.(18)

The Significance of the Evidence of Wrongdoing

It is not the role of this Office to determine whether the President's actions warrant impeachment by the House and removal by the Senate; those judgments are, of course, constitutionally entrusted to the legislative branch.(19) This Office is authorized, rather, to conduct criminal investigations and to seek criminal prosecutions for matters within its jurisdiction.(20) In carrying out its investigation, however, this Office also has a statutory duty to disclose to Congress information that "may constitute grounds for an impeachment," a task that inevitably requires judgment about the seriousness of the acts revealed by the evidence.

From the beginning, this phase of the OIC's investigation has been criticized as an improper inquiry into the President's personal behavior; indeed, the President himself suggested that specific inquiries into his conduct were part of an effort to "criminalize my private life."(21) The regrettable fact that the investigation has often required witnesses to discuss sensitive personal matters has fueled this perception.

All Americans, including the President, are entitled to enjoy a private family life, free from public or governmental scrutiny. But the privacy concerns raised in this case are subject to limits, three of which we briefly set forth here.

First. The first limit was imposed when the President was sued in federal court for alleged sexual harassment. The evidence in such litigation is often personal. At times, that evidence is highly embarrassing for both plaintiff and defendant. As Judge Wright noted at the President's January 1998 deposition, "I have never had a sexual harassment case where there was not some embarrassment."(22) Nevertheless, Congress and the Supreme Court have concluded that embarrassment-related concerns must give way to the greater interest in allowing aggrieved parties to pursue their claims. Courts have long recognized the difficulties of proving sexual harassment in the workplace, inasmuch as improper or unlawful behavior often takes place in private.(23) To excuse a party who lied or concealed evidence on the ground that the evidence covered only "personal" or "private" behavior would frustrate the goals that Congress and the courts have sought to achieve in enacting and interpreting the Nation's sexual harassment laws. That is particularly true when the conduct that is being concealed—sexual relations in the workplace between a high official and a young subordinate employee— itself conflicts with those goals.

Second. The second limit was imposed when Judge Wright required disclosure of the precise information that is in part the subject of this Referral. A federal judge specifically ordered the President, on more than one occasion, to provide the requested information about relationships with other women, including Monica Lewinsky. The fact that Judge Wright later determined that the evidence would not be admissible at trial, and still later granted judgment in the President's favor, does not change the President's legal duty at the time he testified. Like every litigant, the President was entitled to object to the discovery questions, and to seek guidance from the court if he thought those questions were improper. But having failed to convince the court that his objections were well founded, the President was duty bound to testify truthfully and fully. Perjury and attempts to obstruct the gathering of evidence can never be an acceptable response to a court order, regardless of the eventual course or outcome of the litigation.

The Supreme Court has spoken forcefully about perjury and other forms of obstruction of justice:

> *In this constitutional process of securing a witness' testimony, perjury simply has no place whatever. Perjured testimony is an obvious and flagrant affront to the basic*

> *concepts of judicial proceedings. Effective restraints against this type of egregious offense are therefore imperative.(24)*

The insidious effects of perjury occur whether the case is civil or criminal. Only a few years ago, the Supreme Court considered a false statement made in a civil administrative proceeding: "False testimony in a formal proceeding is intolerable. We must neither reward nor condone such a 'flagrant affront' to the truth-seeking function of adversary proceedings. ... Perjury should be severely sanctioned in appropriate cases."(25) Stated more simply, "[p]erjury is an obstruction of justice."(26)

Third. The third limit is unique to the President. "The Presidency is more than an executive responsibility. It is the inspiring symbol of all that is highest in American purpose and ideals."(27) When he took the Oath of Office in 1993 and again in 1997, President Clinton swore that he would "faithfully execute the Office of President."(28) As the head of the Executive Branch, the President has the constitutional duty to "take Care that the Laws be faithfully executed."(29) The President gave his testimony in the Jones case under oath and in the presence of a federal judge, a member of a co-equal branch of government; he then testified before a federal grand jury, a body of citizens who had themselves taken an oath to seek the truth. In view of the enormous trust and responsibility attendant to his high Office, the President has a manifest duty to ensure that his conduct at all times complies with the law of the land.

In sum, perjury and acts that obstruct justice by any citizen—whether in a criminal case, a grand jury investigation, a congressional hearing, a civil trial, or civil discovery—are profoundly serious matters. When such acts are committed by the President of the United States, we believe those acts "may constitute grounds for an impeachment."

The Scope of the Referral

1. *Background of the Investigation.* The link between the OIC's jurisdiction—as it existed at the end of 1997—and the matters set forth in this Referral is complex but direct. In January 1998, Linda Tripp, a witness in three ongoing OIC investigations, came forward with allegations that: (i) Monica Lewinsky was planning to commit perjury in *Jones v. Clinton*, and (ii) she had asked Ms. Tripp to do the same. Ms. Tripp also stated that: (i) Vernon Jordan had counseled Ms. Lewinsky and helped her obtain legal representation in the Jones case, and (ii) at the same time, Mr. Jordan was helping Ms. Lewinsky obtain employment in the private sector.

OIC investigators and prosecutors recognized parallels between Mr. Jordan's relationship with Ms. Lewinsky and his earlier relationship with a pivotal Whitewater-Madison figure, Webster L. Hubbell. Prior to January 1998, the OIC possessed evidence that Vernon Jordan—along with other high-level associates of the President and First Lady—helped Mr. Hubbell obtain lucrative consulting contracts while he was a potential witness and/or subject in the OIC's ongoing investigation. This assistance took place, moreover, while Mr. Hubbell was a target of a separate criminal investigation into his own conduct. The OIC also possessed evidence that the President and the First Lady knew and approved of the Hubbell-focused assistance.

Specifically, in the wake of his April 1994 resignation from the Justice Department, Mr. Hubbell launched a private consulting practice in Washington, D.C. In the startup process, Mr. Hubbell received substantial aid from important public and private figures. On the day prior to Mr. Hubbell announcing his resignation, White House Chief of Staff Thomas "Mack" McLarty attended a meeting at the White House with the President, First Lady, and others, where Mr. Hubbell's resignation was a topic of discussion.

At some point after the White House meeting, Mr. McLarty spoke with Vernon Jordan about Mr. Jordan's assistance to Mr. Hubbell. Mr. Jordan introduced Mr. Hubbell to senior executives at New York-based MacAndrews & Forbes Holding Co. Mr. Jordan is a directorof Revlon, Inc., a company controlled by MacAndrews & Forbes. The introduction was successful; MacAndrews & Forbes retained Mr. Hubbell at a rate of $25,000 per quarter. Vernon Jordan informed President Clinton that he was helping Mr. Hubbell.(30)

By late 1997, this Office was investigating whether a relationship existed between consulting payments to Mr. Hubbell and his lack of cooperation (specifically, his incomplete testimony) with the OIC's investigation.(31) In particular, the OIC was investigating whether Mr. Hubbell concealed information about certain core Arkansas matters, namely, the much-publicized Castle Grande real estate project and related legal work by the Rose Law Firm, including the First Lady.

Against this background, the OIC considered the January 1998 allegations that: (i) Ms. Lewinsky was prepared to lie in order to benefit the President, and (ii) Vernon Jordan was assisting Ms. Lewinsky in the Jones litigation, while simultaneously helping her apply for a private-sector job with, among others, Revlon, Inc.

Based in part on these similarities, the OIC undertook a preliminary investigation. On January 15, 1998, this Office informed the Justice Department of the results of our inquiry. The Attorney General immediately applied to the Special Division of the Court of Appeals for the District of Columbia Circuit for an expansion of the OIC's jurisdiction. The Special Division granted this request and authorized the OIC to determine whether Monica Lewinsky or others had violated federal law in connection with the *Jones v. Clinton* case.

2. Current Status of the Investigation. When the OIC's jurisdiction was expanded to cover the Lewinsky matter in January 1998, several matters remained under active investigation by this Office. Evidence was being gathered and evaluated on, among other things, events related to the Rose Law Firm's representation of Madison Guaranty Savings & Loan Association; events related to the firings in the White House Travel Office; and events related to the use of FBI files. Since the current phase of the investigation began, additional events arising from the Lewinsky matter have also come under scrutiny, including possible perjury and obstruction of justice related to former White House volunteer Kathleen Willey, and the possible misuse of the personnel records of Pentagon employee Linda Tripp.

From the outset, it was our strong desire to complete all phases of the investigation before deciding whether to submit to Congress information—if any—that may constitute grounds for an impeachment. But events and the statutory command of Section 595(c) have dictated otherwise. As the investigation into the President's actions with respect to Ms. Lewinsky and the Jones litigation progressed, it became apparent that there was a significant body of substantial and credible information that met the Section 595(c) threshold. As that phase of the investigation neared completion, it also became apparent that a delay of this Referral until the evidence from all phases of the investigation had been evaluated would be unwise. Although Section 595(c) does not specify when information must be submitted, its text strongly suggests that information of this type belongs in the hands of Congress as soon as the Independent Counsel determines that the information is reliable and substantially complete.

All phases of the investigation are now nearing completion. This Office will soon make final decisions about what steps to take, if any, with respect to the other information it has gathered. Those decisions will be made at the earliest practical time, consistent with our statutory and ethical obligations.

The Contents of the Referral

The Referral consists of several parts. Part One is a Narrative. It begins with an overview of the information relevant to this investigation, then sets forth that information in chronological sequence. A large part of the Narrative is devoted to a description of the President's relationship with Monica Lewinsky. The nature of the relationship was the subject of many of the President's false statements, and his desire to keep the relationship secret provides a motive for many of his actions that apparently were designed to obstruct justice.

The Narrative is lengthy and detailed. It is the view of this Office that the details are crucial to an informed evaluation of the testimony, the credibility of witnesses, and the reliability of other evidence. Many of the details reveal highly personal information; many are sexually explicit. This is unfortunate, but it is essential. The President's defense to many of the allegations is based on a close parsing of the definitions that were used to describe his conduct. We have, after careful review, identified no manner of providing the information that reveals the falsity of the President's statements other than to describe his conduct with precision.

Part Two of the Referral is entitled "Information that May Constitute Grounds for An Impeachment." This "Grounds" portion of the Referral summarizes the specific evidence that the President lied under oath and attempted to obstruct justice. This Part is designed to be understandable if read without the Narrative, although the full context in which the potential grounds for impeachment arise can best be understood if considered against the backdrop of information set forth in Part One.

Several volumes accompany the Referral. The Appendix contains relevant court orders, tables, a discussion of legal and evidentiary issues, background information on the Jones litigation, a diagram of the Oval Office, and other reference material. We next set forth a series of "Document Supplements," which attempt to provide some of the most important support material in an accessible format. Document Supplement A contains transcripts of the President's deposition testimony and grand jury testimony; Document Supplement B contains transcripts of Monica Lewinsky's testimony and interview statements. Document Supplements C, D, and E set forth the full text of the documents cited in the Referral. Although every effort has been made to provide full and accurate quotations of witnesses in their proper context, we urge review of the full transcripts of the testimony cited below.

Narrative

A. Introduction

This Referral presents substantial and credible information that President Clinton criminally obstructed the judicial process, first in a sexual harassment lawsuit in which he was the defendant and then in a grand jury investigation. The opening section of the Narrative provides an overview of the object of the President's cover-up, the sexual relationship between the President and Ms. Lewinsky. Subsequent sections recount the evolution of the relationship chronologically, including the sexual contacts, the President's efforts to get Ms. Lewinsky a job, Ms. Lewinsky's subpoena in *Jones v. Clinton*, the role of Vernon Jordan, the President's discussions with Ms. Lewinsky about her affidavit and deposition, the President's deposition testimony in Jones, the President's attempts to coach a potential witness in the harassment case, the President's false and misleading statements to aides and to the American public after the Lewinsky story became public, and, finally, the President's testimony before a federal grand jury.

B. Evidence Establishing Nature of Relationship

1. Physical Evidence

Physical evidence conclusively establishes that the President and Ms. Lewinsky had a sexual relationship. After reaching an immunity and cooperation agreement with the Office of the Independent Counsel on July 28, 1998, Ms. Lewinsky turned over a navy blue dress that she said she had worn during a sexual encounter with the President on February 28,

1997. According to Ms. Lewinsky, she noticed stains on the garment the next time she took it from her closet. From their location, she surmised that the stains were the President's semen.(1)

Initial tests revealed that the stains are in fact semen.(2) Based on that result, the OIC asked the President for a blood sample.(3) After requesting and being given assurances that the OIC had an evidentiary basis for making the request, the President agreed.(4) In the White House Map Room on August 3, 1998, the White House Physician drew a vial of blood from the President in the presence of an FBI agent and an OIC attorney.(5) By conducting the two standard DNA comparison tests, the FBI Laboratory concluded that the President was the source of the DNA obtained from the dress.(6) According to the more sensitive RFLP test, the genetic markers on the semen, which match the President's DNA, are characteristic of one out of 7.87 trillion Caucasians.(7)

In addition to the dress, Ms. Lewinsky provided what she said were answering machine tapes containing brief messages from the President, as well as several gifts that the President had given her.

4. Documents

In addition to her remarks and email to friends, Ms. Lewinsky wrote a number of documents, including letters and draft letters to the President. Among these documents are (i) papers found in a consensual search of her apartment; (ii) papers that Ms. Lewinsky turned over pursuant to her cooperation agreement, including a calendar with dates circled when she met or talked by telephone with the President in 1996 and 1997; and (iii) files recovered from Ms. Lewinsky's computers at home and at the Pentagon.

5. Consistency and Corroboration

Because of the fashion in which the investigation had unfolded, in sum, a massive quantity of evidence was available to test and verify Ms. Lewinsky's statements during her proffer interview and her later cooperation. Consequently, Ms. Lewinsky's statements have been corroborated to a remarkable degree. Her detailed statements to the grand jury and the OIC in 1998 are consistent with statements to her confidants dating back to 1995, documents that she created, and physical evidence.(18) Moreover, her accounts generally match the testimony of White House staff members; the testimony of Secret Service agents and officers; and White House records showing Ms. Lewinsky's entries and exits, the President's whereabouts, and the President's telephone calls.

C. Sexual Contacts

1. The President's Accounts

a. Jones Testimony

In the Jones deposition on January 17, 1998, the President denied having had "a sexual affair," "sexual relations," or "a sexual relationship" with Ms. Lewinsky.(19) He noted that "[t]here are no curtains on the Oval Office, there are no curtains on my private office, there are no curtains or blinds that can close [on] the windows in my private dining room," and added: "I have done everything I could to avoid the kind of questions you are asking me here today ...."(20)

The President did not dispute his legal representative's assertion that the President and Ms. Lewinsky had had "absolutely no sex of any kind in any manner, shape or form," nor did he dispute the implication that Ms. Lewinsky's affidavit, in denying "a sexual relationship," meant that there was "absolutely no sex of any kind in any manner, shape or form." In subsequent questioning by his attorney, President Clinton testified under oath that Ms. Lewinsky's affidavit was "absolutely true."(22)

b. Grand Jury Testimony

Testifying before the grand jury on August 17, 1998, seven months after his Jones deposition, the President acknowledged "inappropriate intimate contact" with Ms. Lewinsky but maintained that his January deposition testimony was accurate.(23) In his account, "what began as a friendship [with Ms. Lewinsky] came to include this conduct."(24) He said he remembered "meeting her, or having my first real conversation with her during the government shutdown in November of '95." According to the President, the inappropriate contact occurred later (after Ms. Lewinsky's internship had ended), "in early 1996 and once in early 1997."(25)

The President refused to answer questions about the precise nature of his intimate contacts with Ms. Lewinsky, but he did explain his earlier denials.(26) As to his denial in the Jones deposition that he and Ms. Lewinsky had had a "sexual relationship," the President maintained that there can be no sexual relationship without sexual intercourse, regardless of what other sexual activities may transpire. He stated that "most ordinary Americans" would embrace this distinction.(27)

The President also maintained that none of his sexual contacts with Ms. Lewinsky constituted "sexual relations" within a specific definition used in the Jones deposition.(28) Under that definition:

> [A] person engages in "sexual relations" when the person knowingly engages in or causes—(1) contact with the genitalia, anus, groin, breast, inner thigh, or buttocks of any person with an intent to arouse or gratify the sexual desire of any person .... "Contact" means intentional touching, either directly or through clothing.(29)

According to what the President testified was his understanding, this definition "covers contact by the person being deposed with the enumerated areas, if the contact is done with an intent to arouse or gratify," but it does not cover oral sex performed on the person being deposed.(30) He testified:

> [I]f the deponent is the person who has oral sex performed on him, then the contact is with—not with anything on that list, but with the lips of another person. It seems to be self-evident that that's what it is. ... Let me remind you, sir, I read this carefully.(31)

In the President's view, "any person, reasonable person" would recognize that oral sex performed on the deponent falls outside the definition.(32) If Ms. Lewinsky performed oral sex on the President, then—under this interpretation—she engaged in sexual relations but he did not. The President refused to answer whether Ms. Lewinsky in fact had performed oral sex on him.(33) He did testify that direct contact with Ms.

Lewinsky's breasts or genitalia would fall within the definition, and he denied having had any such contact.(34)

2. Ms. Lewinsky's Account

According to Ms. Lewinsky, she and the President had ten sexual encounters, eight while she worked at the White House and two thereafter.(35) The sexual encounters generally occurred in or near the private study off the Oval Office—most often in the windowless hallway outside the study.(36) During many of their sexual encounters, the President stood leaning against the doorway of the bathroom across from the study, which, he told Ms. Lewinsky, eased his sore back.(37)

Ms. Lewinsky testified that her physical relationship with the President included oral sex but not sexual intercourse.(38) According to Ms. Lewinsky, she performed oral sex on the President; he never performed oral sex on her.(39) Initially, according to Ms. Lewinsky, the President would not let her perform oral sex to completion. In Ms. Lewinsky's understanding, his refusal was related to "trust and not knowing me well enough."(40) During their last two sexual encounters, both in 1997, he did ejaculate.(41)

According to Ms. Lewinsky, she performed oral sex on the President on nine occasions. On all nine of those occasions, the President fondled and kissed her bare breasts. He touched her genitals, both through her underwear and directly, bringing her to orgasm on two occasions. On one occasion, the President inserted a cigar into her vagina. On another occasion, she and the President had brief genital-to-genital contact.(42)

Whereas the President testified that "what began as a friendship came to include [intimate contact]," Ms. Lewinsky explained that the relationship moved in the opposite direction: "[T]he emotional and friendship aspects ... developed after the beginning of our sexual relationship."(43)

D. Emotional Attachment

As the relationship developed over time, Ms. Lewinsky grew emotionally attached to President Clinton. She testified: "I never expected to fall in love with the President. I was surprised that I did."(44) Ms. Lewinsky told him of her feelings.(45) At times, she believed that he loved her too.(46) They were physically affectionate: "A lot of hugging, holding hands sometimes. He always used to push the hair out of my face."(47) She called him "Handsome"; on occasion, he called her "Sweetie," "Baby," or sometimes "Dear."(48) He told her that he enjoyed talking to her—she recalled his saying that the two of them were "emotive and full of fire," and she made him feel young.(50) He said he wished he could spend more time with her.(51)

E. Conversations and Phone Messages

Ms. Lewinsky testified that she and the President "enjoyed talking to each other and being with each other." In her recollection, "We would tell jokes. We would talk about our childhoods. Talk about current events. I was always giving him my stupid ideas about what I thought should be done in the administration or different views on things."(54) One of Ms. Lewinsky's friends testified that, in her understanding, "[The President] would talk about his childhood and growing up, and [Ms. Lewinsky] would relay stories about her childhood and growing up. I guess normal conversations that you would have with someone that you're getting to know."(55)

The longer conversations often occurred after their sexual contact. Ms. Lewinsky testified: "[W]hen I was working there [at the White House] ... we'd start in the back [in or near the private study] and we'd talk and that was where we were physically intimate, and we'd usually end up, kind of the pillow talk of it, I guess, ... sitting in the Oval Office ...."(56) During several meetings when they were not sexually intimate, they talked in the Oval Office or in the area of the study.(57)

Along with face-to-face meetings, according to Ms. Lewinsky, she spoke on the telephone with the President approximately 50 times, often after 10 p.m. and sometimes well after midnight.(58) The President placed the calls himself or, during working hours, had his secretary, Betty Currie, do so; Ms. Lewinsky could not telephone him directly, though she sometimes reached him through Ms. Currie.(59) Ms. Lewinsky testified: "[W]e spent hours on the phone talking."(60)

On 10 to 15 occasions, she and the President had phone sex.(62) After phone sex late one night, the President fell asleep mid-conversation.(63)

F. Gifts

Ms. Lewinsky and the President exchanged numerous gifts. By her estimate, she gave him about 30 items, and he gave her about 18.(72) Ms. Lewinsky's first gift to him was a matted poem given by her and other White House interns to commemorate "National Boss Day," October 24, 1995.(73) This was the only item reflected in White House records that Ms. Lewinsky gave the President before (in her account) the sexual relationship began, and the only item that he sent to the archives instead of keeping.(74) On November 20—five days after the intimate relationship began, according to Ms. Lewinsky—she gave him a necktie, which he chose to keep rather than send to the archives.(75) According to Ms. Lewinsky, the President telephoned the night she gave him the tie, then sent her a photo of himself wearing it.(76) The tie was logged pursuant to White House procedures for gifts to the President.(77)

H. Secrecy

1. Mutual Understanding

Both Ms. Lewinsky and the President testified that they took steps to maintain the secrecy of the relationship. According to Ms. Lewinsky, the President from the outset stressed the importance of keeping the relationship secret. In her handwritten statement to this Office, Ms. Lewinsky wrote that "the President told Ms. L to deny a relationship, if ever asked about it. He also said something to the effect of if the two people who are involved say it didn't happen—it didn't happen."(89) According to Ms. Lewinsky, the President sometimes asked if she had told anyone about their sexual relationship or about the gifts they had exchanged; she (falsely) assured him that she had not.(90) She told him that "I would always deny it, I would always protect him," and he responded approvingly.(91) The two of them had, in her words, "a mutual understanding" that they would "keep this private, so that meant deny it and ... take whatever appropriate steps needed to be taken."(92) When she and the President both were subpoenaed to testify in the Jones case, Ms. Lewinsky anticipated that "as we had on every other occasion and every other instance of this relationship, we would deny it."(93)

2. Cover Stories

For her visits to see the President, according to Ms. Lewinsky, "[T]here was always some sort of a cover."(97) ... Later, after she left the White House and started working at the Pentagon, Ms. Lewinsky relied on Ms. Currie to arrange times when she could see the President. The cover story for those visits was that Ms. Lewinsky was coming to see Ms. Currie, not the President.(103)

While the President did not expressly instruct her to lie, according to Ms. Lewinsky, he did suggest misleading cover stories.(104) And, when she assured him that she planned to lie about the relationship, he responded approvingly.

Once she was named as a possible witness in the Jones case, according to Ms. Lewinsky, the President reminded her of the cover stories. After telling her that she was a potential witness, the President suggested that, if she were subpoenaed, she could file an affidavit to avoid being deposed. He also told her she could say that, when working at the White House, she had sometimes delivered letters to him, and, after leaving her White House job, she had sometimes returned to visit Ms. Currie.(106) (The President's own testimony in the Jones case mirrors the recommendations he made to Ms. Lewinsky for her testimony. In his deposition, the President testified that he saw Ms. Lewinsky "on two or three occasions" during the November 1995 government furlough, "one or two other times when she brought some documents to me," and "sometime before Christmas" when Ms. Lewinsky "came by to see Betty."(107))

In his grand jury testimony, the President acknowledged that he and Ms. Lewinsky "might have talked about what to do in a nonlegal context" to hide their relationship, and that he "might well have said" that Ms. Lewinsky should tell people that she was bringing letters to him or coming to visit Ms. Currie.(108) But he also stated that "I never asked Ms. Lewinsky to lie."(109)

3. Steps to Avoid Being Seen or Heard

After their first two sexual encounters during the November 1995 government shutdown, according to Ms. Lewinsky, her encounters with the President generally occurred on weekends, when fewer people were in the West Wing.

II. 1995: Initial Sexual Encounters

The month after her White House internship began, Ms. Lewinsky and the President began what she characterized as "intense flirting."(137) At departure ceremonies and other events, she made eye contact with him, shook hands, and introduced herself.(138) When she ran into the President in the West Wing basement and introduced herself again, according to Ms. Lewinsky, he responded that he already knew who she was.(139)

In the autumn of 1995, an impasse over the budget forced the federal government to shut down for one week, from Tuesday, November 14, to Monday, November 20.(141) Only essential federal employees were permitted to work during the furlough, and the White House staff of 430 shrank to about 90 people for the week. White House interns could continue working because of their unpaid status, and they took on a wide range of additional duties.(142)

During the shutdown, Ms. Lewinsky worked in Chief of Staff Panetta's West Wing office, where she answered phones and ran errands.(143) The President came to Mr. Panetta's office frequently because of the shutdown, and he sometimes talked with Ms. Lewinsky.(144) She characterized these encounters as "continued flirtation."(145) According to Ms. Lewinsky, a Senior Adviser to the Chief of Staff, Barry Toiv, remarked to her that she was getting a great deal of "face time" with the President.(146)

C. November 15 Sexual Encounter

According to Ms. Lewinsky, she and the President made eye contact when he came to the West Wing to see Mr. Panetta and Deputy Chief of Staff Harold Ickes, then again later at an informal birthday party for Jennifer Palmieri, Special Assistant to the Chief of Staff.(150) At one point, Ms. Lewinsky and the President talked alone in the Chief of Staff's office. In the course of flirting with him, she raised her jacket in the back and showed him the straps of her thong underwear, which extended above her pants.(151)

En route to the restroom at about 8 p.m., she passed George Stephanopoulos's office. The President was inside alone, and he beckoned her to enter.(152) She told him that she had a crush on him. He laughed, then asked if she would like to see his private office.(153) Through a connecting door in Mr. Stephanopoulos's office, they went through the President's private dining room toward the study off the Oval Office. Ms. Lewinsky testified: "We talked briefly and sort of acknowledged that there had been a chemistry that was there before and that we were both attracted to each other and then he asked me if he could kiss me." Ms. Lewinsky said yes. In the windowless hallway adjacent to the study, they kissed.(154) Before returning to her desk, Ms. Lewinsky wrote down her name and telephone number for the President.(155)

At about 10 p.m., in Ms. Lewinsky's recollection, she was alone in the Chief of Staff's office and the President approached.(156) He invited her to rendezvous again in Mr. Stephanopoulos's office in a few minutes, and she agreed.(157) (Asked if she knew why the President wanted to meet with her, Ms. Lewinsky testified: "I had an idea."(158))

They met in Mr. Stephanopoulos's office and went again to the area of the private study.(159) This time the lights in the study were off.(160)

According to Ms. Lewinsky, she and the President kissed. She unbuttoned her jacket; either she unhooked her bra or he lifted her bra up; and he touched her breasts with his hands and mouth.(161) Ms. Lewinsky testified: "I believe he took a phone call ... and so we moved from the hallway into the back office .... [H]e put his hand down my pants and stimulated me manually in the genital area."(162) While the President continued talking on the phone (Ms. Lewinsky understood that the caller was a Member of Congress or a Senator), she performed oral sex on him.(163) He finished his call, and, a moment later, told Ms. Lewinsky to stop. In her recollection: "I told him that I wanted ... to complete that. And he said ... that he needed to wait until he trusted me more. And then I think he made a joke ... that he hadn't had that in a long time."(164)

White House records corroborate details of Ms. Lewinsky's account. She testified that her November 15 encounters with the President occurred at about 8 p.m. and 10 p.m., and that in each case the two of them went from the Chief of Staff's office to the Oval Office area.(167) Records show that the President visited the Chief of Staff's office for one minute at 8:12 p.m. and for two minutes at 9:23 p.m., in each case returning to the Oval Office.(168) She recalled that the President took a telephone call during their sexual encounter, and she believed that the caller was a Member of Congress or a Senator.(169) White House records show that after returning to the Oval Office from the Chief of Staff's office, the President talked to two Members of Congress: Rep. Jim Chapman from 9:25 p.m. to 9:30 p.m., and Rep. John Tanner from 9:31 p.m. to 9:35 p.m.(170)

D. November 17 Sexual Encounter

According to Ms. Lewinsky, she and the President had a second sexual encounter two days later (still during the government furlough), on Friday, November 17. ...

Ms. Lewinsky testified:

> We were again working late because it was during the furlough and Jennifer Palmieri ... had ordered pizza along with Ms. Currie and Ms. Hernreich. And when the pizza came, I went down to let them know that the pizza was there and it was at that point when I walked into Ms. Currie's office that the President was standing there with some other people discussing something.
>
> And they all came back to the office and Mr.—I think it was Mr. Toiv, somebody accidentally knocked pizza on my jacket, so I went to go use the restroom to wash it off and as I was coming out of the restroom, the President was standing in Ms. Currie's doorway and said, "You can come out this way."(173)

Ms. Lewinsky and the President went into the area of the private study, according to Ms. Lewinsky. There, either in the hallway or the bathroom, she and the President kissed. After a few minutes, in Ms. Lewinsky's recollection, she told him that she needed to get back to her desk. The President suggested that she bring him some slices of pizza.(174)

A few minutes later, she returned to the Oval Office area with pizza and told Ms. Currie that the President had requested it. Ms. Lewinsky testified: "[Ms. Currie] opened the door and said, 'Sir, the girl's here with the pizza.' He told me to come in. Ms. Currie went back into her office and then we went into the back study area again."(175) Several witnesses confirm that when Ms. Lewinsky delivered pizza to the President that night, the two of them were briefly alone.(176)

Ms. Lewinsky testified that she and the President had a sexual encounter during this visit.(177) They kissed, and the President touched Ms. Lewinsky's bare breasts with his hands and mouth.(178) At some point, Ms. Currie approached the door leading to the hallway, which was ajar, and said that the President had a telephone call.(179) Ms. Lewinsky recalled that the caller was a Member of Congress with a nickname.(180) While the President was on the telephone, according to Ms. Lewinsky, "he unzipped his pants and exposed himself," and she performed oral sex.(181) Again, he stopped her before he ejaculated.(182)

During this visit, according to Ms. Lewinsky, the President told her that he liked her smile and her energy. He also said: "I'm usually around on weekends, no one else is around, and you can come and see me."(183)

Records corroborate Ms. Lewinsky's recollection that the President took a call from a Member of Congress with a nickname. While Ms. Lewinsky was at the White House that evening (9:38 to 10:39 p.m.), the President had one telephone conversation with a Member of Congress: From 9:53 to 10:14 p.m., he spoke with Rep. H.L. "Sonny" Callahan.(184)

III. January–March 1996: Continued Sexual Encounters

President Clinton and Ms. Lewinsky had additional sexual encounters near the Oval Office in 1996. After their sixth sexual encounter, the President and Ms. Lewinsky had their first lengthy conversation. On President's Day, February 19, the President terminated their sexual relationship, then revived it on March 31.

F. March 31 Sexual Encounter

On Sunday, March 31, 1996, according to Ms. Lewinsky, she and the President resumed their sexual contact.(265) Ms. Lewinsky was at the White House from 10:21 a.m. to 4:27 p.m. on that day.(266) The President was in the Oval Office from 3:00 to 5:46 p.m.(267) His only call while in the Oval Office was from 3:06 to 3:07 p.m.(268) Mrs. Clinton was in Ireland.(269)

According to Ms. Lewinsky, the President telephoned her at her desk and suggested that she come to the Oval Office on the pretext of delivering papers to him.(270) She went to the Oval Office and was admitted by a plainclothes Secret Service agent.(271) In her folder was a gift for the President, a Hugo Boss necktie.(272)

In the hallway by the study, the President and Ms. Lewinsky kissed. On this occasion, according to Ms. Lewinsky, "he focused on me pretty exclusively," kissing her bare breasts and fondling her genitals.(273) At one point, the President inserted a cigar into Ms. Lewinsky's vagina, then put the cigar in his mouth and said: "It tastes good."(274) After they were finished, Ms. Lewinsky left the Oval Office and walked through the Rose Garden.(275)

IV. April 1996: Ms. Lewinsky's Transfer to the Pentagon

With White House and Secret Service employees remarking on Ms. Lewinsky's frequent presence in the West Wing, a deputy chief of staff ordered Ms. Lewinsky transferred from the White House to the Pentagon. On April 7—Easter Sunday—Ms. Lewinsky told the President of her dismissal. He promised to bring her back after the election, and they had a sexual encounter.

B. Decision to Transfer Ms. Lewinsky

Ms. Lieberman testified that, because Ms. Lewinsky was so persistent in her efforts to be near the President, "I decided to get rid of her."(293) First she consulted Chief of Staff Panetta. According to Mr. Panetta, Ms. Lieberman told him about a woman on the staff who was "spending too much time around the West Wing." Because of "the appearance that it was creating," Ms. Lieberman proposed to move her out of the White House. Mr. Panetta—who testified that he valued Ms. Lieberman's role as "a tough disciplinarian" and "trusted her judgment"—replied, "Fine."(294) Although Ms. Lieberman said she could not recall having heard any rumors linking the President and Ms. Lewinsky, she acknowledged that "the President was vulnerable to these kind of rumors … yes, yes, that was one of the reasons" for moving Ms. Lewinsky out of the White House.(295) Later, in September 1997, Marcia Lewis (Ms. Lewinsky's mother) complained about her daughter's dismissal to Ms. Lieberman, whom she met at a Voice of America ceremony. Ms. Lieberman, according to Ms. Lewis, responded by "saying something about Monica being cursed because she's beautiful." Ms. Lewis gathered from the remark that Ms. Lieberman, as part of her effort to protect the President, "would want to have pretty women moved out."(296)

Most people understood that the principal reason for Ms. Lewinsky's transfer was her habit of hanging around the Oval Office and the West Wing.(297) In a memo in October 1996, John Hilley, Assistant to the President and Director of Legislative Affairs, reported that Ms. Lewinsky had been "got[ten] rid of" in part "because of 'extracurricular activities'" (a phrase, he maintained in the grand jury, that meant only that Ms. Lewinsky was often absent from her work station).(298)

White House officials arranged for Ms. Lewinsky to get another job in the Administration.(299) "Our direction is to make sure she has a job in an Agency," Patsy Thomasson wrote in an email message on April 9, 1996.(300) Ms. Thomasson's office (Presidential Personnel) sent Ms. Lewinsky's resume to Charles Duncan, Special Assistant to the Secretary of Defense and White House Liaison, and asked him to find a Pentagon opening for her.(301) Mr. Duncan was told that, though Ms. Lewinsky had performed her duties capably, she was being dismissed for hanging around the Oval Office too much.(302) According to Mr. Duncan—who had received as many as 40 job referrals per day from the White House—the White House had never given such an explanation for a transfer.(303)

C. Ms. Lewinsky's Notification of Her Transfer

On Friday, April 5, 1996, Timothy Keating, Staff Director for Legislative Affairs, informed Ms. Lewinsky that she would have to leave her White House job.(304) According to Mr. Keating, he told her that she was not being fired, merely "being given a different opportunity." In fact, she could tell people it was a promotion if she cared to do so.(305) Upon hearing of her dismissal, Ms. Lewinsky burst into tears and asked if there was any way for her to stay in the White House, even without pay.(306) No, Mr. Keating said. According to Ms. Lewinsky, "He told me I was too sexy to be working in the East Wing and that this job at the Pentagon where I'd be writing press releases was a sexier job."(307)

Ms. Lewinsky was devastated. She felt that she was being transferred simply because of her relationship with the President.(308) And she feared that with the loss of her White House job, "I was never going to see the President again. I mean, my relationship with him would be over."(309)

D. Conversations with the President about Her Transfer

1. Easter Telephone Conversations and Sexual Encounter

On Easter Sunday, April 7, 1996, Ms. Lewinsky told the President of her dismissal and they had a sexual encounter. ...

At the White House, according to Ms. Lewinsky, she told Secret Service Officer Muskett that she needed to deliver papers to the President.(313) Officer Muskett admitted her to the Oval Office, and she and the President proceeded to the private study.(314)

According to Ms. Lewinsky, the President seemed troubled about her upcoming departure from the White House: He told me that he thought that my being transferred had something to do with him and that he was upset. He said, "Why do they have to take you away from me? I trust you." And then he told me—he looked at me and he said, "I promise you if I win in November I'll bring you back like that."(315)

He also indicated that she could have any job she wanted after the election.(316) In addition, the President said he would find out why Ms. Lewinsky was transferred and report back to her.(317)

After this Easter Sunday conversation, the President and Ms. Lewinsky had a sexual encounter in the hallway, according to Ms. Lewinsky.(320) She testified that the President touched her breasts with his mouth and hands.(321) According to Ms. Lewinsky: "I think he unzipped [his pants] … because it was sort of this running joke that I could never unbutton his pants, that I just had trouble with it."(322) Ms. Lewinsky performed oral sex. The President did not ejaculate in her presence.(323)

During this encounter, someone called out from the Oval Office that the President had a phone call.(324) He went back to the Oval Office for a moment, then took the call in the study. The President indicated that Ms. Lewinsky should perform oral sex while he talked on the phone, and she obliged.(325) The telephone conversation was about politics, and Ms. Lewinsky thought the caller might be Dick Morris.(326) White House records confirm that the President had one telephone call during Ms. Lewinsky's visit: from "Mr. Richard Morris," to whom he talked from 5:11 to 5:20 p.m.(327)

V. April–December 1996: No Private Meetings

After Ms. Lewinsky began her Pentagon job on April 16, 1996, she had no further physical contact with the President for the remainder of the year. She and the President spoke by phone (and had phone sex) but saw each other only at public functions. Ms. Lewinsky grew frustrated after the election because the President did not bring her back to work at the White House.

VI. Early 1997: Resumption of Sexual Encounters

In 1997, President Clinton and Ms. Lewinsky had further private meetings, which now were arranged by Betty Currie, the President's secretary. After the taping of the President's weekly radio address on February 28, the President and Ms. Lewinsky had a sexual encounter. On March 24, they had what proved to be their final sexual encounter. Throughout this period, Ms. Lewinsky continued to press for a job at the White House, to no avail.

A. Resumption of Meetings with the President

1. Role of Betty Currie

a. Arranging Meetings

In 1997, with the presidential election past, Ms. Lewinsky and the President resumed their one-on-one meetings and sexual encounters. The President's secretary, Betty Currie, acted as intermediary.

According to Ms. Currie, Ms. Lewinsky would often call her and say she wanted to see the President, sometimes to discuss a particular topic.(380) Ms. Currie would ask President Clinton, and, if he agreed, arrange the meeting.(381) Ms. Currie also said it was "not unusual" that Ms. Lewinsky would talk by phone with the President and then call Ms. Currie to set up a meeting.(382) At times, Ms. Currie placed calls to Ms. Lewinsky for President Clinton and put him on the line.(383)

The meetings between the President and Ms. Lewinsky often occurred on weekends.(384) When Ms. Lewinsky would arrive at the White House, Ms. Currie generally would be the one to authorize her entry and take her to the West Wing.(385) Ms. Currie acknowledged that she sometimes would come to the White House for the sole purpose of having Ms. Lewinsky admitted and bringing her to see the President.(386) According to Ms. Currie, Ms. Lewinsky and the President were alone together in the Oval Office or the study for 15 to 20 minutes on multiple occasions.(387)

B. Secrecy

Ms. Currie testified that she suspected impropriety in the President's relationship with Ms. Lewinsky.(404) She told the grand jury that she "had concern." In her words: "[H]e was spending a lot of time with a 24-year-old young lady. I know he has said that young people keep him involved in what's happening in the world, so I knew that was one reason, but there was a concern of mine that she was spending more time than most."(405) Ms. Currie understood that "the majority" of the President's meetings with Ms. Lewinsky were "more personal in nature as opposed to business."(406)

C. Valentine's Day Advertisement

On February 14, 1997, the Washington Post published a Valentine's Day "Love Note" that Ms. Lewinsky had placed. The ad said:

> *HANDSOME*
> *With love's light wings did*
> *I o'er perch these walls*
> *For stony limits cannot hold love out,*
> *And what love can do that dares love attempt.*
> *—Romeo and Juliet 2:2*
>
> *Happy Valentine's Day.*
> *M(421)*

D. February 28 Sexual Encounter

According to Ms. Lewinsky, she and the President had a sexual encounter on Thursday, February 28—their first in nearly 11 months. ... Wearing a navy blue dress from the Gap, Ms. Lewinsky attended the radio address at the President's invitation (relayed by Ms. Currie), then had her photo taken with the President.(429) Ms. Lewinsky had not been alone with the President since she had worked at the White House, and, she testified, "I was really nervous."(430) President Clinton told her to see Ms. Currie after the photo was taken because he wanted to give her something.(431) "So I waited a little while for him and then Betty and the President and I went into the back office," Ms. Lewinsky testified.(432) (She later learned that the reason Ms. Currie accompanied them was that Stephen Goodin did not want the President to be alone with Ms. Lewinsky, a view that Mr. Goodin expressed to the President and Ms. Currie.(433)) Once they had passed from the Oval Office toward the private study, Ms. Currie said, "I'll be right back," and walked on to the back pantry or the dining room, where, according to Ms. Currie, she waited for 15 to 20 minutes while the President and Ms. Lewinsky were in the study.(434) Ms. Currie (who said she acted on her own initiative) testified that she accompanied the President and Ms. Lewinsky out of the Oval Office because "I didn't want any perceptions, him being alone with someone."(435)

In the study, according to Ms. Lewinsky, the President "started to say something to me and I was pestering him to kiss me, because … it had been a long time since we had been alone."(436) The President told her to wait a moment, as he had presents for her.(437) As belated Christmas gifts, he gave her a hat pin and a special edition of Walt Whitman's *Leaves of Grass*.(438)

Ms. Lewinsky described the Whitman book as "the most sentimental gift he had given me … it's beautiful and it meant a lot to me."(439) During this visit, according to Ms. Lewinsky, the President said he had seen her Valentine's Day message in the *Washington Post*, and he talked about his fondness for *Romeo and Juliet*.(440)

Ms. Lewinsky testified that after the President gave her the gifts, they had a sexual encounter:

> [W]e went back over by the bathroom in the hallway, and we kissed. We were kissing and he unbuttoned my dress and fondled my breasts with my bra on, and then took them out of my bra and was kissing them and touching them with his hands and with his mouth.
>
> And then I think I was touching him in his genital area through his pants, and I think I unbuttoned his shirt and was kissing his chest. And then … I wanted to perform oral sex on him … and so I did. And then … I think he heard something, or he heard someone in the office. So, we moved into the bathroom.
>
> And I continued to perform oral sex and then he pushed me away, kind of as he always did before he came, and then I stood up and I said … I care about you so much; … I don't understand why you won't let me … make you come; it's important to me; I mean, it just doesn't feel complete, it doesn't seem right.(441)

Ms. Lewinsky testified that she and the President hugged, and "he said he didn't want to get addicted to me, and he didn't want me to get addicted to him." They looked at each other for a moment.(442) Then, saying that "I don't want to disappoint you," the President consented.(443) For the first time, she performed oral sex through completion.(444)

When Ms. Lewinsky next took the navy blue Gap dress from her closet to wear it, she noticed stains near one hip and on the chest.(445) FBI Laboratory tests revealed that the stains are the President's semen.(446)

E. March 29 Sexual Encounter

According to Ms. Lewinsky, she had what proved to be her final sexual encounter with the President on Saturday, March 29, 1997. Records show that she was at the White House from 2:03 to 3:16 p.m., admitted by Ms. Currie.(450) The President was in the Oval Office during this period (he left shortly after Ms. Lewinsky did, at 3:24 p.m.), and he did not have any phone calls during her White House visit.(451)

According to Ms. Lewinsky, Ms. Currie arranged the meeting after the President said by telephone that he had something important to tell her. At the White House, Ms. Currie took her to the study to await the President. He came in on crutches, the result of a knee injury in Florida two weeks earlier.(452)

According to Ms. Lewinsky, their sexual encounter began with a sudden kiss: "[T]his was another one of those occasions when I was babbling on about something, and he just kissed me, kind of to shut me up, I think."(453) The President unbuttoned her blouse and touched her breasts without removing her bra.(454) "[H]e went to go put his hand down my pants, and then I unzipped them because it was easier. And I didn't have any panties on. And so he manually stimulated me."(455) According to Ms. Lewinsky, "I wanted him to touch my genitals with his genitals," and he did so, lightly and without penetration.(456) Then Ms. Lewinsky performed oral sex on him, again until he ejaculated.(457)

VII. May 1997: Termination of Sexual Relationship

In May 1997, amid indications that Ms. Lewinsky had been indiscreet, President Clinton terminated the sexual relationship.

A. Questions about Ms. Lewinsky's Discretion

In April or May 1997, according to Ms. Lewinsky, the President asked if she had told her mother about their intimate relationship. She responded: "No. Of course not."(468) (In truth, she had told her mother.(469)) The President indicated that Ms. Lewinsky's mother possibly had said something about the nature of the relationship to Walter Kaye, who had mentioned it to Marsha Scott, who in turn had alerted the President.(470)

B. May 24: Break-up

On Saturday, May 24, 1997, according to Ms. Lewinsky, the President ended their intimate relationship. Ms. Lewinsky was at the White House that day from 12:21 to 1:54 p.m.(472) The President was in the Oval Office during most of this period, from 11:59 a.m. to 1:47 p.m.(473) He did not have any telephone calls.(474)

According to Ms. Lewinsky, she got a call from Ms. Currie at about 11 a.m. that day, inviting her to come to the White House at about 1 p.m. Ms. Lewinsky arrived wearing a straw hat with the hat pin the President had given her, and bringing gifts for him, including a puzzle and a Banana Republic shirt. She gave him the gifts in the dining room, and they moved to the area of the study.(475)

According to Ms. Lewinsky, the President explained that they had to end their intimate relationship.(476) Earlier in his marriage, he told her, he had had hundreds of affairs; but since turning 40, he had made a concerted effort to be faithful.(477) He said he was attracted to Ms. Lewinsky, considered her a great person, and hoped they would remain friends. He pointed out that he could do a great deal for her. The situation, he stressed, was not Ms. Lewinsky's fault.(478) Ms. Lewinsky, weeping, tried to persuade the President not to end the sexual relationship, but he was unyielding, then and subsequently.(479) Although she and the President kissed and hugged thereafter, according to Ms. Lewinsky, the sexual relationship was over.(480)

VIII. June–October 1997: Continuing Meetings and Calls

Ms. Lewinsky tried to return to the White House staff and to revive her sexual relationship with the President, but she failed at both.

A. Continuing Job Efforts

Although Ms. Lewinsky was not offered another White House job, some testimony indicates that the President tried to get her one.

According to Betty Currie, the President instructed her and Marsha Scott to help Ms. Lewinsky find a White House job.(482) Ms. Currie testified that she resisted the request, because her opinion of Ms. Lewinsky had shifted over time. At first, she testified, she considered Ms. Lewinsky "a friend" who "had been wronged" and had been "maligned improperly."(483) But "[l]ater on, I considered her as a pain in the neck, more or less."(484) The change of heart resulted in part from Ms. Currie's many phone calls in 1997 from Ms. Lewinsky, who was often distraught and sometimes in tears over her inability to get in touch with the President.(485) Deeming her "a little bit pushy," Ms. Currie argued against bringing Ms. Lewinsky back to work at the White House, but the President told her and Ms. Scott, in Ms. Currie's words, "to still pursue her coming back."(486) Indeed, according to Ms. Currie, the President "was pushing us hard" on the matter.(487) To the best of Ms. Currie's recollection, it was the only time the President instructed her to try to get someone a White House job.(488)

B. July 3 Letter

"[V]ery frustrated" over her inability to get in touch with the President to discuss her job situation, Ms. Lewinsky wrote him a peevish letter on July 3, 1997.(500) Opening "Dear Sir," the letter took the President to task for breaking his promise to get her another White House job.(501) Ms. Lewinsky also obliquely threatened to disclose their relationship. If she was not going to return to work at the White House, she wrote, then she would "need to explain to my parents exactly why that wasn't happening." Some explanation was necessary because she had told her parents that she would be brought back after the election.(502) (Ms. Lewinsky testified that she would not actually have told her father about the relationship—she had already told her mother—but she wanted to remind the President that she had "left the White House like a good girl in April of '96," whereas other people might have threatened disclosure in order to retain the job.(503))

Ms. Lewinsky also raised the possibility of a job outside Washington. If returning to the White House was impossible, she asked in this letter, could he get her a job at the United Nations in New York?(504) It was the first time that she had told the President that she was considering moving.(505)

C. July 4 Meeting

On Friday, July 4, 1997, Ms. Lewinsky had what she characterized as a "very emotional" visit with the President.(508)

In Ms. Lewinsky's recollection, their meeting began contentiously, with the President scolding her: "[I]t's illegal to threaten the President of the United States."(511) He then told her that he had not read her July 3 letter beyond the "Dear Sir" line; he surmised that it was threatening because Ms. Currie looked upset when she brought it to him. (Ms. Lewinsky suspected that he actually had read the whole thing.)(512) Ms. Lewinsky complained about his failure to get her a White House job after her long wait. Although the President claimed he wanted to be her friend, she said, he was not acting like it. Ms. Lewinsky began weeping, and the President hugged her. While they hugged, she spotted a gardener outside the study window, and they moved into the hallway by the bathroom.(513)

There, the President was "the most affectionate with me he'd ever been," Ms. Lewinsky testified. He stroked her arm, toyed with her hair, kissed her on the neck, praised her intellect and beauty.(514) In Ms. Lewinsky's recollection:

> [H]e remarked … that he wished he had more time for me. And so I said, well, maybe you will have more time in three years. And I was … thinking just when he wasn't President, he was going to have more time on his hands. And he said, well, I don't know, I might be alone in three years. And then I said something about … us sort of being together. I think I kind of said, oh, I think we'd be a good team, or something like that. And he … jokingly said, well, what are we going to do when I'm 75 and I have to pee 25 times a day? And … I told him that we'd deal with that. …(515)

Ms. Lewinsky testified that "I left that day sort of emotionally stunned," for "I just knew he was in love with me."(516)

Just before leaving, according to Ms. Lewinsky, she told the President "that I wanted to talk to him about something serious and that while I didn't want to be the one to talk about this with him, I thought it was important he know."(517) She informed him that Newsweek was working on an article about Kathleen Willey, a former White House volunteer who claimed that the President had sexually harassed her during a private meeting in the Oval Office on November 23, 1993. (Ms. Lewinsky knew of the article from Ms. Tripp, who had worked at the White House at the time of the alleged incident and had heard about the incident from Ms. Willey. Michael Isikoff of Newsweek had talked with Ms. Tripp about the episode in March 1997 and again shortly before July 4, and Ms. Tripp had subsequently related the Isikoff conversations to Ms. Lewinsky.(518)) Ms. Lewinsky told the President what she had learned from Ms. Tripp (whom she did not name), including the fact that Ms. Tripp had tried to get in touch with Deputy White House Counsel Bruce Lindsey, who had not returned her calls.(519)

Ms. Lewinsky testified about why she conveyed this information to the President: "I was concerned that the President had no idea this was going on and that this woman was going to be another Paula Jones and he didn't really need that."(520) She understood that Ms. Willey was looking for a job, and she thought that the President might be able to "make this go away" by finding her a job.(521)

The President responded that the harassment allegation was ludicrous, because he would never approach a small-breasted woman like Ms. Willey.(522) He further said that, during the previous week, Ms. Willey had called Nancy Hernreich to warn that a reporter was working on a story about Ms. Willey and the President; Ms. Willey wondered how she could get out of it.(523)

L. News of Job Search Failure

On October 6, 1997, according to Ms. Lewinsky, she was told that she would never work at the White House again. Ms. Tripp conveyed the news, which she indicated had come from a friend on the White House staff. Ms. Lewinsky testified:

Linda Tripp called me at work on October 6th and told me that her friend Kate in the NSC ... had heard rumors about me and that I would never work in the White House again. ... [Kate's] advice to me was "get out of town."(579)

For Ms. Lewinsky, who had previously considered moving to New York, this call was the "straw that broke the camel's back."(580) She was enraged.(581)

When terminating their sexual relationship on May 24, the President had told Ms. Lewinsky that he hoped they would remain friends, for he could do a great deal for her.(583) Now, having learned that he could not (or would not) get her a White House job, Ms. Lewinsky decided to ask him for a job in New York, perhaps at the United Nations—a possibility that she had mentioned to him in passing over the summer. On the afternoon of October 6, Ms. Lewinsky spoke of this plan to Ms. Currie, who quoted the President as having said earlier: "Oh, that's no problem. We can place her in the UN like that."(584)

[Publisher's Note: See Grounds section, Ground VII, for a synopsis of the job-search help Ms. Lewinsky received from the White House.]

F. Early Morning Phone Call

On December 15, 1997, Paula Jones's lawyers served President Clinton with her second set of document requests by overnight mail. These requests asked the President to "produce documents that related to communications between the President and Monica Lewisky" [sic].(790) This was the first Paula Jones discovery request to refer to Monica Lewinsky by name.

Ms. Lewinsky testified that in the early-morning hours of December 17, at roughly 2:00 or 2:30 a.m., she received a call from the President.(791) The call lasted about half an hour.(792)

The President gave Ms. Lewinsky two items of news: Ms. Currie's brother had died in a car accident, and Ms. Lewinsky's name had appeared on the witness list in the Jones case.(793) According to Ms. Lewinsky, the President said "it broke his heart" to see her name on the witness list.(794) The President told her that she would not necessarily be subpoenaed; if she were, he "suggested she could sign an affidavit to try to satisfy [Ms. Jones's] inquiry and not be deposed."(795)

The President told Ms. Lewinsky to contact Ms. Currie in the event she were subpoenaed.(796) He also reviewed one of their established cover stories. He told Ms. Lewinsky that she "should say she visited the [White House] to see Ms. Currie and, on occasion when working at the [White House], she brought him letters when no one else was around."(797) The President's advice "was ... instantly familiar to [Ms. Lewinsky]."(798) She testified that the President's use of this "misleading" story amounted to a continuation of their pre-existing pattern.(799)

Later in the conversation, according to Ms. Lewinsky, the President said he would try to get Ms. Currie to come in over the weekend so that Ms. Lewinsky could visit and he could give her several Christmas presents.(800) Ms. Lewinsky replied that, since Ms. Currie's brother had just died, perhaps they should "let Betty be."(801)

XIII. January 5–January 16, 1998:

The Affidavit

On January 5, 1998, Ms. Lewinsky's attorney, Francis Carter, drafted an affidavit for Ms. Lewinsky in an attempt to avert her deposition. She spoke with the President that evening. On January 6, Ms. Lewinsky talked to Mr. Jordan about the affidavit, which denied any sexual relations between her and the President. On January 7, Ms. Lewinsky signed the affidavit. On January 8, she interviewed for a job in New York City. After the interview went poorly, Mr. Jordan placed a phone call to the company's chairman on her behalf, and Ms. Lewinsky was given a second interview. The following week, after Ms. Lewinsky told Ms. Currie that she would need a reference from the White House, the President asked Chief of Staff Erskine Bowles to arrange one.

January 6: The Draft Affidavit

According to Ms. Lewinsky, in the afternoon of January 6, 1998, she visited Mr. Carter's office and picked up a draft of the affidavit.(934) Later that day, according to Ms. Lewinsky, she and Mr. Jordan discussed the draft by telephone.(936) Ms. Lewinsky testified that having Mr. Jordan review the affidavit was like getting it "blessed" by the President.(937) Ms. Lewinsky testified that she told Mr. Jordan that she was worried about a sentence that implied that she had been alone with the President and thus might incline Paula Jones's attorneys to question her.(938) She eventually deleted it.(939)

In addition, Paragraph 8 of the draft affidavit provided in part:

> I have never had a sexual relationship with the President. ... The occasions that I saw the President, with crowds of other people, after I left my employment at the White House in April, 1996 related to official receptions, formal functions or events related to the U.S. Department of Defense, where I was working at the time.(941)

Deeming the reference to "crowds" "too far out of the realm of possibility,"(942) Ms. Lewinsky deleted the underscored phrase and wrote the following sentence at the end of this paragraph: "There were other people present on all of these occasions."(943) She discussed this proposed sentence, as well as her general anxiety about Paragraph 8, with Mr. Jordan.(944)

When questioned in the grand jury, Mr. Jordan acknowledged that Ms. Lewinsky called him with concerns about the affidavit,(945) but maintained that he told her to speak with her attorney.(946)

Phone records for January 6 show that Mr. Jordan had a number of contacts with Ms. Lewinsky, the President, and Mr. Carter. Less than thirty minutes after Mr. Jordan spoke by phone to Ms. Lewinsky, he talked with the President for thirteen minutes. Immediately after this call, at 4:33 p.m., Mr. Jordan called Mr. Carter. Less than an hour later, Mr. Jordan placed a four-minute call to the main White House number. Over the course of the day, Mr. Jordan called a White House number twice, Ms. Lewinsky three times, and Mr. Carter four times.(947)

Mr. Carter testified that his phone conversations with Mr. Jordan this day and the next "likely" related to Ms. Lewinsky and his litigation strategy for her.(948) In fact, Mr. Carter billed Ms. Lewinsky for time for "[t]elephone conference with Atty Jordan."(949)

When questioned in the grand jury, Mr. Jordan testified that he could not specifically remember the January 6 calls. He said he "assumed" that he talked with Ms. Lewinsky about her job search, and he believed that he called Mr. Carter to see "how he was dealing with this highly emotional lady."(950) He said that he might have talked with the President about Ms. Lewinsky, but he maintained that "there [was] no connection" between his 13-minute conversation with the President and the call he placed immediately thereafter to Mr. Carter.(951)

D. January 7: Ms. Lewinsky Signs Affidavit

Ms. Lewinsky set an appointment with Mr. Carter to finalize the affidavit for 10 a.m. on January 7, 1998.(952) She signed the affidavit; however, she acknowledged in the grand jury that statements in it were false.(953) Mr. Carter indicated to her that he "intend[ed] to hold onto this until after I talk to plaintiff's lawyers." He told her to "keep in touch," and said: "Good luck on your job search."(956)

According to Mr. Jordan, Ms. Lewinsky came to his office on January 7 and showed him the signed affidavit.(957) Over the course of the day, Mr. Jordan placed three calls of significant duration to the White House.(958) He testified: "I knew the President was concerned about the affidavit and whether it was signed or not."(959) When asked whether the President understood that the affidavit denied a sexual relationship, Mr. Jordan testified: "I think that's a reasonable assumption."(960) According to Mr. Jordan, when he informed the President that Ms. Lewinsky had signed the affidavit, the President said, "Fine, good."(961) Mr. Jordan said he was continuing to work on her job, and the President responded, "Good."(962)

Ten days after this conversation, in the Jones deposition, President Clinton was asked whether he knew that Ms. Lewinsky had met with Vernon Jordan and talked about the Jones case. He answered:

> I knew he met with her. I think Betty suggested that he meet with her. Anyway, he met with her. I, I thought that he talked to her about something else. I didn't know that— I thought he had given her some advice about her move to New York. Seems like that's what Betty said.(963)

In his grand jury appearance, however, President Clinton testified that Mr. Jordan informed "us" on January 7 that Ms. Lewinsky had signed an affidavit to be used in connection with the Jones case.(964) The President defended his deposition testimony by stating:

> [M]y impression was that, at the time, I was focused on the meetings. I believe the meetings he had were meetings about her moving to New York and getting a job. I knew at some point that she had told him that she needed some help, because she had gotten a subpoena. I'm not sure I know whether she did that in a meeting or a phone call. And I was not, I was not focused on that. I know that, I know Vernon helped her get a lawyer, Mr. Carter. And I, I believe that he did it after she had called him, but I'm not sure. But I knew that the main source of their meetings was about her move to New York and her getting a job.(965)

E. January 8: The Perelman Call

The day after she signed the affidavit, January 8, 1998, Ms. Lewinsky interviewed in New York with Jaymie Durnan, Senior Vice President and Special Assistant to the Chairman at MacAndrews & Forbes Holdings, Inc. (MFH).(966) Mr. Durnan testified that, although impressive, Ms. Lewinsky was not suited for any MFH opening.(967) He told her that he would pass on her resume to Revlon, an MFH company.(968) Ms. Lewinsky called Mr. Jordan and reported that she felt that the interview had gone "very poorly."(969) Mr. Jordan indicated in response that "he'd call the chairman."(970)

At 4:54 p.m., Mr. Jordan called Ronald Perelman, chairman and chief executive officer of MFH.(971) Mr. Jordan told the grand jury with respect to Mr. Perelman, one "[c]an't get any higher—or any richer."(972) Asked why he chose to call Mr. Perelman, Mr. Jordan responded: "I have spent a good part of my life learning institutions and people, and, in that process, I have learned how to make things happen. And the call to Ronald Perelman was a call to make things happen, if they could happen."(973)

According to Mr. Perelman, Mr. Jordan spoke of "this bright young girl, who I think is terrific," and said that he wanted "to make sure somebody takes a look at her."(977) Mr. Perelman testified that, in the roughly twelve years that Mr. Jordan had been on Revlon's Board of Directors, he did not recall Mr. Jordan ever calling to recommend someone.(978)

After he spoke with Mr. Perelman, Mr. Jordan telephoned Ms. Lewinsky and told her, "I'm doing the best I can to help you out."(982) Ms. Lewinsky soon received a call from Revlon, inviting her to another interview.(984)

Over the course of January 8, Mr. Jordan placed three calls to the White House—twice to a number at the White House Counsel's Office, once to the main White House number.(985) As to the Counsel's Office calls, Mr. Jordan speculated that he was trying to reach Cheryl Mills, Deputy White House Counsel, to express his "frustration" about Ms. Lewinsky.(986)

According to Mr. Jordan, Ms. Mills knew who Ms. Lewinsky was: "[T]hat was no secret, I don't think, around the White House, that I was helping Monica Lewinsky."(987)

F. January 9: "Mission Accomplished"

On the morning of Friday, January 9, 1998, Ms. Lewinsky interviewed with Allyn Seidman, Senior Vice President of MFH, and two individuals at Revlon.(988) Ms. Lewinsky testified that the interviews went well and that Ms. Seidman called her back that day and "informally offered [her] a position, and [she] informally accepted."(989)

Ms. Lewinsky then called Mr. Jordan and relayed the good news.(990) When shown records of a seven-minute call at 4:14 p.m., Mr. Jordan testified: "I have to assume that if she got the job and we have a seven-minute conversation and the day before I had talked to the chairman [Ronald Perelman], I have to assume the Jordan magic worked."(991)

According to Mr. Jordan, he believed that he notified Ms. Currie and the President as soon as he learned that Ms. Lewinsky had obtained an offer: "I am certain that at some point in time I told Betty Currie, 'Mission accomplished.'"(992) Mr. Jordan testified that he also told the President directly that, "'Monica Lewinsky's going to work for Revlon,' and his response was, 'Thank you very much.'"(993)

Grounds

There is Substantial and Credible Information that President Clinton Committed Acts that May Constitute Grounds for an Impeachment.

Introduction

Pursuant to Section 595(c) of Title 28, the Office of Independent Counsel (OIC) hereby submits substantial and credible information that President Clinton obstructed justice during the Jones v. Clinton sexual harassment lawsuit by lying under oath and concealing evidence of his relationship with a young White House intern and federal employee, Monica Lewinsky. After a federal criminal investigation of the President's actions began in January 1998, the President lied under oath to the grand jury and obstructed justice during the grand jury investigation. There also is substantial and credible information that the President's actions with respect to Monica Lewinsky constitute an abuse of authority inconsistent with the President's constitutional duty to faithfully execute the laws.

There is substantial and credible information supporting the following eleven possible grounds for impeachment:

1. President Clinton lied under oath in his civil case when he denied a sexual affair, a sexual relationship, or sexual relations with Monica Lewinsky.

2. President Clinton lied under oath to the grand jury about his sexual relationship with Ms. Lewinsky.

3. In his civil deposition, to support his false statement about the sexual relationship, President Clinton also lied under oath about being alone with Ms. Lewinsky and about the many gifts exchanged between Ms. Lewinsky and him.

4. President Clinton lied under oath in his civil deposition about his discussions with Ms. Lewinsky concerning her involvement in the Jones case.

5. During the Jones case, the President obstructed justice and had an understanding with Ms. Lewinsky to jointly conceal the truth about their relationship by concealing gifts subpoenaed by Ms. Jones's attorneys.

6. During the Jones case, the President obstructed justice and had an understanding with Ms. Lewinsky to jointly conceal the truth of their relationship from the judicial process by a scheme that included the following means: (i) Both the President and Ms. Lewinsky understood that they would lie under oath in the Jones case about their sexual relationship; (ii) the President suggested to Ms. Lewinsky that she prepare an affidavit that, for the President's purposes, would memorialize her testimony under oath and could be used to prevent questioning of both of them about their relationship; (iii) Ms. Lewinsky signed and filed the false affidavit; (iv) the President used Ms. Lewinsky's false affidavit at his deposition in an attempt to head off questions about Ms. Lewinsky; and (v) when that failed, the President lied under oath at his civil deposition about the relationship with Ms. Lewinsky.

7. President Clinton endeavored to obstruct justice by helping Ms. Lewinsky obtain a job in New York at a time when she would have been a witness harmful to him were she to tell the truth in the Jones case.

8. President Clinton lied under oath in his civil deposition about his discussions with Vernon Jordan concerning Ms. Lewinsky's involvement in the Jones case.

9. The President improperly tampered with a potential witness by attempting to corruptly influence the testimony of his personal secretary, Betty Currie, in the days after his civil deposition.

10. President Clinton endeavored to obstruct justice during the grand jury investigation by refusing to testify for seven months and lying to senior White House aides with knowledge that they would relay the President's false statements to the grand jury—and did thereby deceive, obstruct, and impede the grand jury.

11. President Clinton abused his constitutional authority by (i) lying to the public and the Congress in January 1998 about his relationship with Ms. Lewinsky; (ii) promising at that time to cooperate fully with the grand jury investigation; (iii) later refusing six invitations to testify voluntarily to the grand jury; (iv) invoking Executive Privilege; (v) lying to the grand jury in August 1998; and (vi) lying again to the public and Congress on August 17, 1998—all as part of an effort to hinder, impede, and deflect possible inquiry by the Congress of the United States.

The first two possible grounds for impeachment concern the President's lying under oath about the nature of his relationship with Ms. Lewinsky. The details associated with those grounds are, by their nature, explicit. The President's testimony unfortunately has rendered the details essential with respect to those two grounds, as will be explained in those grounds.

I. There is substantial and credible information that President Clinton lied under oath as a defendant in Jones v. Clinton regarding his sexual relationship with Monica Lewinsky.

The detailed testimony of Ms. Lewinsky, her corroborating prior consistent statements to her friends, family members, and counselors, and the evidence of the President's semen on Ms. Lewinsky's dress establish that Ms. Lewinsky and the President engaged in substantial sexual activity between November 15, 1995, and December 28, 1997.(89)

The President, however, testified under oath in the civil case—both in his deposition and in a written answer to an interrogatory—that he did not have a "sexual relationship" or a "sexual affair" or "sexual relations" with Ms. Lewinsky. In addition, he denied engaging in activity covered by a more specific definition of "sexual relations" used at the deposition.(90)

In his civil case, the President made five different false statements related to the sexual relationship. For four of the five statements, the President asserts a semantic defense: The President argues that the terms used in the Jones deposition to cover sexual activity did not cover the sexual activity in which he engaged with Ms. Lewinsky. For his other false statements, the President's response is factual—namely, he disputes Ms. Lewinsky's account that he ever touched her breasts or genitalia during sexual activity.(91)

The President's denials—semantic and factual—do not withstand scrutiny.

First, in his civil deposition, the President denied a "sexual affair" with Ms. Lewinsky (the term was not defined). The President's response to lying under oath on this point rests on his definition of "sexual affair"—namely, that it requires sexual intercourse, no matter how extensive the sexual activities might otherwise be. According to the President, a man could regularly engage in oral sex and fondling of breasts and genitals with a woman and yet not have a "sexual affair" with her.

Second, in his civil deposition, the President also denied a "sexual relationship" with Ms. Lewinsky (the term was not defined). The President's response to lying under oath on this point similarly rests on his definition of "sexual relationship"—namely, that it requires sexual intercourse. Once again, under the President's theory, a man could regularly engage in oral sex and fondling of breasts and genitals with a woman, yet not have a "sexual relationship" with her.

The President's claim as to his interpretation of "sexual relationship" is belied by the fact that the President's own lawyer—earlier at that same deposition—equated the term "sexual relationship" with "sex of any kind in any manner, shape or form." The President's lawyer offered that interpretation when requesting Judge Wright to limit the questioning to prevent further inquiries with respect to Monica Lewinsky. As the videotape of the deposition reveals, the President was present and apparently looking in the direction of his attorney when his attorney offered that statement.(92) The President gave no indication that he disagreed with his attorney's straightforward interpretation that the term "sexual relationship" means "sex of any kind in any manner, shape, or form." Nor did the President thereafter take any steps to correct the attorney's statement.

Third, in an answer to an interrogatory submitted before his deposition, the President denied having "sexual relations" with Ms. Lewinsky (the term was not defined). Yet again, the President's apparent rejoinder to lying under oath on this point rests on his definition of "sexual relations"—that it, too, requires sexual intercourse. According to President Clinton,oral sex does not constitute sexual relations.

Fourth, in his civil deposition, the President denied committing any acts that fell within the specific definition of "sexual relations" that was in effect for purposes of that deposition. Under that specific definition, sexual relations occurs "when the person knowingly engages in or causes contact with the genitalia, anus, groin, breast, inner thigh, or buttocks of any person with an intent to arouse or gratify the sexual desire of any person."(93) Thus, the President denied engaging in or causing contact with the genitalia, breasts, or anus of "any person" with an intent to arouse or gratify the sexual desire of "any person." Concerning oral sex, the President's sole answer to the charge that he lied under oath at the deposition focused on his interpretation of "any person" in the definition. Ms. Lewinsky testified that she performed oral sex on the President on nine occasions. The President said that by receiving oral sex, he would not "engage in" or "cause"(94) contact with the genitalia, anus, groin, breast, inner

315

thigh, or buttocks of "any person" because "any person" really means "any other person." The President further testified before the grand jury: "[I]f the deponent is the person who has oral sex performed on him, then the contact is with—not with anything on that list, but with the lips of another person."(95)

The President's linguistic parsing is unreasonable. Under the President's interpretation (which he says he followed at his deposition), in an oral sex encounter, one person is engaged in sexual relations, but the other person is not engaged in sexual relations.(96)

Even assuming that the definitional language can be manipulated to exclude the deponent's receipt of oral sex, the President is still left with the difficulty that reasonable persons would not have understood it that way. And in context, the President's semantics become even weaker: The Jones suit rested on the allegation that the President sought to have Ms. Jones perform oral sex on him. Yet the President now claims that the expansive definition devised for deposition questioning should be interpreted to exclude that very act.

Fifth, by denying at his civil deposition that he had engaged in any acts falling within the specific definition of "sexual relations," the President denied engaging in or causing contact with the breasts or genitalia of Ms. Lewinsky with an intent to arouse or gratify one's sexual desire. In contrast to his explanations of the four preceding false statements under oath, the President's defense to lying under oath in this instance is purely factual.

As discussed above, Ms. Lewinsky testified credibly that the President touched and kissed her bare breasts on nine occasions, and that he stimulated her genitals on four occasions.(97) She also testified about a cigar incident, which is discussed above. In addition, a deleted computer file from Ms. Lewinsky's home computer contained an apparent draft letter to the President that explicitly referred to an incident in which the President's "mouth [was] on [her] breast" and implicitly referred to direct contact with her genitalia.(98) This draft letter further corroborates Ms. Lewinsky's testimony.

Ms. Lewinsky's prior consistent statements to various friends, family members, and counselors—made when the relationship was ongoing—likewise corroborate her testimony on the nature of the President's touching of her body. Ms. Lewinsky had no apparent motive to lie to her friends, family members, and counselors. Ms. Lewinsky especially had no reason to lie to Dr. Kassorla and Ms. Estep, to whom she related the facts in the course of a professional relationship. And Ms. Lewinsky's statements to some that she did not have intercourse with the President, even though she wanted to do so, enhances the credibility of her statements. Moreover, the precise nature of the sexual activity only became relevant after the President interposed his semantic defense regarding oral sex on August 17, 1998.

By contrast, the President's testimony strains credulity. His apparent "hands-off" scenario—in which he would have received oral sex on nine occasions from Ms. Lewinsky but never made direct contact with Ms. Lewinsky's breasts or genitalia—is not credible. The President's claim seems to be that he maintained a hands-off policy in ongoing sexual encounters with Ms. Lewinsky, which coincidentally happened to permit him to truthfully deny "sexual relations" with her at a deposition occurring a few years in the future. As Ms. Lewinsky noted, it suggests some kind of "service contract—that all I did was perform oral sex on him and that that's all this relationship was."(99)

The President also had strong personal, political, and legal motives to lie in the Jones deposition: He did not want to admit that he had committed extramarital sex acts with a young intern in the Oval Office area of the White House. Such an admission could support Ms. Jones's theory of liability and would embarrass him. Indeed, the President admitted that during the relationship he did what he could to keep the relationship secret, including "misleading" members of his family and Cabinet.(100) The President testified, moreover, that he "hoped that this relationship would never become public."(101)

At the time of his civil deposition, the President also could have presumed that he could lie under oath without risk because—as he knew—Ms. Lewinsky had already filed a false affidavit denying a sexual relationship with the President. Indeed, they had an understanding that each would lie under oath (explained more fully in Ground VI below). So the President might have expected that he could lie without consequence on the belief that no one could ever successfully challenge his denial of a sexual relationship with her.

In sum, based on all of the evidence and considering the President's various responses, there is substantial and credible information that the President lied under oath in his civil deposition and his interrogatory answer in denying a sexual relationship, a sexual affair, or sexual relations with Ms. Lewinsky.(102)

II. There is substantial and credible information that President Clinton lied under oath to the grand jury about his sexual relationship with Monica Lewinsky.

In the foregoing testimony to the grand jury, the President lied under oath three times.

1. The President testified that he believed oral sex was not covered by any of the terms and definitions for sexual activity used at the Jones deposition. That testimony is not credible: At the Jones deposition, the President could not have believed that he was telling "the truth, the whole truth, and nothing but the truth" in denying a sexual relationship, sexual relations, or a sexual affair with Monica Lewinsky.

2. In all events, even putting aside his definitional defense, the President made a second false statement to the grand jury. The President's grand jury testimony contradicts Ms. Lewinsky's grand jury testimony on the question whether the President touched Ms. Lewinsky's breasts or genitalia during their sexual activity. There can be no contention that one of them has a lack of memory or is mistaken. On this issue, either Monica Lewinsky lied to the grand jury, or President Clinton lied to the grand jury. Under any rational view of the evidence, the President lied to the grand jury.

317

First, Ms. Lewinsky's testimony about these encounters is detailed and specific. She described with precision nine incidents of sexual activity in which the President touched and kissed her breasts and four incidents involving contacts with her genitalia.

Second, Ms. Lewinsky has stated repeatedly that she does not want to hurt the President by her testimony.(109) Thus, if she had exaggerated in her many prior statements, she presumably would have said as much, rather than adhering to those statements. She has confirmed those details, however, even though it clearly has been painful for her to testify to the details of her relationship with the President.

Third, the testimony of many of her friends, family members, and counselors corroborate her testimony in important detail. Many testified that Ms. Lewinsky had told them that the President had touched her breasts and genitalia during sexual activity. These statements were made well before the President's grand jury testimony rendered these precise details important. Ms. Lewinsky had no motive to lie to these individuals (and obviously not to counselors). Indeed, she pointed out to many of them that she was upset that sexual intercourse had not occurred, an unlikely admission if she were exaggerating the sexual aspects of their relationship.

Fourth, a computer file obtained from Ms. Lewinsky's home computer contained a draft letter that referred in one place to their sexual relationship. The draft explicitly refers to "watching your mouth on my breast" and implicitly refers to direct contact with Ms. Lewinsky's genitalia.(110) This draft letter further corroborates Ms. Lewinsky's testimony and indicates that the President's grand jury testimony is false.

Fifth, as noted above, the President's "hands-off" scenario—in which he would have received oral sex on nine occasions from Ms. Lewinsky but never made direct contact with Ms. Lewinsky's breasts or genitalia—is implausible. As Ms. Lewinsky herself testified, it suggests that she and the President had some kind of "service contract—that all I did was perform oral sex on him and that that's all this relationship was."(111) But as the above descriptions and the Narrative explain, the nature of the relationship, including the sexual relationship, was far more than that.

Sixth, in the grand jury, the President had a motive to lie by denying he had fondled Ms. Lewinsky in intimate ways. The President clearly sought to deny any acts that would show that he committed perjury in his civil case (implying that the President understood how seriously the public and the courts would view perjury in a civil case). To do that, the President had to deny touching Ms. Lewinsky's breasts or genitalia—no matter how implausible his testimony to that effect might be.

Seventh, the President refused to answer specific questions before the grand jury about what activity he did engage in (as opposed to what activity he did not engage in)—even though at the Jones deposition only seven months before, his attorney stated that he was willing to answer specific questions when there was a sufficient factual predicate.(112) The President's failure in the grand jury to answer specific follow-up questions suggests that he could not supply responses in a consistent or credible manner.

3. Finally, the President made a third false statement to the grand jury about his sexual relationship with Monica Lewinsky. He contended that the intimate

contact did not begin until 1996. Ms. Lewinsky has testified that it began November 15, 1995, during the government shutdown—testimony corroborated by statements she made to friends at the time.(113) A White House photograph of the evening shows the President and Ms. Lewinsky eating pizza.(114) White House records show that Ms. Lewinsky did not depart the White House until 12:18 a.m. and show that the President was in the Oval Office area until 12:35 a.m.(115)

Ms. Lewinsky was still an intern when she says the President began receiving oral sex from her, whereas she was a full-time employee by the time that the President admits they began an "inappropriate intimate" relationship. The motive for the President to make a false statement about the date on which the sexual relationship started appears to have been that the President was unwilling to admit sexual activity with a young 22-year-old White House intern in the Oval Office area. Indeed, Ms. Lewinsky testified that, at that first encounter, the President tugged at her intern pass. He said that "this" may be a problem; Ms. Lewinsky interpreted that statement to reflect his awareness that there would be a problem with her obtaining access to the West Wing.(116)

For all these reasons, there is substantial and credible information that the President lied to the grand jury about his sexual relationship with Monica Lewinsky.(117)

III. There is substantial and credible information that President Clinton lied under oath during his civil deposition when he stated that he could not recall being alone with Monica Lewinsky and when he minimized the number of gifts they had exchanged.

Substantial and credible information demonstrates that the President made three false statements under oath in his civil deposition regarding whether he had been alone with Ms. Lewinsky.

First, the President lied when he said "I don't recall" in response to the question whether he had ever been alone with Ms. Lewinsky. The President admitted to the grand jury that he had been alone with Ms. Lewinsky. It is not credible that he actually had no memory of this fact six months earlier, particularly given that they were obviously alone when engaging in sexual activity.

Second, when asked whether he had been alone with Ms. Lewinsky in the hallway in the Oval Office, the President answered, "I don't believe so, unless we were walking back to the back dining room with the pizza."(149) That statement, too, was false: Most of the sexual encounters between the President and Ms. Lewinsky occurred in that hallway (and on other occasions, they walked through the hallway to the dining room or study), and it is not credible that the President would have forgotten this fact.

Third, the President suggested at his civil deposition that he had no specific recollection of being alone with Ms. Lewinsky in the Oval Office, but had a general recollection that Ms. Lewinsky may have brought him "papers to sign" on certain occasions when she worked at the Legislative Affairs Office.(150) This statement was false. Ms. Lewinsky did not bring him papers for official purposes. To the contrary, "bringing papers" was one of

319

the sham "cover stories" that the President and Ms. Lewinsky had originally crafted to conceal their sexual relationship.(151) The fact that the President resorted to a previously designed cover story when testifying under oath at the Jones deposition confirms that he made these false denials in a calculated manner with the intent and knowledge that they were false.

The President had an obvious motive to lie in this respect. He knew that it would appear odd for a President to have been alone with a female intern or low-level staffer on so many occasions. Such an admission might persuade Judge Wright to deny any motion by Ms. Lewinsky to quash her deposition subpoena. It also might prompt Ms. Jones's attorneys to oppose efforts by Ms. Lewinsky not to be deposed and to ask specific questions of Ms. Lewinsky about the times she was alone with the President. It also might raise questions publicly if and when the President's deposition became public; at least parts of the deposition were likely to become public at trial, if not at the summary judgment stage.

Because lying about their sexual relationship was insufficient to avoid raising further questions, the President also lied about being alone with Ms. Lewinsky—or at least feigned lack of memory as to specific occurrences.(152)

During his civil deposition, the President also was asked several questions about gifts he and Monica Lewinsky had exchanged. The evidence demonstrates that he answered the questions falsely. As with the questions about being alone, truthful answers to these questions would have raised questions about the nature of the relationship. Such answers also would have been inconsistent with the understanding of the President and Ms. Lewinsky that, in response to her subpoena, Ms. Lewinsky would not produce all of the gifts she had received from the President (an issue discussed more fully in Ground V).

The President stated in his civil deposition that he could not recall whether he had ever given any gifts to Ms. Lewinsky;(199) that he could not remember whether he had given her a hat pin although "certainly, I could have"; and that he had received a gift from Ms. Lewinsky only "once or twice."(200) In fact, the evidence demonstrates that they exchanged numerous gifts of various kinds at many points over a lengthy period of time. Indeed, on December 28, only three weeks before the deposition, they had discussed the hat pin. Also on December 28, the President had given Ms. Lewinsky a number of gifts, more than he had ever given her before.

A truthful answer to the questions about gifts at the Jones deposition would have raised further questions about the President's relationship with Monica Lewinsky. The number itself would raise questions about the relationship and prompt further questions about specific gifts; some of the specific gifts (such as Vox and Leaves of Grass) would raise questions whether the relationship was sexual and whether the President had lied in denying that their relationship was sexual. Ms. Lewinsky explained the point: Had they admitted the gifts, it would "at least prompt [the Jones attorneys] to want to question me about what kind of friendship I had with the President and they would want to speculate and they'd leak it and my name would be trashed and he [the President] would be in trouble."(201)

For those reasons, the President had a clear motive when testifying under oath to lie about the gifts.

IV. There is substantial and credible information that the President lied under oath during his civil deposition concerning conversations he had with Monica Lewinsky about her involvement in the Jones case.

President Clinton was asked during his civil deposition whether he had discussed with Ms. Lewinsky the possibility of her testifying in the Jones case. He also was asked whether he knew that she had been subpoenaed at the time he last had spoken to her.

There is substantial and credible information that the President lied under oath in answering these questions. A false statement about these conversations was necessary in order to avoid raising questions whether the President had tampered with a prospective witness in the civil lawsuit against him.

There is substantial and credible information that President Clinton lied under oath in his civil deposition in answering "I'm not sure" when asked whether he had talked to Ms. Lewinsky about the prospect of her testifying. In fact, he had talked to Ms. Lewinsky about it on three occasions in the month preceding his civil deposition, as Ms. Lewinsky's testimony makes clear.

The President's motive to lie in his civil deposition on this point is evident. Had he admitted talking to Ms. Lewinsky about the possibility that she might be asked to testify, that would have raised the specter of witness tampering. Such an admission likely would have led Ms. Jones's attorneys to inquire further into that subject with both the President and Ms. Lewinsky. Furthermore, had the President admitted talking to Ms. Lewinsky about her testifying, that conversation would have attracted public inquiry into the conversation and the general relationship between the President and Ms. Lewinsky.

There is substantial and credible information that the President lied under oath in his civil deposition by answering "I don't know if she had been" subpoenaed when describing his last conversation with Ms. Lewinsky. In fact, he knew that she had been subpoenaed. Given that the conversation with Ms. Lewinsky occurred in the few weeks immediately before the President's civil deposition, he could not have forgotten the conversation. As a result, there is no plausible conclusion except that the President intentionally lied in this answer.

During the civil deposition, the President also falsely dated his last conversation with Ms. Lewinsky as "probably sometime before Christmas," which implied that it might have been before the December 19 subpoena. Because Ms. Lewinsky had been subpoenaed on December 19, that false statement about the date of the conversation was a corollary to his other false statement (that he did not know she had been subpoenaed at the time of their last conversation).

The President's motive to lie in his civil deposition on the subpoena issue is evident. Had he admitted talking to Ms. Lewinsky after her subpoena, that would have raised the specter of witness tampering, which could have triggered legal and public scrutiny of the President.

V. There is substantial and credible information that President Clinton endeavored to obstruct justice by engaging in a pattern of activity to conceal evidence regarding his relationship with Monica Lewinsky from the judicial process in the Jones case. The pattern included:

(i) concealment of gifts that the President had given Ms. Lewinsky and that were subpoenaed from Ms. Lewinsky in the Jones case; and

(ii) concealment of a note sent by Ms. Lewinsky to the President on January 5, 1998.

From the beginning, President Clinton and Monica Lewinsky hoped and expected that their relationship would remain secret. They took active steps, when necessary, to conceal the relationship. The President testified that "I hoped that this relationship would never become public."(222)

Once the discovery process in the Jones case became an issue (particularly after the Supreme Court's unanimous decision on May 27, 1997, that ordered the case to go forward), their continuing efforts to conceal the relationship took on added legal significance. The risks to the President of disclosure of the relationship dramatically increased.

An effort to obstruct justice by withholding the truth from the legal process—whether by lying under oath, concealing documents, or improperly influencing a witness's testimony—is a federal crime.(223) There is substantial and credible information that President Clinton engaged in such efforts to prevent the truth of his relationship with Monica Lewinsky from being revealed in the Jones case.

VII. There is substantial and credible information that President Clinton endeavored to obstruct justice by helping Ms. Lewinsky obtain a job in New York at a time when she would have been a witness against him were she to tell the truth during the Jones case.

The President had an incentive to keep Ms. Lewinsky from jeopardizing the secrecy of the relationship. That incentive grew once the Supreme Court unanimously decided in May 1997 that the case and discovery process were to go forward.

At various times during the Jones discovery process, the President and those working on his behalf devoted substantial time and attention to help Ms. Lewinsky obtain a job in the private sector.

Ms. Lewinsky first mentioned her desire to move to New York in a letter to the President on July 3, 1997. The letter recounted her frustration that she had not received an offer to return to work at the White House.(324)

On October 1, the President was served with interrogatories asking about his sexual relationships with women other than Mrs. Clinton.(325) On October 7, 1997, Ms. Lewinsky couriered a letter expressing dissatisfaction with her job search to the President.(326) In response, Ms. Lewinsky said she received a late-night call from President Clinton on October 9, 1997. She said that the President told her he would start helping her find a job in New York.(327)

The following Saturday, October 11, 1997, Ms. Lewinsky met with President Clinton alone in the Oval Office dining room from 9:36 a.m. until about 10:54 a.m. In that meeting, she furnished the President a list of New York jobs in which she was interested.(328) Ms. Lewinsky mentioned to the President that she would need a reference from someone in the White House; the President said he would take care of it.(329) Ms. Lewinsky also suggested to the President that Vernon Jordan might be able to help her, and President Clinton agreed.(330) Immediately after the meeting, President Clinton spoke with Mr. Jordan by telephone.(331)

According to White House Chief of Staff Erskine Bowles, at some time in the summer or fall of 1997, President Clinton raised the subject of Monica Lewinsky and stated that "she was unhappy where she was working and wanted to come back and work at the OEOB [Old Executive Office Building]; and could we take a look."(332) Mr. Bowles referred the matter to Deputy Chief of Staff John Podesta.(333)

Mr. Podesta said he asked Betty Currie to have Ms. Lewinsky call him, but heard nothing until about October 1997, when Ms. Currie told him that Ms. Lewinsky was looking for opportunities in New York.(334) The Ambassador to the United Nations, Bill Richardson, said that Mr. Podesta told him that Ms. Currie had a friend looking for a position in New York.(335)

According to Ms. Lewinsky, Ambassador Richardson called her on October 21, 1997,(336) and interviewed her soon thereafter. She was then offered a position at the UN.(337) Ms. Lewinsky was unenthusiastic.(338) During the latter part of October 1997, the President and Ms. Lewinsky discussed enlisting Vernon Jordan to aid in pursuing private-sector possibilities.(339)

On November 5, 1997, Ms. Lewinsky met Mr. Jordan in his law office. Mr. Jordan told Ms. Lewinsky that she came "highly recommended."(340) Ms. Lewinsky explained that she hoped to move to New York, and went over her list of possible employers.(341) Mr. Jordan telephoned President Clinton shortly after the meeting.(342)

Ms. Lewinsky had no contact with the President or Mr. Jordan for another month.(343) On December 5, 1997, however, the parties in the Jones case exchanged witness lists. Ms. Jones's attorneys listed Ms. Lewinsky as a potential witness. The President testified that he learned that Ms. Lewinsky was on the list late in the day on December 6.(344)

The effort to obtain a job for Ms. Lewinsky then intensified. On December 7, President Clinton met with Mr. Jordan at the White House.(345) Ms. Lewinsky met with Mr. Jordan on December 11 to discuss specific job contacts in New York. Mr. Jordan gave her the names of some of his business contacts.(346) He then made calls to contacts at MacAndrews & Forbes (the parent corporation of Revlon), American Express, and Young & Rubicam.(347)

Mr. Jordan also telephoned President Clinton to keep him informed of the efforts to help Ms. Lewinsky. Mr. Jordan testified that President Clinton was aware that people were trying to get jobs for her, that Mr. Podesta was trying to help her, that Bill Richardson was trying to help her, but that she wanted to work in the private sector.(348)

On the same day of Ms. Lewinsky's meeting with Mr. Jordan, December 11, Judge Wright ordered President Clinton, over his objection, to answer certain written interrogatories as part of the discovery process in Jones. Those interrogatories required, among other things, the President to identify any government employees since 1986 with whom he had engaged in sexual relations (a term undefined for purposes of the interrogatory).(349) On December 16, the President's attorneys received a request for production of documents that mentioned Monica Lewinsky by name.

On December 17, 1997, according to Ms. Lewinsky, President Clinton called her in the early morning and told her that she was on the witness list, and they discussed their cover stories.(350) On December 18 and December 23, she interviewed for jobs with New York-based companies that had been contacted by Mr. Jordan.(351) On December 19, Ms. Lewinsky was served with a deposition subpoena by Ms. Jones's lawyers.(352) On December 22, 1997, Mr. Jordan took her to her new attorney; she and Mr. Jordan discussed the subpoena, the Jones case, and her job search during the course of the ride.(353)

The President answered the "other women" interrogatory on December 23, 1997, by declaring under oath: "None."(354)

On Sunday, December 28, 1997, Monica Lewinsky and the President met in the Oval Office.(355) During that meeting, the President and Ms. Lewinsky discussed both her move to New York and her involvement in the Jones suit.(356)

On January 5, 1998, Ms. Lewinsky declined the United Nations offer.(357) On January 7, 1998, Ms. Lewinsky signed the affidavit denying the relationship with President Clinton (she had talked on the phone to the President on January 5 about it).(358) Mr. Jordan informed the President of her action.(359)

The next day, on January 8, 1998, Ms. Lewinsky interviewed in New York with MacAndrews & Forbes, a company recommended by Vernon Jordan. The interview went poorly. Mr. Jordan then called Ronald Perelman, the Chairman of the Board at MacAndrews & Forbes. Mr. Perelman said Ms. Lewinsky should not worry, and that someone would call her back for another interview. Mr. Jordan relayed this message to Ms. Lewinsky, and someone called back that day.(360)

Ms. Lewinsky interviewed again the next morning, and a few hours later received an informal offer for a position.(361) She told Mr. Jordan of the offer, and Mr. Jordan then notified President Clinton with the news: "Mission accomplished."(362)

On January 12, 1998, Ms. Jones's attorneys informed Judge Wright that they might call Monica Lewinsky as a trial witness.(363) Judge Wright stated that she would allow witnesses with whom the President had worked, such as Ms. Lewinsky, to be trial witnesses.(364)

In a call on January 13, 1998, a Revlon employee formalized the job offer, and asked Ms. Lewinsky to provide references.(365) Either that day or the next, President Clinton told Erskine Bowles that Ms. Lewinsky "had found a job in the . . . private sector, and she had listed John Hilley as a reference, and could we see if he could recommend her, if asked."(366) Thereafter, Mr. Bowles took the President's request to Deputy Chief of Staff John Podesta, who in turn spoke to Mr. Hilley about writing a letter of recommendation. After speaking with Mr. Podesta, Mr. Hilley agreed to write such a letter, but cautioned it would be a "generic" one.(367) On January 14, at approximately 11:17 a.m., Ms. Lewinsky faxed her letter of acceptance to Revlon and listed Mr. Hilley as a reference.(368)

On January 15, the President responded to the December 15 request for production of documents relating to Monica Lewinsky by answering "none." On January 16, Ms. Lewinsky's attorney sent to the District Court in the Jones case her affidavit denying a "sexual relationship" with the President.(369) The next day, on January 17, the President was deposed and his attorney used her affidavit as the President similarly denied a "sexual relationship."

B. Summary

When a party in a lawsuit (or investigation) provides job or financial assistance to a witness, a question arises as to possible witness tampering. The critical question centers on the intent of the party providing the assistance. Direct evidence of that intent often is unavailable. Indeed, in some cases, the witness receiving the job assistance may not even know that the party providing the assistance was motivated by a desire to stay on good terms with the witness during the pending legal proceeding.(370) Similarly, others who are enlisted in the party's effort to influence the witness's testimony by providing job assistance may not be aware of the party's motivation and intent.

One can draw inferences about the party's intent from circumstantial evidence. In this case, the President assisted Ms. Lewinsky in her job search in late 1997, at a time when she would have become a witness harmful to him in the Jones case were she to testify truthfully. The President did not act half-heartedly. His assistance led to the involvement of the Ambassador to the United Nations, one of the country's leading business figures (Mr. Perelman), and one of the country's leading attorneys (Vernon Jordan).

The question, therefore, is whether the President's efforts in obtaining a job for Ms. Lewinsky were to influence her testimony(371) or simply to help an ex-intimate without concern for her testimony. Three key facts are essential in analyzing his actions: (i) the chronology of events, (ii) the fact that the President and Ms. Lewinsky both intended to lie under oath about the relationship, and (iii) the fact that it was critical for the President that Ms. Lewinsky lie under oath.

There is substantial and credible information that the President assisted Ms. Lewinsky in her job search motivated at least in part by his desire to keep her "on the team" in the Jones litigation.

VIII. There is substantial and credible information that the President lied under oath in describing his conversations with Vernon Jordan about Ms. Lewinsky.

In his civil deposition, the President stated that he had talked to Vernon Jordan about Ms. Lewinsky's job. But as the testimony of Mr. Jordan reveals, and as the President as much as conceded in his subsequent grand jury appearance,(392) the President did talk to Mr. Jordan about Ms. Lewinsky's involvement in the Jones case—including that she had been subpoenaed, that Mr. Jordan had helped her obtain a lawyer, and that she had signed an affidavit denying a sexual relationship with the President. Given their several communications in the weeks before the deposition, it is not credible that the President forgot the subject of their conversations during his civil deposition. His statements "seems like that's what Betty said" and "I didn't know that" were more than mere omissions; they were affirmative misstatements.

The President's motive for making false and misleading statements about this subject in his civil deposition was straightforward. If the President admitted that he had talked with Vernon Jordan both about Monica Lewinsky's involvement in the Jones case and about her job, questions would inevitably arise about whether Ms. Lewinsky's testimony and her future job were connected. Such an admission by the President in his civil deposition likely would have prompted Ms. Jones's attorneys to inquire further into the subject. And such an admission in his deposition would have triggered public scrutiny when the deposition became public.

At the time of his deposition, moreover, the President was aware of the potential problems in admitting any possible link between those two subjects. A criminal investigation and substantial public attention had focused in 1997 on job assistance and payments made to Webster Hubbell in 1994. The jobs and money paid to Mr. Hubbell by friends and contributors to the President had raised serious questions about whether such assistance was designed to influence Mr. Hubbell's testimony about Madison-related matters.(393) Some of Mr. Hubbell's jobs, moreover, had been arranged by Vernon Jordan, which was likely a further deterrent to the President raising both Ms. Lewinsky's job and her affidavit in connection with Vernon Jordan.

IX. There is substantial and credible information that President Clinton endeavored to obstruct justice by attempting to influence the testimony of Betty Currie.

The President referred to Ms. Currie on multiple occasions in his civil deposition when describing his relationship with Ms. Lewinsky. As he himself recognized, a large number of questions about Ms. Lewinsky were likely to be asked in the very near future. The President thus could foresee that Ms. Currie either might be deposed or questioned or might need to prepare an affidavit.

The President called her shortly after the deposition and met with Ms. Currie the next day. The President appeared "concerned," according to Ms. Currie. He then informed Ms. Currie that questions about Ms. Lewinsky had been asked at the deposition.

The statements the President made to her on January 18 and again on January 20 or 21—that he was never alone with Ms. Lewinsky, that Ms. Currie could always hear or see them, and that he never touched Ms. Lewinsky—were false, but consistent with the testimony that the President provided under oath at his deposition. The President knew that the statements were false at the time he made them to Ms. Currie. The President's suggestion that he was simply trying to refresh his memory when talking to Ms. Currie conflicts with common sense: Ms. Currie's confirmation of false statements could not in any way remind the President of the facts. Thus, it is not plausible that he was trying to refresh his recollection.

The President's grand jury testimony reinforces that conclusion. He testified that in asking questions of Ms. Currie such as "We were never alone, right" and "Monica came on to me, and I never touched her, right," he intended a date restriction on the questions. But he did not articulate a date restriction in his conversations with Ms. Currie. Moreover, with respect to some aspects of this incident, the President was unable to devise any innocent explanation, testifying that he did not know why he had asked Ms. Currie some questions and admitting that he was "just trying to reconcile the two statements as best [he could]." On the other hand, if the most reasonable inference from the President's conduct is drawn—that he was attempting to enlist a witness to back up his false testimony from the day before—his behavior with Ms. Currie makes complete sense.

The content of the President's statements and the context in which those statements were made provide substantial and credible information that President Clinton sought improperly to influence Ms. Currie's testimony. Such actions constitute an obstruction of justice and improper influence on a witness.

X. There is substantial and credible information that President Clinton endeavored to obstruct justice during the federal grand jury investigation. While refusing to testify for seven months, he simultaneously lied to potential grand jury witnesses knowing that they would relay the falsehoods to the grand jury.

The President's grand jury testimony followed seven months of investigation in which he had refused six invitations to testify before the grand jury. During this period, there was no indication that the President would admit any sexual relationship with Ms. Lewinsky. To the contrary, the President vehemently denied the allegations.

Rather than lie to the grand jury himself, the President lied about his relationship with Ms. Lewinsky to senior aides, and those aides then conveyed the President's false story to the grand jury.(433)

The President made the following misleading statements to his aides:

➤ The President told Mr. Podesta that he had not engaged in sex "in any way whatsoever" with Ms. Lewinsky, "including oral sex".

➤ The President told Mr. Podesta, Mr. Bowles, and Mr. Ickes that he did not have a "sexual relationship" with Ms. Lewinsky.

➤ The President told Mr. Podesta that "when [Ms. Lewinsky] came by, she came by to see Betty [Currie]."

➤ The President told Mr. Blumenthal that Ms. Lewinsky "came on to him and that he had told her he couldn't have sexual relations with her and that she threatened him."

➤ The President told Mr. Blumenthal that he couldn't remember making any calls to Ms. Lewinsky other than once when he left a message on her answering machine.

During the President's grand jury testimony, the President admitted that his statements to aides denying a sexual relationship with Ms. Lewinsky "may have been misleading."(464) The President also knew his aides likely would be called to testify regarding any communications with him about Ms. Lewinsky. And he presumably expected his aides to repeat his statements regarding Ms. Lewinsky to all questioners, including to the grand jury. Finally, he himself refused to testify for many months. The combination of the President's silence and his deception of his aides had the effect of presenting a false view of events to the grand jury.

The President says that at the time he spoke to his aides, he chose his words with great care so that, in his view, his statements would be literally true because he was referring only to intercourse. That explanation is undermined by the President's testimony before the grand jury that his denials "may have been misleading" and by the contradictory testimony by the aides themselves—particularly John Podesta, who says that the President specifically denied oral sex with Ms. Lewinsky. Moreover, on January 24, 1998, the White House issued talking points for its staff, and those talking points refute the President's literal truth argument: The talking points state as the President's view the belief that a relationship that includes oral sex is "of course" a "sexual relationship."(465)

For all of these reasons, there is substantial and credible information that the President improperly tampered with witnesses during the grand jury investigation.

XI. There is substantial and credible information that President Clinton's actions since January 17, 1998, regarding his relationship with Monica Lewinsky have been inconsistent with the President's constitutional duty to faithfully execute the laws.

Before, during, and after his January 17, 1998, civil deposition, the President attempted to conceal the truth about his relationship with Ms. Lewinsky from the judicial process in the Jones case. Furthermore, the President has since lied under oath to the grand jury and facilitated the provision of false information to the grand jury by others.

The President also misled the American people and the Congress in his public statement of January 26, 1998, in which he denied "sexual relations" with Ms. Lewinsky. The President misled his Cabinet and his senior aides by denying the relationship to them. The Cabinet and senior aides in turn misled the American people and the Congress by conveying the President's denials and professing their belief in the credibility of those denials.

The President promised in January 1998 to cooperate fully with the grand jury investigation and to provide "more rather than less, sooner rather than later." At that time, the OIC was conducting a criminal investigation and was obligated to report to Congress any substantial and credible information that may constitute grounds for an impeachment. The President's conduct delayed the grand jury investigation (and thereby delayed any potential congressional proceedings). He asserted, appealed, withdrew, and reasserted Executive Privilege (and asserted other governmental privileges never before applied in federal criminal proceedings against the government). The President asserted these privileges concerning the investigation of factual questions about which the President already knew the answers. The President refused six invitations to testify voluntarily before the grand jury. At the same time, the President's aides and surrogates argued publicly that the entire matter was frivolous and that any investigation of it should cease.

After being subpoenaed in July, the President made false statements to the grand jury on August 17, 1998. That night, the President again made false statements to the American people and Congress, contending that his answers in his civil deposition had been "legally accurate." The President then made an implicit plea for Congress to take no action: "Our country has been distracted by this matter for too long."(466)

The President has pursued a strategy of (i) deceiving the American people and Congress in January 1998, (ii) delaying and impeding the criminal investigation for seven months, and (iii) deceiving the American people and Congress again in August 1998.

In this case, the President made and caused to be made false statements to the American people about his relationship with Ms. Lewinsky. He also made false statements about whether he had lied under oath or otherwise obstructed justice in his civil case. By publicly and emphatically stating in January 1998 that "I did not have sexual relations with that woman" and these "allegations are false," the President also effectively delayed a possible congressional inquiry, and then he further delayed it by asserting Executive Privilege and refusing to testify for six months during the Independent Counsel investigation. This represents substantial and credible information that may constitute grounds for an impeachment.

Timeline of Scandal in the Clinton Presidency

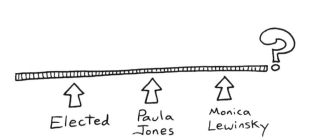

Elected   Paula Jones   Monica Lewinsky

To listen to his enemies, Bill Clinton hasn't had a moral day in his life. The following timeline only covers the troubles that have plagued his Presidency, with an emphasis on the events relating to Monica Lewinsky.

1979   Whitewater Development Corp. is founded.

1985   Loans are extended to Bill Clinton and former Arkansas Governor Jim Guy Tucker from James McDougal's failing Madison Guarantee Savings and Loan.

November 1992   Bill Clinton elected president.

Bill Clinton and Vince Foster (his attorney) sign papers selling Bill Clinton's Whitewater shares to James McDougal.

May 1993   White House Travel Office workers fired (Travelgate). Memos say that Hillary Clinton was behind the firings, which she denies, and rumor says that she was encouraged in this by Harry Thomason, a Hollywood producer, so he could have a piece of the White House charter business. Billy Dale, head of the Travel Office, was aquitted of criminal charges brought against him.

May 1993   Filegate (still being investigated). Alleged improper review of 900 FBI files by the White House of Republican officials in the Bush and Reagan Administrations. The White House calls it an innocent mistake.

Linda Tripp, a holdover from the Bush Administration, becomes Vince Foster's secretary.

July 20, 1993   Linda Tripp is the last person to see Vince Foster alive.

Vince Foster found dead. Death ruled a suicide.

November 22, 1993   Linda Tripp allegedly is told by Kathleen Willey about unwanted sexual advances made by Bill Clinton.

Linda Tripp is approached by New York literary agent Lucianne Goldberg about a Vince Foster homicide conspiracy book.

January 12, 1994   Janet Reno appoints Robert Fiske, Jr. as special prosecutor in Vince Foster investigation.

May 6, 1994   Paula Jones files sexual harassment charges against Bill Clinton in U.S. District Court for the Eastern District of Arkansas, Western Division.

June 30, 1994   Independent prosecutor Robert Fiske, Jr., declares Vince Foster's death a suicide in a preliminary finding.

July 26, 1994   House Banking Committee begins hearings on Whitewater.

July 29, 1994   Senate Banking Committee begins hearings on Whitewater.

August 5, 1994   Kenneth Starr replaces Robert Fiske, Jr. as special prosecutor. Starr continues Whitewater investigation.

Webster Hubbell convicted on fraud charges about the Rose Law firm, where Hillary Clinton was a former partner.

August 21, 1994   Linda Tripp is transferred to the Pentagon, where she later meets Monica Lewinsky.

June 1995   Monica Lewinsky, newly graduated from Lewis and Clark College, arrives at the White House as an unpaid intern in Leon Panetta's office (former Chief of Staff).

November 1995   November 15 and 17 mark the first two sexual encounters between Bill Clinton and Monica Lewinsky.

December 1995   Lewinsky is advanced into a paying position at the Office of Legislative Affairs, where one of her responsibilities is ferrying letters to the Oval Office. According to the Starr report, another sexual encounter with the President happens on December 31.

January 7 and 21, February 4, 1996   Three more sexual encounters between Bill Clinton and Monica Lewinsky.

February 3, 1996   Kenneth Starr concludes that Vince Foster's death was a suicide.

February 19, 1996   Bill Clinton tells Lewinsky that the relationship is over.

March 31, 1996   Lewinsky and Clinton resume their sexual relationship.

April 16, 1996   Monica Lewinsky transfers to a job in public affairs at the Pentagon, where she meets Linda Tripp.

May 30, 1996   White House surrenders Travelgate documents and House starts Filegate hearings.

June 20, 1996   Janet Reno asks Kenneth Starr to look into Filegate.

Summer 1996   Lewinsky reportedly takes Linda Tripp into her confidence about her affair with President Clinton.

September 20, 1996 The House Government Reform and Oversight Committee issues its report on Travelgate and criticizes the president.

February 28, 1997 Another sexual encounter between Bill Clinton and Monica Lewinsky. This is the first one in more than 10 months.

June 25, 1997 Starr pursues questioning of Arkansas state troopers on alleged affairs Clinton had while he was governor.

July 1997 Linda Tripp reports to Paula Jones' lawyers and the media the charge that Bill Clinton made inappropriate sexual advances to Kathleen Willey.

Fall 1997 Tripp tapes 17 hours of conversations with Lewinsky.

October 1997 Tripp tells Lucianne Goldberg of Lewinsky's affair with President Clinton. At Goldberg's suggestion, Tripp begins taping her conversations with Lewinsky.

Clinton allegedly asks Erskine B. Bowles, his Chief of Staff, to get Lewinsky a job.

Lewinsky interviews with U.S. Ambassador to the U.N. Bill Richardson for a position in New York. She later turns the position down.

December 19, 1997 Lewinsky, after being brought to the attention of Paula Jones' lawyers, is subpoenaed in the Jones case.

December 1997 Lewinsky meets with presidential advisor Vernon Jordan and reportedly assures him that she will deny having an affair with Clinton.

Tripp allegedly tells Lewinsky that she will testify about Lewinsky's conversations with her regarding Clinton.

December 28, 1997 Lewinsky meets with Clinton in the Oval Office. He reportedly advises her to be "evasive" in her Paula Jones testimony. Later, Betty Currie drives to Lewinsky's home to take back gifts given to Lewinsky from Clinton.

January 7, 1998 Lewinsky signs an affidavit denying having sex with Clinton. Jordan gets her a job offer with Revlon in New York.

January 12, 1998 Linda Tripp contacts Kenneth Starr and gives him 20 hours of taped conversation with Lewinsky.

January 13, 1998 Tripp has meeting with Lewinsky. Tripp has been wired by the FBI for this meeting.

January 15, 1998 Starr's deputies seek expansion of the independent counsel's White House probe from Attorney General Janet Reno.

January 16, 1998 Janet Reno grants an expansion of the investigation.

U.S. attorneys and the FBI question Lewinsky on her reported affair with Bill Clinton and allegedly offer her immunity from perjury charges related to her affidavit in the Jones case. Her lawyer, William Ginsberg, advises her not to accept immunity deal until they know more.

January 17, 1998   Clinton gives a deposition to Jones lawyers that denies sex with Lewinsky, though he does admit a sexual relationship with Gennifer Flowers, an allegation that he denied during his 1992 campaign.

January 21, 1998   News organizations report the alleged relationship with Lewinsky and the story explodes.

January 22, 1998   Clinton denies the charges of an "improper relationship."

January 23, 1998   Clinton tells his Cabinet that he is innocent.

January 26, 1998   Clinton reiterates his innocence: "I did not have sexual relations with that woman, Ms. Lewinsky. I never told anybody to lie. These allegations are false."

January 29, 1998   Judge Susan Webber Wright rules that Monica Lewinsky is "not essential to the core issues" in the Jones case, and excludes all Lewinsky evidence from the Jones hearings.

February 3, 1998   White House logs show Lewinsky received clearance to visit the White House 37 times, while she was in her Pentagon job.

February 4, 1998   Starr rejects latest written statement by Lewinsky's lawyers seeking immunity for her.

February 10, 1998   Lewinsky's mother, Marcia Lewis, testifies before the grand jury.

February 11, 1998   Retired Secret Service agent Lewis Fox tells the media that he saw Clinton and Lewinsky alone in the Oval Office in late 1995. This directly contradicts the president's testimony.

March 10, 1998   Kathleen Willey, a former White House volunteer, testifies before Ken Starr's grand jury.

March 15, 1998   Kathleen Willey appears on *60 Minutes* with her allegations against Bill Clinton.

March 16, 1998   Clinton denies Kathleen Willey's claims by saying, "Nothing improper happened." The White House releases friendly letters Willey wrote to Clinton after the alleged incident.

March 26, 1998   Over the protest of the Democrats, House Republicans set aside 1.3 million for possible impeachment probe.

April 1, 1998   Judge Susan Webber Wright throws out Jones lawsuit.

April 16, 1998   Paula Jones announces she will appeal the dismissal of her lawsuit.

May 5, 1998   Judge Norma Holloway Johnson rules that executive privilege cannot stop top White House aides Sidney Blumenthal and Bruce Lindsay from testifying before Starr's grand jury.

May 14, 1998   Starr goes to Federal Court to force the Secret Service to testify before the grand jury.

May 26, 1998 Judge Johnson rules that the Secret Service has to testify in the Lewinsky matter.

June 2, 1998 Lewinsky drops her lawyer, William Ginsberg, and replaces him with two more experienced Washington attorneys, Jacob Stein and Plato Cacheris.

June 15, 1998 The editor of Brill's Content, Steven Brill, accuses Ken Starr of illegally leaking information to reporters about the Lewinsky matter. Starr denies the allegation.

June-July 1998 Linda Tripp testifies before the grand jury.

July 7-9, 1998 Maryland's state's attorney opens investigation as to whether Linda Tripp broke Maryland state law by taping Lewinsky without Lewinsky's consent. Lewinsky agrees to cooperate with investigation.

July 21, 1998 U.S. Court of Appeals holds a hearing on the leaks of grand jury information to the media by Ken Starr's office.

July 25, 1998 Negotiations are reported on the subpoena to testify before the grand jury that was served on Bill Clinton. The negotiations center around the timing and format of Clinton's testimony.

July 28, 1998 Lawyers for Starr and Lewinsky announce a full immunity agreement for Monica Lewinsky and her parents in exchange for Lewinsky's testimony before the grand jury.

July 29, 1998 Bill Clinton agrees to testify voluntarily before Starr's grand jury. The testimony is set for August 17, 1998 from the White House.

July 30, 1998 Part of Lewinsky's immunity agreement covers her turning over a stained dress to the FBI lab in order to provide physical evidence of a relationship with Bill Clinton.

August 6, 1998 Monica Lewinsky testifies before the grand jury.

August 17, 1998 Bill Clinton is the first sitting President ever to testify before a grand jury investigating him. He then goes on national TV and admits a "not appropriate" relationship with Monica Lewinsky.

August 20, 1998 Clinton submits a DNA sample to the FBI lab for comparison to the stain in Lewinsky's blue dress.

August 20, 1998 Lewinsky re-testifies in front of the grand jury to show inconsistencies in Clinton's testimony.

September 9, 1998 Starr submits his report and 18 boxes of supporting material to the House.

September 11, 1998 The House votes to release the report to the Internet. The White House issues a preliminary rebuttal to the report.

September 12, 1998 The White House issues a revised rebuttal to the report.

September 21, 1998   The House Judiciary Committee releases the videotape of Clinton's grand jury testimony to the public. In addition 2,800 pages of supporting evidence are released.

September 24, 1998   Representative Henry Hyde (R-IL) House Judiciary Committee Chairman announces that the committee will vote on whether to recommend impeachment hearings for President Clinton no later than October 6, 1998. If the committee votes in the affirmative, the full House will take up the measure by October 8 or 9, 1998.

September 25, 1998   House Judiciary Committee voted to release more evidence pointing to possible impeachment of Bill Clinton, including releasing the tapes made by Linda Tripp of conversations with Monica Lewinsky. The tapes and transcripts thereof will be heavily edited. The scheduled release is October 1, 1998.

September 25, 1998   It was announced that lawyers for Bill Clinton and Paula Jones are negotiating a settlement. Jones reportedly wants 1 million dollars and has dropped her requirement of an apology. Clinton's lawyers have counteroffered with $500,000. Though this case was, in essence, won by Clinton in April 1998 by being thrown out of court, the Appeals Court may reinstate the case due to the testimony that has come out of Ken Starr's grand jury hearings.

September 30, 1998   Republicans release their plan for impeachment proceedings and the wording of their draft resolution initiating the process.

October 5, 1998   The House Judiciary Committee votes to initiate an open-ended inquiry that could lead to impeachment proceedings.

The Cast of Characters

Most of the names listed below come directly from Kenneth Starr's Table of Names at the beginning of the report. The names are in alphabetical order within a number of specific categories. For the more prominent and newsworthy of the people mentioned, brief synopses of their roles in the scandal are included. Most of these people testified before the grand jury, though some were only mentioned in the report.

Karin Joyce Abramson   Former director of the White House Intern Program.

Madeline Albright   Secretary of State; though her feelings about the current revelations in the scandal are not clear, she was a strong supporter of the President when the scandal broke out in January 1998. The charges, she said, "are completely untrue."

Charles Bakaly   Chief spokesman for the Independent Counsel's Office; a lawyer, he devises investigative strategy and coordinates communication of the independent counsel's work to the public.

Bob Barr (R-Georgia)   Another member of the House Judiciary Committee, Barr tried to call for impeachment hearings before the Lewinsky story hit the press.

Stephen Bates   A top Starr deputy, he wrote most of the narrative describing the relationship between Clinton and Lewinsky. A Harvard Law graduate, he is also a journalist, writing for *The Nation*, *The Weekly Standard*, and *The New Republic*. He has also written several nonfiction books.

Jackie Bennett   A top Starr deputy who stands accused of leaking grand-jury testimony to the press.

Robert Bennett   Attorney for President Clinton; a high-powered Washington attorney, he leads the defense in the Jones case. Former clients have included former Representative Dan Rostenkowski and Reagan Defense Secretary Caspar Weinberger.

Robert Bittman   Deputy independent counsel, a high-ranking member of Starr's team.

Andrew Bleiler   Former boyfriend of Monica Lewinsky.

Sidney Blumenthal   Assistant to the President; being a close advisor and friend to the president, Blumenthal became the subject of much legal wrangling. The White House lawyers wanted to limit his testimony to the grand jury due to what they called "executive privilege." This legal theory was ruled against and then dropped by the White House legal team.

Erskine Bowles   White House Chief of Staff; he was planning to resign even before the Lewinsky saga broke in January 1998. He reportedly still wants out.

Ron Brown   Former commerce secretary; a friend of Clinton, as well as a member of the Cabinet, Brown was being investigated himself at the time of his death in an airplane crash.

Lanny Bruer   Special counsel to the President; He takes care of the day-to-day subpoenas and document requests involving the administration.

Plato Cacheris   Attorney for Monica Lewinsky; he was appointed as a new member of the Lewinsky legal team to replace Bill Ginsberg. He is a highly influential lawyer, having represented Iran-Contra witness Fawn Hall and the late attorney general John Mitchell. Cacheris was instrumental in getting Lewinsky immunity, so that she would testify before Starr's grand jury.

Donovan Campbell, Jr.   Paula Jones's lead attorney; he has been instrumental in this crisis by being among the first to consult with Linda Tripp and use her information about Monica Lewinsky against the President. Though the Jones case was dismissed last April, Campbell has been negotiating with the President's lawyers about a settlement for Jones. The President's attorneys are willing to negotiate at this point because of the Starr report and how it proved that Clinton lied in the Jones deposition.

Frank Carter   Monica Lewinsky's first attorney after scandal broke.

James Carville   Former Clinton campaign manager; Carville is an outspoken defender of Bill Clinton and accuses the right wing of conspiring to overturn the electoral wishes of the public through their continued investigations of the President. Carville seems to have a special wrath reserved for Newt Gingrich, who he believes orchestrates the right-wing actions regarding the President.

Hillary Rodham Clinton   First Lady of the United States; she has stayed by Bill Clinton's side through what looks to be a very difficult marriage. However, she has always publicly supported him, though she did remain fairly quiet during some of the darker moments of the Lewinsky scandal.

William Jefferson Clinton   President of the United States in the fight of his political life to defend against the charges that Kenneth Starr has brought in his report.

Larry Cockell   Special agent in charge, Secret Service Presidential Protective Division; he was the lead agent in charge of the Clinton detail.

John Conyers (D-Michigan)   Ranking Democrat of the House Judiciary Committee. Conyers, 69, is one of the founders of the Congressional Black Caucus. The Black Caucus, and the black community in general, have been strong supporters of Clinton during this crisis.

Betty Currie   Personal secretary to the President; she has had much close contact with Lewinsky, from signing her in as a Presidential visitor to calling Vernon Jordan to request help in finding Lewinsky a job, to picking up the gifts that Clinton gave to Lewinsky from Lewinsky's apartment.

Matt Drudge   Drudge Report; a conservative with an Internet publication, Drudge was the first to break the Lewinsky story. He has subsequently been a right-wing voice for many aspects of the story.

Gennifer Flowers   Long a figure connected to Bill Clinton, she claimed a 12-year affair with him. He denied it during the 1992 elections, only admitting that he had "caused pain in his marriage." However, during his deposition in the Jones case, Clinton apparently admitted the affair with Flowers, who is a night-club singer.

Vince Foster   Former deputy White House counsel; Foster committed suicide in the summer of 1996. Linda Tripp was the last person to see him alive. Independent counsels Robert Fiske, Jr., and Kenneth Starr have both led inquiries into rumors of a suspected homicide of Foster; both concluded that the death was a suicide. In the latest twist on the Foster case, the Supreme Court ruled that attorney/client privilege extends beyond the grave, so that Foster's lawyer was not forced to turn over records of his client's conversations to Ken Starr's team.

Lewis Fox   Retired Secret Service uniformed officer; Fox testified that he saw Lewinsky and Clinton alone together in the Oval Office.

Barney Frank (D-Massachusetts)   Outspoken and openly gay member of the House Judiciary Committee. He is a strong presidential supporter.

Newt Gingrich (R-Georgia)   Speaker of the House and longtime Clinton critic. He can dictate the tone and behind-the-scenes maneuvering on this case.

Bill Ginsberg   Monica Lewinsky's former attorney; a personal friend of Lewinsky's father, Ginsberg did not have the Washington experience that might have served well in Lewinsky's defense. His outspokenness and failure to cut an immunity deal probably led to his replacement in the summer of 1998 by more well-connected Washington attorneys.

Lucianne Goldberg   Literary agent; long a right-wing conservative and Clinton-basher, Goldberg first befriended Linda Tripp when she was working on a project about the Vince Foster homicide conspiracy theory. When Tripp later came in contact with Lewinsky and heard her story, Goldberg advised Tripp to tape Lewinsky.

Stephen Goodin   Former aide to President Clinton; he was the aide who kept the President on schedule and carried his personal papers, so he was highly aware of the people surrounding Clinton.

Al Gore   Vice President of the United States; Gore, a former Presidential candidate, is looking toward the 2000 race for another shot at the presidency. His chances for that are widely seen as at least somewhat damaged due to his need to defend Clinton during the current crisis, as well as him being a target for probing himself due to alleged irregularities in campaign financing during the 1996 campaign.

David Grobanie   Owner of Briarwood Bookstore.

Orrin Hatch (R-Utah)   Senate Judiciary Committee Chair, he is a strong conservative who will make key decisions in how the case is conducted in the Senate.

Nancy Hernreich   Deputy assistant to the President and director of Oval Office operations; she shares an office with Bettie Currie, so she was in a position to see the comings and goings of presidential visitors.

John Hilley   Assistant to the President and director of legislative affairs; Monica Lewinsky's supervisor in the White House for her first paying job there (after her internship).

Sydney Hoffman   An associate of Plato Cacheris, Hoffman is credited with being pivotal to closing the Lewinsky immunity deal. He attended a secret meeting with Lewinsky and the Starr lawyers, and later accompanied Lewinsky to her grand-jury testimony.

Henry Hyde (R-Illinois)   Chairman of the House Judiciary Committee. Hyde is seen as an honorable lawmaker. Recent revelations of a past love affair may prejudice him against the Clinton team, but it is unclear whether the uncovering of the affair was directed by the White House.

Harold Ickes   Former deputy chief of staff; he was rather abruptly taken off staff when Erskine Bowles became the Chief of Staff. Now Ickes has been asked to direct a political response to the Starr report.

Michael Isikoff   Reporter, *Newsweek* magazine; he was working on the Lewinsky story and was reportedly at a meeting with Tripp and Goldberg listening to the Lewinsky tapes. *Newsweek* decided not to publish the story initially.

Hon. Norma Holloway Johnson   Chief judge, U.S. District Court for the District of Columbia; she presides over Ken Starr's grand jury. She has ruled in Starr's favor many times, and been upheld in especially her rulings against privileged communication by higher courts. She has ruled against Starr in the matter of alleged media leaks of grand-jury testimony—he will be required to cooperate with an investigation into that.

Paula Corbin Jones   Plaintiff in a civil sexual harassment suit against President Clinton; the Lewinsky investigation came about in part because Lewinsky's relationship to Bill Clinton came to the attention of the Jones lawyers, who wanted to use it to prove a negative pattern of behavior on the part of the President that would uphold the merits of the case. It is Bill Clinton's denial of the Lewinsky affair in his deposition in the Jones case that is the heart of the perjury charge against him.

Vernon Jordan   Friend of President Clinton, and partner at the law firm of Akin, Gump, Strauss, Hauer & Feld; he helped to secure Lewinsky a job in New York, allegedly at the behest of the President.

Mickey Kantor   Clinton family attorney for the Lewinsky case; he is a trusted friend of the Clintons.

Dr. Irene Kassorla   Therapist to Monica Lewinsky.

Brett Kavanaugh   Starr deputy; at 33 he is one of the youngest members of the Starr team. He was highly involved in the writing of the report, and was also key in rebutting the "privileged" communication claims by the White House, so that certain parties would not have to testify in front of the grand jury. Kavanaugh also led the investigation into the death of Vince Foster.

Walter Kaye   Family friend of Monica Lewinsky; he helped Monica Lewinsky get a White House internship in the first place. He is a prominent Democratic contributor.

Janis Kearney   Special assistant to the President and records manager; she testified before the grand jury.

Timothy Keating   Special assistant to the President and staff director for Legislative Affairs; He hired Monica Lewinsky and was her immediate supervisor in the White House for her first paying job there (after her internship).

David Kendall   Attorney for President Clinton; he is the lead attorney in the Lewinsky matter, and is a highly respected Washington lawyer.

Ted Kennedy (D-Massachusetts)   Senator who can rally liberal support for the President.

Joseph Lieberman (D-Connecticut)   Senator who is a Clinton backer, but who was the first figure on Capitol Hill to issue a stinging indictment of the President's behavior.

Dr. Bernard Lewinsky   Monica Lewinsky's father; divorced from Monica's mother, Dr. Lewinsky lives in California. A close friend of his, Bill Ginsberg, served for a time as Monica's legal counsel, but was replaced by more well-connected Washington attorneys. Bernard Lewinsky was covered by his daughter's immunity deal with Kenneth Starr and did not have to testify before Kenneth Starr's grand jury.

Monica Lewinsky   Former White House intern and employee; at the center of the latest controversy surrounding President Clinton, Lewinsky may unintentionally bring down Bill Clinton's presidency.

Ann Lewis   Director, White House communications; one of the main Clinton defenders in the media.

Marcia Lewis   Mother of Monica Lewinsky; she did appear before the grand jury because she is a confidante of her daughter's, but was not required to testify later because she was covered by Monica's immunity deal.

Evelyn Lieberman   Former deputy chief of staff; she told *The New York Times* that Lewinsky's transfer to the Pentagon was for her "inappropriate and immature behavior."

Bruce Lindsey   Deputy White House counsel, and top Clinton deputy, they were friends from the time they both attended Georgetown University. Lindsey was caught up in the controversy of whether he had to answer all the questions before the grand jury due to "lawyer/client privilege." The Supreme Court eventually ruled that the White House lawyer was not protected by that legal principal and he had to testify.

Joe Lockhart   White House press secretary; he recently replaced Mike McCurry and will take over the role of fielding press inquiries into the President.

Glen Maes   White House steward to President Clinton, stationed in the pantry and kitchen area in the West Wing of the White House with a view of the presidential adjoining study.

Bill McCollum (R-Florida)   A member of the House Judiciary Committee, he thinks that the charges levelled against Clinton are impeachable.

Mike McCurry   Former White House press secretary; he was responsible for answering the press's incessant questions on the Lewinsky matter. McCurry stepped down from this post on October 1, 1998.

Lewis Merletti   Director, Secret Service; he was at the center of the battle against Starr.

Eleanor Mondale   Reporter, CBS News; apparently a report made to Monica Lewinsky that the President was unavailable to talk to Lewinsky because he had Mondale in his office put Lewinsky into a furious rage.

James Moody   Attorney for Linda Tripp.

Bayani Nelvis   White House steward to President Clinton, stationed in the pantry and kitchen area in the West Wing of the White House with a view of the presidential adjoining study.

Jennifer Palmieri   Former special assistant to the chief of staff; she supervised Lewinsky when Lewinsky was an intern.

Leon Panetta   Former White House chief of staff; he was consulted by Eleanor Lieberman, a deputy, to transfer Lewinsky out of the White House. Panetta agreed to the transfer.

John Podesta   Deputy White House Chief of Staff, is currently assembling a group of lobbyists and fund-raisers to put pressure on Hill Democrats to support Clinton. Podesta referred Lewinsky to Bill Richardson at the U.N. for a job. Podesta testified that Clinton denied having sex with Lewinsky.

Ashley Raines   Friend of Monica Lewinsky and White House director of Office and Policy Development Operations and Special Liaison.

William Rehnquist   Chief Justice of the Supreme Court. He will preside over a Senate trial, if the case gets that far. Rehnquist is a conservative who unilaterally ruled against the White House this summer in several cases of privileged communications claims by the Clinton defense team.

Janet Reno   Attorney General of the United States; she has been accused of protecting the President, though she readily acceded to Kenneth Starr's request to open the grand jury to include the Lewinsky testimony in his investigations.

Hon. Bill Richardson   U.S. Ambassador to the United Nations; at the request of John Podesta, he interviewed Monica Lewinsky for a job at the U.N. in New York. Offered a job, Lewinsky turned it down.

Richard Mellon Scafie   Heir to the Mellon Bank fortune; personal wealth estimated between $800 million and $1.5 billion. Financial backer of many conservative groups and causes, like the Landmark Legal Fund, which offered to assist Paula Jones' attorneys. The Landmark Legal Fund teamed up with Ken Starr in the aforementioned school-voucher case. Furthermore, Landmark has links to attorney James Moody, the man who represents...Linda Tripp!

Marsha Scott   Deputy director of personnel.

Arlen Specter (R-Pennsylvania)   Right-wing Clinton critic will look to do as much damage to Clinton as he can.

Nathaniel Speights   An attorney for Monica Lewinsky.

Kenneth Starr   Independent counsel; he is at the center of much controversy. When he was first appointed to replace Robert Fiske, Jr., to investigate Whitewater, Starr had a reputation for fairness. As the investigation has proceeded, he has been seen as highly partisan, and willing to do almost anything to make charges stick to Bill Clinton. With this current report, he may succeed in having the President impeached, which is why he is championed by Bill Clinton's enemies.

Jacob Stein   An attorney for Monica Lewinsky; Stein and Cacheris took over the Lewinsky case from Bill Ginsberg. Stein is a high-profile Washington attorney.

George Stephanopoulous   Former senior advisor for policy and strategy, now a TV and print journalist, his opinion is that Clinton will not resign, but will fight for his political life.

Peter Strauss   Husband of Marcia Lewis.

Linda Tripp   "Friend" of Monica Lewinsky (quotations added); Linda Tripp has had a pivotal role in this investigation. She taped many hours of conversation with Lewinsky, reportedly encouraging her in the affair with Clinton. She then turned the tapes over to the Starr inquiry. Her betrayal of Lewinsky has made her an unpopular figure on the left and a darling of the right.

Natalie Rose Ungvari   High school friend of Monica Lewinsky.

Robert Wexler (D-Florida)   A member of the House Judiciary Committee, Wexler is no fan of Kenneth Starr.

Kathleen Willey   Former White House volunteer; she testified to the grand jury (and on TV's *60 Minutes*) that the President kissed and fondled her in a surprising and unwelcome incident.

Michael Williams   Former White House intern.

Hon. Susan Webber Wright   U.S. District Judge presiding over *Jones v. Clinton* civil suit. This judge, a Republican appointed by President George W. Bush, threw the Jones case out of court last April before going to trial because the suit did not prove harm to Jones either emotionally or in her career. Wright had ruled earlier that a sitting president could be tried in a court of law.

Dale Young   Family friend of Monica Lewinsky.

Further Reading

Much of the reading about Bill Clinton is highly partisan, which becomes obvious when reading the titles of the books listed below. Reading up on the Andrew Johnson impeachment and the near-impeachment of Richard Nixon will help you understand how presidential scandals both serious and trivial have been handled before. At this writing, an impeachment certainly seems possible, so the titles covering the impeachment process, and how other scandals fit into that process, would be highly informative.

Bill Clinton

Aitkin, Jonathan, *Nixon: A Life* (Washington, DC: Regnery Publishing) 1996.

Anonymous, *Primary Colors: A Novel of Politics* (New York: Random House) 1996.

Barr, Bob, R. Emmett Tyrrell (intro.), *The Impeachment of William Jefferson Clinton: A Political Docu-Drama* (Washington, DC: Regnery Publishing) 1997.

Becht, Kenneth R., and Duran Crain (ed.), *Just the Facts - a Case for Impeachment: Over 200 Documented Lies, Misrepresentations & Contradictory Statements by William Jefferson Clinton* (Putting America First) 1997.

Becht, Kenneth R., *Just The Facts: A Case for Impeachment* (Putting America First) 1997.

Bennett, William J., *Death of Outrage: Bill Clinton and the Assault on American Ideals* (New York: Simon and Schuster) 1998.

Berman, William C., *America's Right Turn: From Nixon to Clinton* (Baltimore, MD: Johns Hopkins University Press) 1998.

Brummett, John, *Highwire: From the Back Roads to the Beltway: The Education of Bill Clinton* (New York: Hyperion) 1995.

Bugliosi, Vincent, *No Island of Sanity: Paula Jones V. Bill Clinton: The Supreme Court on Trial* (New York: Ballantine Books) 1998.

Clinton, Bill, *Between Hope and History: Meeting America's Challenges for the 21st Century*, Vol. 1 (New York: Times Books) 1996.

Clinton, Bill, et al, *Preface to the Presidency: Selected Speeches of Bill Clinton, 1974-1992* (Fayetteville, AR: University of Arkansas Press) 1996.

Cockburn, Alexander and Ken Silverstein, *Washington Babylon* (New York: Verso Books) 1996.

Coulter, Ann, *High Crimes and Misdemeanors: The Case Against Bill Clinton* (Lanham, MD: National Book Network) 1998.

Drew, Elizabeth, *Showdown: The Struggle Between the Gingrich Congress and the Clinton White House* (New York: Touchstone Books) 1997.

Evans Pritchard, Ambrose, *The Secret Life of Bill Clinton: The Unreported Stories* (Washington, DC: Regnery Publishing) 1997.

Fick, Paul M. PhD, *The Dysfunctional President: Inside the Mind of Bill Clinton* (Secaucus, NJ: Carol Publishing Group) 1995.

Flowers, Gennifer, *Sleeping With the President: My Intimate Years With Bill Clinton* (Anonymous) 1998.

Graham, Tim, et al, *Pattern of Deception: The Media's Role in the Clinton Presidency* (Washington, DC: Media Research Center) 1996.

Greenberg, Paul, *No Surprises: Two Decades of Clinton-Watching* (New York: Brasseys) 1996.

Gross, Martin Louis, *The Great Whitewater Fiasco: An American Tale of Money, Power, and Politics* (New York: Ballantine Books) 1994.

Hohenberg, John, *The Bill Clinton Story: Winning the Presidency* (Syracuse, NY: University of Syracuse Press) 1994.

In Arkansas (Amherst, NY: Prometheus Books) 1993.

Kurtz, Howard, *Spin Cycle: Inside the Clinton Propaganda Machine* (New York: Free Press) 1998.

Larve, L. H., *Political Discourse: A Case Study of the Watergate Affair* (Athens, GA: University of Georgia Press) 1988.

Lawson, Don, *Famous Presidential Scandals* (Springfield, NJ: Enslow Publishing) 1990.

Levin, Jerome David, *The Clinton Syndrome: The President and the Self-Destructive Nature of Sexual Addiction* (Rocklin, CA: Prima Publishing) 1998.

Lyons, Gene, *Fools for Scandal: How the Media Invented Whitewater* (New York: Franklin Square Press) 1996.

Maraniss, David, *First in His Class: The Biography of Bill Clinton* (New York: Simon and Schuster) 1996.

McDougal, Jim, et al, *Arkansas Mischief: The Birth of a National Scandal* (New York: Henry Holt and Company, Inc.) 1998.

Moldea, Dan E., *A Washington Tragedy: How the Death of Vincent Foster Ignited a Political Firestorm* (Washington, DC: Regnery Publishing) 1998.

Portis, Jonathan, et al, *Comeback Kid: The Life and Career of Bill Clinton* (Secaucus, NJ: Birch Lane Press) 1992.

Reel, Guy, *Unequal Justice: Wayne Dumond, Bill Clinton, and the Politics of Rape in Arkansas* (Amherst, NY: Prometheus Books) 1993.

Rehshon, Stanley A., *High Hopes: The Clinton Presidency and the Politics of Ambition* (New York: Routledge Press) 1998.

Roberts, Robert N. and Marion T. Doss, Jr., *From Watergate to Whitewater: The Public Integrity War* (Westport, CT: Praeger Publishers) 1997.

Ruddy, Christopher, *The Strange Death of Vincent Foster: An Investigation* (New York: Free Press) 1997.

Sabato, Larry J., *When Should the Watchdogs Bark?: Media Coverage of the Clinton Scandals* (Washington, DC: Center for Media and Public Affairs) 1994.

Stewart, James B., *Blood Sport: The President and His Adversaries* (New York: Touchstone Books) 1997.

Stone, Deborah J., and Christopher Manion, *Slick Willie: Why America Still Cannot Trust Bill Clinton* (Annapolis, MD: Annapolis Press) 1994.

Thomas, Evan (ed.), *Back from the Dead: How Clinton Survived the Republican Revolution* (New York: Grove/Atlantic Monthly Press) 1997.

Tyrrell, R. Emmett Jr., *Boy Clinton: The Political Biography* (Washington, DC: Regnery Publishing) 1997.

Walker, Martin, *The President We Deserve: Bill Clinton and the New American* (New York: Crown) 1996.

Watson, Kevin H., *The Clinton Record: Everything Bill and Hillary Want You to Forget* (New York, Merrill Press) 1996.

Woodward, Bob and Julie Rubenstein (eds.), *The Agenda: Inside the Clinton White House* (New York: Pocket Books) 1995.

Woodward, Bob, *The Choice: How Clinton Won* (New York, Touchstone) 1997

Richard Nixon and Watergate/Impeachment

Barrer, Lester A. and Myra E. Barrer (eds.), Documentation Index to the Richard M. Nixon Impeachment Proceedings: Including the "Watergate" and Related Investigations, Hearings, and Prosecutions (Triangle News Service) 1975.

Boyan, Stephen A., *Constitutional Aspects of Watergate: Documents and Materials* (Dobbs Ferry, NY: Oceana Publications) 1976.

Emery, Fred, *Watergate: The Corruption of American Politics and the Fall of Richard Nixon* (New York: Simon and Schuster) 1995.

Garza, Hedda (ed.), Watergate Investigation Index: House Judiciary Committee Hearings & Report on Impeachment (St. Clair Shores, MI: Scholarly Press) 1985.

Woodward, Bob, and Carl Bernstein, The Final Days: *The Classic, Behind-the-Scenes Account of Richard Nixon's Last Days in the White House* (New York, Touchstone Books) 1994.

Zeifman, Jerry, *Without Honor: Crimes of Camelot and the Impeachment of Richard Nixon* (New York, Thunder's Mouth Press) 1996.

Impeachment

Barth, Alan (ed.), *Presidential Impeachment* (Washington DC: Public Affairs Press) 1974.

Berger, Raoul, *Impeachment: The Constitutional Problems* (Cambridge, MA: Harvard University Press) 1973.

Bushnell, Eleanore, *Crimes, Follies, and Misfortunes: The Federal Impeachment Trials* (Champaign, IL: University of Illinois Press) 1992.

Colondny, Len, and Robert Gettlin, *Silent Coup: The Removal of a President* (New York, Acacia Press) 1991.

Gerhardt, Michael J., *The Federal Impeachment Process: A Constitutional & Historical Analysis* (Princeton, NJ: Princeton University Press) 1996.

Hoffer, Peter Charles, and N.E.H. Hull, *Impeachment in America, 1635-1805* (New Haven, CT: Yale University Press) 1984.

Keisling, William, *We All Fall Down: A Chronicle of an Impeachment Foretold,* (Airville, PA: Yardbird Books) 1996.

Labovitz, John R., *Presidential Impeachment* (New Haven, CT: Yale University Press) 1978.

Melton, Buckner F., *First Impeachment: The Constitution's Framers and the Case of Senator William Blount* (Macon, GA: Mercer University Press) 1998.

Andrew Johnson

Les Benedict, Michael, *The Impeachment and Trial of Andrew Johnson* (New York: W. W. Norton and Company) 1990.

Political Scandals

Feinberg, Barbara Silberdick, *American Political Scandals Past and Present* (Danbury, CT: Franklin Watts) 1992.

Hagood, Wesley O., *Presidential Sex: From the Founding Fathers to Bill Clinton* (Secaucus, NJ: Citadel Press) 1998.

Kessler, Ronald, *Inside Congress: The Power, the People & the Scandals of Congress* (New York: Pocket Books) 1997.

Williams, Robert, *Political Scandals in the United States* (Chicago: Fitzroy Dearborn Publishers) 1998.

Glossary

It's all a bunch of mumbo-jumbo, right? Here's a collection of terms that are likely to pop up again and again as the political crisis in Washington rolls to its conclusion.

attorney general   The highest-ranking law-enforcement person in the country. Appointed by the President, the attorney general is charged with enforcing federal laws.

autocracy   A government in which one person possesses unlimited power.

censure   The formal resolution of a legislative body reprimanding and condemning a person, normally a member, for specified conduct.

Common Law   Has its origins in England and grows from ever-changing custom and tradition.

complaint   All lawsuits begin when the party allegedly harmed (the "plaintiff") files a complaint against the defendant. The complaint alleges what the plaintiff thinks happened and how he or she was harmed as a result. It may or may not be true. That is the point of a trial. The trial determines what really happened; the complaint is unsubstantiated.

conflict of interest   A clash between the public interest and the private financial gain of the person involved.

conspiracy   A group of two or more persons with a common design and common plan to achieve their goals.

contempt of court   Any act that is calculated to embarrass, hinder, or obstruct court administration of justice, or that is calculated to lessen its authority or dignity. If a judge orders you to pay child support and you don't, you can be found guilty of contempt of court. Your actions show disrespect for the court and its authority.

cross-examination   The process whereby the opposing lawyer asks leading, intense, and often confrontational questions of the witness in order to better reveal the truth. There is no cross-examination of witnesses in a grand jury. The Starr Report was based almost exclusively upon grand jury testimony.

damages   In order to be awarded damages, a plaintiff in a lawsuit must be able to prove injury in some way. The injury could be physical, emotional, or economic. The dollar amount a jury awards for those injuries are the "damages."

deponent   In a civil lawsuit, the person who is having his deposition taken, under oath.

deposition   A main tool of discovery; the taking of someone's sworn testimony under oath outside of a courtroom.

discovery   The phase in a civil lawsuit, in which each party finds out what the other party in the case knows about the facts of the case.

"Enemies List"   In 1973, the American public learned of President Nixon's list of people who opposed him. Names on that list included Bill Cosby, Paul Newman, and then-CBS newsman Daniel Schorr. The administration planned on having these people audited by the IRS and investigated by the FBI.

exculpatory evidence   Shows the innocence of the accused and thereby contradicts the charges alleged.

extortion   Obtaining property from another by the wrongful use of actual or threatened force, violence, or fear.

friend of the court brief   Sometimes people or organizations beyond the two parties directly involved may be interested in a particular case because of the precedent the case may set. In these circumstances, the court allows those interested entities to lobby on behalf of one side or another. These arguments are called friend of the court briefs.

guilt   Means that the defendant was found to have committed the acts alleged by the prosecution "beyond a reasonable doubt." In most jurisdictions, guilt must be agreed upon by a unanimous verdict of all jurors.

indictment   When a prosecutor believes he has enough evidence to charge a defendant with a crime, he does so by issuing an indictment listing the charges.

internship   A non-paying position similar to an apprenticeship where an inexperienced person gains experience.

jurisdiction   The right and power of a court to adjudicate a matter pending before it.

law journal   A periodical that publishes scholarly legal articles, run by the top students of any law school.

misdemeanor   An offense lower than a felony and generally punishable by fine, or imprisonment other than in a penitentiary.

Most Favored Nation (MFN) status   A designation made by the federal government that allows certain countries, "most favored" countries, tax and tariff breaks when exporting to the U.S.

obstruction of justice   Impeding or obstructing those who seek justice in court or those who are conducting an official investigation. For example, if you lie to a prosecutor to protect a friend of yours who committed a crime, you are obstructing justice.

pleading the Fifth   The Fifth Amendment of the Bill of Rights in the Constitution gives all citizens the right not to testify against themselves if they don't want to. Pleading the Fifth means you are using your right against self-incrimination. Juries are told that no inference, either positively or negatively, should be drawn when a person invokes this right.

poll   A random survey of people designed to elicit general opinions. Almost all politicians now use polls before they announce any policy action.

reasonable doubt   For a jury to be convinced beyond a reasonable doubt, it must be fully satisfied that the person is guilty. This is the highest level of proof required and is used only in criminal trials. It does not mean "convinced 100 percent," but it comes close.

simple majority   More than half of the voting members of any group. In the 435 member House of Representatives, 218 members make up a simple majority. Republicans alone number more than that figure.

slush fund   An informal name given to an account whose funds cannot easily be traced back to their original source.

solicitor general   In charge of representing the government before the Supreme Court. He or she decides what cases the government should ask the Court to review and what position the government should take in cases before the Court.

subornation of perjury   The crime of asking or forcing another person to lie under oath. And again, the lie must be about a material matter. If Clinton asked Monica Lewinsky to deny her sexual relationship in Lewinsky's Jones affidavit, that is subornation of perjury. It would have been a lie about a material matter.

subpoena   A command to appear at a certain time and place and give testimony regarding a certain matter.

summary judgment   When there is a summary judgment motion, the judge considers the evidence on both sides and determines whether a reasonable jury could conclude the contrary of the movant's evidence. Since a judge decides law, and a jury decides facts, when no evidence showing that facts are disputed are proffered by the non-movant, no trial is needed. The judge can then decide the case by this type of motion.

transactional immunity   A sort of blanket immunity. It prevents any prosecution relating to any matter surrounding the testimony.

treason   As defined in the U.S. Constitution, a crime committed by a U.S. citizen who helps a foreign government to overthrow, make war against, or seriously injure the U.S.

use immunity   Only prevents prosecution from the testimony itself. Any other matter surrounding the testimony would still be a potential cause for criminal prosecution.

war room   In a political campaign, the place where all the main decisions are made, where the candidate and his advisers meet, where they review polls and strategies.

wiretap   Information is obtained by intercepting messages by wiretapping, radio surveillance, and other means. In some states, it is illegal to tape conversations without both parties' consent. For instance, if you tap into and tape your neighbor's cordless-phone telephone calls, you may be guilty of illegal wiretapping.

zine   An Internet magazine. As such, it can only be read online and cannot be found in bookracks.

Index

A

Abramson, Karin Joyce, 337
Abscam scandal, 102
abuse of power, charges in Starr report, 250-252
Accuracy in Media (AIM), 132
ACLU (American Civil Liberties Union), 147
Adams, John Quincy (elected office after Presidency), 259
admissibility of evidence, 91
admission of adultery speech, Bill Clinton, 3, 4-6
adultery
  admission of by Bill Clinton, 3-6
  Bill Clinton's history of, 72
    Arkansas state troopers's role in, 73-74
    Dolly Browning, 72-73
    Gennifer Flowers, 74-76
    Kathleen Willey, 76-79
    Paula Jones, 79
  Dick Morris, 180
  historical accounts, 161-162
    Alexander Hamilton, 260
    Arthur Brown, 7
    Franklin D. Roosevelt, 166-168
    George Washington, 5
    Grover Cleveland, 164-165
    James Buchanan, 163-164
    John F. Kennedy, 168-169, 176
    Lyndon Baines Johnson, 56, 169-171
    Thomas Jefferson, 162-163
    Warren Harding, 165-166
    William Taulbee, 88
  see also sexual harassment; sexual relationship with Monica Lewinsky

affidavits in Jones case
  Linda Tripp, 200-202
  Monica Lewinsky, 202-203
    draft, 310
    signing, 311
    Starr Report, 309-312
Agnew, Spiro (vice president to Nixon), resignation during Watergate scandal, 110
AIM (Accuracy in Media), 132
Albright, Madeline, 337
alcoholic step-father, effect on Bill Clinton, 41-42
Aldrich, Gary (role in right-wing conspiracy), 134
All The President's Men, 113
amendments, Fifth Amendment, 111
American Civil Liberties Union (ACLU), 147
American Spectator, 133
appointment
  independent counsels, 119-120
  Kenneth Starr, 155-157
approval ratings
  of Bill Clinton at end of first term, 68
  of President George Bush, 62
Arab-scam (Abscam), 102
Arkansas state troopers, role in Bill Clinton's affairs, 73-74
articles of impeachment, *see* impeachment
assassination of John F. Kennedy, conspiracy surrounding, 130
Attorney General, 118
  appointment of independent counsels, 119-120
  Janet Reno, *see* Reno, Janet
  powers of independent counsels, 120-121
authority of independent counsels, 120-121
autocracy, 15

B

Babcock, Orville (exhonerated in Whiskey-Ring scandal), 100
Bakaly, Charles, 337
Baker, Senator Howard (questioned about Nixon's knowledge of Watergate), 11
Barr, Bob (member of House Judiciary Committee), 261, 337
Barrett, Thomas (member of House Judiciary Committee), 263
Bates, John D. (fomer deputy to Starr), 140
Bates, Stephen, 337
Belknap, William (impeachment of), 37
Bennett, Jackie, 337
Bennett, Robert, 337
Berman, Howard (member of House Judiciary Committee), 263
Bernstein, Carl (investigator of Watergate scandal), 108, 110
"beyond a reasonable doubt", 27
Bittman, Robert, 337
Blair, Jim (cattle futures trading), 58-59
Bleiler, Andrew, 338
Blount, Senator William (impeachment of), 31-32
blue dress, evidence of Clinton-Lewinsky affair, 184-185
Blumenthal, Sidney, 338
Bono, Mary (member of House Judiciary Committee), 262
Bork, Robert, 111
Bowles, Erskine, 338
Boys Nation, Bill Clinton in, 43
Bradley, Anna (mistress of Senator Arthur Brown), 7
branches of government
  executive branch, 18-20
  "The Federalist Papers", 20

judiciary branch, 16
  role in impeachment
    process, 28-29
  legislative branch, 16-18
  separation of powers, 15-16
Brandeis, Justice Louis
  (separation of powers), 15
Britton, Nan (mistress of Warren
  Harding), 165
Brostow, Benjamin (uncovered
  Whiskey-Ring scandal), 100
Brown, Jerry, 63
Brown, L.D. (Arkansas state
  trooper), deposition against Bill
  Clinton, 73
Brown, Ron, 338
Brown, Senator Arthur
  (mistress of), 7
Browning, Dolly (claimed to
  have sexual relationship with
  Bill Clinton), 72-73
Bruer, Lanny, 338
Bryant, Ed (member of House
  Judiciary Committee), 262
Buchanan, James (historical
  account of sex scandal),
  163-164, 233
budget deficit reduction plan
  (Bill Clinton), 67
Bush, George
  approval rating of, 62
  involvement in Iran-Contra
    affair, 102-106
  presidential election in 1992,
    62-63
Byck, Samuel (plan to assassinate
  Richard Nixon), 27

C

Cacheris, Plato, 236, 338
Callender, James (sedition case
  against), 33
campaign contributions
  limits on, 113
  taxpayer, 114
campaign finance reports, 114
campaign laws, 113-115
campaign spending limits, 114
campaign strategies of Bill
  Clinton (presidential election
  of 1992), 63-65
Campbell, Donovan, Jr., 338
Canaday, Charles (member of
  House Judiciary Committee), 262

Carter, Francis (attorney for
  Monica Lewinsky), 309, 338
Carter, Jimmy
  current activities of, 275
  Ethics in Government Act, 119
Carville, James, 64, 232, 338
cattle futures trading of Hillary
  Clinton, 58-59
CBS News, 236
censure, 258
  of Andrew Jackson, 38
  of Bill Clinton, 256
Chappaquiddick Island
  scandal, 192
charges
  House Judiciary Committee
    report, 252
  Starr report, 242-243
    abuse of power, 250-252
    final analysis of, 253
    obstruction of justice,
      247-250
    perjury, 243-247
    witness tampering, 250
Chase, Justice Samuel
  (impeachment of), 32-34
Checkers speech (President
  Richard Nixon), 5
Chicago, importance to election
  of John F. Kennedy, 52
childhood
  of Bill Clinton, 41-42
  of Hillary Rodham, 52-53
Cleveland, Grover (historical
  account of sex scandal),
  164-165
Clifford, Clark (statesman for
  Jack Kennedy), 193
Clinton, Bill, 338
  censure, possible courses of
    action, 256
  charges against in Starr report,
    242-243
    abuse of power, 250-252
    final analysis of, 253
    obstruction of justice,
      247-250
    perjury, 243-247
    witness tampering, 250
  childhood of, 41-42
  as "Comeback Kid", 48
  Democratic Presidential
    primary election in 1992,
    62-63
    60 Minutes appearance, 76

draft dodging of, 44-45
education of, 43-44
election history of (in
  Arkansas), 47-48
Filegate scandal, 154
future of, 277-279
general election in 1992
  campaign strategy, 63-65
  Perot candidacy, 63
grand-jury testimony, 244-245
Hillary's dedication to,
  221-224
history of adultery, 72
  Arkansas state troopers'
    role in, 73-74
  Dolly Browning, 72-73
  Gennifer Flowers, 74-76
  Kathleen Willey, 76-79
  Paula Jones, 79
House Judiciary Committee
  charges, 252
"I did not inhale" statement,
  79-80
impeachment
  aftermath of, 267-269
  chances in Congress of,
    259-260
  debate about strength of
    case for, 260
  House of Representatives
    role in, 264
  possible courses of action,
    255-258
  question about necessity
    of, 11-12
  resources on impeaching,
    345-347
  Senate role in, 265-267
  Supreme Court role in,
    260-261
inauguration of, 66-67
interviews
  with Jim Lehrer, 7
  with *Rollcall*, 8
Jones case, *see* Jones case
legacy of, 6
lies, significance of, 83
love for Hillary, 226-228
meeting Hillary Rodham for
  first time, 46
meeting President John F.
  Kennedy, 43
political promises of, 80-83
political scandals, *see* political
  scandals

presidency of
 approval rating at end of
  first term, 68
 deficit reduction plan, 67
 gays in the military
  policy, 66
 timeline of events that
  have plagued, 331-336
as professor at University of
 Arkansas Law School, 46-47
relationship with Monica
 Lewinsky, *see* sexual
 relationship with Monica
 Lewinsky
resignation option, 258-259
right-wing hatred of, 65-66
speeches
 admission of adultery, 3-6
 denial of sexual
  relationship with Monica
  Lewinsky, 6-8
 nomination of Michael
  Dukakis, 61-62
successes as Arkansas
 governor, 48-49
Travelgate scandal, 150-153
 death of Vince Foster,
  153-154
Vernon Jordan, *see* Jordan,
 Vernon
wedding of, 47, 57-58
Whitewater, 146
 appointment of Kenneth
  Starr, 155-157
 convictions of the
  McDougals and Jim
  Tucker, 146-148
 Webster Hubbell, 148-150
at Yale Law School, 45-46
The Clinton Chronicles, 135
Clinton, Hillary Rodham,
 239-240, 338
 60 Minutes appearance during
  Democratic Presidential
  primary elections, 76
 cattle futures trading, 58-59
 dedication to Bill Clinton,
  221-224, 226-228
 private life of, 224-225
 public appearance of, 222-224
 reaction to Starr Report, 129,
  135, 225-226
 at Rose Law Firm, 58
 successes of, 59

"vast right-wing
 conspiracy", 129
 legality of actions of, 135
Whitewater, 146
 convictions of the
  McDougals and Jim
  Tucker, 146-148
 Webster Hubbell, 148-150
 see also Rodham, Hillary
Clinton, Roger, Sr., 42
Cockell, Larry, 338
Cohen, Richard (syndicated
 columnist), 142
Coleman, Anne (mistress of
 James Buchanan), 163
Coleman, Robert, 163
college, *see* education
"Comeback Kid," Bill Clinton as,
 48, 277-279
Common Law, 25
complaint (in lawsuits), 87
conclusion of investigation, Starr
 Report, 11
confidentiality, lawyer-client
 privilege, 275-276
conflict of interest, 131
 Kenneth Starr, 130-132
Congress, 15, 16-18
 Bill Clinton's chances of
  impeachment, 259-260
 expelling members of, 279
 House of Representatives,
  16-18
  Democratic control of, 68
  impeachment of Senator
   William Blount, 31-32
  reprimands, 273
  Republican control of, 68
  role in impeachment
   process, 264
 members of House Judiciary
  Committee, 261-264
 Senate, 16-18
  Ethics rules, 113
  impeachment of Senator
   William Blount, 31-32
  role in impeachment
   process, 265-267
conservatism
 hatred of Bill Clinton, 65-66
 Kenneth Starr criticisms,
  139-143
consistency and corrobaration,
 cited as evidence in Starr
 Report, 292

conspiracy, 66, 234, 238
 The Clinton Chronicles, 135
 Gary Aldrich's role in, 134
 John F. Kennedy
  assassination, 130
 Kenneth Starr's role in,
  139-140
  conflict of interest,
   130-132
 legal definition of, 130
 Linda Tripp's role in, 133-134
 Lucianne Goldberg's role in,
  133-134
 Richard Mellon Scafie's role
  in, 132-133
 "vast right-wing conspiracy",
  129
  legality of actions of, 135
conspiracy to obstruct justice,
 charges in House Judiciary
 Committee report, 252
Constitution
 executive branch, 18-20
 judiciary branch, 16
 legislative branch, 16-18
 see also impeachment
constitutionality of independent
 counsel statute, 124
contempt of court, 93, 234
Contents of the Referral (Starr
 Report), 290-291
 Grounds
  Introduction, 313-325
  Summary, 325-329
 Narrative
  1995: Initial Sexual
   Encounters, 297-299
  April 1996: Lewinsky's
   Transfer to the Pentagon,
   300-302
  April-December 1996: No
   Private Meetings, 302
  Conversations and Phone
   Messages, 294-295
  Early 1997: Resumption of
   Sexual Encounters,
   302-305
  Emotional Attachment, 294
  Evidence Establishing
   Nature of Relationship,
   291-292
  Gifts, 295
  Introduction, 291
  January 5-January 16,
   1998, 309-313

January-March 1996: Continued Sexual Encounters, 299-300

June-October 1997: Continuing Meetings and Calls, 306-309

May 1997: Termination of Sexual Relationship, 305-309

Secrecy, 295-296

Sexual Contacts, 292-294

Conversations and Phone Messages (Narrative in Starr Report), 294-295

convictions in Whitewater scandal, 146-148

Conyers, John (member of House Judiciary Committee), 261, 339

Cornelius, Catherine (handled campaign travel), involvement in Travelgate, 151-153

Cossack, Roger (CNN legal analyst), 141

cost of investigations of independent counsels, 123

court, *see* Supreme Court

Couter, Ann (author of High Crimes and Misdemeanor), 154

Cox, Archibald (prosecutor in Watergate scandal), 110, 118-119

Credit Mobiler scandal of 1872, 99-100

CREEP (Campaign to Re-elect President), 108, 110

crimes
conspiracy, 234, 238
contempt of court, 234
Jordon, Vernon, legal problems, 238
obstruction of justice, 234, 236, 238
perjury, 233-234, 236
subornation of perjury, 234, 238
wiretapping, 234

criminal indictments, as legal remedies, 233

cross-examination, 78

Crowley, Candy (CNN spokesperson), 142

Currie, Betty (Bill Clinton's secretary), 238, 339
refusal to allow Monica Lewinsky's return to White House, 188-189

role in Clinton-Lewinsky affair, 182-183

Starr report charges against Bill Clinton, witness tampering, 250

D

Dale, Billy R. (head of Travelgate in 1982), 151

damages (in lawsuits), 93

De Vane, William Rufus, 164

Dean, John (involvement in Watergate scandal investigation), 110

death
of James McDougal, 147
of Vince Foster, 153-154

Declaration of Independence, 14-15

Deep Throat (inside source for Watergate scandal), 108-110
identity of, 112-113

deficit reduction plan, Bill Clinton, 67

Definition of Sexual Relations, 205

Delahunt, William (member of House Judiciary Committee), 263

democracy, 280

Democratic Party
control of House of Representatives, 68
effect of Clinton-Lewinsky scandal on, 276-277
members of House Judiciary Committee, 261-264
Presidential primary election of 1992, 62-63, 76

denial of sexual relationship with Monica Lewinsky, Bill Clinton, 6-8

denouncement of media, 213-214

deponent, 9

depositions, 72
Arkansas state troopers, 73-74
Bill Clinton
Jones case, 8-9, 205-208
perjury charges in Starr report, 245
Kathleen Willey, 77-79

discovery (civil lawsuits), 72
Jones case, 90-91

dismissal of Jones case, 92-94

"distinguishing characteristics" of Bill Clinton, Jones case, 247

Doar, John (study on impeachment), 25-26

documents cited as evidence in Starr Report, 292

dogding draft, Bill Clinton, 44-45

Douglas, Justice William O., 16

draft dodging of Bill Clinton, 44-45

Drudge, Matt (Drudge Report), 208, 216, 339

Dukakis, Michael, nomination, 61-62

E

economy, deficit reduction plan of Bill Clinton, 67

Edeleman, Marian Wright, 56

education
of Bill Clinton
early years, 43-44
Yale Law School, 45-46
of Hillary Rodham
early years, 53
Wellesley College, 53-55
Yale Law School, 55

elections
Bill Clinton
in Arkansas, 47-48
as "Comeback Kid", 48
Presidential election in 1992, 62-65, 76
John F. Kennedy, importance of Chicago to, 52
popular vote percentages, 65

Ellsberg, Daniel (pro-war staffer), 108

Emotional Attachment (Narrative in Starr Report), 294

EOP (Executive Office of the President), 20

Ethics in Government Act, 119

Ethics rules, 113

evidence
admissibility of, 91
"beyond a reasonable doubt", 27
blue dress, 184-185

establishing nature of relationship (Starr Report), 291-292
consistency and corrobaration, 292
documents, 292
physical evidence, 291-292
lack of in Jones case, 94
of wrongdoing, Starr Report, 286
required for impeachment, 27-28
exculpatory, 232
executive branch, 18-20
Executive Office of the President (EOP), 20
expansion of investigations of independent counsels, 121-122
expelling members of Congress, 279
extortion, 38

F

factual background (Starr Report), 284-285
Fairfax, Sarah "Sally" (mistress of President George Washington), 5
Fall, Albert B. (involvement in Teapot-Dome scandal), 101
Falwell, Jerry (*The Clinton Chronicles*), 135
family life
Bill Clinton, 41-42
Hillary Clinton, 59
Kenneth Starr, 138-139
FBI sting operations, Abscam, 102
FBI tapes, recording Monica Lewinsky conversation with Linda Tripp, 205
Federal Rules of Criminal Procedure, Rule 6(e), 235
"The Federalist Papers", 20
Ferguson, Danny (Arkansas state trooper)
deposition against Bill Clinton, 74
role in Jones case, 87
Fifth Amendment, 111
Filegate, 154
financial disclosure forms, 113
First Ladies, college educations of, 54

Fiske, Robert B. (dismissal of), 155-157
Flowers, Gennifer (claim of sexual relationship with Bill Clinton), 74-76, 339
Floyd, John, 233
Foster, Vince, 339
death of, 68, 153-154
Fox, Lewis, 339
Frank, Barney (member of House Judiciary Committee), 262, 339
Fries, John (treason case against), 33
Fulbright, Senator William J. (Bill Clinton working for), 44
future
of Bill Clinton, 277-279
of independent counsel law, 273-274
of Kenneth Starr, 271-273

G

gays in the military policy, 66
Gekas, George (member of House Judiciary Committee), 262
general elections, Presidential election in 1992
Bill Clinton campaign strategy, 63-65
Perot candidacy, 63
"gentlemen's agreement", 212
Gerth, Jeff (New York Times reporter), Whitewater investigation, 146
gifts exchanged between Bill Clinton and Monica Lewinsky
Banana Republic shirt, 186
Leaves of Grass, 184
Narrative in Starr Report, 295
puzzle, 186
Gilbert, Arthur (authored full page ad in L.A. Times denouncing media), 213
Gingrich, Newt (member of House Judiciary Committee), 262, 339
Ginsburg, William, 236, 339
Goldberg, Lucianne (literary agent), 198, 339
relationship with Linda Tripp, 197-198
role in right-wing conspiracy, 133-134

"Golden Fleece Awards", 131
Goldwater, Barry, 53
Goodin, Stephen, 339
Gore, Al (Vice President to Bill Clinton), 340
background of, 267-269
government
Declaration of Independence, 14-15
executive branch, 18-20
"The Federalist Papers", 20
independent counsel, 21
judiciary branch, 16
role in impeachment process, 28-29
legislative branch, 16-18
operation of, 13
scandals, *see* political scandals
separation of powers, 15-16
see also impeachment
governor, Bill Clinton's successes as, 48-49
Graham, Lindsey (member of House Judiciary Committee), 263
grand juries, 232
Bill Clinton testimony, 244-245
Grant, Ulysses S. (involvement in Whiskey-Ring scandal), 100-101
Grobanie, David, 340
Grounds (Contents of Referral)
Introduction, 313-325
Summary, 325-329

H

Haldeman, H. R., 239
Halpin, Maria (mistress of Grover Cleveland), 164
Hamilton, Alexander (adultery of), 260
Harding, Warren, G.
historical account of sex scandal, 165-166
involvement in Teapot-Dome scandal, 101-102
Hastings, Judge Alcee L. (impeachment of), 38
Hatch, Orrin, 233, 340
hearings, McCarthy hearings, 17
Hemings, Sally (mistress of Thomas Jefferson), 163
Hernreich, Nancy, 340

Hickock (mistress of Eleanor Roosevelt), 167
"high crimes and misdemeanors", 24-26, 154
Hilley, John (Assistant to President), 340
  role in transferring Monica Lewinsky to Pentagon (Starr Report), 300
historical accounts
  impeachment, 23-24
  independent counsel statute, 118-119
  media's role in scandals, 212-213
  national consciousness, 212-213
  political scandals
    Abscam, 102
    Andrew Jackson, 150
    Chappaquiddick Island scandal, 192
    Credit Mobilier scandal of 1872, 99-100
    Iran-Contra affair, 102-106
    Teapot Dome, 101-102
    Watergate, *see* Watergate
    Whiskey-Ring scandal, 100-101
  sex scandals
    Buchanan, James, 163-164
    Cleveland, Grover, 164-165
    Dick Morris, 180
    Franklin D. Roosevelt, 166-169
    George Washington, 162
    John F. Kennedy, 176
    Lyndon Baines Johnson, 169-171
    media involvement, 171
    Thomas Jefferson, 162-163
    Warren G. Harding, 165-166
Hoffman, Sydney, 340
house, Ethics rules, 113
House Government Reform and Oversight Committee, investigation of Webster Hubbell, 149
House Judiciary Committee
  charges against Bill Clinton, 252
  charges in Starr report, 242-243
  members of, 261-264
House of Representatives, 16-18
  Democratic control of, 68
  impeachment of Senator William Blount, 31-32

reprimands, 273
Republican control of, 68
role in impeachment process, 264
Hubbell, Webster, 237
  role in Whitewater scandal, 148-150
Humphreys, Judge West Hughes (impeachment of), 37
Hutchinson, Asa (member of House Judiciary Committee), 263
Hyde, Henry (member of House Judiciary Committee), 262, 340

I

"I did not inhale" statement (Bill Clinton), 79-80
Ickes, Harold, 340
illegal acts in relation to impeachment, 10-11
immunity
  transactional, 236
  use, 236
impeachment, 23
  Bill Clinton
    aftermath of, 267-269
    chances in Congress of, 259-260
    debate about strength of case for, 260
    possible courses of action, 255-256, 257-258
  evidence required for, 27-28
  "high crimes and misdemeanors", 24-26
  history of, 23-24
  House of Representatives, role of, 264
  Judge Alcee L. Hastings, 38
  Judge Charles Swayne, 37
  Judge Halsted L. Ritter, 37
  Judge John Pickering, 37
  Judge Walter Nixon, 38
  Judge West Hughes Humphreys, 37
  of Justice Samuel Chase, 32-34
  as legal remedy, 233
  necessity of, 11-12
  as political process, 34
  practical process of, 27-28
  President Andrew Johnson, 34-37

resources on, 345-348
  Andrew Johnson, 348
  Bill Clinton, 345-347
  Richard Nixon, 347-348
role in political process, 10-11
role of Senate in, 265-267
role of Supreme Court in, 260-261
Senator William Blount, 31-32
Starr Report Grounds section
  Introduction, 313-325
  Summary, 325-329
study on history of, 25-26
Supreme Court's role in, 28-29
theoretical process of, 26-27
Watergate, resources on, 347-348
William Belknap, 37
see also political scandals
inauguration of Bill Clinton, 66-67
independent counsel statute, 117-118, 235
  constitutionality of, 124
  Ethics in Government Act, 119
  flaws in, 127
  future of, 273-274
  history of, 118-119
  reauthorization of, 123-124
independent counsels, 21
  appointment of, 119-120
  cost of investigations, 123
  expansion of investigations of, 121-122
  investigating, 235
  Kenneth Starr, *see* Starr, Kenneth
  legal tactics of, 126
  list of investigations of Bill Clinton Administration, 124-126
  list of prior investigations, 122-123
  powers of, 120-121
indictments, 126
infidelity, *see* adultery
Information Superhighway, *see* Internet
Inglis, Bob (member of House Judiciary Committee), 262
Internet
  Matt Drudge, *see* Drudge, Matt
  media, 216-218
internship, 174

interrogatories, 90
interviews, Bill Clinton
   with Jim Lehrer, 7
   with Rollcall (italic), 8
introduction (Starr Report),
   283-284
investigations
   conclusion of Starr Report, 11
   grand juries, 232
   independent counsels, *see*
     independent counsel statute;
     independent counsels
   legal ramifications, 232-233
   Starr Report, *see* Starr Report
   summary of investigations of
     Clintons by Kenneth Starr,
     156-157, 157
   Watergate scandal, *see*
     Watergate
   Webster Hubbell, 148-150
   see also Whitewater
Iran-Contra affair, 102-106
Isikoff, Michael (investigative
   reporter for *Newsweek*),
   208, 340

J

Jackson, President Andrew
   censure of, 38
   political scandal, 150
Janet Reno, *see* Reno, Janet
   (Attorney General)
Jefferson, President Thomas
   accomplishments of, 42
   historical account of sex
     scandal, 162-163
   schools named after, 44
Jenkins, William (member of
   House Judiciary Committee), 263
job transfer
   Bettie Currie's refusal to allow
     return to White House,
     188-189
   Monica Lewinsky's transfer to
     Pentagon, 180-181, 300-302
Johnson, Judge Norma
   Holloway, 340
Johnson, President Lyndon
   Baines, historical account of sex
     scandal, 56, 169-171
Johnson, Norma Holloway
   (Judge), 235

Johnson, President Andrew
   impeachment of, 34-37
   resources on impeaching, 348
Jones case, 68, 71, 79, 85
   account of sexual contacts in
     Starr Report, *see* Starr Report
   background for, 85-88
   Browning affidavit in, 72-73
   charges in Starr report
     obstruction of justice,
       247-250
     perjury, 243-247
   damage done by, 94-95
   Definition of Sexual Relations,
     205-206
   deposition of Bill Clinton,
     8-9, 205-208
     media aftermath, 208- 211
   deposition of Kathleen Willey,
     77-79
   discovery process, 90-91
   dismissal of, 92-94
   "distinguishing characteris-
     tics" of Bill Clinton, 247
   lack of evidence in, 94
   Linda Tripp's role in, 133-134,
     199-202
   Monica Lewinsky's role in,
     91-92, 198-199
   "Points to make in an
     Affidavit", 200-202
   Richard Mellon Scafie's
     association with, 132-133
   subpoenas
     Linda Tripp, 199-200
     Monica Lewinsky, 198-199
   Supreme Court ruling, 89-90
   see also Clinton, Bill;
     Lewinsky, Monica;
     Tripp, Linda
Jones, Paula Corbin, 340
   claim of sexual harassment by
     Bill Clinton, 79
   see also Jones case
Jordon, Vernon (lawyer and
   friend of Bill Clinton), 341
   connection with Monica
     Lewinsky's job offer
     from MacAndrews &
       Forbes Holdings, Inc.,
       203-204, 311-312
     role in giving Monica
       Lewinsky job contacts,
       195-196
   initial contact with Monica
     Lewinsky, 191-193

legal problems, 238
relationships with Bill Clinton
   and Monica Lewinsky,
   237-238
Revlon, 237
journalism, *see* media
judges
   impeachment of, 37-38
   see also individual names of
     judges
Judicial Watch, 133
judiciary branch, 16
   role in impeachment process,
     28-29
Judiciary Committtee, *see* House
   Judiciary Committee
jurisdiction, 32

K

Kantor, Mickey, 341
Kassorla, Dr. Irene, 341
Kavanaugh, Brett, 341
Kaye, Walter, 341
Kearney, Janis, 341
Keating, Timothy, 341
Kelly, Virginia (mother of Bill
   Clinton), 42
Kendall, David, 233-234, 341
Kennedy, Jacqueline Bouvier, 168
Kennedy, President John F.
   Bill Clinton meeting of, 43
   conspiracy to assassinate, 130
   election of, importance of
     Chicago to, 52
   schools named after, 44
   sexual encounters before
     debates, 176
Kennedy, Senator Ted, 341
   Chappaquiddick Island
     scandal, 192
Kenneth Starr, *see* Starr, Kenneth;
   Starr Report
Kissinger, Henry (National
   Security Advisor), 212

L

L.A. Times, Arthur Gilbert full
   page ad denouncing media, 213
land deals (John Floyd), 233
Landmark Legal Fund, 133

law journal, 46
law professors
    Bill Clinton as, 46-47
    McLain, Lynn (University of
        Baltimore), 239
    Sargentich, Thomas, 235
    schools, *see* University of
        Arkansas Law School; Yale
        Law School
laws
    campaign, 113-115
    Federal Rules of Criminal
        Procedure Rule 6(e), 235
    independent counsel statutes,
        235, 273-274
    Maryland wiretap laws,
        238-239
lawsuits (Jones case), *see*
    Jones case
lawyer-client privilege, 275-276
lawyers
    Cacheris, Plato, 236
    Ginsburg, William, 236
    Jordan, Vernon, *see* Jordan,
        Vernon
    Kendall, David, 233, 234
    Stein, Jacob, 236
leaks to news media, 234-236
Leaves of Grass, 184
legacy of Bill Clinton, 6
legal problems of Vernon
    Jordan, 238
legal ramifications of
    investigation, 232-233
legal remedies
    criminal indictments, 233
    impeachment, 233
legal tactics of independent
    counsels, 126
legalities
    transactional immunity, 236
    use immunity, 236
legislative branch, 16-18
LeHand, Marguerite (mistress of
    Franklin D. Roosevelt, 166
Lehrer, Jim (interview with Bill
    Clinton), 7
Lewinsky, Monica, 341
    affidavit in Jones case,
        202-203
        draft, 310
        signing, 311
        Starr Report, 309-312
    deal with Kenneth Starr, 236

job offer from MacAndrews &
    Forbes Holdings, Inc.,
    203-204, 311-312
motives prior to receiving
    subpoena in Jones case,
    198-199
relationship with Linda Tripp
    at Pentagon, 187-188
relationship with Vernon
    Jordan, 191-193, 203-204,
    237-238, 311-312
Revlon, 237
role in Jones case, 91-92
talking points, 202-203, 236
Tripp, Linda, 238-239
see also sexual relationship
    with Monica Lewinsky
Lewinsky, Dr. Bernard, 237, 341
Lewis, Ann, 341
Lewis, Marcia, 341
Liddy, Gordon (Watergate
    burgler), 110
Lieberman, Evelyn, 342
Lieberman, Joseph, 341
lies
    Bill Clinton
        "I did not inhale"
            statement, 79-80
        political promises, 80-83
        see also adultery, Bill
            Clinton's history of
    lying under oath, compared
        to perjury, 246-247
    significance of, 83
    see also charges; perjury
Limbaugh, Rush, 66
Lincoln, President Abraham,
    impeachment of President
    Andrew Johnson, 34
Lindsey, Bruce, 342
Livingstone, Craig (involvement
    in Filegate scandal), 154
lobbyists, Ken Starr as, 18, 131
Lockhart, Joe, 342
Lofgren, Zoe (member of House
    Judiciary Committee), 262
Lowell, Abbe (counsel for
    Democrats on House Judiciary
    Committee), 242

M

MacAndrews & Forbes Holdings,
    Inc., 203
    Starr Report, 311-312
Madison Guaranty, 67
Maes, Glen, 342
The Manchurian Candidate, 130
Marceca, Anthony (involvement
    in Filegate scandal), 154
margin call, 58
marijuana, Bill Clinton's "I did
    not inhale" statement, 79-80
marriage of Bill Clinton and
    Hillary Rodham, 57-58
Martens, Darnell (partner of
    Hollywood producer Harry
    Thomason), 151
Maryland wiretap laws, 238-239
Matlain, Mary, 232
McCarthy, Eugene, 54
McCarthy, Senator Joseph
    (hearings of), 17
McCollum, Bill (member of
    House Judiciary Committee),
    262, 342
McCurry, Mike, 342
McDougal, James
    conviction for involvement in
        Whitewater scandal, 147
    death of, 147
    involvement in Whitewater
        scandal, 146
McDougal, Susan
    conviction for involvement in
        Whitewater scandal, 147
    involvement in Whitewater
        scandal, 146
McFarlane, Robert (National
    Security Advisor to Ronald
    Reagan), involvement in
    Iran-Contra affair, 103, 105
McLain, Lynn (University of
    Baltimore), 239
media
    CBS News, 236
    coverage after Monica
        Lewinsky affair is
        discovered, 208-210, 211
    denouncement of, 213-214
    historical account of role in
        scandals, 212-213
    Internet and, 216-218

involvement in reporting of sex scandals, 171
leaks to, 234-236
  Starr, Kenneth, 234-236
NBC Nightly News, 235
New York Times, 235
O.J. Simpson and, 214
rules of civility, 218-219
sensationalism, 171, 214-216, 218
Watergate aftermath, 114
see also newspapers
members of House Judiciary Committee, 261-264
Mercer, Lucy Page (mistress of Franklin D. Roosevelt), 166
Merletti, Lewis, 342
MFN (Most Favored Nation) status, 81
middle-class tax cut, lack of in Bill Clinton's initial budget plan, 67
military services
  Bill Clinton's avoidance of, 44-45
  gays in the military policy, 66
misdemeanors, 257
  definition of, 24
mistresses
  Arthur Brown, 7
  George Washington, 5
  Grover Cleveland, 164
  James Buchanan, 163
  John F. Kennedy, 168-169
  Lyndon Baines Johnson, 169
  Thomas Jefferson, 163
  Warren Harding, 165
Mitchell, John (involvement in Watergate scandal), 108-110
Mondale, Eleanor, 342
Monica Lewinsky, *see* Lewinsky, Monica
Moody, James, 342
moral leadership of Presidency, 280
Morris, Dick
  Bill Clinton political consultant, 47
  sex scandals, 180
Most Favored Nation (MFN) status, 81
movies
  All The President's Men, 113
  Primary Colors, 224
  Wag the Dog, 249

N

Nadler, Jerrold (member of House Judiciary Committee), 263
Narrative (Contents of Referral)
  1995: Initial Sexual Encounters, 297-299
  April 1996: Lewinsky's Transfer to the Pentagon, 300-302
  April-December 1996: No Private Meetings, 302
  Conversations and Phone Messages, 294-295
  Early 1997: Resumption of Sexual Encounters, 302-305
  Emotional Attachment, 294
  Evidence Establishing Nature of Relationship, 291-292
    consistency and corrobaration, 292
    documents, 292
    physical evidence, 291-292
  Gifts, 295
  Introduction, 291
  January 5-January 16, 1998, 309-313
  January-March 1996: Continued Sexual Encounters, 299-300
  June-October 1997: Continuing Meetings and Calls, 306-309
  May 1997: Termination of Sexual Relationship, 305-309
  Secrecy, 295-296
  Sexual Contacts, 292-294
    Bill Clinton's account in Jones case, 292-293
    Grand Jury testimony of Bill Clinton, 293-294
    Monica Lewinsky's testimony, 294
national consciousness
  effect of Clinton-Lewinsky scandal on, 276-277
  historical account of, 212-213
  sensationalism of the media, 214-218
  Watergate aftermath, 114
National Enquirer, 214
NBC Nightly News, 235
necessity of impeachment, question about, 11-12

Nelvis, Bayani, 342
Net, *see* Internet
New York Times, 215, 235
news media, *see* media
newspapers
  L.A. Times, 213
  National Enquirer, 214
  New York Times, 215
  Photoplay, 167
  Richmond Recorder, 162
  Washington Post
    account of Watergate scandal, 108-110
    love poem from Monica Lewinsky to Bill Clinton, 184, 303
  see also media
Newsweek, Isikoff, Michael (investigative reporter), 208
Nixon, Judge Walter, impeachment of, 28-29, 38
Nixon, President Richard
  effect of resignation on, 258
  impeachment study during administration of, 25-26
  resignation over Watergate scandal, 111
  resources on impeaching, 347-348
  Samuel Byck's plan to assassinate, 27
  speeches, Checkers speech, 5
  tapes, 236, 239
  Watergate scandal, *see* Watergate
nomination of Michael Dukakis, Bill Clinton speech, 61-62
North, Oliver (involvement in Iran-Contra affair), 103, 105

O

O.J. Simpson and the media, 214
obstruction of justice, 234, 236, 238
  charges in Starr report, 247-250
"old boy" network, 212
oral sex, *see* sexual relationship with Monica Lewinsky
order of succession, 268-269
Oval Office tapes (Watergate tapes), 110-111
oversight investigations, 17

P

PACs (political action committees)
campaign contributions, 113
Palmieri, Jennifer, 342
Panetta, Leon, 342
partisanship and Kenneth Starr,
139-143
Pel, Scott, 236
Pentagon, Monica Lewinsky's
transfer to, 180-181, 188-189,
300-302
"Pentagon Papers", 108
Perelman, Ronald (chairman and
CEO of MacAndrews & Forbes
Holdins, Inc.), 203-204
Lewinsky's job offer, 203-204
Starr Report, 311-312
perjury, 12, 83, 95, 233-234, 236
charges in Starr report,
243-247
compared to lying under
oath, 246-247
Perot, Ross (Presidential
candidacy of), 63
phone conversations (taped),
see tapes
phone sex, Clinton-Lewinsky
affair, 181-182
Photoplay, 167
physical evidence
cited in Starr Report, 291-292
see also evidence
Pickering, Judge John
(impeachment of), 37
"Pleading the Fifth", 111
Podesta, John, 342
poem from Monica Lewinsky to
Bill Clinton, 184, 303
"Points to make in an Affidavit",
202-203, 236
political action committees
(PACs) campaign
contributions, 113
political elections, *see* elections
political parties, *see* Democratic
Party; Republican Party
political process, impeachment
as, 10-11, 28-29, 34
possible courses of action
against Bill Clinton, 255-256
question about necessity of,
11-12
role of Supreme Court,
260-261

political scandals
Filegate, 154
historical accounts of, *see*
historical accounts
resources on, 348
sex scandals, *see* adultery;
sexual relationship with
Monica Lewinsky
Travelgate, 68, 150-154
Watergate, *see* Watergate
Whiskey-Ring, 100-101
Whitewater, *see* Whitewater
see also impeachment
polls, 48
approval rating of President
George Bush, 62
character and integrity of
presidents, 6
Hillary's knowledge of Bill
Clinton's affair, 223
private versus public matter of
Clinton-Lewinsky affair, 252
popular vote percentages,
presidential elections, 65
powers of independent counsels,
120-121
presents, *see* gifts exchanged
between Bill Clinton and
Monica Lewinsky
Presidency, 18-20
ability to be sued in civil
court, Supreme Court ruling,
89-90
Bill Clinton
approval rating at end of
first term, 68
deficit reduction plan, 67
gays in the military
policy, 66
timeline of events that
have plagued, 331-336
see also Clinton, Bill
effect of Starr investigation
on, 274-276
lawyer-client privilege,
275-276
legal ramifications of
investigation, 232-233
requirements for office, 280
presidential elections, *see*
elections
presidential order of succession,
268-269
presidents, *see* individual names
of presidents

press, *see* media
Primary Colors, 224
primary elections
Democratic Presidential
primary election in 1992,
62-63
Presidential primary election
of 1992, 76
privacy issues, Starr Report,
287, 288
private life of Hillary Rodham
Clinton, 224-225
probes, *see* investigations
professor of law, Bill Clinton as,
46-47
promises of politicians, 67
Bill Clinton, 80-83
proof, *see* evidence
prosecutors
grand juries, 232
Kenneth Starr, *see* Starr,
Kenneth
special, 113
see also independent counsels;
individual names of
prosecutors
Proxmire, Senator William,
"Golden Fleece Awards", 131
public appearance of Hillary
Rodham Clinton, 222-224
puzzle (gift from Monica
Lewinsky), 186

Q-R

Raines, Ashley, 342
Reagan, Ronald, 237
involvement in Iran-Contra
affair, 102-106
"reasonable doubt", 27
reauthorization of independent
counsel statute, 123-124
Rehnquist, Chief Justice William,
33, 343
religion and Kenneth Starr, 138
Reno, Janet (Attorney
General), 343
grants permission to extend
Starr investigation, 285
reporters, *see* media
reports
Kenneth Starr, *see* Starr Report
Matt Drudge, *see* Drudge, Matt

reprimands (House of Representatives), 273
Republican Party
    control of House of Representatives, 68
    effect of Clinton-Lewinsky scandal on, 276-277
    members of House Judiciary Committee, 261-264
    right-wing politicians, hatred of Bill Clinton, 65-66
resignations
    Bill Clinton's option for, 258-259
    forced (James Watt), 237
    Watergate, 111-112
resources
    on impeachment, 345-348
        Andrew Johnson, 348
        Bill Clinton, 345-347
        Richard Nixon, 347-348
    on political scandals, 348
Revlon, 237
Rhodes Scholarship, 44
Richardson, Hon. Bill, 343
Richmond Recorder, 162
right-wing conspiracy, *see* conspiracy
right-wing politicians, hatred of Bill Clinton, 65-66
risks of angering Kenneth Starr, 231-232
Ritter, Judge Halsted L. (impeachment of), 37
Ritz-Carlton Hotel, 238
Robertson, Pat (host of 700 Club), 150
Rodham, Hillary
    childhood of, 52-53
    education of, 53
        Wellesley College, 53-55
        Yale Law School, 55
    meeting Bill Clinton for first time, 46
    political activities during law school, 55-57
    role in Nixon impeachment inquiry, 46
    wedding of, 47, 57-58
    work on impeachment study, 25
    see also Clinton, Hillary Rodham
Rogan, James (member of House Judiciary Committee), 263

Rollcall, Bill Clinton interview with, 8
Roosevelt, Eleanor, 167
Roosevelt, Franklin D. (historical account of sex scandal), 166-169
Rose Law Firm, 58
    Webster Hubbell and Hillary Rodham Clinton, 148-150
Ross, Senator Edmund G. (impeachment of President Andrew Johnson), 36
rules of civility (media), 218-219
Rutherford Institute, 135

S

Sargentich, Thomas (American University, Washington College of Law), 235
"Saturday Night Massacre", 111
Scafie, Richard Mellon, 343
    role in right-wing conspiracy, 132-133
scandals, *see* political scandals
Schippers, David P. (chief investigative counsel for House Judiciary Committee), 242
school, *see* education
Schumer, Charles (member of House Judiciary Committee), 263
Scope of Referral (Starr Report)
    background of investigation, 288-290
    current status of investigation, 289-290
Scott, Bobby (member of House Judiciary Committee), 263
Scott, Marsha, 343
Secrecy (Narrative in Starr Report), 295-296
Secret Service
    suspicions of Clinton-Lewinsky affair, 179-180
    testimony of, 179, 276
sedition (James Callender case), 33
Senate, 16-18
    Ethics rules, 113
    impeachment of Senator William Blount, 31-32
    role in impeachment process, 265-267

sensationalism of media, 214-216, 218
Sensenbrenner, James (member of House Judiciary Committee), 263
separation of powers, 15-16
Sexual Contacts (Narrative in Starr Report), 292-294
    Bill Clinton's account in Jones case, 292-293
    Grand Jury testimony of Bill Clinton, 293-294
    Monica Lewinsky's testimony, 294
sexual harassment, *see* adultery; Jones case
"sexual relations," definition in Paula Jones case, 8-9
sexual relationship with Monica Lewinsky
    Bettie Currie's role, 182-183
    Bill Clinton's account in Jones case (Starr Report), 292-293
    blue dress, 184-185
    Definition of Sexual Relations, 205-206
    denial of, 6-8
    future effect on country, 276-277
    Grand Jury testimony of Bill Clinton, 293-294
    initial contacts, 173-174, 297-299
    January-March 1996: Continued Sexual Encounters, 299-300
    job search with Vernon Jordan, 195-196
    job transfer to Pentagon, 180-181, 300-302
    letters of frustration to Bill Clinton, 194-195
    love poem from Monica Lewinsky in Washington Post, 303-305
    plea to return to White House, 188-189
    phone sex, 181-182
    resumption of affair in 1997, 302-305
    Secret Service suspicions, 179-180
    summary of encounters, 174-177
    terminations of relationship, 178, 186, 305-309

testimony of Monica
Lewinsky, 294
threats from Monica Lewinsky
to reveal relationship,
189-191
timeline of events, 331-336
Vernon Jordan's initial
contact with Monica
Lewinsky, 191-193
see also adultery
simple majority, 264
Simpson, O.J., and the media, 214
60 Minutes appearance, Bill
Clinton and Hillary Clinton, 76
slush finds, 109
special prosecutors, *see*
independent counsels
Specter, Arlen, 343
speeches
Bill Clinton
admission of adultery, 3-6
denial of sexual
relationship with Monica
Lewinsky, 6-8
nomination of Michael
Dukakis, 61-62
Richard Nixon, Checkers
speech, 5
Speights, Nathaniel, 343
Stanton, Edwin M., President
Andrew Johnson's firing of, 34
Stanton, Justice Edwin, 16
Star, Gennifer Flowers'
allegations in, 74
Starr, Kenneth, 343
appointment of, 155-157
conflict of interest, 130-132
conservatism of, 139-143
criticisms of, 139-143
deal with Monica
Lewinsky, 236
family upbringing, 138-139
future of, 271-273
initial contact with Linda
Tripp, 204-205
media leaks, 234-236
risks of angering, 231-232
Starr Report, *see* Starr Report
summary of investigations of
Clintons, 156-157
support for, 139-143
as tobacco lobbyist, 18,
130-132

Starr Report, 9-10, 283
charges in, 242-243
abuse of power, 250-252
final analysis of, 253
obstruction of justice,
247-250
perjury, 243-247
witness tampering, 250
conclusion of investigation, 11
Contents of the Referral, *see*
Contents of the Referral
effect of investigation on
Presidency, 274-276
factual background, 284-285
introduction, 283-284
investigation, 285-288
background of, 288-289
current status of, 289-290
privacy concerns, 287, 288
reaction of Hillary Rodham
Clinton to, 225-226
Scope of Referral, 288-290
significance of evidence of
wrongdoing, 286-288
state troopers, *see* Arkansas state
troopers
Stein, Jacob, 236, 343
Stephanopoulous, George, 64, 343
Strauss, Peter, 343
subornation of perjury, 234, 238
subpoenas in Jones case, 9
Linda Tripp, 199-200
"Points to make in an
Affidavit", 200-202
Monica Lewinsky, 198-199
"Points to make in an
Affidavit", 202-203
suicide of Vince Foster, 68
summary judgment, 92
Supreme Court, 16
constitutionality of
independent counsel
statute, 124
impeachment of Justice
Samuel Chase, 32-34
role in impeachment process,
28-29, 260-261
ruling on proceeding of Jones
case, 89-90
Swayne, Judge Charles
(impeachment of), 37

T

talking points, 236
taped phone conversations
(Linda Tripp), 238-239
tapes
Linda Tripp's recordings of
Monica Lewinsky,
199-200, 205
Richard Nixon, 236, 239
Watergate tapes, 110-111
Taulbee, Representative William
(adultery of), 88
tax cut, lack of in Bill Clinton's
initial budget plan, 67
taxpayer campaign funding, 114
Teapot Dome scandal, 101-102
telephone sex, *see* phone sex
television, *see* media
Tenure of Office Act, 35
testimony
Betty Currie, refusal to allow
Monica Lewinsky's return to
White House, 188-189
Bill Clinton
grand-jury testimony,
244-245, 293-294
Jones case, 292-293
Monica Lewinsky, 294
"Pleading the Fifth", 111
Secret Service, 179, 276
theocracy, 280
Thomas, Evan (Newsweek
spokesperson), 142
Thomason, Harry (Hollywood
producer and friend of Bill
Clinton), 8, 151
timeline of events surrounding
Bill Clinton's relationship with
Monica Lewinsky, 331-336
tobacco lobbyist, Kenneth Starr
as, 18, 131
transactional immunity, 236
Travelgate scandal, 68, 150-153
death of Vince Foster, 153-154
treason, 24
John Fries case, 33
Tripp, Linda, 238-239, 343
affidavit in Jones case,
200-202
call to Jones's lawyers, 91
initial contact with Kenneth
Starr, 204-205

Maryland wiretap laws,
238-239
"Points to make in an
Affidavit", 200-202
relationship with Monica
Lewinsky at Pentagon,
187-188
relationship with Lucianne
Goldberg (literary agent),
197-198
role in right-wing conspiracy,
133-134
subpoena in Jones case,
199-200
talking points, 236
tape recordings of Monica
Lewinsky, 199-200
troopers, *see* Arkansas state
troopers
Tucker, Jim Guy (convicted in
Whitewater scandal), 147
Turow, Scott (lawyer and
author), 142
Tyson Foods, cattle futures
trading of Hillary Clinton,
58-59

U-V

Ungvari, Natalie Rose, 343
United States government, *see*
government
University of Arkansas Law
School, Bill Clinton as professor
at, 46-47
use immunity, 236

Valentine's Day advertisement
from Monica Lewinsky,
184, 303
Van Sustern, Greta (CNN legal
analyst), 141
"vast right-wing conspiracy," *see*
right-wing conspiracy
Vernon Jordan, *see* Jordan,
Vernon
Vietnam War, draft dodging of
Bill Clinton, 44-45

W-Z

Wag the Dog, 249
Walsh, Lawrence (Former
Independent Counsel), 142
war room, 64
Washington, George
historical account of sex
scandal, 162
mistress of, 5
Washington Post
account of Watergate scandal,
108-110
Monica Lewinsky love poem,
184, 303
Watergate, 107
compared to Clinton-
Lewinsky scandal, 115
Deep Throat (inside source for
Watergate scandal), 108, 110
identity of, 112-113
effect on independent counsel
statute, 118-119
investigators of scandal,
108, 110
media aftermath, 114
Nixon resignation, 111
politcal aftermath, 113-115
resignations from, 112
resources on, 347-348
"Saturday Night Massacre", 111
summary of events, 110-111
Washington Post account,
108-110
Waters, Maxine (member of House
Judiciary Committee), 262
Watt, James, 237
Watt, Melvin (member of House
Judiciary Committee), 263
wedding of Bill Clinton and
Hillary Rodham, 47, 57-58
Wellesley College, Hillary
Rodham at, 53-55
Wexler, Robert (member of
House Judiciary Committee),
263, 344
Whiskey-Ring scandal, 100-101

Whitewater, 67, 146, 232
appointment of Kenneth
Starr, 155-157
convictions of McDougals and
Jim Tucker, 146-148
Webster Hubbell,
148-150, 237
Willey, Kathleen, 236, 344
claim of sexual harassment by
Bill Clinton, 76-79
Williams, Michael, 344
wiretapping, 234
laws in Maryland, 238-239
witness tampering, charges in
Starr report, 250
Wolff, Craig T. (jounalism
professor), 217
Woodruff, Judy (journalist), 215
Woods, Joseph (study on
impeachment), 25-26
Woodward, Bob (investigator of
Watergate scandal), 108, 110
Woodward, C. Vann (study of
impeachment), 25
Wright, Betsey, 56
Wright, Judge Susan Webber, 344
decision to admit evidence of
Bill Clinton's sexual
relationships in Jones
case, 284
dismissal of Jones case, 92-94
wrongdoing, evidence of (Starr
Report), 286-288

Yale Law School
Bill Clinton at, 45-46
Hillary Rodham at, 55
Young, Dale, 344

About the Authors

Steven D. Strauss is a political analyst, attorney, and author. He has worked on two national presidential campaigns (Hart in 1984 and Dukakis in 1988). Strauss has appeared on the Family Channel, the Talk America Radio Network, and numerous local radio and television stations. He has also been featured in *Inc.* magazine, *Glamour*, *McCalls*, *Twist*, *American Benefactor*, and the *Chicago Tribune*. His previous books include the user-friendly *Ask A Lawyer* series of legal advice books. Titles in the series include *Debt and Bankruptcy*, *Wills and Trusts*, *Landlord and Tenant*, and *Divorce and Child Custody*.

Strauss received a bachelors degree in political science from UCLA, a masters degree in public policy analysis from the Claremont Graduate School, and was a Coro Foundation Fellow in Public Affairs.

He is a practicing attorney and owner of the Strauss Law Firm, with offices in Sacramento and San Francisco, California. You can reach him, or receive free legal advice, at www.stevenstrauss.com.

Spencer Strauss is a native of Southern California. He received a bachelors degree from California State University, Fullerton, and is a graduate of the American Academy of Dramatic Arts. He also attended the McGeorge School of Law and used that education for a career in business. In his principle career, Strauss is an investment property broker. He is also an ardent follower of the American political scene, an interest inherited from his beloved father. This is his first book.

The Cast of Characters...continued

Michael Isikoff   Reporter, *Newsweek* magazine; he was working on the Lewinsky story and was reportedly at a meeting with Tripp and Goldberg listening to the Lewinsky tapes. *Newsweek* decided not to publish the story initially.

Paula Corbin Jones   Plaintiff in a civil sexual harassment suit against President Clinton; the Lewinsky investigation came about in part because Jones's lawyers wanted to use Lewinsky's relationship to Bill Clinton to prove a negative pattern of behavior on the part of the president. Bill Clinton's denial of the Lewinsky affair in his deposition in the Jones case is the heart of the perjury charge against him.

Vernon Jordan   Friend of President Clinton, and partner at Law Firm of Akin, Gump, Strauss, Hauer & Feld; he helped to secure Lewinsky a job in New York, allegedly at the behest of the president.

David Kendall   Attorney for President Clinton; he is the lead attorney in the Lewinsky matter, and is a highly respected Washington lawyer.

Joseph Lieberman (D-Connecticut)   Senator who is a Clinton backer, but who was the first figure on Capitol Hill to issue a stinging indictment of the President's behavior.

Dr. Bernard Lewinsky   Monica Lewinsky's father; divorced from Monica's mother, Dr. Lewinsky lives in California. A close friend of his, Bill Ginsberg, served for a time as Monica's legal counsel.

Monica Lewinsky   Former White House intern and employee; at the center of the latest controversy surrounding President Clinton, Lewinsky may unintentionally bring down Bill Clinton's Presidency.

Marcia Lewis   Mother of Monica Lewinsky; she did appear before the grand jury because she is a confidante of her daughter's, but was not required to testify later because she was covered by Monica's immunity deal.

Evelyn Lieberman   Former deputy chief of staff; she told *The New York Times* that Lewinsky's transfer to the Pentagon was for her "inappropriate and immature behavior."

Mike McCurry   Former White House press secretary; he was responsible for answering the press' incessant questions on the Lewinsky matter. McCurry stepped down from this post on October 1, 1998.

Leon Panetta   Former White House chief of staff; he was consulted by Eleanor Lieberman, a deputy, to transfer Lewinsky out of the White House. Panetta agreed to the transfer.

Janet Reno   Attorney General of the United States; she has been accused of protecting the president, though she readily acceded to Kenneth Starr's request to open the grand jury to include the Lewinsky testimony in his investigations.

Kenneth Starr   Independent counsel; he is at the center of much controversy. When he was first appointed to investigate Whitewater, Starr had a reputation for fairness. As the investigation has proceeded, he has been seen as a highly partisan, and willing to do almost anything to make charges stick to Bill Clinton.

George Stephanopoulous   Former senior advisor for policy and strategy, now a TV and print journalist, his opinion is that Clinton will not resign, but will fight for his political life.

Linda Tripp   "Friend" of Monica Lewinsky (quotations added); taped many hours of conversation with Lewinsky, reportedly encouraging her in the affair with Clinton, then turned the tapes over to the Starr inquiry.

Kathleen Willey   Former White House volunteer; she testified to the grand jury (and on TV's *60 Minutes*) that the president kissed and fondled her in an unwelcome incident.

Hon. Susan Webber Wright   U.S. District Judge presiding over *Jones v. Clinton* civil suit; threw the Jones case out of court last April because the suit did not prove emotional or professional harm to Jones.

The Complete Idiot's Reference Card

The Cast of Characters

Stephen Bates　A top Starr deputy, he wrote most of the narrative describing the relationship between Clinton and Lewinsky. A Harvard Law graduate, he is also a journalist, writing for *The Nation*, *The Weekly Standard*, and *The New Republic*. He has also written several nonfiction books.

Robert Bennett　Attorney for President Clinton; a high-powered Washington attorney, he leads the defense in the Jones case.

Sidney Blumenthal　Assistant to the President; being a close advisor and friend to the president, Blumenthal became the subject of much legal wrangling.

Erskine Bowles　White House chief of staff; he was planning to resign even before the Lewinsky saga broke in January 1998. He reportedly still wants out.

James Carville　Former Clinton campaign manager; Carville is an outspoken defender of Bill Clinton and accuses the right wing of conspiring to overturn the electoral wishes of the public.

Bill Clinton　President of the United States in the fight of his political life to defend against the charges that Kenneth Starr has brought in his report.

Hillary Rodham Clinton　First Lady of the United States; she has stayed by Bill Clinton's side, though she did remain fairly quiet during some of the darker moments of the Lewinsky scandal.

John Conyers (D-Michigan)　Ranking Democrat of the House Judiciary Committee. Conyers, 69, is one of the founders of the Congressional Black Caucus.

Betty Currie　Personal secretary to the President; she has had much close contact with Lewinsky, from signing her in as a Presidential visitor to calling Vernon Jordan to request help in finding Lewinsky a job, to picking up the gifts that Clinton gave to Lewinsky from Lewinsky's apartment.

Matt Drudge　Drudge Report; a conservative with an Internet publication, Drudge was the first to break the Lewinsky story. He has subsequently been a right-wing voice for many aspects of the story.

Gennifer Flowers　Long a figure connected to Bill Clinton, she claimed a 12-year affair with him. He denied it during the 1992 elections, but during his deposition in the Jones case, apparently admitted the affair.

Vince Foster　Former deputy White House counsel; Foster committed suicide in the summer of 1996. Linda Tripp was the last person to see him alive. Independent counsels Robert Fiske, Jr., and Kenneth Starr have both concluded that the death was a suicide.

Newt Gingrich (R-Georgia)　Speaker of the House and longtime Clinton critic. He can dictate the tone and behind-the-scenes maneuvering on this case.

William Ginsberg　Monica Lewinsky's former attorney; a personal friend of Lewinsky's father, his outspokenness and failure to cut an immunity deal probably led to his replacement in the summer of 1998 by more well-connected Washington attorneys.

Lucianne Goldberg　Literary agent; long a right-wing conservative and Clinton-basher, Goldberg first befriended Linda Tripp when she was working on a project about the Vince Foster homicide conspiracy theory. When Tripp came in contact with Lewinsky and heard her story, Goldberg advised Tripp to tape Lewinsky.

Orrin Hatch (R-Utah)　Senate Judiciary Committee Chair, he is a strong conservative who will make key decisions in how the case is conducted in the Senate.

Henry Hyde (R-Illinois)　Chairman of the House Judiciary Committee. Hyde is seen as an honorable lawmaker. Recent revelations of a past love affair may prejudice him against the Clinton team, but it is unclear whether the uncovering of the affair was directed by the White House.

continues

alpha
books